IMAGES OF ORGANIZATION

For my parents
Idris and Rachel Morgan

Gareth Morgan

IMAGES OF ORGANIZATION

SAGE Publications
International Educational and Professional Publisher
Newbury Park London New Delhi

For information address:

SAGE Publications, Inc.
2455 Teller Road
Newbury Park, California 91320
E-mail: order@sagepub.com

SAGE Publications Ltd.
6 Bonhill Street
London EC2A 4PU
United Kingdom

SAGE Publications India Pvt. Ltd.
M-32 Market
Greater Kailash I
New Delhi 110 048 India

Printed in the United States of America

Library of Congress Cataloging-in-Publication Data

Morgan, Gareth
    Images of organization.

    Bibliography: p.
    Includes index.
    1. Organization. 2. Organizational behavior.
    3. Management. I. Title.
    HD31.M628 1986   658.4   86-6663
    ISBN 0-8039-2830-0
    ISBN 0-8039-2831-9 (pbk.)

        96 97 98 99 25 24 23 22 21

Contents

Acknowledgments

I have worked on this book for a long time and owe so much to so many people. Special thanks are due to my colleagues and students at Lancaster, Penn State, and York. They have shared in the evolution of the ideas, and their enthusiasm and insights have proved a constant source of energy and inspiration. While it is impossible to thank them all by name, I am very grateful.

Gibson Burrell, Bob Cooper, Peter Frost, Vic Murray, Linda Smircich, Wayne Tebb, and Eric Trist have made very special contributions to the development of my work, and I am lucky to have them as both friends and colleagues.

The Social Sciences and Humanities Research Council of Canada provided help at a critical stage of the writing by providing a Research-Leave Fellowship. At York University, Vicki Keller and Paula Ironi have provided me with outstanding secretarial support. And as always, my friends at Sage have proved excellent partners.

Finally, I am lucky to have the support of a wonderful family. My wife Karen has contributed to this book in so many ways, and has helped to make the writing a happy and rewarding experience.

—*Gareth Morgan*
Toronto

1

Introduction

Effective managers and professionals in all walks of life, whether they be business executives, public administrators, organizational consultants, politicians, or trade unionists, have to become skilled in the art of "reading" the situations that they are attempting to organize or manage.

This skill usually develops as an intuitive process, learned through experience and natural ability. Though at times a person may actually declare that he or she needs to "read what's happening at X," or to "get a handle on Y," the process of reading and rereading often occurs at an almost subconscious level. For this reason it is often believed that effective managers and problem solvers are born rather than made, and have a kind of magical power to understand and transform the situations that they encounter.

If we take a closer look at the processes used, however, we find that this kind of mystique and power is often based on an ability to develop deep appreciations of the situations being addressed. Skilled readers develop the knack of reading situations with various scenarios in mind, and of forging actions that seem appropriate to the readings thus obtained.

They have a capacity to remain open and flexible, suspending immediate judgments whenever possible, until a more comprehensive view of the situation emerges. They are aware of the fact that new insights often arise as one reads a situation from "new angles," and that a wide and varied reading can create a wide and varied range of action possibilities. Less effective managers and problem solvers, on the other hand, seem to interpret everything from a fixed standpoint. As a result, they frequently hit blocks that they can't get around; their actions and behaviors are often rigid and inflexible and a source of conflict. When problems and differences of opinion arise, they usually have no alternative but to hammer at issues in the same old way and to create consensus by convincing others to "buy into" their particular view of the situation.

There is a close relationship between this process of reading organizational life and the process known as organizational analysis. The formal analysis and diagnosis of organizations, like the process of reading, always rests in applying some kind of theory to the situation being considered. For theories, like readings, are interpretations of reality. We theorize about or "read" situations as we attempt to formulate images and explanations that help us to make sense of their fundamental nature. And an effective analysis, like an effective reading, rests in being able to do this in ways that take account of rival theories or explanations, rather than being committed to a fixed and unshakable point of view.

This book explores and develops the art of reading and understanding organizations. First, it seeks to show how many of our conventional ideas about organization and management build on a small number of taken-for-granted images, especially mechanical and biological ones. Second, by exploring these and a number of alternative images, it seeks to show how we can create new ways of thinking about organization. Third, it seeks to show how this general method of analysis can be used as a practical tool for diagnosing organizational problems, and for the management and design of organizations more generally. And fourth, it seeks to explore the implications raised by this kind of analysis.

The basic premise on which the book builds is that our theories and explanations of organizational life are based on metaphors that lead us to see and understand organizations in distinctive yet partial ways. Metaphor is often just regarded as a device for embellishing discourse, but its significance is much greater than this. For the use of metaphor implies *a way of thinking* and *a way of seeing* that pervade how we understand our world generally. For example, research in a wide variety of fields has demonstrated that metaphor exerts a formative influence on science, on our language and on how we think, as well as on how we express ourselves on a day-to-day basis.

We use metaphor whenever we attempt to understand one element of experience in terms of another. Thus, metaphor proceeds through implicit or explicit assertions that A *is* (or is like) B. When we say "the man is a lion," we use the image of a lion to draw attention to the lion-like aspects of the man. The metaphor frames our understanding of the man in a distinctive yet partial way.

One of the interesting aspects of metaphor rests in the fact that it always produces this kind of one-sided insight. In highlighting certain interpretations it tends to force others into a background role. Thus in drawing attention to the lionlike bravery, strength, or ferocity of the man, the metaphor glosses the fact that the same person may well also be a chauvinist pig, a devil, a saint, a bore, or a recluse. Our ability to achieve a comprehensive "reading" of the man depends on an ability to see how these different aspects of the person may coexist in a com-plementary or even a paradoxical way.

It is easy to see how this kind of thinking has relevance for under-standing organization and management. For organizations are com-plex and paradoxical phenomena that can be understood in many different ways. Many of our taken-for-granted ideas about organiza-tions are metaphorical, even though we may not recognize them as such. For example, we frequently talk about organizations *as if* they were machines designed to achieve predetermined goals and objec-tives, and which should operate smoothly and efficiently. And as a result of this kind of thinking we often attempt to organize and manage them in a mechanistic way, forcing their human qualities into a back-ground role.

By using different metaphors to understand the complex and para-doxical character of organizational life, we are able to manage and de-sign organizations in ways that we may not have thought possible before. The following chapters illustrate how this can be done by ex-ploring the implications of different metaphors for thinking about the nature of organization. While some of the metaphors tap familiar ways of thinking, others develop insights and perspectives that will be rather new.

Thus Chapter 2 examines the image of organizations as machines and illustrates how this style of thought underpins the development of bureaucratic organization. When managers think of organizations as machines they tend to manage and design them as machines made up of interlocking parts that each play a clearly defined role in the func-tioning of the whole. While at some times this can prove highly effec-tive, at others it can have many unfortunate results. One of the most basic problems of modern management is that the mechanical way of thinking is so ingrained in our everyday conceptions of organization that it is often very difficult to organize in any other way. In demonstrating this, the chapter helps us to become more open to other ways of thinking.

Chapter 3 examines the idea that organizations are like organisms. This popular metaphor focuses attention on understanding and managing organizational "needs" and environmental relations. We come to see different types of organization as belonging to different species, of which the bureaucratic type is just one. We see that different species are suited for coping with the demands of different environments, and we are able to develop interesting theories about organization-environment relations. We are encouraged to understand how organizations are born, grow, develop, decline, and die, and how they are able to adapt to changing environments. We are also encouraged to consider relations between species, and the evolutionary patterns found in the interorganizational ecology. As in the case of the mechanical metaphor, this kind of imagery leads us to see and understand organizations from a unique perspective that has already contributed a great deal to the theory of modern management.

In Chapter 4 we pursue the implications of yet another metaphor. What if we view organizations as brains? What if we attempt to design them as brains? The metaphor draws attention to the importance of information processing, learning, and intelligence, and provides a frame of reference for understanding and assessing modern organizations in these terms. And it points to a set of design principles for enhancing these qualities. In the history of brain research different metaphors have been used for thinking about the brain, and our chapter explores two of these. The first treats the brain as a kind of information-processing computer; the second, as a hologram. These images, especially the latter, highlight important principles of self-organization for designing organizations in which a high degree of flexibility and innovation is needed.

Chapter 5 explores the idea that organizations are cultures. Organization is now seen to reside in the ideas, values, norms, rituals, and beliefs that sustain organizations as socially constructed realities. This focus, which has received increasing attention over the last few years from writers on corporate culture, gives us yet another way of managing and designing organizations: through the values, beliefs, and other patterns of shared meaning that guide organizational life.

In Chapter 6 we use a political metaphor to focus on the different sets of interests, conflicts, and power plays that shape organizational activities. The chapter explores organizations as systems of government drawing on various political principles to legitimize different kinds of rule, as well as the detailed factors shaping the politics of organizational life.

In Chapter 7 the focus of attention shifts to a more abstract metaphor: the idea that organizations are "psychic prisons" where people become trapped by their own thoughts, ideas, and beliefs, or by preoccupations originating in the unconscious mind. Could it be that our favored modes of organizing manifest an unconscious preoccupation with control? Or a form of repressed sexuality? Or a fear of death? Or a desire to minimize or avoid anxiety-provoking situations? Could it be that our ways of organizing are designed to protect us from ourselves? Could it be that we often become prisoners of our thoughts, confined and controlled by the way we think? Could it be that we are prisoners of ideologies that confine us in alienating modes of life? The image of a psychic prison invites us to examine organizational life to see if, and in what ways, we have become trapped by conscious and unconscious processes of our own creation. In doing so, the metaphor offers many important insights about the psychodynamic and ideological aspects of organization.

Chapter 8 investigates another metaphor requiring a twist in imagination. This time we are invited to understand organization as flux and transformation. The secret of understanding organization, from this perspective, rests in understanding the logics of change shaping social life. The chapter examines three different logics. One emphasizes how organizations are self-producing systems that create themselves in their own image. Another emphasizes how they are produced as a result of circular flows of positive and negative feedback. And a third suggests that they are the product of a dialectical logic whereby every phenomenon tends to generate its opposite. The insights generated can help us to understand and manage organizational change, and to understand forces shaping the nature of organization at a societal level.

Chapter 9 explores the idea that organizations are instruments of domination. Here the focus is on the potentially exploitative aspects of organization. The chapter shows how organizations often use their employees, their host communities, and the world economy to achieve their own ends, and how the essence of organization rests in a process of domination where certain people impose their will on others. An extension of the political metaphor examined in Chapter 6, the image of domination helps us to understand the aspects of modern organization that have radicalized labor-management relations in many parts of the world. This metaphor is particularly useful for understanding organizations from the perspective of exploited groups, and for understanding how actions that are rational from one viewpoint can prove exploitative from another.

Each of the above chapters explores a *way of thinking* about organization, on the premise that we can use the ideas and concepts thus generated to understand organizations in specific settings. Chapter 10 shows how this can be done through the analysis of a case study. The chapter develops a twofold approach that uses the insights generated by different metaphors to produce a *diagnostic reading* of the situation being analyzed, and then moves to a *critical evaluation* of how the various insights relate. In this way the general idea of reading organization is developed as a concrete method of analysis that allows us to explore and deal with the complexity of organizational life in a very practical manner.

Finally, Chapter 11 focuses on the possibility of developing an approach to organization that builds on the transformative potential of the ideas and analysis developed in earlier chapters.

Each chapter is accompanied by a set of bibliographic notes that appear toward the end of the book, and allow the reader to follow points of interest in greater depth.

Overall, the book thus stands as a treatise on metaphorical thinking that contributes to both the theory and practice of organizational analysis. Frequently, the discussion ranges well beyond the confines of organization theory, for the metaphors and general ideas considered are drawn from diverse sources. Thus in one chapter we may be exploring biology and in another psychoanalysis, or holography, or political thought. In each case the chapter explores the nature of the metaphor being considered, then focuses on the concrete implications for understanding organizational practice and the general strengths and limitations of the perspective thus created.

The metaphors discussed have been selected to illustrate a broad range of ideas and perspectives, but, of course, by no means exhaust the possibilities. This is why it is important to understand that the mode of analysis developed here rests in a *way of thinking* rather than in the mechanistic application of a small set of clearly defined analytical frameworks. While the book focuses on a number of key metaphors that have relevance for understanding a wide range of organizational situations, there are others that can produce their own special insight. Effective organizational analysis must always remain open to this possibility.

We live in a world that is becoming increasingly complex. Unfortunately, our styles of thinking rarely match this complexity. We often end up persuading ourselves that everything is more simple than it actually is, dealing with complexity by presuming that it does not really exist. This is very evident in the way fad and fashion dominate approaches to organizational analysis and problem-solving, an interest in one type of solution or set of techniques quickly giving way to another.

The approach to organizational analysis developed in this book stands against this general trend, in the belief that organizations are generally complex, ambiguous, and paradoxical. The real challenge is to learn to deal with this complexity. The method of analysis offered here points to a way in which we can begin to take up this challenge by relying on the most valuable asset we have: our capacity for critical thinking. I believe that by building on the use of metaphor—which is basic to our way of thinking generally—we have a means of enhancing our capacity for creative yet disciplined thought, in a way that allows us to grasp and deal with the many-sided character of organizational life. And in doing so, I believe that we can find new ways of organizing and new ways of approaching and solving organizational problems.

2

Mechanization Takes Command

Organizations as Machines

The Chinese sage Chuang-tzu, who lived in the fourth century B.C., relates the following story:

> As Tzu-gung was traveling through the regions north of river Han, he saw an old man working in his vegetable garden. He had dug an irrigation ditch. The man would descend into the well, fetch up a vessel of water in his arms, and pour it out into the ditch. While his efforts were tremendous, the results appeared to be very meager.
>
> Tzu-gung said, "There is a way whereby you can irrigate a hundred ditches in one day, and whereby you can do much with little effort. Would you not like to hear of it?" Then the gardener stood up, looked at him, and said, "And what would that be?"
>
> Tzu-gung replied, "You take a wooden lever, weighted at the back and light in front. In this way you can bring up water so quickly that it just gushes out. This is called a draw-well."
>
> Then anger rose up in the old man's face, and he said, "I have heard my teacher say that whoever uses machines does all his work like a machine. He who does his work like a machine grows a heart like a machine, and he who carries the heart of a machine in his breast loses his simplicity. He who has lost his simplicity becomes unsure in the strivings of his soul.
>
> "Uncertainty in the strivings of the soul is something which does not agree with honest sense. It is not that I do not know of such things; I am ashamed to use them."

If the old man were to visit the modern world he would no doubt be very dismayed. For machines now influence virtually every aspect of our existence. While they have increased our productive abilities many thousandfold, they have also done much more, shaping almost every aspect of our lives. The debate initiated by Tzu-gung and the old man continues. In the view of many, mechanization has brought mainly gain, raising mankind from competitors with nature to virtual masters of nature. For others, the old man's vision of human alienation recurs in various forms, as they contemplate the high price of mechanical progress in terms of the transition from craft to factory production, the exchange of rural community for urban sprawl, the general degradation of the environment, and the assault of rationalism upon the human spirit.

Regardless of the stand one takes, the wisdom of the old man's vision regarding the pervasive influence of machines remains beyond dispute. The use of machines has radically transformed the nature of productive activity and has left its mark on the imagination, thoughts, and feelings of humans throughout the ages. Scientists have produced mechanistic interpretations of the natural world, and philosophers and psychologists have articulated mechanistic theories of human mind and behavior. Increasingly, we have learned to use the machine as a metaphor for ourselves and our society, and to mold our world in accordance with mechanical principles.

This is nowhere more evident than in the modern organization.

Consider, for example, the mechanical precision with which many of our institutions are expected to operate. Organizational life is often routinized with the precision demanded of clockwork. People are frequently expected to arrive at work at a given time, perform a predetermined set of activities, rest at appointed hours, then resume their tasks until work is over. In many organizations one shift of workers replaces another in methodical fashion so that work can continue uninterrupted twenty-four hours a day, every day of the year. Often the work is very mechanical and repetitive. Anyone who has observed work in the mass-production factory, or in any of the large "office factories" processing paper forms such as insurance claims, tax returns, or bank checks, will have noticed the machinelike way in which such organizations operate. They are designed like machines, and their employees are in essence expected to behave as if they were parts of machines.

Fast-food restaurants and service organizations of many kinds operate in accordance with similar principles, with every action preplanned in a minute way, even in areas where personal interactions with others are concerned. Employees are frequently trained to interact with customers according to a detailed code of instructions, and are monitored

Greeting the customer	Yes	No
1. There is a smile.		
2. It is a sincere greeting.		
3. There is eye contact.		
Other:		
Taking the order	**Yes**	**No**
1. The counter person is thoroughly familiar with the menu ticket. (No hunting for items.)		
2. The customer has to give the order only once.		
3. Small orders (four items or less) are memorized rather than written down.		
4. There is suggestive selling.		
Other:		
Assembling the order	**Yes**	**No**
1. The order is assembled in the proper sequence.		
2. Grill slips are handed in first.		
3. Drinks are poured in the proper sequence.		
4. Proper amount of ice.		
5. Cups slanted and finger used to activate.		
6. Drinks are filled to the proper level.		
7. Drinks are capped.		
8. Clean cups.		
9. Holding times are observed on coffee.		
10. Cups are filled to the proper level on coffee.		
Other:		
Presenting the order	**Yes**	**No**
1. It is properly packaged.		
2. The bag is double folded.		
3. Plastic trays are used if eating inside.		
4. A tray liner is used.		
5. The food is handled in a proper manner.		
Other:		
Asking for & receiving payment	**Yes**	**No**
1. The amount of the order is stated clearly and loud enough to hear.		
2. The denomination received is clearly stated.		
3. The change is counted out loud.		
4. Change is counted efficiently.		
5. Large bills are laid on the till until the change is given.		
Other:		
Thanking the customer & asking for repeat business	**Yes**	**No**
1. There is always a thank you.		
2. The thank you is sincere.		
3. There is eye contact.		
4. Return business was asked for.		
Other:		

Exhibit 2.1. A management observation checklist used to evaluate the performance of counter staff in a fast-food restaurant

in their performance. Even the most casual smile, greeting, comment, or suggestion by a sales assistant is often programmed by company policy and rehearsed to produce authentic results. The management observation checklist used by a famous fast-food restaurant to monitor employee performance (Exhibit 2.1) indicates the degree to which a simple task like serving a customer can be mechanized, observed, and evaluated in a mechanical way.

Machines, mechanical thinking, and the rise of bureaucratic organization

Organizations that are designed and operated as if they were machines are now usually called bureaucracies. But most organizations are bureaucratized in some degree, for the mechanistic mode of thought has shaped our most basic conceptions of what organization is all about. For example, when we talk about organization we usually have in mind a state of orderly relations between clearly defined parts that have some determinate order. Although the image may not be explicit, we are talking about a set of mechanical relations. We talk about organizations as if they were machines, and as a consequence we tend to expect them to operate as machines: in a routinized, efficient, reliable, and predictable way.

In certain circumstances, which we will discuss in the concluding section of this chapter, a mechanical mode of organization can provide the basis for effective operation. But in others it can have many unfortunate consequences. It is thus important to understand how and when we are engaging in mechanistic thinking, and how so many popular theories and taken-for-granted ideas about organization support this thinking. For one of the major challenges facing many modern organizations is to replace this kind of thinking with fresh ideas and approaches, such as those to be discussed in subsequent chapters. Let us turn, therefore, to the story behind the development of our mechanistic concepts of organization.

THE ORIGINS OF MECHANISTIC ORGANIZATION

Organizations are rarely established as ends in themselves. They are instruments created to achieve other ends. This is reflected in the origins of the word organization, which derives from the Greek *organon*, meaning a tool or instrument. No wonder, therefore, that ideas about tasks, goals, aims, and objectives have become such fundamental organizational concepts. For tools and instruments are mechanical devices invented and developed to aid in performing some kind of goal-oriented activity.

This instrumentality is evident in the practices of the earliest formal organizations of which we know, such as those that built the great pyramids, empires, churches, and armies. However, it is with the invention and proliferation of machines, particularly along with the industrial revolution in Europe and North America, that concepts of organization really became mechanized. For the use of machines, especially in industry, required that organizations be adapted to the needs of machines.

If we examine the changes in organization accompanying the industrial revolution, we find an increasing trend towards the bureaucratization and routinization of life generally. Many self-employed family groups and skilled artisans gave up the autonomy of working in their homes and workshops to work on relatively unskilled jobs in factory settings. At the same time, factory owners and their engineers realized that the efficient operation of their new machines ultimately required major changes in the design and control of work. Division of labor at work, which was praised by the Scottish economist Adam Smith in his book *The Wealth of Nations* (1776), became intensified and increasingly specialized as manufacturers sought to increase efficiency by reducing the discretion of workers in favor of control by their machines and their supervisors. New procedures and techniques were also introduced to discipline workers to accept the new and rigorous routine of factory production.

Much was learned from the military, which since at least the time of Frederick the Great of Prussia had emerged as a prototype of mechanistic organization. Frederick, who ruled from 1740 to 1786, inherited an army composed for the most part of criminals, paupers, foreign mercenaries, and unwilling conscripts—an unruly mob. He was determined to change this, and quickly set about making reforms. He borrowed much from the practice of Roman legions and the reformed European armies of the sixteenth century, but also introduced numerous innovations of his own. Many of these were inspired by the mechanical inventions of his day.

In particular Frederick was fascinated by the workings of automated toys such as mechanical men, and in his quest to shape the army into a reliable and efficient instrument he introduced many reforms that actually served to reduce his soldiers to automata. Among these reforms were the introduction of ranks and uniforms, the extension and standardization of regulations, increased specialization of tasks, the use of standardized equipment, the creation of a command language, and systematic training which involved army drill. Frederick's aim was to shape the army into an efficient mechanism operating through means of standardized parts. Training procedures allowed these parts to be forged from almost any raw material, thus allowing the parts to be easily replaced when necessary, an essential characteristic for wartime operation. To ensure that his military machine operated on command, Frederick fostered the principle that the men must be taught to fear their officers more than the enemy. And to ensure that the military machine was used as wisely as possible, he developed the distinction between advisory and command functions, freeing specialist advisers (staff) from the line of command to plan activities. In time, further refinements were introduced, including the idea of decentralizing controls to create greater autonomy of parts in different combat situations.

Many of these ideas and practices had great relevance for solving problems created by the development of factory systems of production and were adopted in a piecemeal fashion throughout the nineteenth century, as entrepreneurs struggled to find organizational forms suited to machine technology. The new technology was thus accompanied and reinforced by mechanization of human thought and action. Organizations that used machines became more and more like machines. Frederick the Great's vision of a "mechanized" army gradually became a reality in factory and office settings as well.

During the nineteenth century a number of attempts were made to codify and promote the ideas that could lead to the efficient organization and management of work. Thus Adam Smith's praise of the division of labor was followed in 1801 by Eli Whitney's public demonstration of mass production, showing how guns could be assembled from piles of interchangeable parts. And in 1832 Charles Babbage, inventor of one of the earliest forms of the mathematical computer, published a treatise advocating a scientific approach to organization and management and emphasizing the importance of planning and an appropriate division of labor. However, it was not until the early twentieth century that these ideas and developments were synthesized in a comprehensive theory of organization and management.

One major contribution to this theory was made by the German sociologist Max Weber, who observed the parallels between the mechanization of industry and the proliferation of bureaucratic forms of organization. He noted that the bureaucratic form routinizes the process of administration exactly as the machine routinizes production. In his work we find the first comprehensive definition of bureaucracy as a form of organization that emphasizes precision, speed, clarity, regularity, reliability, and efficiency achieved through the creation of a fixed division of tasks, hierarchical supervision, and detailed rules and regulations.

As a sociologist Weber was interested in the social consequences of the proliferation of bureaucracy and, rather like the old man in Chuang-tzu's story, was concerned about the effect it would have on the human side of society. He saw that the bureaucratic approach had the potential to routinize and mechanize almost every aspect of human life, eroding the human spirit and capacity for spontaneous action. And he also recognized that it could have grave political consequences in undermining the potential for more democratic forms of organization. His writings on bureaucracy are thus pervaded by a great skepticism, of which we will have more to say in Chapter 9.

The other major contribution was made by a group of management theorists and practitioners in North America and Europe who set the basis for what is now known as "classical management theory" and "scientific management." In contrast with Weber, they were firm advocates of bureaucratization and devoted their energies to identifying detailed principles and methods through which this kind of organization could be achieved. While the classical management theorists focused on the design of the total organization, the scientific managers focused on the design and management of individual jobs. It is through the ideas of these theorists that so many mechanistic principles of organization have become entrenched in our everyday thinking. It is thus worth examining their work in some detail.

CLASSICAL MANAGEMENT THEORY: DESIGNING BUREAUCRATIC ORGANIZATIONS

Typical of the classical theorists were the Frenchman Henri Fayol, the American F. W. Mooney, and the Englishman Col. Lyndall Urwick. They were all interested in problems of practical management and sought to codify their experience of successful organization for others to follow. The basic thrust of their thinking is captured in the idea that management is a process of planning, organization, command, coordination, and control. Collectively they have set the basis for many modern management techniques, such as management by objectives (MBO); planning, programming, budgeting systems (PPBS); and other methods stressing rational planning and control. Each theorist codified his insights, drawing on a combination of military and engineering principles. Exhibit 2.2 summarizes some of the general principles of classical management theory.

Unity of command: an employee should receive orders from only one superior.

Scalar chain: the line of authority from superior to subordinate, which runs from top to bottom of the organization; this chain, which results from the unity-of-command principle, should be used as a channel for communication and decision making.

Span of control: the number of people reporting to one superior must not be so large that it creates problems of communication and coordination.

Staff and line: staff personnel can provide valuable advisory services, but must be careful not to violate line authority.

Initiative: to be encouraged at all levels of the organization.

Division of work: management should aim to achieve a degree of specialization designed to achieve the goal of the organization in an efficient manner.

Authority and responsibility: attention should be paid to the right to give orders and to exact obedience; an appropriate balance between authority and responsibility should be achieved. It is meaningless to make someone responsible for work if they are not given appropriate authority to execute that responsibility.

Centralization (of authority): always present in some degree, this must vary to optimize the use of faculties of personnel.

Discipline: obedience, application, energy, behavior, and outward marks of respect in accordance with agreed rules and customs.

Subordination of individual interest to general interest: through firmness, example, fair agreements, and constant supervision.

Equity: based on kindness and justice, to encourage personnel in their duties; and fair remuneration which encourages morale yet does not lead to overpayment.

Stability of tenure of personnel: to facilitate the development of abilities.

Esprit de corps: to facilitate harmony as a basis of strength.

These principles, many of which were first used by Frederick the Great and other military experts to develop armies into "military machines," provided the foundation of management theory in the first half of this century. And their use is very widespread today.

Exhibit 2.2. Principles of classical management theory

If we implement these principles, we arrive at the kind of organization represented in the familiar organization chart (Exhibit 2.3): a pattern of precisely defined jobs organized in a hierarchical manner through precisely defined lines of command or communication. And if we examine these principles closely, we find that the classical theorists were in effect designing the organization exactly as if they were designing a machine.

When an engineer designs a machine the task is to define a network of interdependent parts arranged in a specific sequence and anchored by precisely defined points of resistance or rigidity. The classical theorists were attempting to achieve a similar design in their approach to organization. We see this in the way the organization is conceived as a network of parts: functional departments such as production, marketing, finance, personnel, and research and development, which are further specified as networks of precisely defined jobs. Job responsibilities interlock so that they complement each other as perfectly as possible, and are linked together through the scalar chain of command expressed in the classical dictum "one man one boss."

The motions of the organizational structure thus produced are made to operate as precisely as possible through patterns of authority, e.g., in terms of job responsibilities and the right to give orders and to exact obedience. Patterns of authority serve as points of resistance and coordinate activities by restricting activity in certain directions while encouraging it in others. By giving detailed attention to patterns of authority, and to the general process of direction, discipline, and subordination of individual to general interest, the classical theorists sought to ensure that when commands were issued from the top of the organization they would travel throughout the organization in a precisely determined way, to create a precisely determined effect.

These principles are basic to both centralized bureaucracy (illustrated in Exhibit 2.3) and the modified form found in the divisionalized organization, where various units are allowed to operate in a semiautonomous manner, under the general rather than the detailed supervision and control of those with ultimate authority. Just as the military introduced decentralization to cope with difficult combat situations, the classical management theorists recognized the necessity of reconciling the contrary requirements of centralization and decentralization to preserve an appropriate flexibility in different parts of large organizations.

The ability to achieve this kind of decentralization has been greatly advanced during the course of the twentieth century through the development of management techniques like MBO and PPBS and the design of sophisticated management information systems (MIS), which

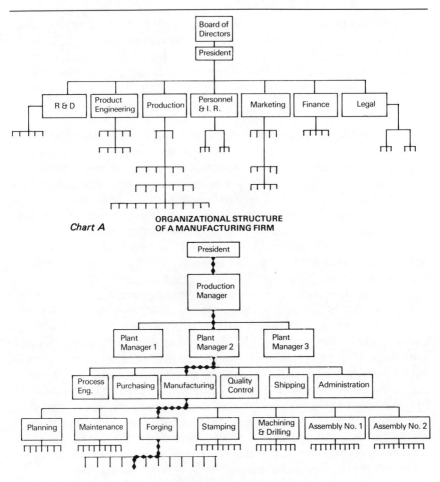

Chart A — **ORGANIZATIONAL STRUCTURE OF A MANUFACTURING FIRM**

Chart B — **DETAILED STUCTURE OF THE PRODUCTION DEPARTMENT**

Chart A illustrates an organization divided on the principle of functional specialization. Each functional department has its own hierarchical mode of organization. Chart B illustrates details relating to the production department. Note the chain of command which runs from top to bottom of the organization. From any place at the bottom of the hierarchy there is only one route to the top, a reflection of the principle that each subordinate should have no more than one superior. An example is indicated by the highlighted line. Note the different "spans of control." The chief executive in Chart A has a span of control equal to seven. The foreman of the forging section in the production department (Charts A and B) has a span of control of twelve. The production manager has a span of three. Note how the advisory or "staff" departments (e.g., finance, personnel, legal, R & D) have no direct authority over "line" departments such as the production department.

Exhibit 2.3. Organization chart illustrating the principles of classical management theory and bureaucratic organization

are often used to establish the kinds of "top-down" control advocated by the classical theorists. For example, MBO is now often used to impose a mechanistic system of goals and objectives on an organization. These are then used to control the direction in which managers and employees can take the organization, e.g., through the development of performance targets consistent with these goals. The same often happens with PPBS and other budgeting systems, with MIS being used to provide the detailed information necessary to implement the controls on a monthly, weekly, and even daily basis.

In this way the ideas of the classical management theorists are reinforced under the guise of modern management. This often occurs because the people designing these management systems have come to think about organization mechanistically and are unaware of other ways in which these techniques could be used—for example, to promote the kind of organizational learning and inquiry discussed in Chapter 4, or the participative corporate cultures or systems of organizational democracy discussed in Chapters 5 and 6.

The whole thrust of classical management theory and its modern application is to suggest that organizations can or should be rational systems that operate in as efficient a manner as possible. While many will endorse this as an ideal, it's easier said than done, because we are dealing with people, not inanimate cogs and wheels. In this regard it is significant that the classical theorists gave relatively little attention to the human aspects of organization. While they frequently recognized the need for leadership, initiative, benevolence, equity, esprit de corps, and other factors that might influence human motivation, organization as such was mainly understood as a technical problem. The classical theorists recognized that it was important to achieve a balance or harmony between the human and technical aspects of organization, especially through appropriate selection and training procedures, but their main orientation was to make humans fit the requirements of mechanical organization. And as we will see, for this they have been much criticized.

SCIENTIFIC MANAGEMENT

In Frederick the Great's approach to military organization we thus find many of the basic principles later elaborated by the classical management theorists. We also find many of the principles elaborated by the other great Frederick of organization theory, Frederick Taylor, who pioneered what is now known as scientific management.

Taylor was an American engineer and a flamboyant if somewhat disturbed personality. By his death in 1915 he had gained a reputation as a major "enemy of the working man," having been summoned in 1911 to defend his system of management before a committee of the U.S. House of Representatives. While one of the most maligned and criticized of all organization theorists, he has also proved to be one of the most influential. His principles of scientific management provided the cornerstone for work design throughout the first half of this century, and in many situations prevail right up to the present day.

Taylor advocated five simple principles, which can be summarized as follows:

1. *Shift all responsibility for the organization of work from the worker to the manager;* managers should do all the thinking relating to the planning and design of work, leaving the workers with the task of implementation.
2. *Use scientific methods* to determine the most efficient way of doing work; design the worker's task accordingly, specifying the *precise* way in which the work is to be done.
3. *Select* the best person to perform the job thus designed.
4. *Train* the worker to do the work efficiently.
5. *Monitor* worker performance to ensure that appropriate work procedures are followed and that appropriate results are achieved.

In applying these principles Taylor advocated the use of time-and-motion study as a means of analyzing and standardizing work activities. His scientific approach called for detailed observation and measurement of even the most routine work, to find the optimum mode of performance. Under Taylor's system menial tasks such as pig-iron handling and earth shoveling became the subjects of science. He fused the perspective of an engineer with an obsession for control.

Prominent models of his approach to scientific management are found in numerous manufacturing firms, retail organizations, and offices. Consider, for example, the fast-food chains serving hamburgers, pizzas, and other highly standardized products. Here work is often organized in the minutest detail on the basis of designs that analyze the total process of production, find the most efficient procedures, and then allocate these as specialized duties to people trained to perform them in a very precise way. All the "thinking" is done by the managers and designers, leaving all the "doing" to the employees. The management observation checklist presented in Exhibit 2.1 provides the perfect illustration of Taylor's approach to management, showing how a simple job such as taking and serving a customer's order can be split into many separate elements which can each be observed and evaluated. Taylor would have been well pleased with such a system of work evaluation.

The same approach to work design is also found in assembly-line manufacture. Here Taylor's ideas are built into the technology itself, making the workers servants or adjuncts to machines that are in complete control of the organization and pace of work.

We also see Taylor's methods influencing the organization of office work through "organization and methods" and "work study" projects. These projects break integrated tasks into specialized components that can then be allocated to different employees. Thus in processing an insurance claim form, one employee may be responsible for checking the claim against the policy, another may initiate an evaluation process, another may conduct the evaluation, yet another may evaluate the evaluation, and so on. Systematically applied, Taylor's five principles lead to the development of "office factories" where people perform fragmented and highly specialized duties in accordance with an elaborate system of work design and performance evaluation.

The effect of Taylor's scientific management on the workplace has been enormous, increasing productivity manyfold while accelerating the replacement of skilled craftspeople by unskilled workers. And it is for these reasons that it has been so influential yet so maligned. For the increases in productivity have often been achieved at great human cost, reducing many workers to automatons, just as the army reforms of Frederick the Great did to his soldiers over 150 years earlier.

The human problems resulting from such methods of production have been glaringly obvious ever since they were first introduced, especially when built into assembly-line technology. For example, when Henry Ford established his first assembly line to produce the Model T, employee turnover rose to approximately 380 percent per annum. Only by doubling wages to his famous "$5 a day" was he able to stabilize the work situation and persuade workers to accept the new technology. In periods of high employment when jobs are plentiful, workers still often shun the assembly line, as witnessed in the early 1970s when turnover in some plants, such as Ford's at Wixom, was running at almost 100 percent p.a. For most people assembly-line work is simply boring or alienating. Job cycles are often very short, with workers sometimes being asked to complete work involving seven or eight separate operations every forty or fifty seconds, seven or eight hours a day, fifty weeks a year. When General Motors decided to tighten up on efficiency in its Lordstown plant in the late 1960s, the speed of the assembly line was raised to increase output from 60 to 100 cars per hour. At this new pace each worker had thirty-six seconds to perform at least eight different operations, such as walking, lifting, handling, raising a carpet, bending to fasten bolts, fastening them by air gun, replacing the carpet, and putting a sticker on the hood.

The principle of separating the planning and design of work from its execution is often seen as the most pernicious and far-reaching element of Taylor's approach to management, for it effectively "splits" the worker, advocating the separation of hand and brain. As Taylor was fond of telling his workers, "You are not supposed to think. There are other people paid for thinking around here." Men were no more than "hands" or "manpower," the energy or force required to propel the organizational machine. The jobs they were required to perform were simplified to the ultimate degree so that workers would be cheap, easy to train, easy to supervise, and easy to replace. Just as the system of mass production required that products be assembled from interchangeable parts, Taylor's system rationalized the workplace so that it could be "manned" by interchangeable workers.

Over the years Taylor's approach to management has been extended and refined in many ways. For example, his contemporaries Frank and Lillian Gilbreth carried out important studies of human motion in the performance of work. The essence of mechanization rests in reducing complex procedures to sets of separate motions, which can then be reproduced mechanically at will. The Gilbreths focused on this aspect of work activity, designing jobs for maximum efficiency in the use of effort. Along with Taylor, they made important contributions to the principles employed in assembly-line production and to the science of ergonomics, which studies the use of energy in the workplace. Interestingly, Taylor's principles have crossed many ideological barriers, being extensively used in the USSR as well as in capitalist countries. This fact signifies that Taylorism is as much a tool for securing general control over the workplace as a means toward the generation of profit. Though the USSR is not averse to profitable use of productive resources, one of the great attractions of Taylorism rests in the power it confers to those in control.

While Taylor is often seen as the villain who created scientific management, it is important to realize that he was really part of a much broader social trend involving the mechanization of life generally. For example, the principles underlying Taylorism are now found on the football field and athletics track, in the gymnasium, and in the way we rationalize and routinize our personal lives. Taylor gave voice to a particular aspect of the trend towards mechanization, specialization, and bureaucratization that Max Weber saw as such a powerful social force. Taylorism was typically imposed on the work-force. But many of us impose forms of Taylorism on ourselves as we train and develop specialized capacities for thought and action and shape our bodies to conform with preconceived ideals. Under the influence of the same kind of mechanism that has helped make Taylorism so powerful, we often think about and treat ourselves as if we were machines.

The really distinctive feature of Taylorism thus is not the fact that Taylor tried to mechanize the organization of people and work, but the *degree* to which he was able to do this. For Taylor's workers were expected to be as reliable, predictable, and efficient as the robots that are now replacing them. History may well judge that Taylor came before his time. His principles of scientific management make superb sense for organizing production when robots rather than human beings are the main productive force, when organizations can truly become machines.

Strengths and limitations of the machine metaphor

"**S**et goals and objectives and go for them."

"Organize rationally, efficiently, and clearly."

"Specify every detail so that everyone will be sure of the jobs that they have to perform."

"Plan, organize, and control, control, control."

These and other similar ideas are often ingrained in our way of thinking about organization and in the way we read and evaluate organizational practice. For many people it is almost second nature to organize by setting up a structure of clearly defined activities linked by clear lines of command, communication, coordination, and control. Thus when a manager designs an organization he or she frequently designs a formal structure of jobs into which people can then be fitted. Or, if the people are available first, it is a question of finding everyone a clearly defined role to play. When a vacancy arises in an organization, managers frequently talk about having "a slot" to fill. Much of our training and education is often geared to making us "fit in" and feel comfortable in our appointed place, so that organization can proceed in a rational and efficient way.

Classical management theory and scientific management were each pioneered and sold to managers as the "one best way to organize." The early theorists believed that they had discovered *the* principles of organization, which, if followed, would more or less solve managerial problems forever. Now, we only have to look at the contemporary organizational scene to find that they were completely wrong on this score.

And indeed, if we look closely, we find that their management principles often lie at the basis of many modern organizational problems.

Images or metaphors only create partial ways of seeing. For in encouraging us to see and understand the world from one perspective they discourage us from seeing it from others. This is exactly what has happened in the course of developing mechanistic approaches to organization. For in understanding organization as a rational, technical process, mechanical imagery tends to underplay the human aspects of organization, and to overlook the fact that the tasks facing organizations are often much more complex, uncertain, and difficult than those that can be performed by most machines.

The strengths and limitations of the machine as a metaphor for organization are reflected in the strengths and limitations of mechanistic organization in practice.

The strengths can be stated very simply. For mechanistic approaches to organization work well only under conditions where machines work well: (a) when there is a straightforward task to perform; (b) when the environment is stable enough to ensure that the products produced will be appropriate ones; (c) when one wishes to produce exactly the same product time and again; (d) when precision is at a premium; and (e) when the human "machine" parts are compliant and behave as they have been designed to do.

Some organizations have had spectacular success using the mechanistic model, because these conditions are all fulfilled. Take for example the McDonald's hamburger chain, which has established a solid reputation for excellent performance in the fast-food industry. The firm has mechanized the organization of all its franchise outlets all over the world so that each can produce a uniform product. The firm serves a carefully targeted mass market in a perfectly regular and consistent way, with all the precision that "hamburger science" can provide. (The firm actually has its own "Hamburger U" for teaching this science to its managers, and has a detailed operating manual to guide franchises in the daily operations of the McDonald's system.) The firm is exemplary in its adoption of Tayloristic principles and recruits a nonunionized labor force, often made up of high school and college students, that will be happy to fit the organization as designed. And the "machine" works perfectly most of the time. Of course, the company also has a dynamic and innovative character, but this is for the most part confined to its central staff who do the thinking, i.e., the policy development and design work, for the corporation as a whole.

Many franchising systems have used the same Tayloristic approach with great effect, centralizing the design and development of products or services and decentralizing implementation in a highly controlled way. The use of scientific methods to determine the work to be performed, manuals that set standards and codify performance in minute detail, well-developed recruitment and training plans, and comprehensive systems of job evaluation often provide the recipe for success, provided that the service or product is amenable to definition and control in this way.

Surgical wards, aircraft maintenance departments, finance offices, courier firms, and other organizations where precision, safety, and clear accountability are at a premium are also often able to implement mechanistic approaches successfully, at least in certain aspects of their operations.

However, despite these successes, mechanistic approaches to organization often have severe limitations. In particular they: (a) can create organizational forms that have great difficulty in adapting to changing circumstances; (b) can result in mindless and unquestioning bureaucracy; (c) can have unanticipated and undesirable consequences as the interests of those working in the organization take precedence over the goals the organization was designed to achieve; and (d) can have dehumanizing effects upon employees, especially those at the lower levels of the organizational hierarchy.

Mechanistically structured organizations have great difficulty adapting to changing circumstances because they are designed to achieve predetermined goals; they are not designed for innovation. This should come as no surprise, for machines are usually single-purpose mechanisms designed to transform specific inputs into specific outputs and can engage in different activities only if they are explicitly modified or redesigned to do so.

Changing circumstances call for different kinds of action and response. Flexibility and capacities for creative action thus become more important than narrow efficiency. It becomes more important to do the right thing in a way that is timely and "good enough" than to do the wrong thing well, or the right thing too late. In these respects, mechanistic organization falls victim to the kind of "segmentalism" that Rosabeth Moss Kanter has shown plagues so many modern corporations. The compartmentalization created by mechanistic divisions between different hierarchic levels, functions, roles, and people tends to create barriers and stumbling blocks.

For example, when new problems arise they are often ignored because there are no ready-made responses. Or they are approached in a fragmented rather than a holistic way so that they can be tackled through existing organizational policies, procedures, and patterns of expertise. But standardized procedures and channels of communication are often unable to deal effectively with new circumstances, necessitating numerous ad hoc meetings and committees, which, because they have to be planned to fit rather than disrupt the normal mode of operation, are often too slow or too late for dealing with issues. Problems of inaction and lack of coordination thus become rife. In such circumstances the organization frequently becomes clogged with backlogs of work because normal routine has been disrupted, and complex issues float up the organizational hierarchy as members at each level find in turn that they are unable to solve them. On the way, information often gets distorted, as people hide errors and the true nature and magnitude of problems for fear of being held responsible for them. Those in command of the organization thus frequently find themselves facing issues that are inappropriately defined, and which they have no real idea of how to approach. They are often forced to delegate them to special task forces or teams of staff experts or consultants—who, since they are often remote from the concrete problems being experienced, further increase the delay and inadequacy of response. The difficulty of achieving effective responses to changing circumstances is often further aggravated by the high degree of specialization in different functional areas within the organization (e.g., production, marketing, finance, product engineering). Interdepartmental communications and coordination are often poor, and people often have a myopic view of what is occurring, there being no overall grasp of the situation facing the enterprise as a whole. As a result the actions encouraged by one element of the organization often entail negative consequences for others, so that one element ends up working against the interests of another.

These problems are often compounded by the fact that mechanistic definitions of job responsibilities encourage many organizational members to adopt mindless, unquestioning attitudes such as "it's not my job to worry about that" or "that's his responsibility, not mine" or "I'm here to do what I'm told." Though often seen as employee attitudes, they are actually inherent in the mechanistic approach to organization. Defining work responsibilities in a clear-cut manner has the advantage of letting everyone know what is expected of them. But it also lets them know what is *not* expected of them. Detailed job descriptions have this two-edged character, creating many problems when the organization faces changing circumstances that call for initiative and flexibility in response.

This institutionalized passivity and dependency can even lead people to make and justify deliberate mistakes on the premise that they're obeying orders. The hierarchical organization of jobs builds on the idea that control must be exercised *over* the different parts of the organization (to ensure that they are doing what they are designed to do), rather than being built *into* the parts themselves. Supervisors and other hierarchical forms of control do not just monitor the performance of workers—they also remove responsibility from workers, because their function really becomes operational only when problems arise. In a similar way, a system of quality control on a production line often institutionalizes the production of defective goods. People realize that they are allowed a quota of errors, developing the attitude that "I won't bother to correct that one—I'll leave it for the inspectors."

Much of the apathy, carelessness, and lack of pride so often encountered in the modern workplace is thus not coincidental: it is fostered by the mechanistic approach to organization that dominates work life. The rationality underlying mechanistic design is what may be described as a "functional" or "instrumental" rationality. It derives from the way people and jobs fit together in a fixed design. This kind of rationality contrasts with the "substantial rationality" of systems where people are encouraged to determine whether what they are doing is appropriate and to adjust actions accordingly. Whereas under the bureaucratic ethos actions are rational because of their place *within* the whole, substantial rationality requires actions that are informed by intelligent awareness of the complete situation. Whereas bureaucratic rationality is mechanical, substantial rationality is reflective and self-organizing. Mechanistic organization discourages initiative, encouraging people to obey orders and keep their place rather than to take an interest in, challenge, and question what they are doing. People in a bureaucracy who question the wisdom of conventional practice are viewed more often than not as troublemakers. Therefore apathy often reigns, as people learn to feel powerless about problems which collectively they understand and ultimately have the power to solve.

These difficulties are often linked to another set of problems: the development of subgoals and sets of interests that undermine the organization's ability to meet its primary objectives. The functional specialization in which elements of the organization's overall mission are broken down and made the responsibility of separate people or departments creates a structure that is supposed to be a system of cooperation but often turns out as a system of competition. The intention of mechanistic-bureaucratic organization is that the parts should contribute to the goals and objectives of the whole. But interpreted from a wider perspective the hierarchical structure is not just a network of jobs and roles, but also a career system in which individuals compete for limited places higher up the hierarchy. Competition also occurs because resources available to the organization are often limited, so that developments in one area (e.g., the marketing department) may exclude developments in others. As a consequence, the mechanistic organization can produce behavior which, while rational for the individuals involved in specific activities (e.g., the development of the marketing function), may prove irrational for the whole. Empire building, careerism, the defense of departmental interests and pet projects, and the padding of budgets to create slack resources may subvert the working of the whole. If the organization is staffed by rational men and women who behave in accordance with the formal interests and aims of the total organization, "fitting in" rather than using the organization for other purposes, then this may not occur. But humans are human, and the best-laid plans have a habit of turning in ways never intended by their creators. Formal organizations thus often become guided toward the achievement of informal ends, some of which may be quite contrary to the aims underlying the original design.

A final set of problems relate to human consequences. The mechanistic approach to organization tends to limit rather than mobilize the development of human capacities, molding human beings to fit the requirements of mechanical organization rather than building the organization around their strengths and potentials. Both employees and organizations lose from this arrangement. Employees lose opportunities for personal growth, often spending many hours a day on work they neither value nor enjoy, while organizations lose the creative and intelligent contributions that most employees are capable of making, given the right opportunities.

Mechanistic approaches to organization have proved incredibly popular, partly because of their efficiency in the performance of certain tasks, but also because of their ability to reinforce and sustain particular patterns of power and control. The machine metaphor has special appeal for individuals and groups who wish to exercise a close control over people and their activities; and as we will see in Chapters 6, 7, and 9, its popularity and use are often supported by a complex set of factors. However, there can be little doubt that the increasing rate of societal flux and change poses many problems for organizations based on mechanical designs. Mechanistic organizations may well in the end prove to be but one specific kind of organization, generated by, yet only imperfectly suited to, the requirements of the mechanical age. Now that we are entering an age with a completely new technological base drawing on microelectronics, new organizational principles are likely to become of increasing importance. The images of organization considered in the following chapters give a glimpse of what may be both possible and appropriate for managing these new times.

3

Nature Intervenes

Organizations as Organisms

$\mathbf{L}$et's think about organizations as if they were organisms.

We find ourselves thinking about them as living systems, existing in a wider environment on which they depend for the satisfaction of various needs. And as we look around the organizational world we begin to see that it is possible to identify different species of organization in different kinds of environment. Just as we find polar bears in arctic regions, camels in deserts, and alligators in swamps, we notice that certain species of organization are better "adapted" to specific environmental conditions than others. We find that bureaucratic organizations tend to work most effectively in environments that are stable or protected in some way and that very different species are found in more competitive and turbulent regions, such as the environments of high-tech firms in the aerospace and microelectronics industries.

In this simple line of inquiry we find the crux of many of the most important developments in organization theory over the last fifty years. For the problems of mechanistic visions of organization have led many organization theorists away from mechanical science and toward biology as a source of ideas for thinking about organization. In the process, organization theory has become a kind of biology in which the distinctions and relations among *molecules, cells, complex organisms, species,* and *ecology* are paralleled in those between *individuals, groups, organizations, populations (species) of organizations,* and their *social ecology*. And in pursuing this line of inquiry, organization theorists have generated many new ideas for understanding how organizations function, and the factors that influence their well-being.

In this chapter we will explore these ideas, showing how the organismic metaphor has helped organization theorists to identify and study different organizational needs, organizations as "open systems," the process of adapting organizations to environments, organizational life cycles, the factors influencing organizational health and development, different species of organization, and the relations between species and their ecology.

Collectively, these ideas have had an enormous impact on the way we now think about organization. Under the influence of the machine metaphor, organization theory was locked into a form of engineering preoccupied with relations between goals, structures, and efficiency. The idea that organizations are more like organisms has changed all this, guiding our attention toward the more general issues of survival, organization-environment relations, and organizational effectiveness. Goals, structures, and efficiency now become subsidiary to problems of survival and other more "biological" concerns.

Discovering organizational needs

Not surprisingly, organization theory began its excursion into biology by developing the idea that employees are people with complex needs that must be satisfied if they are to lead full and healthy lives and to perform effectively in the workplace. In retrospect, this hardly appears a profound insight, because from a modern perspective this seems an obvious fact of life. We all know that employees work best when motivated by the tasks they have to perform, and that the process of motivation hinges on allowing people to achieve rewards that satisfy their personal needs. However, in the early part of this century, this idea was by no means obvious. For many people work was a basic necessity, and those who designed and managed early organizations treated it as such. Hence, as we saw in the previous chapter, people like Frederick Taylor and the other classical management theorists were able to view the design of organizations as a *technical* problem, and the task of encouraging people to comply with the requirements of the organizational machine was reduced to a problem of "paying the right rate for the job." While esprit de corps was viewed as a valuable aid to management, management was viewed primarily as a process of controlling and directing employees in their work.

Much of organization theory since the late 1920s has rested in overcoming the limitations of this perspective. We can start the story with the Hawthorne Studies. These were conducted in the 1920s and 1930s under the leadership of Elton Mayo, at the Hawthorne Plant of the Western Electric Company in Chicago. At the outset the studies were primarily concerned with investigating the relation between conditions of work and the incidence of fatigue and boredom among employees. As the research progressed, however, it left this narrow Taylorist perspective to focus on many other aspects of the work situation as well, including the attitudes and preoccupations of employees and factors in the social environment outside work. The studies are now famous for identifying the importance of social needs in the workplace and the way work groups can satisfy these needs by restricting output and engaging in all manner of unplanned activities. In identifying that an "informal organization" based on friendship groups and unplanned interactions can exist alongside the formal organization documented in the "blueprints" designed by management, the studies dealt an important blow to classical management theory. They showed quite clearly that work activities are influenced as much by the nature of human beings as by formal design, and that organization theorists must pay close attention to this human side of organization.

With the Hawthorne Studies, the whole question of work motivation thus became a burning issue, as did the relations between individuals and groups. A new theory of organization began to emerge, built on the idea that individuals and groups, like biological organisms, operate most effectively only when their needs are satisfied.

Theories of motivation such as that pioneered by Abraham Maslow presented the human being as a kind of psychological organism struggling to satisfy its needs in a quest for full growth and development. This theory, which suggested that humans are motivated by a hierarchy of needs progressing through the physiological, the social, and the psychological, had very powerful implications, for it suggested that bureaucratic organizations which sought to motivate employees through money, or by merely providing a secure job, confined human development to the lower levels of the need hierarchy. Many management theorists were quick to see that jobs and interpersonal relations could be redesigned to create conditions for personal growth that would simultaneously help organizations to achieve their aims and objectives.

Thus the idea of integrating the needs of individuals and organizations became a powerful force. Organizational psychologists like Chris Argyris, Frederick Herzberg, and Douglas McGregor began to show how bureaucratic structures, leadership styles, and work organization generally could be modified to create "enriched," motivating jobs that would encourage people to exercise their capacities for self-control and creativity. Under their influence, alternatives to bureaucratic organization began to emerge.

Particular attention was focused on the idea of making employees feel more useful and important by giving them meaningful jobs, and by giving as much autonomy, responsibility, and recognition as possible as a means of getting them involved in their work. Job enrichment, combined with a more participative, democratic, and employee-centered style of leadership, arose as an alternative to the excessively narrow, authoritarian, and dehumanizing work orientation generated by scientific management and classical management theory.

Developed in countless ways, these ideas provided a powerful framework for the development of what is now known as human-resource management. Employees were to be seen as valuable resources that could contribute in rich and varied ways to an organization's activities if given an appropriate chance. Maslow's theory suggested a whole repertoire of means (summarized in Exhibit 3.1) through which employees could be motivated at all levels of the need hierarchy. Much of this theorizing has proved extremely attractive in management circles, for it offered the possibility of motivating employees through "higher-level" needs without paying them any more money.

During the 1960s and 1970s management and organizational researchers thus gave much attention to shaping the design of work as a means of increasing productivity and job satisfaction, improving work quality, reducing absenteeism and turnover, and incidentally, often getting a lot of good publicity for doing so. The famous experiments in work design by Volvo in Sweden present one of the more prominent examples, the much-publicized idea that Volvo workers are happy in their jobs spilling over into the idea that perhaps therefore they make better-quality cars.

This dual focus on the technical and human aspects of organization is now reflected in the view that organizations are best understood as

TYPE OF NEED

Self actualizing
- Encouragement of complete employee commitment.
- The job becomes a major expressive dimension of employee's life.

Ego
- Creation of jobs with scope for achievement, autonomy, responsibility and personal control.
- Work enhancing personal identity.
- Feedback and recognition for good performance, e.g. promotions, "employee of the month" awards.

Social
- Work organization that permits interaction with colleagues.
- Social and sports facilities.
- Office and factory parties outings.

Security
- Pension and health care plans.
- Job tenure.
- Emphasis on career paths within the organization.

Physiological
- Salaries and wages.
- Safe and pleasant working conditions.

Exhibit 3.1. Examples of how organizations can satisfy needs at different levels of Maslow's hierarchy "sociotechnical systems." The term was coined in the 1950s by members of the Tavistock Institute of Human Relations in England to capture the interdependent qualities of the social and technical aspects of work. In their view, these aspects of work are inseparable, because the nature of one element in this configuration *always* has important consequences for the other. When we choose a technical system (whether organizational structure, leadership style, or technology) it always has human consequences, and vice versa. This has been particularly well illustrated in many Tavistock studies, such as that conducted by Eric Trist and Ken Bamforth on technological change in coal mining in England in the late 1940s. The attempt to mechanize the mining process through the introduction of the "long-wall method," which in effect bought assembly-line coal cutting to the coal face, created severe problems by destroying the informal fabric of social relations present in the mine. The new technology promised increases in efficiency yet brought all the social problems now associated with the modern factory, compounded many times by much worse physical conditions. The resolution of the problems rested in finding a means of reconciling human needs and technical efficiency.

Work in most parts of the world has now shown that in designing or managing any kind of social system, whether it be a small group, an organization, or a society, the interdependence of technical and human needs must be kept firmly in mind. This is now clearly recognized in most popular theories of organization, leadership, and group functioning, all of which usually build on sociotechnical principles in one way or another.

Recognizing the importance of environment: organizations as open systems

When we recognize that individuals, groups, and organizations have needs that must be satisfied, attention is invariably drawn to the fact that they depend on a wider environment for various kinds of sustenance. It is this kind of thinking that now underpins the "systems approach" to organization, which takes its main inspiration from the work of a theoretical biologist, Ludwig von Bertalanffy. Developed simultaneously on both sides of the Atlantic in the 1950s and 1960s, the systems approach builds on the principle that organizations, like organisms, are "open" to their environment and must achieve an appropriate relation with that environment if they are to survive.

Developed at a theoretical level, the open-systems approach has generated many new concepts for thinking about organizations (Exhibit 3.2). These are often presented as general principles for thinking about *all* kinds of systems, since von Bertalanffy developed the principles of *General Systems Theory* as a means of linking different scientific disciplines. However, he achieved this integration by taking the living organism as a model for understanding complex open systems, thus reproducing ideas primarily developed for understanding biological systems in order to understand the world at large. Early systems theory thus developed as a biological metaphor in disguise.

At a pragmatic level, the open-systems approach usually focuses on a number of key issues.

First, there is the emphasis on the environment in which organizations exist. Surprising as it may now seem, the classical management theorists devoted relatively little attention to the environment. They treated the organization as a "closed" mechanical system and became preoccupied with principles of internal design. The open-systems view has changed all this, suggesting that we should always organize with the environment in mind. Thus much attention has been devoted to understanding the immediate "task environment" defined by the organization's direct interactions, (e.g., with customers, competitors, suppliers, labor unions, and government agencies), as well as the broader "contextual" or "general environment." All this has important implications for organizational practice, stressing the importance of being able to scan and sense changes in task and contextual environments, of being able to bridge and manage critical boundaries and areas of interdependence, and of being able to develop appropriate strategic responses. Much of the widespread interest in corporate strategy is a product of this realization that organizations must be sensitive to what is occurring in the world beyond.

A second focus of the open-systems approach defines an organization in terms of interrelated subsystems. Systems are like Chinese boxes in that they always contain wholes within wholes. Thus organizations contain individuals (who are systems on their own account), who belong to groups or departments, which belong to larger organizational divisions. And so on. If we define the whole organization as a system, then the other levels can be understood as subsystems, just as molecules, cells, and organs can be seen as subsystems of a living organism, even though they are complex open systems on their own account.

These principles, derived primarily from the study of biological systems, are now often used in the analysis of organizations as systems:

The concept of an "open system." Organic systems at the level of the cell, complex organism, and population of organisms exist in a continuous exchange with their environment. This exchange is crucial for sustaining the life and form of the system, since environmental interaction is the basis of self-maintenance. It is thus often said that living systems are "open systems," characterized by a continuous cycle of input, internal transformation (throughout), output, and feedback (whereby one element of experience influences the next). The idea of openness emphasizes the key relationships between the environment and the internal functioning of the system. Environment and system are to be understood as being in a state of interaction and mutual dependence. The open nature of biological and social systems contrasts with the "closed" nature of many physical and mechanical systems, though the degree of openness can vary, since some open systems may only be responsive to a relatively narrow range of inputs from the environment. Towers, bridges, or even clockwork toys with predetermined motions are closed systems. A machine that is able to regulate its internal operation in accordance with variations in the environment may be considered a partially open system. A living organism, organization, or social group is a fully open system. (But note the critique of the concept of openness presented in Chapter 8.)

Homeostasis. The concept of homeostasis refers to self-regulation and the ability to maintain a steady state. Biological organisms seek a regularity of form and distinctness from the environment while maintaining a continuous exchange with that environment. This form and distinctness is achieved through homeostatic processes that regulate and control system operation on the basis of what is now called "negative feedback," where deviations from some standard or norm initiate actions to correct the deviation. Thus when our body temperature rises above normal limits, certain bodily functions operate to try and counteract the rise, e.g., we begin to perspire and breathe heavily. Social systems also require such homeostatic control processes if they are to acquire enduring form.

Entropy/negative entropy. Closed systems are entropic in that they have a tendency to deteriorate and run down. Open systems, on the other hand, attempt to sustain themselves by importing energy to try and offset entropic tendencies. It is thus said that they are characterized by negative entropy.

Structure, function, differentiation, and integration. The relationship between these concepts is of crucial importance for understanding living systems. It is easy to see organization as a structure of parts and to explain system behavior in terms of relations between the parts, causes and effects, stimulus and response. Our understanding of living systems warns against such reduction, emphasizing that structure, function, behavior and all other features of system operation are closely intertwined. Though it is possible to pursue the study of organisms through study of anatomy, a full understanding of such systems calls for much more. Even the life of the simple cell is dependent on a complex web of relations between cellular structure, metabolism, gas exchange, the acquisition of nutrients, and numerous other functions. The cell as a system is a system of functional interdependence that is not reducible to a simple structure. Indeed, the structure at any one time depends on the existence of these functions and in many respects is only a manifestation of them. The same is true of more complex organisms, which reflect increased differentiation and specialization of function, e.g., with specialized organs performing specific functions— and which thus require more complex systems of integration to maintain the system as a whole, e.g., through the operation of a brain. Similar relationships between structure, function, differentiation, and integration can also be seen in social systems such as organizations.

Requisite variety. Related to the idea of differentiation and integration is the principle of requisite variety, which states that the internal regulatory mechanisms of a system must be as diverse as the environment with which it is trying to deal. For only by incorporating required variety into internal controls can a system deal with the variety and challenge posed by its environment. Any system that insulates itself from diversity in the environment tends to atrophy and lose its complexity and distinctive nature. Thus requisite variety is an important feature of living systems of all kinds.

Equifinality. This principle captures the idea that in an open system there may be many different ways of arriving at a given end state. This is in contrast to more closed systems where system relations are fixed in terms of structure to produce specific patterns of cause and effect. Living systems have flexible patterns of organization that allow the achievement of specific results from different starting points with different resources in different ways. The structure of the system at a given time is no more than an aspect or manifestation of a more complex functional process; it does not determine that process.

System evolution. The capacity of a system to evolve depends on an ability to move to more complex forms of differentiation and integration, greater variety in the system facilitating its ability to deal with challenges and opportunities posed by the environment. As we will discuss later, this involves a cyclical process of variation, selection, and retention of the selected characteristics.

Exhibit 3.2. A glossary of some open-systems concepts

Systems theorists are fond of thinking about intra- and interorganizational relations in these terms, using configurations of subsystems to depict key patterns and interconnections. One popular way of doing this is to focus on the key sets of needs which the organization must satisfy to survive, and emphasize the importance of managing relations between them. Thus the sociotechnical view of organization discussed earlier is often expanded to take account of relations between technical, social, managerial, strategic, and environmental requirements (Exhibit 3.3). As we will see, this way of thinking has helped us to recognize how everything depends on everything else, and to find ways of managing the relations between critical subsystems and the environment.

A third focus in the pragmatic use of the systems approach rests in the attempt to establish congruencies between different systems, and to identify and eliminate potential dysfunctions. Just as a sociotechnical approach to work design emphasizes the importance of matching human and technical requirements, open-systems theory more generally encourages a matching of the kind of subsystems illustrated in Exhibit 3.3. Here the principles of requisite variety, differentiation and integration, and other systems ideas (discussed in Exhibit 3.2) can be brought into play. For example, the principle of requisite variety is particularly important in designing control systems or for the management of internal and external boundaries—for these must embrace the complexity of the phenomena being controlled or managed to be effective. And, as we shall see later, the principle of differentiation and integration is useful for organizing different kinds of task within the same organization.

Collectively, these ideas have pointed the way to theories of organization and management that allow us to break free of bureaucratic thinking, and to organize in a way that meets the requirements of the environment. These insights are now usually marshaled under the perspective known as "contingency theory," and in the practice of organizational development.

Contingency theory: adapting organization to environment

"Organizations are open systems that need careful management to satisfy and balance internal needs and to adapt to environmental circumstances."

Organizations, like organisms, can be conceived of as sets of interacting subsystems. These subsystems can be defined in many ways. Here is one example stressing relations between the different variables that influence the functioning of an organization, thereby providing a useful diagnostic tool.

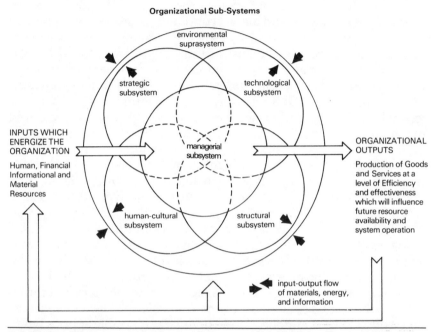

Organizational Sub-Systems

Exhibit 3.3. How an organization can be seen as a set of independent subsystems
SOURCE: Adapted from CONTINGENCY VIEWS OF ORGANIZATION AND MANAGEMENT by Fremont E. Kast and James E. Rosenzweig. © 1973, Science Research Associates, Inc. Reprinted by permission of the publisher.

"There is no one best way of organizing. The appropriate form depends on the kind of task or environment with which one is dealing."

"Management must be concerned, above all else, with achieving 'good fits'. Different approaches to management may be necessary to perform different tasks within the same organization, and quite different types or 'species' of organization are needed in different types of environment."

In a nutshell, these are the main ideas underlying the contingency approach to organization, which has established itself as a dominant perspective in modern organizational analysis.

One of the most influential studies establishing the credentials of this approach was conducted in the 1950s by two British researchers,

Tom Burns and G. M. Stalker. Their work is famous for establishing the distinction between "mechanistic" and "organic" approaches to organization and management.

Focusing on firms in a variety of industries, e.g., man-made fibers, engineering, and electronics, Burns and Stalker illustrated that when change in the environment becomes the order of the day, as when changing technological and market conditions pose new problems and challenges, open and flexible styles of organization and management are required. Exhibit 3.4 attempts to capture salient aspects of their study, illustrating patterns of organization and management in four successful firms experiencing different rates of environmental change.

The rayon mill faced a relatively stable environment, employed a technology that was routine and well understood, and was organized in a highly mechanistic way. The firm had a "Factory Bible," held by every head of department, and defining required action in almost every situation. People in the organization thus knew precisely what was expected of them and attended to their job responsibilities in a narrow yet efficient way, to create a competitively priced product. The firm was relatively successful in meeting the demands placed upon it, treating problematic situations as temporary deviations from the norm, and doing whatever it could to stabilize its operating environment. For example, the sales office was sometimes asked to restrain sales in the interests of sustaining an even and trouble-free production schedule.

In other successful organizations facing more uncertain and turbulent environmental conditions, the mechanistic approach to organization tended to be abandoned; more organic and flexible approaches to organization were required for successful operation. Thus in a switchgear firm operating in an area of the engineering industry where product developments hinged on improvements in design and cutting costs, and where products were frequently made to customer specifications, systems of authority, communication, and work organization were geared to the contingencies of changing situations. Great use was made of meetings as a means of exchanging information and identifying problems, particularly those relating to the coordination of work, so that an alternative system of organization existed alongside the formal hierarchy defining relationships between specialist tasks.

In successful firms in the electronics industry the departure from the mechanistic mode was even more pronounced. For example, in a firm involved in radio and television manufacture, at the more stable end of the electronics spectrum, the need to keep abreast of market and technological change through frequent product modification, and the need to link developments in research and production, called for free and open collaboration and communication across departments and levels of seniority. Meetings were again a central feature, driving and dominating day-to-day work activities. This approach to organization has grown in prominence in the twenty-five years since the publication of Burns and Stalker's work. It is most evident in the "project" or "matrix" form of organization, which makes use of project teams to deal with the continuous flow of problems and projects associated with changes in corporate policy and in characteristics of the environment.

In successful organizations in even more unpredictable areas of the electronics field, where the need to innovate was an essential condition for survival, the mode of organization was even more open. Here, jobs were allowed to shape themselves, people being appointed to the organization for their general ability and expertise and allowed and encouraged to find their own place and to define the contribution that they could make. This style of open, "organic" management is fully consistent with the way the electronics industry has evolved. When the first commercial electronics firms began operating at the end of World War II, there was no commercial market for electronics products to speak of, since peacetime applications of this newly emerging technology had yet to be found. The electronics industry literally had to invent both products and markets, and at the same time to cope with the rapid technological change that in about thirty years converted computers from room-size giants into devices that fit our pockets. As we are all so well aware, countless new applications have been found for the basic technology. From the start, firms in this industry operated in an organic and flexible manner, searching for opportunities in the environment and adapting themselves to take advantage of these opportunities. Thus in the firms observed by Burns and Stalker the process of finding out what one should be doing in one's job proved unending, defining a mode of organization linking inquiry and action. Successful electronics firms avoided organizational hierarchies and avoided narrow departmentation, defining and redefining roles in a collaborative manner in connection with the tasks facing the organization as a whole. They created a form of organization having more in common with that of an amoeba than a machine.

Burns and Stalker's idea that it is possible to identify a continuum of organizational forms ranging from mechanistic to organic, and that more flexible forms are required to deal with changing environments, received support from other studies conducted in the late 1950s and early 1960s. For example, Joan Woodward, in a study of firms in England, discerned a relationship between technology and the structure of successful organizations. She showed that the principles of classical management theory were not always the right ones to follow, since different technologies impose different demands on individuals and or-

	Rayon Mill	Switchgear firm	Radio & Television firm	Electronics firm
Nature of environment	Relatively stable: technological and market conditions well understood	Moderate rate of change: expanding market coupled with opportunities for improved products	High degree of change: dynamic technological and market conditions with predictable rate of novelty	Highly unpredictable: rapid technological advance and boundless market opportunities
Nature of task facing the firm	Efficient production of standard product	Efficient production and sale of basic product, subject to modification according to customer requirements	Efficient design, production, and marketing of new products in highly competitive environment	Exploitation of rapid technical change through innovation and exploration of new market situations
Organization of work	Clearly defined jobs arranged in hierarchical pattern	Rough division of job responsibilities according to a functional and hierarchical pattern, modified to meet contingencies. No stable division of functions	Consistent blurring of organizational positions; every section of management concerned with the focal task of competitive selling	Deliberate attempt to avoid specifying individual tasks; jobs defined by the individuals concerned through interaction with others

	MECHANISTIC			ORGANIC
Nature of authority	Clearly defined and vested in formal position in hierarchy; seniority important	Not clearly defined but following the hierarchy except in specially convened committees and meetings	Limits of authority and responsibility not defined; authority vested in people with ability to solve problems at hand	Pattern of authority informal and constantly changing as roles become redefined with changing circumstances; vested in individuals with appropriate skills & abilities
Communications system	According to pattern specified in various rules and regulations; mainly vertical	according to rules and conventions, but supplemented by regular system of committees and meetings. Junior staff free to consult with top management group	Frequent meetings in a context of constant consultation across all levels and parts of the firm	Completely free and informal; the process of communication was unending and central to the concept of organization
Nature of employee commitment	Commitment to responsibilities associated with their own particular jobs; loyalty and obedience important	Commitment to own job but recognizing the need for flexibility in dealing with contingencies arising from the total situation	Commitment to demands of own functional positions reconciled with wider demands for cooperation and flexible interpretation of function	Full commitment to the central tasks facing the concern as a whole and an ability to deal with considerable stress and uncertainty

MECHANISTIC ◄──────────────────► ORGANIC

Exhibit 3.4. Patterns of organization and management in four successful organizations facing different rates of environmental change
SOURCE: Based on Burns and Stalker (1961).

ganization that have to be met through *appropriate* structure. Her evidence suggested that bureaucratic-mechanistic organization might be appropriate for firms employing mass-production technologies, but that firms with unit, small-batch, or process systems of production needed a different approach. Woodward's findings also suggested that given any technology a range of possible organizational forms may be employed. Though suggesting that successful organizations matched structure and technology, she demonstrated that this relationship was ultimately one of strategic choice. Burns and Stalker also made a similar point in stressing that there was absolutely no guarantee that firms would find the appropriate mode of organization for dealing with their environment. Their study emphasized that successful adaptation of organization to environment depended on the ability of top management to interpret the conditions facing the firm in an appropriate manner, and to adopt relevant courses of action. Both these studies thus demonstrated that in the process of organizing a lot of choices have to be made, and were at one in suggesting that effective organization depends on achieving a balance or compatibility between strategy, structure, technology, the commitments and needs of people, and the external environment.

We find here the essence of modern contingency theory. But it took an important study by several Harvard researchers, led by Paul Lawrence and Jay Lorsch, to hammer the point home. Their research was built around two principal ideas. First, that different kinds of organizations are needed to deal with different market and technological conditions. Second, that organizations operating in uncertain and turbulent environments need to achieve a higher degree of internal differentiation, e.g., between departments, than those in environments that are less complex and more stable. To test their ideas they studied high- and low-performance organizations in three industries experiencing high, moderate, and low rates of growth and technological and market change. The plastics industry was selected as an example of a turbulent environment and the standardized-container industry as an example of a stable environment, with the food industry in between. Lawrence and Lorsch's results supported their hypotheses, showing that successful firms in each environment achieved an appropriate degree of differentiation and integration, and that the degree of differentiation between departments tended to be greater in the plastics industry than in the food industry, which was in turn greater than that in the standardized container industry.

The Lawrence and Lorsch study thus refined the contingency approach by showing that styles of organization may need to vary between organizational subunits because of the detailed characteristics of their subenvironments. Production departments typically face task environments characterized by more clear-cut goals and shorter time horizons, and can adopt more formal or bureaucratic modes of interpersonal interaction than sales departments. Research and development departments, especially those engaged in fundamental as opposed to applied research, face even more ambiguous goals, have even longer time horizons, and often adopt even less formalized modes of interaction. The study showed that the degree of required differentiation in managerial and organizational styles between departments varied according to the nature of the industry and its environment, and that an appropriate degree of integration was also needed to tie the differentiated parts together again.

The study also yielded important insights on modes of integration. For example, in relatively stable environments, conventional bureaucratic modes of integration such as hierarchy, rules, and so on appeared to work quite well. But in more turbulent environments they needed to be replaced by other modes, such as the use of multidisciplinary project teams and the appointment of personnel skilled in the art of coordination and conflict resolution. The successful use of these integrative devices was also shown to be dependent on achieving an intermediate stance between the units being coordinated; on the power, status, and competence of those involved; and on the presence of a structure of rewards favoring integration.

Lawrence and Lorsch gave a precision and refinement to the general idea that certain organizations need to be more organic than others, suggesting that the degree of organicism required varies from one organizational subunit to another. Using their ideas, we can appreciate that even in the dynamic context of an electronics firm, where the dominant ethic may be to remain open, flexible, and innovative, there may be exceptions to the rule. For example, certain aspects of production or financial administration may require clearer definition and control than work in other areas.

The Lawence and Lorsch study thus reinforced and developed the ideas emerging from the other studies discussed above, marking an important turning point in favor of contingency theory. This work served to popularize the idea that in different environmental circumstances some species of organization are better able to survive than others, and that since the relations between organization and environment are the product of human choices, they may become maladapted. In such cases, organizations are likely to experience many problems both in dealing with the environment and in their internal functioning. Such ideas naturally give rise to a desire to know more about the nature of organizational species and the requirements for designing and maintaining healthy organizations. And not surprisingly, these concerns have been an important feature of recent research.

The variety of the species

The ideas discussed in the previous sections go a long way toward showing us what species of organization are successful and under what conditions. But between the 1960s and the 1980s hundreds of research studies have further addressed the job of specifying organizational characteristics and their success in dealing with different tasks and environmental conditions. These studies have added rich insight to the mechanistic-organic continuum developed by Burns and Stalker.

Consider, for example, the work of Henry Mintzberg of McGill University, which identifies five configurations or species of organization: the *machine bureaucracy,* the *divisionalized form,* the *professional bureaucracy,* the *simple structure,* and the species that we refer to as the *"adhocracy."* The thrust of his work, which has been extended and refined in many ways by his colleagues Danny Miller and Peter Friesen, is to show that effective organization depends on developing a cohesive set of relations between structural design; the age, size, and technology of the firm; and the conditions of the industry in which it is operating.

The work of the McGill researchers confirms that the machine bureaucracy and the divisionalized form (both of which were discussed in Chapter 2) tend to be ineffective except under conditions where tasks and environment are simple and stable. Their highly centralized systems of control tend to make them slow and ineffective in dealing with changing circumstances. While appropriate for firms that are "production" or "efficiency driven," they are often inappropriate for firms that are "market" or "environment driven."

The professional bureaucracy modifies the principles of centralized control to allow greater autonomy to staff and is appropriate for dealing with relatively stable conditions where tasks are relatively complicated. This is an appropriate structure for universities, hospitals, and other professional organizations where the people with the key skills and abilities need a large measure of autonomy and discretion to be effective in their work. The structure of the professional bureaucracy tends to be fairly flat, tall hierarchies being replaced by a decentralized system of authority. Standardization and integration are achieved through professional training and the acceptance of key operating norms, rather than through more direct forms of control.

The simple structure and "adhocracy" tend to work best in unstable environmental conditions. The former usually comprises a chief executive, often the founder or an entrepreneur, who may have a group of support staff, and a group of operators who do the basic work. Organization is very informal and flexible and, though run in a highly centralized way by the chief executive, is ideal for achieving quick changes and maneuvers. This form of organization works very well in entrepreneurial organizations where speedy decision making is at a premium, provided that tasks are not too complex. It is typical of successful young and innovative companies.

The "adhocracy," a term coined by Warren Bennis to characterize organizations that are temporary by design, approximates Burns and Stalker's organic form of organization. It is a form highly suited for the performance of complex and uncertain tasks in turbulent environments. The adhocracy usually involves project teams that come together to perform a task and disappear when the task is over, with members regrouping in other teams devoted to other projects. Adhocracies now abound in innovative firms in the aerospace and electronics industries, in all kinds of project-oriented companies such as consulting firms and advertising agencies, and in the movie industry. This form of organization also sometimes emerges as a differentiated unit of a larger organization: e.g., an ad hoc task group or project team performing a limited assignment or contributing to the strategic planning and development of the organization as a whole. It is also frequently used in R & D work.

Many adhocracies utilize what is often known as "matrix organization," though this is best regarded as a species of organization with a high degree of variation. While some approaches to matrix organization can be so highly formalized that they operate as modified bureaucracies, others are closer to free-flowing organic forms.

The term matrix organization was coined to capture a visual impression of organizations that systematically attempt to combine the kind of functional or departmental structure of organization found in a bureaucracy with a project-team structure (Exhibit 3.5). The functional units are equivalent to the columns of a matrix, while the teams form the rows.

The fully developed matrix is team-driven in that priority is given to business, program, product, or project areas, with functional specialisms providing support. And in this form it is like the adhocracy, since the focus on an end product rather than on functional contributions encourages flexible, innovative, and adaptive behavior. In some matrix organizations, however, the functional divisions retain most of the control, so that the teams are set within a bureaucratic structure from which it is often difficult to break free. As a result, they often fail to innovate and perform their project tasks in an effective way.

Matrix organizations, sometimes described as "project organizations," adapt the functional-bureaucratic form to meet the demands of special situations through the establishment of subunits or teams with membership drawn from different functional areas or departments:

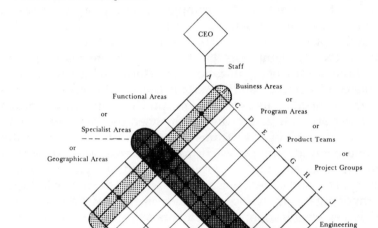

General Form of a Matrix Organization

Exhibit 3.5. Matrix organization
SOURCE: Diagram from Kolodny (1981: 20). Copyright, 1981, by the Foundation for the School of Business at Indiana University. Reprinted by permission.

Matrix organization provides a means of breaking down the barriers between specialisms and allowing members from different functional specialisms to fuse their skills and abilities in an attack on common problems. Organizations may establish project teams to cope with the design and production of specific products, to tackle a corporate planning problem, or to deal with ad hoc issues such as the relocation of a plant or offices. While some organizations may establish few teams, others may be dominated by team activity. Teams may be temporary and be treated as a departure from normal operations, or may be seen as a feature of the way business ought to be done.

Matrix organization typically increases the adaptability of organizations in dealing with their environments, improves coordination between functional specialisms, and makes good use of human resources. The approach also diffuses influence and control, allowing people at the middle and lower levels of an organization to make contributions that might otherwise be denied. The fusion of functional expertise with product orientation also helps to create a healthy competition for internal resources between product areas while preserving a product-oriented focus in relation to the external environment.

Problems do arise, however, especially in relation to conflicts between departmental and team loyalties and responsibilities. This is particularly true where project teams are superimposed on a strong bureaucratic style of organization. Team members are often seen as *representatives* of functional departments and held accountable for their actions by departmental heads upon whose favor their career may depend. They are often confined to "sitting in" and "reporting back," and thus may find it difficult to become fully committed members of their team. The dual loyalties and responsibilities erode the effectiveness of the teams. In more fully developed matrix organizations this tension of dual responsibility is often resolved in favor of an emphasis on team commitment, backed by appropriate rewards. Also, matrix organizations often tend to be dominated by meetings, which may seem to be very time consuming. They require close attention to the inevitable conflicts and a high degree of collegiality and interpersonal skill in their members.

Our discussion of the varieties of matrix organization illustrates some of the difficulties encountered in attempting to identify discrete types of organization. For unlike in nature, where species are distinguished by discrete clusters of attributes, organizational characteristics are often distributed in a more continuous way. One form often tends to blend with another, producing organizations that have hybrid characteristics. However, as Henry Mintzberg and the early contingency theorists have shown, if we focus on successful organizations, their specieslike character becomes much clearer. For successful organizations seem to share distinctive characteristics that are appropriate for dealing with their environment.

Interestingly, this is supported by two very influential studies that lie outside the contingency tradition. In their 1982 book, *In Search of Excellence*, Thomas Peters and Robert Waterman document the characteristics of what they regard as excellent U.S. companies. Most of these organizations are innovative, market-driven, operating in dynamic environments. And not surprisingly, most of them adopt organizational designs that have much in common with the adhocracy/organic forms of organization. (The major exception is the McDonald's corporation, which, as discussed in Chapter 2, adopts a highly mechanistic mode of organization. But as Peters and Waterman show, its relatively small and innovative *headquarters* employs a much more open and flexible form of management.) The eight principles of excellence identified by Peters and Waterman (Exhibit 3.6) do much to refine earlier ideas on how adhocracies/organic organizations operate in practice, and add powerful weight to the insights of the early contingency theorists.

In her book *The Change Masters*, Rosabeth Moss Kanter of Yale University also identifies the characteristics of successful corporations dealing with changing environments, and makes many further contributions to our understanding of adhocracies and the organic approach to management. The distinction that she draws between "segmentalist" and "integrative" organizations parallels the distinction between Burns and Stalker's concepts of mechanistic and organic organization. And her insights on the pathologies which segmentalist organizations encounter in dealing with change, and on the processes through which integrative organizations manage learning and novelty, add much to our understanding of the problems that have preoccupied contingency theorists over the last few decades.

Both Peters and Waterman's and Kanter's books delineate a species of successful organization. Thus, even though they do not devote much attention to the contingency theorists' dictum that successful organization rests in a fit between organization and environment, and that in practice there may thus be many varieties of "excellent" organizations, their work makes a valuable contribution to the contingency perspective.

Organizational health and development

How does one achieve a good "fit" in practice? It's all very well to talk about the need to adapt organizations to environmental circumstances, and about the need to ensure that internal relations are balanced and appropriate, but what does this mean in operational terms?

These and related questions have become the focus of attention for numerous consultancy-oriented researchers working in the field of or-

In their study of "excellent" U.S. companies (firms in high-technology, consumer goods, service, resource, project-management, and general industrial categories), Peters and Waterman identify eight basic practices as characteristic of successfully managed companies:

A bias for action
- Project teams that tend to be small, fluid, ad hoc, and problem/action-focused.
- Communications are of the essence, and there is an important commitment to learning and experimentation.
- Complex problems are tackled through a willingness to shift resources to where they are needed to encourage fluidity and action (chunking).

Close to the customer
- The market-driven principle of commitment to service, reliability, and quality, based on an appreciation of "nichemanship" and the ability to custom-tailor a product or service to a client's needs.

Autonomy and entrepreneurship
- A principle which champions innovation, decentralization, the delegation of power and action to the level where they are needed, and a healthy tolerance of failure.

Productivity through people
- The principle that employees are people and a major resource, and should be trusted, respected, inspired, and made "winners."
- Organizational units should be small-scale to preserve and develop a people-oriented quality.

Hands-on, value-driven
- Organization guided by a clear sense of shared values, mission, and identity, relying on inspirational leadership rather than bureaucratic control.

Stick to the knitting
- The principle of building on strengths and knowledge of one's niche.

Simple form, lean staff
- Avoid bureaucracy; build main commitments to projects or product division rather than to the dual lines of responsibility found in formal matrix organizations; use small organizational units.

Simultaneous loose-tight properties
- The principle that reconciles the need for overall control with a commitment to autonomy and entrepreneurship.

Exhibit 3.6. Organizing for action and innovation
SOURCE: Based on Peters and Waterman (1982: 89-327).

ganizational development, popularly known as "OD." They have helped to bring the insights generated by the contingency theorists, and the systems approach generally, right down to earth by developing diagnostic and prescriptive models to identify organizational ailments and to prescribe some kind of cure. In effect, they have adopted the role of organizational doctors.

Given an understanding of the ideas discussed in previous sections it is easy to see how such diagnosis and prescription can proceed. For all we really need to do is pose a series of questions about the existing relations between organization and environment:

1. *What is the nature of the organization's environment?* Is it simple and stable or complex and turbulent? Is it easy to see interconnections between various elements of the environment? What changes are occurring in the economic, technological, market, labor-relations, and sociopolitical dimensions? What is the chance of some development transforming the whole environment—some development that will create a new opportunity or challenge the viability of existing operations?

2. *What kind of strategy is being employed?* Is the organization adopting a nonstrategy, simply reacting to whatever change comes along? Is the organization attempting to defend a particular niche that it has created in the environment? Is the organization systematically analyzing the environment to identify new threats and opportunities? Is the organization adopting an innovative, proactive stance, constantly searching for new opportunities and evaluating existing activities? Is the stance towards the environment competitive or collaborative?

3. *What kind of technology (mechanical and nonmechanical) is being used?* Are the processes used to transform inputs into outputs standardized and routinized? Does the technology create jobs with high or low scope for responsibility and autonomy? Does the technology rigidify operations, or is it flexible and open-ended? What technological choices face the organization? Can it replace rigid systems with more flexible forms?

4. *What kind of people are employed, and what is the dominant "culture" or ethos within the organization?* What orientations do people bring to their work? Is a narrow "I'm here for the money" commitment the norm, or are people searching for challenge and involvement? What are the core values and beliefs shaping patterns of corporate culture and subculture?

5. *How is the organization structured, and what are the dominant managerial philosophies?* Is the organization bureaucratic, or are matrix/organic

forms of organization the norm? Is the dominant managerial philosophy authoritarian, stressing accountability and close control, or more democratic, encouraging initiative and enterprise throughout the organization? Does the philosophy stress safe but sure approaches, or is it innovative and risk-taking?

This scheme of questioning can be used to identify organizational characteristics and to determine the compatibility between the different elements. In asking these questions we are building on the idea that the organization consists of interrelated subsystems of a strategic, human, technological, structural, and managerial nature (see Exhibit 3.3 discussed earlier), which need to be internally consistent and adapted to environmental conditions. Our answers can be plotted as shown in Exhibit 3.7, to reveal congruencies and incongruencies.

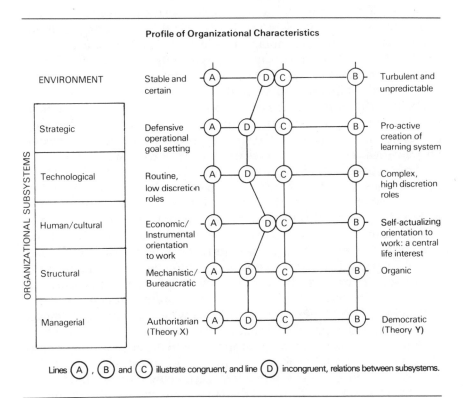

Profile of Organizational Characteristics

Lines (A), (B) and (C) illustrate congruent, and line (D) incongruent, relations between subsystems.

Exhibit 3.7. Congruence and incongruence between organizational subsystems
SOURCE: Adapted from Burrell and Morgan (1979:177).

Three examples of congruent relations between organizational and environmental characteristics are represented by the positions (A), (B), and (C) in Exhibit 3.7. In accordance with the conclusions of contingency theory, each is likely to be highly effective. Position (A) represents an organization in a stable environment adopting a defensive strategy to protect its niche. Perhaps it is an organization commanding a secure market on the basis of a good-quality product produced in a cost-efficient way. The organization employs a mass-production technology, and is structured and managed mechanistically. The people employed are content with their narrowly defined roles, and the organization operates in an efficient and trouble-free manner.

Position (C) represents an organization encountering a moderate degree of change in its environment. Technological developments are occurring at a regular pace, and markets are in a constant state of transition. The organization has to keep abreast of these developments, analyzing emergent trends, updating production methods, and creating a flow of product modifications, rather like the radio and television firm in Burns and Stalker's study. It is not on the cutting edge of innovation. Its competitive advantage rests in being able to produce a better product in a cost-effective way. The organization adopts an effective project-driven matrix organization, and commands the required flexibility and commitment from its staff.

Position (B) represents the case of a firm in a highly turbulent environment where products and technologies are constantly changing and often have a very short life span. This means that it has to search for new ideas and opportunities on a continuous basis. The firm is a kind of "prospector," always looking for new places where it can strike gold. It relies on getting there first, recognizing that type (C) organizations will soon move in with a competitive product. Innovation is the lifeblood of this organization. It employs people who are prepared to make massive commitments to their work and who are motivated and managed in an organic way. The company would probably qualify as one of Peters and Waterman's excellent companies, using many of the management practices identified in Exhibit 3.6. Again, this organization is balanced internally and in relation to its environment.

Position (D) presents a set of relations where the strategic stance, technology, and approach to organization and management are incongruent with the nature of the environment and the general orientations of the people within the organization. The situation is characteristic of an organization that is overbureaucratized, being more inclined to defend the position it has achieved than to search out new opportunities. It is a frustrating place in which to work, because the employees are looking for more open and demanding jobs than the strategy, technology, organization, and managerial style allow. The organization should be designed and managed like organization (C), and if a way can be found to allow the people who are highly involved with the organization to initiate changes in the required direction, it could achieve a much more effective configuration of relations. At present the incongruencies get in the way of effective operations, and the organization is likely to find difficulty in sustaining its position within the industry.

The kind of analytical diagnosis presented above can first be conducted at the level of a total organization or major division. But it will also need to be conducted at the level of subunits within the organization, to take account of Lawrence and Lorsch's point about the need for appropriate differentiation and integration. The analysis at this level will identify the pattern of relations necessary for dealing with various subenvironments, and show the required differentiation and integration. However, in an analysis at this subunit level, care must be taken to ensure that the requirements of the parts do not take priority over those of the whole, and that critical competencies are kept firmly in mind. For example, in organizations where front-line innovation is the basis of survival, the design and management of subunits must accommodate the primary task of innovation, rather than the reverse.

Our discussion thus demonstrates how contingency theory and an understanding of organizational needs can provide the basis for a detailed organizational analysis. The analysis helps us to describe detailed patterns of organizational relations, and it shows us possible solutions to the problems revealed. For example, organizational development practitioners confronted with the situation in organization (D) could attempt to improve the alignment of relations by persuading management to move closer to a (C) configuration. This organizational change strategy could involve action on a number of fronts—in relation to strategy, technology, organization structure, and management style. It would also involve an attempt to change the culture of the organization, i.e., the systems of belief and practice that hold the organization in its ineffective configuration.

The task of successful organizational change and development thus often hinges on bringing variables into closer alignment so that the organization can meet the challenges and opportunities posed by the environment. In nature we find that organisms are endowed with a harmonious pattern of internal and external relations as a result of evolution. In organizations, however, the degree of internal harmony and fit with the environment is a product of human decision, action, and inaction, so that incongruence and conflict are often the rule. As a result, there are usually many problems to keep the organizational doctors busy.

Natural selection:
the population-ecology view
of organizations

Up to now our use of the organismic metaphor has focused on organizations as the key units of analysis. We have discussed how organizations and their members can be seen as having different sets of "needs," and examined how organizations can develop patterns of relations that allow them to adapt to their environment. Survival has been presented as a problem of adaptation, and contingency theory offered as a means of identifying patterns of "good fit" and showing how these can be achieved.

Popular as this approach has been, in the last few years it has attracted growing criticism from theorists and researchers subscribing to a "natural-selection" view of organizations. In their opinion the idea that organizations can adapt to their environment attributes too much flexibility and power to the organization and too little to the environment as a force in organizational survival. They advocate that we must counteract this imbalance by focusing on the way environments "select" organizations, and that this can best be done by analysis at the level of *populations* of organizations and their wider ecology.

This "population-ecology" view of organization brings Darwin's theory of evolution right into the center of organizational analysis. In essence, the argument is as follows. Organizations, like organisms in nature, depend for survival on their ability to acquire an adequate supply of the resources necessary to sustain existence. In this effort they have to face competition from other organizations, and since there is usually a resource scarcity, only the fittest survive. The nature, numbers, and distribution of organizations at any given time is dependent on resource availability and on competition within and between different species of organizations. The environment is thus the critical factor in determining which organizations succeed and which fail, "selecting" the most robust competitors through elimination of the weaker ones.

As Darwin frequently emphasizes in his writings, though selection may be the mechanism through which evolution occurs, it depends on there being variation in individual characteristics. For without variation there is nothing to select. Most applications of Darwin's theory thus build on a cyclical model that allows for the *variation, selection, retention,* and *modification* of species characteristics. Variations in a species arise as a result of cross-reproduction and random variation of characteristics. Some of these variations may confer a competitive advantage in the survival process. These fitter varieties thus stand a better chance of selection. Since they now provide the foundation for the next stage of reproduction, there is a strong chance that the new characteristics will be retained as a more highly evolved feature of the species. In turn, these characteristics will be subject to random modification, creating the variety that allows the process to continue. In this way, new species evolve from variations in the old.

Though evolution occurs through modification of individual members of a species, the population ecologists argue that it is more important to understand evolutionary dynamics at the level of the population. Because ultimately, when the environment changes or when a new species makes an inroad on the resource niche traditionally held by another, the change is reflected in population structure. Since members of a species tend to share similar strengths and weaknesses, it is the whole species that tends to survive or fail. While some individual members may be fitter than others, they are often not as fit as the incoming species, and thus tend to share the fate of their population in the long run.

This population perspective opens many new avenues of inquiry, for it encourages us to understand the dynamics influencing whole populations of organizations. Thus as Howard Aldrich, John Freeman, Michael Hannan, and others who have popularized the approach suggest, organizational analysis shifts from explaining how individual organizations adapt to their environments to understanding how different species rise and decline in importance. Why are there so many different kinds of organizations? What factors influence their numbers and distribution? What factors influence a population's ability to acquire or retain a resource niche?

Under the influence of these and related questions the population ecologists have begun to develop a form of organizational demography. Numerous research studies are attempting to identify species or populations (typically defined as sets of organizations sharing certain characteristics or a common fate with regard to environmental circumstances), and the birth rates, death rates, and general factors influencing organizational life cycles, growth, and decline. Considerable attention has also been devoted to understanding organizations and their environments in terms of "resource dependencies" and the patterning and availability of resource niches.

The perspective has created many interesting insights. For example, in critiquing the "adaptation" view of organization the population ecologists have highlighted the importance of inertial pressures that often prevent organizations from changing in response to their environment. Specialization of production plants and personnel, established ideas and "mind-sets" of top managers, inadequate information, the difficulty of restructuring technology and personnel in unionized plants, the force of tradition, barriers to entry created by legal, fiscal, and other circumstances, and many other factors may make it impossible for organizations to engage in timely and efficient changes. Faced with new kinds of competition or environmental circumstances, whole industries or types of organization may come and go. Large traditional steel mills may give way to small, technologically advanced competitors. Department stores may give way to specialty stores in shopping malls. Coal mines and oil companies may give way to entrepreneurial solar-energy firms. Bureaucracies may give way to more flexible project-oriented firms. In the population ecologists' view, it is the ability to obtain a resource niche and outperform one's competitors that is all-important, and in the long run, relative superiority in being able to command resources applies to whole populations of organizations. While one particularly skillful or efficient steel mill or department store may be able to hold off new forms of competition a little longer than other members of their species, in the long run they too may become extinct as a result of environmental changes that they are ill equipped to deal with, compared with species of better fit.

Two other important insights generated by the population-ecology approach are the importance of resource limitations in shaping the growth, development, and decline of organizations, and the role of successful innovations in shaping new species of organization. An awareness of the changing structure of critical resource niches and patterns of resource dependencies can make important contributions to our understanding of the success and power of different organizations. And the way new populations of organizations can emerge through the dissemination of innovations or new practices, as happened in the Silicon Valley computer phenomenon, does much to explain the changing structure of industry.

However, while there is much to commend the population-ecology view, many organization theorists believe that it is far too deterministic a theory to provide a satisfactory explanation of how organizations actually evolve. For example, if we accept at face value the theory that environments select organizations for survival, then in the long run it really doesn't matter what managers and decision makers do. Even efficient and successful firms that adapt to their environment are liable to fail as the result of environmental changes that influence the structure of their resource niche. Not surprisingly, therefore, the population-ecology view has been much criticized for downplaying the importance of the choice of strategic direction for an organization. Despite inertial pressures, an organization may be able to transform itself from one kind of organization into another. While small organizations can often fall victim to the forces of their environment, larger organizations are often far more robust. Their ability to command vast resources often buffers them from dramatic environmental changes, allowing them time to reorganize themselves to cope with threats that might have eliminated less robust competitors.

The population-ecology approach has developed to counteract the adaptation bias generated by contingency theory. As a result, the view of organizational evolution has tended to be rather one-sided, emphasizing resource scarcity and competition, which lie at the basis of selection, and ignoring the facts that resources can be abundant and self-renewing and that organisms collaborate as well as compete. When these neglected aspects of population ecology are brought into consideration, then a more balanced view of the ecology of organizations begins to emerge.

Organizational ecology: the creation of shared futures

The population-ecology and contingency views of organization both view organizations as existing in a state of tension or struggle with their environments. Both presume that organizations and environments are separate phenomena. Under the influence of developments in modern systems theory, however, this kind of assumption has attracted increasing criticism. For organizations, like organisms, are not really discrete entities, even though it may be convenient to think of them as such. They do not live in isolation and are not self-sufficient. Rather, they exist as elements in a complex ecosystem.

Many biologists now believe that it is the whole ecosystem that evolves, and that the process of evolution can really be understood only at the level of the total ecology. This has important implications, because it suggests that organisms do not evolve by adapting to environmental changes, or as a result of these changes selecting the organisms that are to survive. Rather, it suggests that evolution is always evolution of a pattern of relations embracing organisms *and* their environments. It is the *pattern*, not just the separate units comprising this pattern that evolves. Or as Kenneth Boulding has put it, evolution involves the "survival of the fitting," not just the survival of the fittest.

When we attempt to understand the ecology of organizations with this perspective in mind, it becomes necessary to understand that organizations and their environments are engaged in a pattern of cocreation, where each produces the other. For just as in nature the environment of an organism is composed of other organisms, organizational environments are in large measure composed of other organizations. And once we recognize this, it becomes clear that organizations are in principle able to influence the nature of their environment. They can play an active role in shaping their future, especially when acting in concert with other organizations. Environments then become in some measure always negotiated environments, rather than independent external forces.

If we look at the organizational world, we find that, as in nature, collaboration is often as common as competition. Organizations in the same industry frequently get together under the umbrella of trade and professional associations to collaborate in relation to shared interests. Formal and informal cartels for price fixing, agreements regarding areas of competition and market sharing, and the joint sponsorship of lobbies designed to influence government legislation are obvious examples. The Tobacco Trust, which was established by leading U.S. tobacco companies to help shape research on the link between cancer and smoking, presents a particularly striking example of cooperation between firms that are normally engaged in fierce competition. The joint manufacturing projects established in the auto industry between firms like General Motors and Toyota present another.

Examples of collaborative relations between organizations in different industries or in different parts of the same industry are also very common. For example, firms often cultivate interlocking directorships to create a measure of shared decision making and control, engage in joint ventures to pool expertise or share risk, strike agreements with suppliers or manufacturers to achieve a measure of "vertical integration" of production, and engage in numerous kinds of informal networking. They also sometimes establish informal joint organizations to link firms that have an interest in special problems or lines of development. For example, in the financial-services industry it is not uncommon for banks, trust companies, insurance firms, and other interested agencies to offer joint services, in effect creating a new form of organization at the level of the industry. Similar developments can be seen in many other areas as well.

An ecological perspective that emphasizes collaboration can make an important contribution to how we understand and manage the world of organizations. Under the influence of interpretations of evolution that emphasize the survival of the fittest, competition is often encouraged as the basic rule of organizational life. Under the influence of more ecological interpretations stressing the "survival of the fitting," the ethic of collaboration receives much more attention.

A number of social scientists led by Eric Trist have now begun to develop this view of organizational ecology, investigating the possibility of developing new patterns of interorganizational relations that can help shape the future in a proactive way. Building on the observation that these relations emerge as a natural response to complexity and turbulence in the environment, Trist argues that they should be encouraged to help make the turbulence more manageable. In several "action projects" he and his colleagues have sought to develop "referent organizations," such as industry associations and labor-management committees, to regulate relations between stakeholders in broad-based "domains." The idea of such domain-based organizations is to embrace the organization-environment relations of a whole set of constituent organizations, so that what were once external relations—e.g., between competing or interdependent firms, or between labor and management—now in some measure become internal relations that are open to collaborative action. Trist and his colleagues also focus on informal learning networks that can generate domain-based exchange and discussion, promote shared appreciations of concerns and problems, facilitate the emergence of common values and norms, and thus possibly find new solutions to shared problems.

The concern in both cases is to allow the ecology of organizational relations to evolve and survive. Just as natural ecologists are concerned about the disastrous effects of industrial pollution on the natural world, Trist believes that our organizational ecology is menaced by highly individualistic lines of action that threaten to make the social world completely unmanageable. The concept of organizational ecology is thus marshaled as a new and creative way of thinking and acting in relation to these problems.

Strengths and limitations of the organismic metaphor

We began this chapter with the invitation to view organizations as organisms. And we have ended up with a review of some of the central ideas of modern organization theory. This is because most modern organization theorists have looked to nature to understand organizations and organizational life. The ideas identified provide an excellent illustration of how a metaphor can open our minds to a systematic and novel way of thinking. By exploring the parallels between organisms and organizations in terms of organic functioning, relations with the environment, relations between species, and the wider ecology, it has been possible to produce different theories and explanations that have very practical implications for organization and management.

Given the rich and varied insights thus generated it is difficult to identify strengths and limitations that apply equally to all variations of the metaphor. However, there are a number of important commonalities.

One of the main strengths of the metaphor stems from the emphasis placed on understanding relations between organizations and their environments. The mechanical theories explored in Chapter 2 more or less ignored the role of the environment, treating organizations as relatively closed systems that could be designed as clearly defined structures of parts. In contrast, the ideas considered in this chapter stress that organizations are open systems and are best understood as ongoing *processes* rather than as collections of parts. Using the image of an organism in constant exchange with the environment, we are encouraged to take an open and flexible view of organization. We can recognize that so long as key processes are functioning in an effective manner, everything may be going well.

This leads us to a second strength of the metaphor: the management of organizations can often be improved through systematic attention to the "needs" that must be satisfied if the organization is to survive. The metaphor emphasizes survival as the key aim or primary task facing any organization. This contrasts with the classical focus on specific operational goals. Survival is a process, whereas goals are often targets or end points to be achieved. This reorientation gives management an increased flexibility, since if survival is seen as the primary orientation, specific goals are framed by a more basic and enduring process that helps prevent them from becoming ends in themselves, a common fate in many organizations. The focus on the use and acquisition of resources also helps to emphasize that the process of organizing is much broader and more basic than the task of achieving specific goals.

The focus on "needs" also encourages us to see organizations as interacting processes that have to be balanced internally as well as in relation to the environment. Thus we see strategy, structure, technology, and the human and managerial dimensions of organization as subsystems with living needs that must be satisfied in a mutually acceptable way. Otherwise, the openness and health of the overall system suffers. Imagine a sociotechnical system where human needs characteristic of the higher reaches of Maslow's need hierarchy meet assembly-line technology characterized by routine, boring, low-discretion jobs. The result is one of human boredom and alienation where game playing and sabotage emerge as means of gaining self-respect. The abrasive interaction between subsystems in this case is likely to produce an ongoing battle between workers and management, high absenteeism, job turnover when new jobs are freely available, poor-quality products, and low organizational and self-image. The sociotechnical approach suggests that by accommodating and balancing basic needs, strategic management can create a much more harmonious and productive work environment.

A third principal advantage of the metaphor is that in identifying different "species" of organization, we are alerted to the fact that in organizing we always have a range of options. The ideas relating to matrix and organic forms of organization, and the research showing how effective organization is contingent on environmental circumstances, emphasize that managers and those involved in organization design always have choice, and that effective organization depends on the quality of choice. Though those favoring a population-ecology perspective may adopt the rather pessimistic stance that this choice will never count for much, because environmental forces ultimately have the upper hand in determining the fate of an organization, the contingency view offers a new flexibility of approach.

A fourth major strength of the metaphor is that it stresses the virtue of organic forms of organization in the process of innovation. It would be an exaggeration to suggest that mechanistic organizations do not innovate, but the point contains an important kernel of truth. The ideas explored in this chapter are at one in suggesting that if innovation is a priority, then flexible, dynamic, project-oriented matrix or organic forms of organization will be superior to the mechanistic-bureaucratic.

Another obvious strength of the organismic metaphor rests in its contributions to the theory and practice of organizational development, especially through the contingency approach. The metaphor has also had a major impact upon the theory and practice of corporate strategy, which for the most part now focuses on achieving an appropriate fit between organization and environment.

Finally, the metaphor is making important contributions through a focus on "ecology" and interorganizational relations. Researchers adopting ecological views have reinforced the idea that a theory of interorganizational relations is necessary if we are to understand how the world of organization actually evolves. And if the organizational ecologists are correct, it may also be necessary to create new forms of interorganizational relations to deal with the complex environments that modern organizations now face.

Sometimes it is said that a way of seeing is a way of not seeing. Now that the organismic image of organization has established its powerful credentials, it is difficult to see how the classical theorists could have given so little attention to the influence of the environment. And it is difficult to see how they could have believed that there are uniform principles of management worthy of universal application. However, the organizational world was much simpler then. The rise in importance of the organismic metaphor is in many respects a product of changing times that have undermined the efficiency of bureaucratic organizations. Organization theorists did not simply discover the organismic metaphor; they needed it to keep abreast of developments, and as we have seen, they have exploited its insights in many different ways.

This said and done, the metaphor does have major limitations, most of which are associated with the basic way of seeing that the metaphor encourages. The first of these is the fact that we are led to view organizations and their environments in a way that is far too concrete. We know that organisms live in a natural world with material properties that determine the life and welfare of its inhabitants. We can see this world. We can touch and feel it. Nature presents itself as being objective and real in every aspect. But this image breaks down when applied to society and organization, because organizations and their environments can, at least to some extent, be understood as socially constructed phenomena. As we will discuss in some detail in Chapter 5, organizations are very much products of visions, ideas, norms, and beliefs, so that their shape and structure is much more fragile and tentative than the material structure of an organism. True, there are many material aspects of organization, such as the land, buildings, machines, and money. But organizations fundamentally depend for life—in the form of ongoing organizational activity—upon the creative actions of human beings. Organizational environments can also be seen as being a product of human creativity, since they are made through the actions of the individuals, groups, and organizations who populate them.

In view of this, it can be said that it is misleading to suggest that organizations need to "adapt" to their environment, as do the contingency theorists, or that environments "select" the organizations that are to survive, as do the population ecologists. Both views tend to make organizations and their members dependent upon forces operating in an external world, rather than recognizing that they are active agents operating with others in the construction of that world. The natural-selection view of organizational evolution in particular gives the individual organization little influence in the struggle for survival. This view undermines the power of organizations and their members to help make their own futures. Organizations, unlike organisms, have a choice as to whether they are to compete or to collaborate. While we may agree that an organization acting in isolation can have little impact on the environment, and hence that the environment presents itself as external and real in its effects, it is quite a different matter when we consider the possibility of organizations collaborating in pursuit of plural interests to shape the environment they desire. Some organizational ecologists have already grasped the importance of this point, on which we will have more to say in Chapter 8.

A second limitation of the organismic metaphor rests in its assumption of "functional unity." If we look at organisms in the natural world we find that they are characterized by a functional interdependence where every element of the system under normal circumstances works for all the other elements. Thus in the human body the blood, heart, lungs, arms, and legs normally work together to preserve the homeostatic functioning of the whole. The system is unified and shares a common life and a common future. Circumstances when one element works in a way that sabotages the whole, as when appendicitis or a heart attack threatens one's life, are exceptional and potentially pathological.

If we look at most organizations, however, we find that the times at which their different elements operate with the degree of harmony discussed above are often more exceptional than normal. For most organizations are not as functionally unified as organisms. The different elements of an organization are usually capable of living separate lives, and often do so. While organizations *may* at times be highly unified, with people in different departments working in a selfless way for the organization as a whole, they may at other times be characterized by schism and major conflict.

The organismic metaphor has had a subtle yet important impact on our general thinking by encouraging us to believe that the unity and harmony characteristic of organisms can be achieved in organizational life. We often tend to equate organizational well-being with a state of unity where everyone is "pulling together." This style of thought usually leads us to see "political" and other self-interested activity as abnormal or dysfunctional features that should be absent in the healthy organization. As will become apparent from discussion in Chapter 6, where we will be examining organizations as political systems, the emphasis upon unity rather than conflict as the normal state of organization may be an inherent weakness of the organismic metaphor. In recent years those favoring the metaphor have begun to recognize this weakness by giving more attention to the role of power in organizations, but they rarely have gone so far as to abandon the ideal of functional unity. There are good reasons for this, since the idea that organizations can work in a functionally unified way is popular, particularly among managers charged with the task of holding organizations together.

The above point brings us to the final limitation of the organismic metaphor to be considered here: the danger of the metaphor becoming an ideology. This is always a problem in applied social science where images or theories come to serve as normative guidelines for shaping practice. We have already seen the impact of the machine metaphor on classical management theory: the idea that the organization is a machine sets the basis for the idea that it ought to be run like a machine. With the organismic metaphor this "ought" takes a number of forms. For example, the fact that organisms are functionally integrated can easily set the basis for the idea that organizations *should* be the same way. Much of organizational development attempts to achieve this ideal by finding ways of integrating individual and organization, e.g., by designing work that allows people to satisfy their personal needs *through* the organization. While Frederick Taylor's scientific management provided an ideology based on the idea that "efficiency and productivity is in the interests of all," ideologies associated with "OD" tend to emphasize that we can live full and satisfying lives if we fulfill our personal needs through the organizations that dominate the contemporary scene. Many argue that this style of thinking runs the danger of producing an organizational society populated by the "organization man" and the "organization woman." People become resources to be developed, rather than human beings who are valued in themselves and who are encouraged to choose and shape their own future. This issue directs attention to the values that underlie much organizational development, and by implication to the values associated with the use of the organismic metaphor as a basis for theorizing.

Another important ideological dimension of some of the theories discussed in this chapter is found in their links with the social philosophy of the nineteenth century. For example, the population-ecology view of organizations revives the ideology of social Darwinism, which stressed that social life is based on the laws of nature and that only the fittest will survive. Social Darwinism arose as an ideology supporting the early development of capitalism in which small firms competed for survival on a free and open basis. The population-ecology view of organization in effect develops an equivalent ideology for modern times, holding up a mirror to the organizational world and suggesting that the view we see reflects a law of nature. In effect, natural law is invoked to legitimize the organization of society. Obviously, there are real dangers in doing this because when we take the parallels between nature and society too seriously, we fail to see that human beings in principle have a large measure of influence and choice over what their world can be.

4

Toward Self-Organization

Organizations as Brains

In his book *The Natural History of the Mind*, science writer G. R. Taylor offers the following observations on some of the differences between brains and machines:

> In a famous experiment, the American psychologist Karl Lashley removed increasing quantities of the brains of rats which had been taught to run in a maze. He found that, provided he did not remove the visual cortex and thus blind them, he could remove up to ninety percent of their cortex without significant deterioration in their power to thread their way through the maze. There is no man-made machine of which this is true. Try removing nine-tenths of your radio and see if it still brings in a signal! It would seem that each specific memory is distributed in some way over the brain as a whole.

> Similarly, you can remove considerable amounts of the motor cortex without paralyzing any one group of muscles. All that happens is a general deterioration of motor performance. The evolutionary advantages of such an arrangement are manifest: when pursued, it is better to run clumsily than not at all. But how this remarkable distribution of function is achieved we do not really understand. We see, at all events, that the brain relies on patterns of increasing refinement and not (as man-made machines do) on chains of cause and effect.

> The fact is, the brain is not comparable with anything else.

Taylor's comments raise an intriguing question. Is it possible to design organizations so that they have the capacity to be as flexible, resilient, and inventive as the functioning of a brain? As we have seen in previous chapters, most of our current thinking conceives of organization as a relationship between specialized parts linked by lines of communication, command, and control. Even when attempts are made to leave the mechanistic model behind, as in the creation of matrix and organic forms, we seem able only to find new ways of linking the organizational parts. In the matrix organization this is achieved by combining dual patterns of authority and responsibility and by encouraging more democratic styles of management. In the organic form this is achieved by allowing different organizational elements degrees of freedom in which to find their own mode of integration.

The organic organization probably comes closest to the functioning of a brain in that it approximates a principle of self-organization, but there is little in the theory of organicism that tells us how we can bring such organizations into being. Contingency theorists suggest that we can best proceed by appointing "the right people" to the job we have in mind, and by creating flexible authority, communications, and reward structures that will motivate them to satisfy their own needs through the achievement of organizational goals. Studies of successful organic organizations contribute valuable ideas on what may be required in practice, but there is little in the organic metaphor itself that articulates a relevant theory. At best, we have to rely on the idea that successful institutional leadership will generate an appropriate organizational strategy, structure, and style of day-to-day management for motivating creativity and inventiveness.

It is possible that by using the brain as a metaphor for organization we may improve our ability to organize in a manner that promotes flexible and creative action. To the extent that we build organizations on mechanistic principles, we develop what we described in Chapter 2 as an "instrumental" rationality, where people are valued for their ability to fit in and contribute to the efficient operation of a predetermined structure. This is fine for performing a fixed task in stable circumstances; but, as we have seen, when these conditions are violated, organizations designed along these lines encounter many problems. Under changing circumstances it is important that elements of organization be able to question the appropriateness of what they are doing and to modify their action to take account of new situations. This requires an organizing capacity that is "substantially" rational, in the sense that action manifests intelligence of the relations within which the action is set: substantially rational action is not undertaken blindly but in an awareness that it is appropriate. Interestingly, it is for precisely this kind of capacity that the brain is renowned. As a system for initiating intelligent action the brain stands supreme among all the natural and man-made systems of which we are aware. Certainly, no man-made system comes close to matching the sophistication of even simple kinds of brain.

The brain thus offers itself as an obvious metaphor for organization, particularly if our concern is to improve capacities for organizational intelligence. Many managers and organization theorists have readily grasped this point. But for the most part they have limited their attention to the idea that organizations need a brain or brainlike function— e.g., in the form of corporate planning teams, think tanks, or centralized research and decision-making units—that will be able to think for the rest of the organization and control and integrate overall organizational activity. Much of the literature on corporate planning and strategy formulation uses the brain metaphor in this way, viewing the process of strategic management and control as equivalent to the brain and nervous system of an organism. In contrast, it is far less common to think about organizations *as if they were brains,* and to see if we can create new forms of organization that disperse brainlike capacities throughout an enterprise, rather than just confine them to special units or parts. This is a challenge for the future, and a special focus of attention in this chapter.

Images of the brain

In a 1983 *Newsweek* article on the functioning of the brain, science writer Sharon Begley noted the paradox that in the 2,400 years since Hippocrates located the seat of intellect in the skull, humans have been presented with increasing evidence that their greatest thoughts and achievements, and even their deepest emotions, may stem from a three-pound glob of matter with the consistency of Jell-O and the color of day-old slush. Through persistent research, especially over the last hundred years, scientists and philosophers of all kinds have gradually begun to probe and reveal the mysterious workings of this prized area of anatomy. And as might be expected, numerous metaphors ranging from the mystical to the mechanical have been summoned to shape our understanding.

Many of these images focus on the idea that the brain is an information-processing system. For example, the brain has been conceived as a control system similar to a complex computer or telephone switchboard, transmitting information through electronic impulses; as a kind of television system with a capacity to reassemble coherent patterns and images from millions of separate pieces of data; as a sophisticated library or memory bank for data storage and retrieval; as a complex system of chemical reactions that transmit messages and initiate actions; as a mysterious "blackbox" linking stimuli and behavior; as a linguistic system operating through a neural code which translates information into thoughts, ideas, and actions through chemical and electrical changes, rather like the code represented in an alphabet can be converted into prose through words and sentences.

Most recently, the brain has been compared with a holographic system, one of the marvels of laser science. Holography, invented in 1948 by Dennis Gabor, uses a lenseless camera to record information in a way that stores the whole in all the parts. Interacting beams of light create an "interference pattern" that scatters the information being recorded on a photographic plate, known as a hologram, which can then be illuminated to recreate the original information. One of the interesting features of the hologram is that if it is broken, any single piece can be used to reconstruct the entire image. Everything is enfolded in everything else, just as if we were able to throw a pebble into a pond and see the whole pond and all the waves, ripples, and drops of water generated by the splash *in each and every one of the drops of water thus produced.*

Holography demonstrates in a very concrete way that it is possible to create processes where the whole can be encoded in all the parts, so that each and every part represents the whole. Neuroscientist Karl Pribram of Stanford University has suggested that the brain functions in accordance with holographic principles: that memory is distributed throughout the brain and can thus be reconstituted from any of the parts. If he is correct, this may explain why the rats in Karl Lashley's experiments were able to function reasonably well even when major portions of their brain had been removed.

In this chapter we will use the brain as a metaphor for understanding organization in the two ways discussed above. First, we will explore the implications of the idea that organizations are information-processing systems capable of learning to learn. Second, we will explore the idea that organizations can be designed to reflect holographic principles. This will lead us to examine some of the ideas emerging from modern brain research, and to explore possible ideas for designing organizations of the future.

Organizations as information-processing brains

If one thinks about it, every aspect of organizational functioning depends on information processing of one kind or another. Bureaucrats make decisions by processing information with reference to predetermined rules. Strategic managers make decisions through formalized or ad hoc processes, producing policies and plans that then provide a point of reference or framework for the information processing and decision making of others. Organizations are information systems. They are communications systems. And they are decision-making systems. In mechanistic organizations these systems are highly routinized. And in matrix and organic organizations they are more ad hoc and free flowing. We can thus go a long way toward understanding organizations, and the variety of organizational forms in practice, by focusing on their information-processing characteristics.

INFORMATION PROCESSING, DECISION MAKING, AND ORGANIZATIONAL DESIGN

This approach to understanding organization, now often known as "the decision-making approach," was pioneered in the 1940s and 1950s by Nobel Prize-winner Herbert Simon and colleagues like James March while at the Carnegie Institute of Technology (now Carnegie-Mellon University). Exploring the parallels between human decision making and organizational decision making, Simon argued that organizations can never be perfectly rational, because their members have limited information-processing abilities. Arguing that people (a) usually have to act on the basis of incomplete information about possible courses of action and their consequences, (b) are able to explore only a limited number of alternatives relating to any given decision, and (c) are unable to attach accurate values to outcomes, Simon suggested that at best they can achieve only limited forms of rationality. In contrast to the assumptions made in economics about the optimizing behavior of individuals, he concluded that individuals and organizations settle for a "bounded rationality" of "good enough" decisions based on simple rules of thumb and limited search and information.

In Simon's view these limits on human rationality are institutionalized in the structure and modes of functioning of our organizations. Hence his theory of decision making leads us to understand organizations as kinds of institutionalized brains that fragment, routinize, and bound the decision-making process in order to make it manageable. As we look at organizations from this vantage point, we come to see that the various job, departmental, and other divisions within an organization do not just define a structure of work activity. They also create a structure of attention, interpretation, and decision making that exerts a crucial influence on an organization's daily operation. Departmental and job divisions segment the organization's environment, compartmentalize responsibilities, and thus simplify the domains of interest and decision making of managers and operatives. Organizational hierarchies perform a similar function, providing channels of problem solving to help make life more manageable. Those at the lower levels of the hierarchy can be made responsible for routine information and decision making, allowing those at higher levels to focus on unusual or particularly significant information and decisions. Policies, programs, plans, rules, and standard operating procedures again help to simplify organizational reality. And special problems are often posted to units like corporate planning teams, task forces, and consultants, again in an attempt to simplify and manage the complexity of the work situation.

In the thirty-odd years since Simon first introduced this way of thinking about organizations, numerous researchers have devoted considerable attention to understanding organization from this information-processing standpoint. Much of this work has focused on how organizations deal with the complexity and uncertainty presented by their environment. For example, organizational theorist and consultant Jay Galbraith has given attention to the relationship between uncertainty, information processing, and organization design. Uncertain tasks require that greater amounts of information be processed between decision makers during task performance. The greater the uncertainty, the more difficult it is to program and routinize activity by preplanning a response. This helps explain why organizations in different task situations place different kinds of emphasis on rules and programs, hierarchy, and goals and targets as a means of integrating and controlling activity. As uncertainty increases, organizations typically find ways of controlling outputs (e.g., by setting goals and targets) rather than controlling behaviors (e.g., through rules and programs). Hierarchy provides an effective means for controlling situations that are fairly certain, but in uncertain situations can encounter information and decision overload. The information-processing perspective thus provides a means of accounting for differences between mechanistic and more organic forms of organization. While the former are based on information and decision-making systems that are highly programmed and preplanned, the latter are typically based on processes which are more flexible and ad hoc. In organic organizations greater scope is created for discretion and judgment, and more reliance placed on feedback rather than on programming as a means of control.

Galbraith's approach identifies two complementary design strategies for dealing with uncertainty. The first involves procedures for reducing the need for information—e.g., through the creation of slack resources and self-contained tasks. The second involves increasing capacities to process information—e.g., by investing in sophisticated information systems and improving lateral relations through the use of coordinator roles, task forces, and matrix designs. Together with the use of rules and programs, hierarchy, and goal setting, they create a range of possible means whereby organizations can help to reduce and cope with uncertainties generated by the environment. Organizations may also adopt other strategies to control or shield themselves from uncertainty; for example, by attempting to control their market or source of supplies, or by producing various kinds of scheduling devices to smooth demands on the system. They also often engage in mergers and acquisitions and develop coalitions to eliminate the uncertainties associated with competition, and to acquire control over key resources or earlier stages of the production process.

The decision-making approach to organization has thus created a new way of thinking about how organizations really operate and has made contributions to our understanding of organizational design. But there is another implication of the information-processing metaphor that will probably be even more important in the long run. If organization is indeed a product or reflection of information-processing capacities as Herbert Simon has suggested, then new capacities will lead to new organizational forms. Indeed, we can already see this in industries where electronic information processing has assumed a major role, e.g., in airlines, banking, insurance, the media, retailing, and hotels; in high-technology firms such as those in the electronics, computing, and aerospace industries; and in many branches of manufacturing. The introduction of computers and microprocessing has created radical changes in the nature and style of organization. All kinds of functions once performed by skilled and semiskilled people are performed electronically, making complete sections or levels of organization quite redundant, and others more valuable. Networks of relations between humans give way to "interface" between electronic devices supported by new kinds of operators, programmers, and other information specialists.

Consider, for example, how computerized stock-control and check-out facilities in supermarkets and other large retail stores transform their organization. In applying a laser beam to precoded labels on the items being sold, the sales assistant records price and product and inputs data into various kinds of financial analyses, sales reports, inventory controls, reordering procedures, and numerous other automated information and decision-making activities of relevance to the future operations of the firm. The system of organization embedded in the design of such information systems replaces more traditional modes of human interaction, eliminating armies of clerks, stock-room attendants, and middle managers.

Organization in such circumstances increasingly rests *in* the information system.

In the longer term, it is possible to see organizations becoming synonymous with their information systems, since microprocessing facilities create the possibility of organizing without having an organization in physical terms. This new technology creates a capacity for decentralizing the nature and control of work, allowing white-collar workers engaged in related tasks to work in remote locations while being linked on a continuous basis through on-line information networks which maintain a fully integrated system. Many organizations of the future may have no fixed location, with members interacting through personal computers and audiovisual devices to create a network of exchange and interrelated activity, perhaps with remote-controlled robots performing physical work.

The evolution of organizations into information systems is thus capable of transforming them structurally and spatially. The really big question raised by the brain metaphor, however, is whether organizations will also become more intelligent. Is information-based organization necessarily characterized by the bounded rationality found in bureaucracies? Or can it transcend this constraint? Much will depend on the kind of learning abilities built into the organizations thus produced.

CYBERNETICS, LEARNING, AND LEARNING TO LEARN

How can one design systems that are capable of learning in a brainlike way? This question has been of special concern to a group of information theorists who have interested themselves in problems of artificial intelligence under the umbrella of what is now known as cybernetics.

Cybernetics is a relatively new interdisciplinary science focusing upon the study of information, communication, and control. The term was coined in the 1940s by MIT mathematician Norbert Wiener as a metaphorical application of the Greek *kubernetes*, meaning "steersman." The Greeks had developed the concept of steersmanship, probably from their understanding of the processes involved in the control and navigation of watercraft, and extended its use to the process of government and statecraft. Wiener used this imagery to characterize processes of information exchange through which machines and organisms engage in self-regulating behaviors that maintain steady states.

The origins of modern cybernetics are diverse, but are to be found most concretely in the research activities of Wiener and his colleagues during the Second World War, particularly in the attempt to develop and refine devices for the control of gunfire. The problem of firing a gun at a moving target, such as an airplane, presents a difficult problem of steersmanship involving complex statistical forecasting and computation. In addition to considering the speed and position of the plane at a given time and the direction and speed of the missile to be fired, allowance must also be made for variable wind effects and the likelihood that the plane will engage in diversionary flight patterns. To design a gun that can approximate such computations and guide and monitor its own behavior required an ability to design a machine that was able to engage in behavior as flexible and adaptive as that of a living brain. Cybernetics emerged from this design challenge, as scientists expert in mathematics, communications theory, engineering, and social and medical science combined their skills and insights to create machines with the adaptive capacities of organisms.

The core insight emerging from this early work was that the ability of a system to engage in self-regulating behavior depends on processes of information exchange involving *negative feedback*. This concept is central to the process of steersmanship. If we shift a boat off course by taking the rudder too far in one direction, we can get back on course again only by moving it in the opposite direction. Systems of negative feedback engage in this kind of error detection and correction automatically, so that movements beyond specified limits in one direction initiate movements in the opposite direction to maintain a desired course of action.

The concept of negative feedback explains many kinds of routine behavior in a very unconventional way. For example, when we pick up an object from a table we typically assume that our hand, guided by our eye, moves directly towards the object. Cybernetics suggests not. This action occurs through a process of error elimination whereby deviations between hand and object are reduced *at each and every stage of the process* so that in the end no error remains. We pick up the object by avoiding not picking it up (Exhibit 4.1).

These cybernetic principles are evident in many kinds of system. The "governor" regulating the speed of the steam engine invented by James Watt in the nineteenth century provides an early example. Two steel balls were suspended from a central shaft attached to the engine. The shaft rotated with the speed of the engine, swinging the balls in an outward direction as speed increased, thus closing the throttle. The re-

We pick up an object by avoiding not picking it up!

In a similar way, we manage to ride a bicycle by means of a system of information flows and regulatory actions that help us to avoid falling off.

Negative feedback eliminates error: it creates desired system states by avoiding noxiant states.

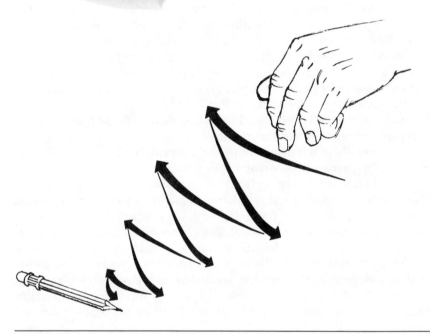

Exhibit 4.1. Negative feedback in practice

verse actions occurred when speed was reduced. In this way the machine acted as a form of communication system in which an increase in speed initiated actions leading to a decrease in speed and vice versa. This is negative feedback: more leads to less, and less to more. Similar principles are incorporated in a house thermostat. And living organisms operate in a parallel manner. When our body heat rises, the brain and central nervous system initiate action which leads us to slow down, sweat, and breathe heavily, in order to initiate changes in the opposite direction. Similarly, when we get cold we are led to shiver, stamp, and attempt to increase body temperature, keeping body functioning within the critical limits necessary for survival.

Cybernetics thus leads to a theory of communication and learning stressing four key principles. First, that systems must have the capacity to sense, monitor, and scan significant aspects of their environment. Second, that they must be able to relate this information to the operating norms that guide system behavior. Third, that they must be able to detect significant deviations from these norms. And fourth, that they must be able to initiate corrective action when discrepancies are detected.

If these four conditions are satisfied, a continuous process of information exchange is created between a system and its environment, allowing the system to monitor changes and initiate appropriate responses. In this way the system can operate in an intelligent, self-regulating manner. However, the learning abilities thus defined are limited in that the system can maintain only the course of action determined by the operating norms or standards guiding it. This is fine so long as the action defined by those standards is appropriate for dealing with the changes encountered. But when this is not the case, the "intelligence" of the system breaks down, for the process of negative feedback ends up trying to maintain an inappropriate pattern of behavior.

This has led modern cyberneticians to draw a distinction between the process of learning and the process of learning to learn. Simple cybernetic systems like house thermostats are able to learn in the sense of being able to detect and correct deviations from predetermined norms. But they are unable to question the appropriateness of what they are doing. For example, a thermostat is unable to determine what level of temperature is appropriate to meet the preferences of the inhabitants of a room and to make adjustments to take account of this. More complex cybernetic systems such as the human brain or advanced computers have this capacity. They are often able to detect and correct errors in operating norms and thus influence the standards that guide their detailed operations. It is this kind of self-questioning ability that underpins the activities of systems that are able to learn to learn and self-organize. The essential difference between these two types of learning is sometimes identified in terms of a distinction between "single-loop" and "double-loop" learning (Exhibit 4.2).

CAN ORGANIZATIONS LEARN AND LEARN TO LEARN?

All the above ideas raise very important questions about modern organizations. Are our organizations able to learn in an ongoing way? Is this learning single-loop or double-loop? What are the main barriers to learning? Are they intrinsic to the nature of human organization, or can they be overcome?

Clearly, it is difficult to answer these questions in an abstract way, because learning capacities vary from one organization to another. But certain general conclusions can be drawn.

Single-loop learning rests in an ability to detect and correct error in relation to a given set of operating norms:

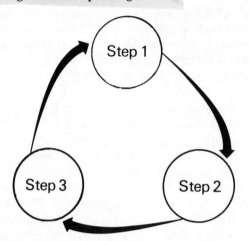

Double-loop learning depends on being able to take a "double look" at the situation by questioning the relevance of operating norms:

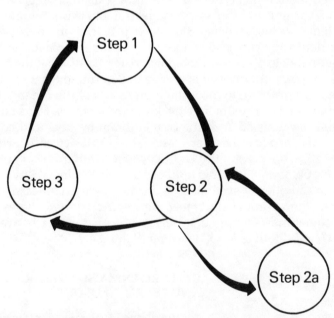

Step 1 = the process of sensing, scanning, and monitoring the environment.
Step 2 = the comparison of this information against operating norms.
Step 2a = the process of questioning whether operating norms are appropriate.
Step 3 = the process of initiating appropriate action.

Exhibit 4.2. Single and double-loop learning

For example, many organizations have become proficient at single-loop learning, developing an ability to scan the environment, to set objectives, and to monitor the general performance of the system in relation to these objectives. This basic skill is often institutionalized in the form of information systems designed to keep the organization "on course." For example, budgets often maintain single-loop learning by monitoring expenditures, sales, profits, and other indications of performance to ensure that organizational activities remain within the limits established through the budgeting process. Advances in computing have done much to foster the use of this kind of single-loop control. Through the use of "exception reports," which highlight critical deviations, managers and employees are often able to zero in on potential problems. Interestingly, a memory function is also often built into these single-loop controls, previous levels of achievement being used as standards to control current levels.

However, the ability to achieve proficiency at double-loop learning often proves more elusive. While some organizations have been successful in institutionalizing systems that review and challenge basic norms, policies, and operating procedures in relation to changes occurring in their environment—e.g., by encouraging ongoing debate and innovation—many fail to do so. This failure is especially true of bureaucratic organizations, since their fundamental organizing principles often operate in a way that actually *obstructs* the learning process. Three of these obstructions are worthy of special attention, and are often found in nonbureaucratic organizations as well.

First there is the general problem that bureaucratic approaches to organization impose fragmented structures of thought on their members and do not really encourage employees to think for themselves. Organizational goals, objectives, structures, and roles create clearly defined patterns of attention and responsibility, fragmenting interest in and knowledge of what the organization is doing. Where hierarchical and horizontal divisions within the organization are particularly powerful, information and knowledge rarely flow in a free manner, so that different sectors of the organization often operate on the basis of different pictures of the total situation, and can pursue subunit goals almost as ends in themselves, unaware of or disinterested in the way they fit the wider picture. The existence of such divisions tends to emphasize the distinctions between different elements of the organization, and foster the development of political systems that place yet further barriers in the way of learning. The bounded rationality inherent in organizational design thus actually *creates* boundaries! Moreover, employees are usually encouraged to occupy and keep a predefined place within the whole, and are rewarded for doing so. Situations in which policies and operating standards are challenged thus tend to be exceptional rather than the rule. For example, a person in a business firm challenging the relevance of a bottom-line profit or loss focus in a particular decision may well be deemed suspect in overall values and orientation. Given these circumstances, it is interesting to note that highly sophisticated single-loop learning systems may actually serve to keep the organization on the wrong course, since people are unable or not prepared to challenge underlying assumptions. The existence of single-loop learning systems, especially when used as controls over employees, may thus prevent double-loop learning from occurring.

A second major barrier to double-loop learning is often associated with the principle of bureaucratic accountability. To the extent that employees are held responsible for their performance within a system that rewards success and punishes failure, they have an incentive to engage in various forms of deception to protect themselves. Thus employees often tend to find ways of obscuring issues and problems that will place them in a bad light. They find ways of deflecting attention and of covering up, as well as of engaging in forms of impression management that make the situations for which they are responsible look better than they actually are. In addition, there is often a temptation to tell managers exactly what one thinks they want to hear.

When systems of accountability foster this kind of defensiveness an organization is rarely able to tolerate high levels of uncertainty. Managers and their employees also have a tendency to want to "tie things down" and be "on top of the facts." This frequently leads them to create oversimplified interpretations of the situations with which they are dealing. They tend to be interested in problems only if there are solutions at hand. Complex issues that are difficult to address are thus often discussed or downplayed in importance to create time for solutions to emerge, or in the hope that problems they pose will disappear. Bearers of bad news are rarely made welcome and are often fired. Under such circumstances, operating assumptions are rarely challenged in an effective way.

A third major barrier to double-loop learning stems from the fact that there is often a gap between what people say and what they do. Chris Argyris of Harvard and Donald Schon of MIT have referred to this as a distinction between "espoused theory" and "theory in use." Many managers and employees attempt to meet problems with rhetoric or rationalizations that convey the impression that they know what they are doing. This may not be just to impress others, but also to convince themselves that all is well and that they have the ability to cope. They also often engage in diversionary behavior, consciously or unconsciously, as when threats to a basic mode of practice lead an individual to deflect blame elsewhere and to tighten up on that practice, intensifying rather than questioning its nature and effects. In such circumstances it becomes increasingly difficult for the manager to confront and deal with the realities of a situation. Developments here may be reinforced by social processes such as "groupthink": group mindsets developed on the basis of social reinforcement, which are often very difficult to break. Individuals, groups, and departments may thus develop espoused theories that effectively prevent them from understanding and dealing with their problems. Double-loop learning requires that we bridge this gulf between theory and reality so that it becomes possible to challenge the values and norms embedded in the theories in use, as well as those that are espoused.

These examples of how organizations often inhibit double-loop learning also indicate how it can be facilitated. In essence, a new philosophy of management is required, to root the process of organizing in a process of open-ended inquiry. As has been shown, the whole process of learning to learn hinges on an ability to remain open to changes occurring in the environment, and on an ability to challenge operating assumptions in a most fundamental way. The following four guidelines summarize how this learning-oriented approach to organization and management can be developed.

First, encourage and value an openness and reflectivity that accepts error and uncertainty as an inevitable feature of life in complex and changing environments. This principle is fundamental for allowing members of an organization to deal with uncertainty in a constructive way. This is particularly important in turbulent environments where the problems that organizations face are frequently large, complex, and unique, and hence difficult to analyze and address. Rather than create conditions which lead employees to hide or deny error and to avoid asking problematic questions, as often happens under bureaucratic systems of accountability, it is necessary to encourage them to understand and accept the problematic nature of the situations with which they are dealing. A philosophy that "it is admissible to write off legitimate error against experience," and that "negative events and discoveries can serve as a source of knowledge and wisdom of great practical value," is an example of the kind of stance required. Note here that we are talking about legitimate error, which is distinct from mistakes that could and should have been avoided. Legitimate error stems from the uncertainty in a situation, as when unique or unexpected circumstances arise for reasons that cannot be predicted or controlled, and does not necessarily reflect badly on those involved. Legitimate error under this philosophy provides a potential lesson rather than an occasion to allocate blame.

Second, encourage an approach to the analysis and solution of complex problems that recognizes the importance of exploring different viewpoints. This principle helps to define a means of framing and reframing issues and problems so that they can be approached in an open-ended way. Given that many of the issues faced by organizations in turbulent environments are unclear and multidimensional, one of the major problems is usually that of defining the nature of the problems with which one is faced. This is best facilitated by managerial philosophies that recognize the importance of probing the various dimensions of a situation, and allow constructive conflict and debate between advocates of competing perspectives. In this way issues can be fully explored, and perhaps redefined so that they can be approached and resolved in new ways. This kind of inquiry helps an organization absorb and deal with the uncertainty of its environment rather than trying to avoid or eliminate it. As an example here we can take those situations where competing action strategies lead to a consideration of the organization's mission, and perhaps a reformulation of that mission. For example, business firms confronted by competing opportunities are often forced to reflect on the question "What business are we in?" The process of learning to learn requires that organizations keep themselves open to such deep and challenging questions, rather than trying to develop fixed foundations for action.

Third, avoid imposing structures of action upon organized settings. This principle relates to the importance of inquiry-driven action. In contrast with traditional approaches to planning, which tend to *impose* goals, objectives, and targets, it is important to devise means where intelligence and direction can emerge from ongoing organizational processes. When goals and objectives have a predetermined character they tend to provide a framework for single-loop learning but discourage double-loop learning. In such cases there is a danger that the organization will fail to keep abreast of the requirements of changing environments. More double-loop learning can be generated by encouraging a "bottom-up" or participative approach to the planning process. But cybernetics also emphasizes the central role played by norms and standards in the learning process, and stresses that double-loop learning develops as we question the relevance and desirability of these norms and standards as guidelines for action. Cybernetics shows us that these guidelines are of significance as limits to be placed on system behavior, rather than as specific targets to be achieved. Double-loop learning is thus best understood as a process which, in essence, questions the limits that are to be placed on action.

We find here a radically new means of approaching the planning process. Whereas the traditional philosophy is to produce a master plan with clear-cut targets, cybernetics suggests that it may be systemically wiser to focus on defining and challenging constraints. Intelligent strategy making thus involves a choice of limits (the negative-feedback "noxiants" one wishes to avoid) rather than just a choice of ends. Instead of just specifying profit objectives or desired market shares, an organization should also plan what it wishes to avoid, e.g., excessive dependence on one product or market segment, excessive reliance on a particular source of supplies, inflexibility of production systems, or employee layoffs. The effect of this approach to strategy is to define an evolving space of possible actions that satisfy critical limits. This leaves room for specific action plans to be generated on an ongoing basis and tested against these constraints for viability.

Interestingly, aspects of this approach to strategic management are found in many aspects of Japanese management practice, such as the ritual of *ringi*, a collective decision-making process in which a policy document passes from manager to manager for approval. The effect of this process is to explore the premises and values underlying the decision proposal. If a manager disagrees with what is being proposed he is typically free to amend the decision proposal and to allow the document to circulate again. In this way the decision process explores the decision domain until a proposal satisfies all critical parameters. This can be extremely time-consuming, since in important decisions a very large number of managers may be involved. But when the decision is made, one can be fairly certain that most errors will have been detected and corrected, and that the decision will carry the commitment of those involved.

The *ringi* is as much a process for exploring and reaffirming values as it is for setting a direction. Cybernetics shows us that coherent direction can emerge from a domain defined in terms of values, and the *ringi* provides an illustration in practice. By contrast, the emphasis placed in Western management on the achievement of specific objectives or ends forces the role of values as standards or guidelines for action into the background. This is one reason why Western management is a lot more mechanistic in orientation than Japanese management, which reveals a good intuitive grasp of cybernetic principles. The difference between Western and Eastern management is vividly reflected in management writer William Ouchi's report of how American and Japanese managers view objectives (Exhibit 4.3).

In the American view objectives should be hard and fast and clearly stated for all to see. In the Japanese view they emerge from a more fundamental process of exploring and understanding the values through which a firm is or should be operating. A knowledge of these values, the limits that are to guide action, defines a set of possible actions. An action chosen from this set may not be the very best, but it will satisfy parameters deemed crucial for success.

In the Japanese *ringi* we thus find the basis of a cybernetic approach to organization. In the Japanese context, the process is often used to affirm standards rather than to question them, but the basic principle

William Ouchi reports on differences in the style of American and Japanese managers working in the U.S. headquarters of a Japanese bank:

> The basic mechanisms of management control in a Japanese company are so subtle, implicit, and internal that they often appear to an outsider not to exist. That conclusion is a mistake. The mechanisms are thorough, highly disciplined and demanding, yet very flexible. Their essence could not be more different from methods of managerial control in Western organizations.
>
> In an interview with the American vice-presidents, I asked how they felt about working for this Japanese bank. "They treat us well, let us in on the decision making, and pay us well. We're satisfied." "You're very fortunate," I continued, "but tell me, if there were something that you could change about this Japanese bank, what would it be?" The response was quick and clearly one that was very much on their minds: "These Japanese just don't understand objectives, and it drives us nuts!"
>
> Next I interviewed the president of this bank, an expatriate Japanese who was on temporary assignment from Tokyo headquarters to run the United States operation, and asked about the two American vice-presidents. "They're hard working, loyal, and professional. We think they're terrific," came the reply. When asked if he would like to change them in any way, the president replied, "These Americans just don't seem to be able to understand objectives."
>
> With each side accusing the other of inability to understand objectives, there was a clear need for further interviewing and for clarification. A second round of interviews probed further into the issue. First the American vice-presidents: "We have all the necessary reports and numbers, but we can't get specific targets from him. He won't tell us how large a dollar increase in loan volume or what percent decrease in operating costs he expects us to achieve over the next month, quarter, or even year. How can we know whether we're performing well without specific targets to shoot for?" A point well taken, for every major American company and government bureau devotes a large fraction of its time to the setting of specific, measurable performance targets. Every American business school teaches its students to take global, fuzzy corporate goals and boil them down to measurable performance targets. Management by objective (MBO), program planning and evaluation, and cost-benefit analysis are among the basic tools of control in modern American management.
>
> When I returned to reinterview the Japanese president, he explained, "If only I could get these Americans to understand our philosophy of banking. To understand what the business means to us—how we feel we should deal with our customers and our employees. What our relationship should be to the local communities we serve. How we should deal with our competitors, and what our role should be in the world at large. If they could get that under their skin, then they could figure out for themselves what an appropriate objective would be for any situation, no matter how unusual or new, and I would never have to tell them, never have to give them a target."

Exhibit 4.3. American and Japanese styles of management: the contrast between mechanistic and cybernetic styles of decision making
SOURCE: William Ouchi, THEORY Z, © 1981, Addison-Wesley, Reading, Massachusetts. Pgs. 33 through 34 (adapted material). Reprinted with permission.

remains the same. By encouraging an approach to management that explores and defines appropriate limits or values, we have a means of promoting continued double-loop learning whereby actions are always evaluated in relation to relevant standards. Action emerges as a result of the learning process: it is not imposed.

The fourth principle facilitating the development of learning to learn relates to the need to make interventions and create organizational structures and processes that help implement the above principles. This brings us to the topic of our next section: the holographic approach to organization. As we will see, this provides many interesting and practical insights into the qualities that organizations must possess if they are to have the flexible self-organizing capacities of a brain.

Brains and organizations as holographic systems

To compare the brain with a hologram may seem to be stretching reason beyond the limits. However, the way a holographic plate enfolds all the information necessary to produce a complete image in each of its parts has much in common with the functioning of a brain. And it is possible to extend this image to create a vision of organization where capacities required in the whole are enfolded in the parts, allowing the system to learn and self-organize, and to maintain a complete system of functioning even when specific parts malfunction or are removed. Some highly innovative organizations have already begun organizing in this way. But the principles on which they build are usually intuitive rather than explicit. It is thus fruitful to look to some of the ideas emerging from modern brain research to help clarify how holographic systems work, so that these ideas can have a greater impact on how we design organizations of the future. Recognizing that a somewhat speculative and futuristic stance is required for dealing with this issue, let us explore.

The holographic character of the brain is most clearly reflected in the patterns of connectivity through which each neuron (nerve cell) is connected with hundreds of thousands of others, allowing a system of functioning that is both generalized *and* specialized. Different regions of the brain seem to specialize in different activities, but the control and execution of specific behaviors is by no means as localized as was once thought. Thus, while we can distinguish between the functions performed by the cortex (the captain or master planner which controls all nonroutine activity, and perhaps memory), the cerebellum (the computer or automatic pilot taking care of routine activity), and the midbrain (the center of feelings, smell, and emotion), we are obliged to recognize that they are all closely interdependent and capable of acting on behalf of each other when necessary. We see this, and also how memory may be distributed rather than localized, in the resilient behavior of Lashley's rats discussed at the very beginning of the chapter. We also know that right and left brains combine to produce patterns of thought, and that the distinction between the functions of these hemispheres as the domains of creative and analytic capacities is accompanied by more general patterns of connectivity. For example, the creative or analogical right brain is richly joined to the limbic system and the emotions. The principle of connectivity and generalized function is also reflected in the way neurons serve both as communication channels and as a locus of specific activity or memory recall. It is believed that each neuron may be as complex as a small computer and capable of storing vast amounts of information. The pattern of rich connectivity between neurons allows simultaneous processing of information in different parts of the brain, a receptivity to different kinds of information at one and the same time, and an amazing capacity to be aware of what is going on elsewhere.

The secret of the brain's capacities seems to depend more on this connectivity, which is the basis of holographic diffusion, than on differentiation of structure. The brain is composed of repetitive units of the same kind (there may only be three basic types of brain cell), so that we find different functions being sustained by very similar structures. The importance of connectivity in accounting for complexity of functioning is also reinforced by comparisons between human and animal brains. For example, elephants have much larger brains than humans, but they are by no means so richly joined.

An interesting aspect of this connectivity rests in the fact it creates a much greater degree of cross-connection and exchange than may be needed at any given time. However, this redundancy is crucial for creating holographic potential and for ensuring flexibility in operation. The redundancy allows the brain to operate in a probabilistic rather than a deterministic manner, allows considerable room to accommodate random error, and creates an excess capacity that allows new activities and functions to develop. In other words, it facilitates the process of self-organization whereby internal structure and functioning can evolve along with changing circumstances.

This self-organizing capacity has been demonstrated in numerous ways. For example, when brain damage occurs it is not uncommon for different areas of the brain to take on the functions which have been impaired, as in the case of Lashley's rats. Similar self-organizing capacities are also evident in the way activity can be modified to take account of new situations. This capacity was demonstrated dramatically by psychologist G. W. Stratton, who tried wearing spectacles that turned the world upside down. After just a few days vision was adjusted by restoring familiar images to their usual position. What is most surprising, however, is that when the spectacles were eventually removed, everything turned upside down again until Stratton's senses reorganized themselves to cope with life as usual.

The brain has this amazing capacity to organize and reorganize itself to deal with the contingencies it faces. Experiments have shown that the more we engage in a specific activity, e.g., playing tennis, typing, or reading, the more the brain adjusts itself to facilitate the kind of functioning required. The simple idea that "practice makes perfect" is underwritten by a complex capacity for self-organization whereby the brain forges or revises patterns of neuronic activity. For example, experiments where monkeys were trained to use a finger to press a lever thousands of times a day showed that the area of the brain controlling that finger increased in size and changed in organization. Our awareness leads us to see the brain as a system which, in no small measure, has played an important role in designing itself in the course of evolution.

Now to our basic problem: how can we use these insights about the holographic character of the brain to create organizations that are able to learn and self-organize in the manner of a brain?

Our discussion provides many clues. For example, it suggests that by building patterns of rich connectivity between similar parts we can create systems that are both specialized and generalized, and that are capable of reorganizing internal structure and function as they learn to meet the challenges posed by new demands. The holographic principle has a great deal running in its favor. For the capacities of the brain are already distributed throughout modern organizations. All the employees have brains, and computers are in essence simulated brains. In this sense, important aspects of the whole are already embodied in the parts. The development of more holographic, brainlike forms of organization thus rests in the realization of a potential that already exists.

FACILITATING SELF-ORGANIZATION: PRINCIPLES OF HOLOGRAPHIC DESIGN

Get the whole into the parts.

Create connectivity and redundancy.

Create simultaneous specialization and generalization.

Create a capacity to self-organize.

These are the things that have to be done to create holographic organization.

Our task now is to examine the means. Much can be learned from the way the brain is organized, and much can be learned from cybernetic principles. I find it helpful to think in terms of the four interacting principles identified in Exhibit 4.4. The principle of *redundant functions* shows a means of building wholes into parts by creating redundancy, connectivity, and simultaneous specialization and generalization. The principle of *requisite variety* helps to provide practical guidelines for the design of part-whole relations by showing exactly how much of the whole needs to be built into a given part. And the principles of *learning to learn* and *minimum critical specification* show how we can enhance capacities for self-organization.

Any system with an ability to self-organize must have an element of redundancy: a form of excess capacity which, appropriately designed and used, creates room for maneuver. Without such redundancy, a system has no real capacity to reflect on and question how it is operating, and hence to change its mode of functioning in constructive ways. In other words, it has no capacity for intelligence in the sense of being able to adjust action to take account of changes in the nature of relations within which the action is set.

Australian systems theorist Fred Emery has suggested that there are two methods for designing redundancy into a system. The first involves *redundancy of parts,* where each part is precisely designed to perform a specific function, special parts being added to the system for the purpose of control and to back up or replace operating parts whenever they fail. This design principle is mechanistic, and the result is typically a hierarchical structure where one part is responsible for controlling another.

If we look around the organizational world it is easy to see evidence of this kind of redundancy: the supervisor who spends his or her time ensuring that others are working; the maintenance team that "stands by" waiting for problems to arise; the employee idly passing time because there's no work to do; employee X passing a request to colleague Y "because that's his job not mine"; the quality controller searching for defects which, under a different system, could much more easily be rectified by those who produced them. Under this design principle the capacity for redesign and change of the system rests with the parts assigned this function; for example, production engineers, planning

Holographic design rests in implementing four interrelated principles:

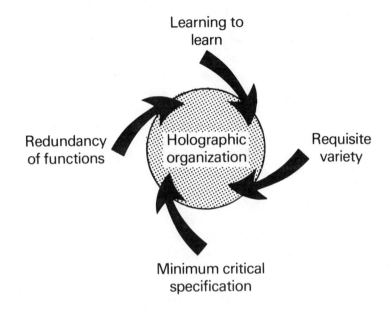

Exhibit 4.4. Principles of holographic design

teams, and systems designers. Such systems are organized and can be reorganized, but they have little capacity to self-organize.

The second design method incorporates a *redundancy of functions*. Instead of spare parts being added to a system, extra functions are added to each of the operating parts, so that each part is able to engage in a range of functions rather than just perform a single specialized activity. An example of this design principle is found in organizations employing autonomous work groups, where members acquire multiple skills so that they are able to perform each other's jobs and substitute for each other as the need arises. At any one time, each member possesses skills that are redundant in the sense that they are not being used for the job at hand. However, this organizational design possesses flexibility and a capacity for reorganization within each and every part of the system.

Systems based on redundant functions are holographic in that capacities relevant for the functioning of the whole are built into the parts. This creates a completely new relationship between part and whole. In a design based on redundant parts, e.g., an assembly line where production workers, supervisors, efficiency experts, and quality controllers have fixed roles to perform, the whole is the sum of predesigned parts. In the holographic design, on the other hand, the parts reflect the nature of the whole, since they take their specific shape at any one time in relation to the contingencies and problems arising in the total situation. When a problem arises on an assembly-line it is typically viewed as "someone else's problem," since those operating the line often do not know, care about, or have the authority to deal with the problems posed. Remedial action has to be initiated and controlled from elsewhere. A degree of passivity and neglect is thus built into the system. This contrasts with systems based on redundant functions, where the nature of one's job is set by the changing pattern of demands with which one is dealing. Needless to say, the two design principles create qualitatively different relationships between people and their work. Under a system of redundant parts involvement is partial and instrumental, and under the principle of redundant functions more holistic and all-absorbing.

In implementing this kind of organizational design one inevitably runs into the question, how much redundancy should be built into any given part? While the holographic principle suggests that we should try and build everything into everything else, in many human systems this is an impossible ideal. For example, in many modern organizations the range of knowledge and skills required is such that it is impossible for everybody to become skilled in everything. So what do we do?

It is here that the idea of *requisite variety* becomes important. This is the principle, originally formulated by the English cybernetician W. Ross Ashby, that suggests that the internal diversity of any self-regulating system must match the variety and complexity of its environment if it is to deal with the challenges posed by that environment (see Exhibit 3.7). Or to put the matter slightly differently, any control system must be as varied and complex as the environment being controlled. In the context of holographic design, this means that all elements of an organization should embody critical dimensions of the environment with which they have to deal, so that they can self-organize to cope with the demands they are likely to face.

The principle of requisite variety thus gives clear guidelines as to how the principle of redundant functions should be applied. It suggests that redundancy (variety) should always be built into a system where it is *directly* needed, rather than at a distance. This means that close attention must be paid to the boundary relations between organizational units and their environments, to ensure that requisite variety always falls within the unit in question. What is the nature of the environment being faced? Can all the skills for dealing with this environment be possessed by every individual? If so, then build around multifunctioned people, as in the model of the autonomous work group discussed earlier. If not, then build around multifunctioned teams that collectively possess the requisite skills and abilities and where each individual member is as generalized as possible, creating a pattern of overlapping skills and knowledge bases in the team overall. It is here that we find a means of coping with the problem that everybody can't be skilled in everything. Organization can be developed in a cellular manner around self-organizing, multidisciplined groups that have the requisite skills and abilities to deal with the environment in a holistic and integrated way.

The principle of requisite variety has important implications for the design of almost every aspect of organization. Whether we are talking about the creation of a corporate planning group, a research department, or a work group in a factory, it argues in favor of a proactive embracing of the environment in all its diversity. Very often managers do the reverse, reducing variety in order to achieve greater internal consensus. For example, corporate planning teams are often built around people who think along the same lines, rather than around a diverse set of stakeholders who can actually represent the complexity of the problems with which the team ultimately has to deal.

The principles of redundant functions and requisite variety create systems that have a capacity for self-organization. For this capacity to be realized and to assume coherent direction, however, two further organizing principles also have to be kept in mind: the principles of *minimum critical specification* and of *learning to learn*.

The first of these principles reverses the bureaucratic principle that organizational arrangements need to be defined as clearly and as precisely as possible. For in attempting to organize in this way one eliminates the capacity for self-organization. The principle of minimum critical specification suggests that managers and organizational designers should primarily adopt a facilitating or orchestrating role, creating "enabling conditions" that allow a system to find its own form. It thus has close links with the idea of "inquiry-driven action," discussed earlier. One of the advantages of the principle of redundant functions is that it creates a great deal of internal flexibility. The more one attempts to specify or predesign what should occur, the more one erodes this flexibility. The principle of minimum critical specification attempts to preserve flexibility by suggesting that, in general, one should specify no more than is absolutely necessary for a particular activity to occur.

For example, in running a meeting it may be necessary to have someone to chair the meeting and to take notes, but it is not necessary to institutionalize the process and have a chairperson and secretary.

Roles can be allowed to change and evolve according to circumstances. In a group or project bureaucratic patterns of fixed hierarchical leadership can be replaced by a heterarchical pattern, where the dominant element at any given time depends on the total situation. Different people can take the initiative on different occasions according to the contribution they are able to make. Instead of making roles clear and separate, roles can be left deliberately ambiguous and overlapping, so that they can be clarified through practice and inquiry. The basic idea is to create a situation where inquiry rather than predesign provides the main driving force. This helps to keep organization flexible and diversified, while capable of evolving structure sufficient and appropriate to deal with the problems that arise.

The principle of minimum critical specification thus helps preserve the capacities for self-organization that bureaucratic principles usually erode. The danger of such flexibility, however, is that it has the potential to become chaotic. This is why the principle of *learning to learn* must be developed as a fourth element of holographic design.

As will be recalled from earlier discussion, a system's capacity for coherent self-regulation and control depends on its ability to engage in processes of single- and double-loop learning. These allow a system to guide itself with reference to a set of coherent values or norms, while questioning whether these norms provide an appropriate basis for guiding behavior. For a holographic system to acquire integration and coherence and to evolve in response to changing demands, these learning capacities must be actively encouraged. In an autonomous work group, for example, members must both value the activities in which they are engaged and the products that they produce, and remain open to the kinds of learning that allow them to question, challenge, and change the design of these activities and products. Given that there are so few predetermined rules for guiding behavior, direction and coherence must come from the group members themselves as they set and honor the shared values and norms that evolve along with changing circumstances.

One of the most important functions of those responsible for designing and managing the kind of "enabling conditions" referred to earlier is that of helping to create a context that fosters this kind of shared identity and learning orientation.

Herbert Simon has suggested that hierarchy is the adaptive form for finite intelligence to assume in the face of complexity. He illustrates this principle with a tale of two watchmakers. Both make good watches, but one is far more successful because instead of assembling the watches piece by piece as if he were building a mosaic, he constructs his watches by forming subassemblies of about ten parts each, which can then be joined with other subassemblies to create subsystems of a higher order. These can then be assembled to form the complete watch. In other words, the successful watchmaker has discovered the principle of hierarchy. By organizing in this way the watchmaker can exercise great control over the process of assembly and tolerate frequent interruptions and setbacks. He can thus achieve a much greater rate of productivity than his competitor, who, when interrupted, has to start all over again. It can be shown mathematically that if the watch comprises a thousand parts, and the assembly process is interrupted an average of once in every hundred assembling operations, the mosaic method will take four thousand times longer than the systems approach to assemble a single watch. Simon uses the parable to illustrate the importance of hierarchy in complex systems, and to argue that systems will evolve much more rapidly if there are stable intermediate forms. Cybernetician W. Ross Ashby has made the similar point that no complex adaptive system can succeed in achieving a steady state in a reasonable period of time unless the process can occur subsystem by subsystem, each subsystem being relatively independent of the others.

The same is true of self-organizing systems. If their organization is completely random they will take an almost infinite amount of time to complete any complex task. If, however, they use their autonomy to learn how to find appropriate patterns of connectivity, they can develop a remarkable ability to find novel and increasingly progressive solutions to complex problems. Such systems typically find and adopt a pattern graded in a hierarchical manner, in that sets of subsystems link to higher-order systems, but the pattern is emergent rather than imposed.

The principles of holographic organization attempt to create the conditions through which such patterns of order can emerge.

HOLOGRAPHIC ORGANIZATION IN PRACTICE

Is holographic organization just a pipe dream? Clearly not. Mention has already been made of the holographic characteristics found in many autonomous work groups. And some highly innovative organizations have begun to extend this principle to restructure major sections of their operations.

Consider, for example, a well-known computer firm that has reorganized many of its factories along lines that reflect the principles of holographic design. For example, in one plant employing almost 200 people the organization has been broken down into teams of 14 to 18 people. These operating teams have complete responsibility for production, from the arrival of supplies in the plant to the shipment of finished products. Every employee becomes certified in the twenty or so operating tasks needed to produce the whole product. The teams meet daily to make decisions about production, to divide work, and to attend to special issues such as improvements in work design, problems in supplies or shipping, or the hiring of new members. Members of the team are responsible for setting their own hours of work and production schedules, and conduct their own quality control. They even administer skills-certification tests to their colleagues. Each operating team has a leader or manager who acts as a resource, coach, and facilitator, and who has special concern for the team's identity.

In addition to the operating teams there are also administrative and technical teams who provide support systems, services, and materials. The technical staff also play an important function in helping the operating teams integrate new products, processes, and equipment into daily operations, so that the plant can remain at the front of technological developments.

The whole ethos of plant operations is characterized by holographic integration. The work design was stimulated by a desire to create a holistic relationship between people and their work, so that employees would acquire a sense of identity with the firm and its products. Each and every worker knows almost everything about the products and processes with which the plant is concerned, and becomes involved with the productive process in the fullest sense. Employees are bound together in their common endeavor through extensive training and orientation programs that help them to develop common values and a sense of shared purpose, and are rewarded for their achievements in terms of skill levels. The results have been spectacularly successful, improving productivity, quality, innovation, and work life in almost every aspect.

Examples of piecemeal moves toward holographic organization are found in numerous other firms as well. In many of the highly innovative firms studied by Thomas Peters and Robert Waterman in their "search for excellence," the rigorous predesign and close control of work give way to more experimental, learning-through-action processes that have much in common with holographic self-management (see Exhibit 3.6). The emphasis that Peters and Waterman place on the ability of these organizations to develop a shared sense of identity, mission, and "corporate culture" also resonates with the holographic model. For it is by building this shared sense of the corporate whole into each and every employee that holographic organization achieves its coherence. Though not usually discussed in this way, the role of corporate culture is important in modern organizations because of its holographic potential.

Strong holographic tendencies are also being created in modern organizations through the introduction of microprocessing technologies that diffuse information, communications, and control. Microprocessing creates a capacity for networks of information exchange and interlocking controls that make many aspects of hierarchy unnecessary. Under its influence many areas of middle management are thus becoming redundant and replaced by more integrated work systems like those of the computer firm discussed above.

However, despite the emergence of these holographic characteristics and potentials, it would be an exaggeration to suggest that the holographic image accurately describes many organizations at the present time.

Strengths and limitations of the brain metaphor

Discussion in much of this chapter has looked to the future. We started cautiously enough, examining organizations as information-processing systems reflecting the bounded rationality of their members, but as the chapter progressed we became increasingly involved with the idea that it is possible to design them so that they can learn and self-organize in the manner of a fully functioning brain.

The main strengths of the ideas explored are their contributions to our understanding of organizational learning and capacities for self-organization. In the discussion of the organismic metaphor much was made of the importance of creating organizations that are able to innovate and evolve and thus meet the challenges and demands of changing environments. The ideas presented in this chapter offer concrete guidelines as to how this can be achieved.

In particular, they suggest that innovative organizations must be designed as learning systems that place primary emphasis on being open to inquiry and self-criticism. The truly innovative organization will need an ethos and holographic spirit where the innovative attitudes and abilities desired of the whole are enfolded in the parts. The challenge to design organizations that can innovate is thus really a challenge to design organizations that can self-organize. For unless an organization is able to change itself to accommodate the ideas it produces and values, it is likely eventually to block its own innovations.

Another major strength of the ideas considered in this chapter hinges on their contribution to our understanding of how strategic management can be designed to facilitate learning to learn. Traditional strategic planning models tend to emphasize setting goals and targets to help an organization respond to the threats and opportunities presented by the environment. As discussed, this tends to inhibit the kind of inquiry that challenges basic operating assumptions. In contrast, the ideas explored in this chapter suggest using cybernetic principles to create degrees of freedom within which the organization can evolve, formulating organizational mission in terms of "noxiants" to be avoided rather than in terms of targets to be achieved.

But isn't this just playing with words? Doesn't attempting to survive amount to the same thing as avoiding threats to survival? Doesn't the pursuit of desired goals or targets amount to the same thing as avoiding noxiants? Aren't we just talking about two sides of the same coin?

Cybernetics suggest not. The process of pursuing a specific goal and the process of identifying and avoiding noxiants are qualitatively different modes of action that impact organization and environment in very different ways. When one pursues a specific goal one orients action toward a fixed point of reference, and in the process narrows one's understanding of and interest in the environment to suit these specific concerns. As a result, relationships with the environment are usually seen and manipulated in an instrumental way. Much of the turbulence of modern environments is actually created by this kind of strategic action, as organizations jostle for position and attempt to create conditions that will help them achieve their targets. In this process independent and often conflicting lines of action combine to make the achievement of desired goals increasingly difficult. And even when an organization is successful, another goal soon becomes appropriate and the scramble starts again. Though we typically take goal-oriented strategy as a necessity of organizational life, it is in point of fact a socially constructed necessity, characteristic of a mechanical mentality.

In contrast, a strategy based on the avoidance of noxiants involves a choice of limits and constraints rather than a choice of ends, creating degrees of freedom that allow meaningful direction to emerge. This cybernetic principle underlies many aspects of social life. It is no coincidence that most of our great codes of behavior are framed in terms of "thou shalt *not*." Whether we examine the Ten Commandments or contemporary legal systems, we find the principles of avoiding noxiants defining a space of acceptable behaviors within which individuals can self-organize. As new noxiants are identified, or old ones deemed less of a threat, they are typically added to or removed from the list, thus modifying the space of action in an evolving manner. Cybernetics suggests that this basic principle could be usefully applied to help organizations learn and evolve, and to help reduce the environmental turbulence with which they have to deal.

Though the concept of avoiding noxiants seems counterintuitive, it is in point of fact highly consistent with some aspects of current management practice. Managers frequently guide their actions with a view to possible negative consequences, scanning their context for possible problems and proceeding within the limits thus defined. However, this kind of cybernetic insight is often implicit rather than explicit and runs counter to what many management theorists encourage them to do: "set goals and go for them." Many managers thus find themselves denying their cybernetic sense in favor of the idea that ideally they should be more goal-oriented than they currently are. With time, however, as knowledge of cybernetics increases, we may well find that the management theorists have the most to learn here. The Japanese view of management and objectives (Exhibit 4.3), and *ringi* decision making, demonstrate the power and utility of the cybernetic approach to management. The differences between Japanese and Western management are as much cybernetic as they are cultural.

A third major strength of the perspective developed in this chapter is that it provides a means by which we can move beyond the bounded rationality that characterizes so many organizations of the present time. While Herbert Simon has made much of the link between bounded rationality and the limited cognitive capacities of human beings, there are grounds for believing that his scenario is a somewhat pessimistic one. Most organizations reflect a bounded rationality because they are bureaucratized, not because they are populated by people. Bureaucratization builds bounded rationality into its structure *by design*. The design reflects the limited capacities of a *single individual* to exercise control over activities and decision processes that require the contribution of a significant number of people. The design also reflects a mechanical and linear approach to complex problems, as in a decision tree. The hierarchical thought structure reflected in a bureaucracy and in a decision tree are identical. Both provide a means of fragmenting attention and action so that complex phenomena can be ordered and controlled in a manageable way.

Thus, Simon's valuable reinterpretation of the nature of bureaucratic organization from an information-processing perspective is probably best understood as providing a rationalization for bureaucracy, rather than as demonstrating limits on the nature of organizational rationality. Holographic and other organizational designs that break free of bureaucratic controls show that organizations can deal with uncertain and complex problems in ways that go well beyond the capacities of any single individual. Also, modern brain research shows that there is another side to cognitive capacity: the holistic, analogical, intuitive, and creative capacities of the brain's right hemisphere. If new organizational designs can tap these creative possibilities they will provide further means of extending and transforming organizational capacities for rational action.

A final strength of the perspective developed in this chapter is that it provides a valuable means of thinking about how developments in computing and other microprocessing technology can be used to facilitate new styles of organization. In many organizations the full implications of this technology are not always realized, because new information-processing systems are often used to reinforce bureaucratic principles. Thus we often find computing facilities increasing centralization and hierarchical, top-down control. The technology is in effect reinforcing the single-loop learning characteristics of bureaucracy. This may confer certain advantages to those in control of bureaucratic organizations and yield efficiencies in terms of the quality of management information. And where microprocessors and robots replace people, reduced staffing and improved quality control may also result. However, insofar as we use the new technology to implement old ways of doing things, we are probably falling short of its potential. As Marshall McLuhan observed, "the medium is the message." Bureaucracy belongs to the age of the written word and the industrial revolution. Microprocessing belongs to the age of electronic communication, and we can expect this new technology to be accompanied by modes of organization fashioned in its own image. The principles of cybernetics, organizational learning, and holographic self-organization provide valuable guidelines regarding the direction this change might take.

Against all these strengths of the brain metaphor, it is necessary to identify two major weaknesses. First, there is a danger of overlooking important conflicts between the requirements of learning and self-organization on the one hand, and the realities of power and control on the other. Any move away from bureaucracy toward self-organization has major implications for the distribution of power and control within an organization, since the increase in autonomy granted to self-organizing units undermines the ability of those with ultimate power to keep a firm hand on day-to-day activities and developments. Moreover, the process of learning requires a degree of openness and self-criticism that is foreign to traditional modes of management. And the principles of requisite variety and minimum critical specification run counter to the inclination of managers who stress secrecy, exclusion, and the need to keep a tight rein on operations. Such attitudes and practices signify the presence of important countervailing forces that may prevent many modes of organizational learning and self-organization from becoming a reality.

A second weakness, evident in the above, is the fact that since any move toward self-organization must be accompanied by a major change in attitudes and values, the realities of power may be reinforced by an inertia stemming from existing assumptions and beliefs. Learning and self-organization generally call for a reframing of attitudes, emphasizing the importance of activeness over passiveness, autonomy over dependence, flexibility over rigidity, collaboration over competition, openness over closedness, and democratic inquiry over authoritarian belief. For many organizations this may call for a "personality change" that can only be achieved over a considerable period of time.

5

Creating Social Reality

Organizations as Cultures

Ever since the rise of Japan as a leading industrial power, organization theorists and managers alike have become increasingly aware of the relationship between culture and management. During the 1960s the confidence and impact of American management and industry seemed supreme. Gradually, but with increasing force, through the 1970s the performance of Japanese automobile, electronics, and other manufacturing industries began to change all this. Japan began to take command of international markets, establishing a solid reputation for quality, reliability, value, and service. With virtually no natural resources, no energy, and over 110 million people crowded in four small mountainous islands, Japan succeeded in achieving the highest growth rate, the lowest level of unemployment and, at least in some of the larger and more successful organizations, one of the best-paid and healthiest working populations in the world. Out of the ashes of the Second World War the country built an industrial empire second to none.

While different theorists have argued about the reasons for this transformation, most agree that the culture and general way of life of this mysterious Eastern country have played a major role. The changing balance of world power associated with the OPEC oil crisis of 1973, and the growing internationalization of the large corporations, have also increased interest in understanding the relationship between culture and organizational life.

Culture and organization

But what is this phenomenon we call culture? The word has been derived metaphorically from the idea of cultivation, the process of tilling and developing land. When we talk about culture we are typically referring to the pattern of development reflected in a society's system of knowledge, ideology, values, laws, and day-to-day ritual. The word is also frequently used to refer to the degree of refinement evident in such systems of belief and practice. Both these usages derive from nineteenth-century observations of "primitive" societies conveying the idea that different societies manifest different levels and patterns of social development. Nowadays, however, the concept of culture does not necessarily carry this old evaluative stance, being used more generally to signify that different groups of people have different ways of life.

When talking about society as a culture we are thus using an old agricultural metaphor to guide our attention to very specific aspects of social development. And it is a metaphor that has considerable relevance for our understanding of organizations.

In this chapter we will first explore the idea that organization is itself a cultural phenomenon that varies according to a society's stage of development. Second, we will focus on the idea that culture varies from one society to another, and examine how this helps us to understand cross-national variations in organizations. Third, we will explore patterns of corporate culture and subculture between and within organizations. After this, we will take a detailed look at how patterns of culture are created and sustained, and how organizations are socially constructed realities.

ORGANIZATION AS A CULTURAL PHENOMENON

Political scientist Robert Presthus has suggested that we now live in an "organizational society." Whether in Japan, Germany, Hong Kong, Britain, Russia, the United States, or Canada, large organizations are likely to influence most of our waking hours in a way that is completely alien to life in a remote tribe in the jungles of South America. This may seem to be stating the obvious, but many characteristics of culture rest in the obvious. For example, why do so many people build their lives around distinct concepts of work and leisure, follow rigid routines five or six days a week, live in one place and work in another, wear uniforms, defer to authority, and spend so much time in a single spot performing a single set of activities? To an outsider, daily life in an organizational society is full of peculiar beliefs, routines, and rituals that identify it as a distinctive cultural life when compared with that in more traditional societies.

Anthropologists and sociologists have long observed these differences. For example, in societies where households rather than formal organizations are the basic economic and productive units we find that work has a completely different meaning, and often occupies far less of a person's time. The distinctions drawn between means and ends, between occupational activities and general economic and social organization, tend to be far more blurred, and systems of attitude and belief much more cohesive. The French sociologist Emile Durkheim has shown that the development of organizational societies is accompanied by a disintegration of traditional patterns of social order, as common ideals, beliefs, and values give way to more fragmented and differentiated patterns of belief and practice based on the occupational structure of the new society. The division of labor characteristic of industrial societies creates a problem of integration, or what may be more accurately described as a problem of "cultural management." Ways have to be found of binding the society together again. Government, religion, the media, and other institutions and individuals concerned with shaping opinion and belief play important roles in this process.

In a sense, we can thus say that people working in factories and offices in Detroit, Leningrad, Liverpool, Paris, Tokyo and Toronto all belong to the same industrial culture. They are all members of organizational societies. Their work and life experience seem qualitatively different from those of individuals living in more traditional societies dominated by domestic systems of production. If nothing else, modern office and factory workers share basic expectations and skills that allow organizations to operate on a day-to-day basis. Though we often regard the routine of organizational life as just that, routine, it does in point of fact rest on numerous skillful accomplishments. Being a factory or office worker calls on a depth of knowledge and cultural practice which, as members of an organizational society, we tend to take for granted.

For these reasons some social scientists believe that it is often more useful to talk about the culture of industrial *society*, rather than of industrial societies, since the detailed differences between countries often mask more important commonalities. Many of the major cultural similarities and differences in the world today are occupational rather than national, the similarities and differences associated with being a factory worker, a janitor, a government official, a banker, a store assistant, or an agricultural worker being as significant as those associated with national identity. Important dimensions of modern culture are rooted in the structure of industrial society, the organization of which is itself a cultural phenomenon.

ORGANIZATION AND CULTURAL CONTEXT

However, though all modern societies share much in common, it would be a mistake to dismiss cross-national differences in culture as being of little significance. The course of history has fashioned many variations in national social characteristics and views of the meaning of life, and in national styles and philosophies of organization and management. The recent success of Japan, the decline of industrial Britain, the fame of American enterprise, and the distinctive characteristics of many other organizational societies are all crucially linked with the cultural contexts in which they have evolved.

For example, if we examine the Japanese concept of work and the relations between employees and their organizations we find that they are very different from those prevailing in the West. The organization is viewed as a collectivity to which employees belong, rather than just a workplace comprising separate individuals. The collaborative spirit of a village or commune pervades work experience, and there is considerable emphasis on interdependence, shared concerns, and mutual help. Employees frequently make lifelong commitments to their organization, which they see as an extension of their family. Authority relations are often paternalistic and highly traditional and deferential. Strong links exist between the welfare of the individual, the corporation, and the nation. For example, at Matsushita, one of Japan's largest and most successful corporations, these principles permeate company philosophy (Exhibit 5.1).

An Australian expert on Japan, Murray Sayle, has offered an intriguing theory of the historical factors accounting for this solidarity. He believes that Japanese organizations combine the cultural values of the rice field with the spirit of service of the samurai. While the former is crucial for understanding solidarity in the factory, the latter accounts for many characteristics of management and for the pattern of interorganizational relations that has played such a crucial role in Japan's economic success.

Rice growing in Japan has always been a precarious activity because of the scarcity of land and the short growing season. In retrospect, the process of building a civilization on this crop appears to be a prototype

Basic business principles
To recognize our responsibilities as industrialists, to foster progress, to promote the general welfare of society, and to devote ourselves to the further development of world culture.

Employees' creed
Progress and development can be realized only through the combined efforts and cooperation of each member of our Company. Each of us, therefore, shall keep this idea constantly in mind as we devote ourselves to the continuous improvement of our Company.

The seven "spiritual" values
1. National Service Through Industry
2. Fairness
3. Harmony and Cooperation
4. Struggle for Betterment
5. Courtesy and Humility
6. Adjustment and Assimilation
7. Gratitude

These values, taken to heart, provide a spiritual fabric of great resilience. They foster consistent expectations among employees in a work force that reaches from continent to continent. They permit a highly complex and decentralized firm to evoke an enormous continuity that sustains it even when more operational guidance breaks down.

"It seems silly to Westerners," says one executive, "but every morning at 8:00 a.m., all across Japan, there are 87,000 people reciting the code of values and singing together. It's like we are all a community."

Exhibit 5.1. Company philosophy at Matsushita Electric Company
SOURCE: Pascale and Athos (1981: 75-76, 73). Reprinted by permission.

of the Japanese ability to take on projects that seem impossible. Above all else, traditional rice cultivation is a cooperative affair. As Sayle has observed, there is no such thing as a solitary, independent, pioneering rice farmer. The growing process calls for intensive teamwork in short back-breaking bursts of planting, transplanting, and harvest. Everyone is expected to perform to the best of their ability to ensure that the collective outcome is as good as it can be. If one family fails to maintain their irrigation ditches in good repair, the whole system suffers. When the crop fails, as it often does because of disastrous weather conditions, the whole group is punished. There are no individual winners or losers. Under such circumstances, conformity and tradition is favored over opportunism and individuality. Respect for and dependence on one another are central to the way of life. It is this rice culture that we now see in the Japanese factory.

Rice farmers in Japan have always been willing to share their crop with those who are able to look after them. Such was the case in relation to the samurai, the "men of service" who depended on the farmers for their rice and physical existence. They played an important role in Japanese military and bureaucratic history and are now paralleled in the managerial "clans" or elites that run Japanese society. Protection of one's employees, service to each other, and acceptance of one's place in and dependence on the overall system are dominant characteristics. This service orientation extends to relations between organizations and the wider society, as reflected in the Matsushita philosophy. It is also crucial in explaining the close and collaborative relations between the banking system and Japanese industry. In contrast with the West, where the banks tend to act as independent judges and controllers of corporate investment, in Japan they assume a responsibility to provide help when and where it is needed.

Coupled with an amazing capacity to borrow and adapt ideas from elsewhere, first from China, and now from the West, the cultures of the rice field and of the samurai blend to create a hierarchical yet harmonious form of social organization within a modern industrial context. The managerial echelons are elitist and highly meritocratic, as they have been for centuries. Workers readily contribute to the material goals of their industrial masters and defer to their authority, because that has always been the traditional relationship between worker and samurai. No surprise, therefore, that so many people are prepared to sing the company song and commit a lifetime to the corporate family.

The system of organization is feudal rather than modern, and from outside the culture seems distinctly oppressive, particularly since mobility between ranks is highly restricted, being determined for each individual from a very early age. However, it is important to realize that the kind of submissiveness and deference to authority found in Japan is not necessarily experienced as demeaning. Hierarchy in a Japanese corporation is as much a system of mutual service as one of top-down control. As Robert Dore, a well-known commentator on Japanese society, has noted, there seem to be different relations between subordination and self-respect in Japan. In many Western countries individualistic culture leads us to seek and gain self-respect by competing with others, or against the wider "system," thus emphasizing our uniqueness and separateness. In Japan, on the other hand, cultural conditions allow workers to achieve self-respect through service *within* the system, even though there may be many aspects of the system which they find distasteful. In this regard, the spirit of the samurai pervades the whole culture.

In many accounts of Japanese organization some of the more distasteful aspects of work experience have been more or less ignored. Dazzling success stories tell of the way the Japanese arrive at work early or stay late to find ways of improving efficiency through the activities of voluntary "quality circles," or of how the dedicated Honda workman straightens the windshield-wiper blades on all the Hondas he passes on his way home each evening. Far less attention is devoted to the disgruntlement with which many workers accept the burdens of factory life. In this regard, the firsthand account of work in a Toyota factory by Japanese journalist Satoshi Kamata helps to provide a refreshing balance. Though perhaps untypical of Japanese industry as a whole, it shows how Toyota's relentless drive for success in the early 1970s was accompanied by much personal deprivation on the part of many workers, particularly those living hundreds of miles away from their families in camps rigidly policed by company guards. While the workplace was characterized by the genuine spirit of cooperation found in the rice field, it was also characterized by constant pressures to achieve demanding work targets and to fulfill the requirements of company values and norms. The exercise of company authority—whether in the form of an arbitrary transfer from one workplace to another, of a call for extra work effort, or of canceled leave—was often resented, though accepted with a grumble and a joke as an inevitable feature of life. Kamata's account suggests that day-to-day life in a Japanese factory can be at least as grueling as that in any Western manufacturing plant. The important difference is that the Japanese seem to have a greater capacity to grin and bear it!

Many discussions of Japanese management tend to ignore the cultural-historical circumstances that allow Japanese management to flourish as it does. They tend to overestimate the ease with which techniques and policies can be transplanted from one context to another, for it is the context that often makes the difference between success and failure. Debates regarding the merits of the Japanese system continue. For some writers it offers a model for practice throughout the world. For others it represents the remnants of a feudal system that may well be on the verge of major transformation as a restless youth culture, exposed to Western rather than samurai and rice-field values, exerts its influence on work and society.

Our focus on Japan is intended to be no more than illustrative. The point is that culture, whether Japanese, Arabian, British, Canadian, Chinese, French, or American, shapes the character of organization. Thus in Britain, generations of social change and class conflict often perpetuate antagonistic divisions in the workplace that no amount of conciliation and management technique seem able to overcome. In contrast with the Japanese, the British factory worker often defines himself in opposition to a system he perceives to have exploited his ancestors as it now exploits him. Managerial elites often assume a basic right to rule workers, who they see as having a "duty to obey" (Exhibit 5.2). Where the Protestant work ethic that dominated Victorian En-

The antagonism that often runs throughout the British workplace is gently yet clearly illustrated in the following account offered by management writer Charles Handy:

When auntie came to dinner

My aunt by marriage is a splendid character, but from a bygone age. Her father never worked, nor his father before him, nor, of course, had she ever earned a penny in her life. Their capital worked for them, and they managed their capital. Work was done by workers. She sees all governments today as insanely prejudiced against capital, all workers as inherently greedy and lazy, and most managements as incompetent. No wonder the world is in a mess and she getting poorer every day.

Tony is a friend from work. His father was a postman. He started life as a draftsman in a large engineering firm. He grew up believing that inherited capital was socially wrong. He had never met any man who did not or had not worked for his living.

They met, by chance, at my house over a meal. It started quietly, politely. Then she inquired what he did. It transpired that he had recently joined his staff union. Auntie had never met a union member.

"Good heavens, how could you?" she said.

"It makes very good sense," said Tony, "to protect your rights."

"What rights? What poppycock is this? If people like you spent more time at their work and less looking after their own interests, this country wouldn't be in its present mess."

"Don't you," said Tony, "spend your time looking after your rights?"

"Of course," she said, "but then, I've got rights. I provide the money that makes it possible for people like you to live."

"I provide the labor that keeps your money alive, although why I should work to preserve the capital of rich people whom I've never met is something that puzzles me."

"You talk like a Communist, young man, although you dress quite respectably. Do you know what you're saying?"

"You don't have to be a Communist to question the legitimacy of inherited wealth."

My aunt turned to me.

"You see why I'm worried about this country?" she said.

Each regarded the other as an example of an unnatural species. Given their opposed "core beliefs," no proper argument or dialogue was possible, only an exchange of slogans or abuse. It is a score which is replicated at negotiating tables as well as dinner tables.

Exhibit 5.2. Antagonistic attitudes and the workplace
SOURCE: From C. Handy, GODS OF MANAGEMENT, Souvenir Books of London, 1978, pp.161-162. Reprinted by permission of the publisher.

gland still exerts a major influence, however, work relationships can still be as paternalistic and compliant (though with less advanced technology not usually as productive) as those in many a Japanese factory. It is the cultural context that seems decisive.

If we turn to the United States for illustrations of how culture shapes management, the ethic of competitive individualism is probably the one that stands out most clearly. Many American corporations and their employees are preoccupied with the desire to be "winners" and with the need to reward and punish successful and unsuccessful behavior. In this regard, it is significant that the American expert on Japan, Ezra Vogel, poses the Japanese challenge in an American way, titling his book *Japan as Number One*. From an American perspective, industrial and economic performance is often understood as a kind of game. And the general orientation in many organizations is to play the game for all it's worth: set objectives, clarify accountability, and "kick ass" or reward success lavishly and conspicuously.

In an essay written in the early 1940s on the relation between morale and national character, anthropologist Gregory Bateson drew attention to differences among parent-child relations in North America, England, and elsewhere. He noted the American practice of encouraging certain forms of boastful and exhibitionistic behavior on the part of children still in a dependent and subordinate position, whereas in England children were encouraged to be submissive spectators in adult company and rewarded for being "seen but not heard." Bateson suggests that these child-rearing practices have considerable implications for later life, in the American case creating a great deal of room for self-appreciation and self-congratulation as a basis for independence and strength. We see this in the "We're No. 1" syndrome. And we find it in an organizational context in the opportunities created for conspicuous achievement on the part of those in subordinate roles, combined with expressive congratulation from those in superior roles.

Significantly, in their "search for excellence" in American corporations Thomas Peters and Robert Waterman place considerable emphasis on the importance of positive reinforcement (the reward for desirable behavior). Successful organizations in the United States seem to find ways of rewarding and motivating their employees so that they come to see themselves as winners. For example, Thomas Watson, Sr., of IBM is said to have made a practice of writing out a check on the spot for achievements he observed in wandering about the organization. At Tupperware the process of positive reinforcement is ritualized every Monday night, when all the saleswomen attend a "Rally" for their distributorship. At Rally, everyone marches up on stage in the reverse order of last week's sales, a process known as "Count Up," while their peers celebrate them by joining in "All Rise." Almost anyone who has done anything at all receives a pin or badge, or several pins and badges. The ceremony combines head-on competition with a positive tone that suggests that everyone wins. Applause and hoopla surround the entire event. The whole system, in essence, recreates the pattern for reinforcing desirable behavior evident in so many American parent-child relations.

The above examples provide splendid illustrations of Gregory Bateson's point. However, the most colorful example emerging from the Peters and Waterman research is found in the early years of a company named Foxboro, where a technical advance was desperately needed for survival. Late one evening, a scientist rushed into the president's office with a working prototype. Dumbfounded at the elegance of the solution, and bemused about how to reward it, the president rummaged through the drawers in his desk, found something, and leaning towards the scientist said "Here!" In his hand was a banana, the only reward he could immediately put his hands on. As Peters and Waterman report, from that day on a small "gold banana" pin has been the highest accolade for scientific achievement at Foxboro.

Positive reinforcement is practiced in many Japanese, British, French and other non-American corporations, often with considerable influence on employee motivation and performance. However, the U.S.A. stands supreme in the extent to which a concern for winning and direct reward for appropriate behavior have established themselves as important features of the culture and corporate life.

By understanding the cultural factors that shape individuals and their organizations we have a means of understanding important cross-national differences in organizational behavior. In addition to understanding the peculiarities of foreign practice, we also have a better means of understanding the peculiarities of our own. For one of the characteristics of culture is that it creates a form of ethnocentricism. In providing taken-for-granted codes of action that we recognize as "normal," it leads us to see activities that do not conform with these codes as abnormal. A full awareness of the nature of culture, however, shows us that we are all equally abnormal in this regard. By adopting the standpoint of the cultural stranger, we can see organizations, their employees, their practices, and their problems in a refreshingly new perspective.

CORPORATE CULTURES AND SUBCULTURES

The influence of a host culture is rarely uniform. Just as individuals in a culture can have different personalities while sharing much in common, so too with groups and organizations.

It is this phenomenon that is now recognized as "corporate culture." Organizations are mini-societies that have their own distinctive patterns of culture and subculture. Thus one organization may see itself as a tight-knit team or family that believes in working together. Another may be permeated by the idea that "we're the best in the industry and intend to stay that way." Yet another may be highly fragmented, divided into groups that think about the world in very different ways, or that have different aspirations as to what their organization should be. Such patterns of belief or shared meaning, fragmented or integrated, and supported by various operating norms and rituals, can exert a decisive influence on the overall ability of the organization to deal with the challenges that it faces.

One of the easiest ways of appreciating the nature of culture and subculture is simply to observe the day-to-day functioning of a group or organization to which one belongs, *as if one were an outsider*. Adopt the role of anthropologist. The characteristics of the culture being observed will gradually become evident as one becomes aware of the patterns of interaction between individuals, the language that is used, the images and themes explored in conversation, and the various rituals of daily routine. And as one explores the rationale for these aspects of culture, one usually finds that there are sound historical explanations for the way things are done.

An excellent illustration of this kind of analysis has been provided by my colleague Linda Smircich, who studied the top executive group of an American insurance company. The company was a division of a much larger organization serving agriculture, and offered a broad range of insurance services to agriculture and to the general public. Sustained observation of day-to-day management generated two key impressions. First, the company seemed to emphasize cooperative values and an identity rooted in the world of agriculture rather than in that of competitive business. The staff were polite and gracious and always seemed prepared to give help and assistance wherever it was needed. This ethos was reflected in one of the company mottoes: "We grow friends." However, coexisting with this surface of friendly cooperation was a second dimension of organizational culture that suggested that the cooperative ethos was at best superficial. Meetings and other public forums always seemed dominated by polite yet disinterested exchange. Staff rarely got involved in any real debate and seemed to take very little in-depth interest in what was being said. For example, hardly anyone took any notes, and the meetings were in effect treated as ritual occasions. This superficiality was confirmed by observed differences between the public and private faces of the organization. Whereas in public the ethos of harmony and cooperation ruled, in private people often expressed considerable anger and dissatisfaction with various staff members and with the organization in general.

Many organizations have fragmented cultures of this kind, where people say one thing and do another. One of the interesting features of Linda Smircich's study was that she was able to identify the precise circumstances that had produced the fragmentation within the company, and was able to show why it continued to operate in its somewhat schizophrenic fashion. Ten years earlier, when the organization was just four years old, it had passed through a particularly "traumatic" period that witnessed the demotion of its president, the hiring and firing of his successor, and the appointment of a group of professionals from the insurance industry at large. These events led to the development of separate subcultures. The first of these was represented by the original staff, or the "inside group" as they came to be known; the second by the new professionals—"the outside group." Most of the outside group had been recruited from the same rival insurance company and brought with them very strong beliefs as to what was needed in their new organization. "This was how we did it at . . ." became a frequent stance taken in discussion. They wanted to model the new organization on the old.

The new president, appointed after the firing of the second, was a kind and peace-loving man. He set out to create a team atmosphere that would bind the organization together. However, rather than encourage a situation where organizational members could explore and resolve their differences in an open manner, he adopted a style of management that really required organizational members to put aside or repress their differences. The desire for harmony was communicated in a variety of ways, particularly through use of specific rituals. For example, at special management meetings the staff became an Indian tribe. Each member was given an Indian name and a headband with a feather. The aim was to forge unity between inside and outside groups. During this ritual, the practice of levying a fifty-cent fine on anyone who mentioned the name of the rival insurance firm was introduced.

In both subtle and more obvious ways, the president continued to send messages about the need for harmony. He introduced regular staff meetings to review operations at which calm, polite cooperation quickly established itself as a norm. As some staff members reported,

We sit in the same seats, like cows always go to the same stall.

It's a real waste of time. It's a situation where you can say just about anything and no one will refute it.

> People are very hesitant to speak up, afraid to say too much. They say what everyone else wants to hear.

Harmony and teamwork were also sought through the use of imagery to define the desired company spirit—for example, the slogan "wheeling together." The logo of a wagon wheel was spread through the company. The idea of "putting one's shoulder to the wheel" or "wheeling together" featured in many discussions and documents. And an actual wagon wheel, mounted on a flat base, was moved from department to department.

The effect of this leadership style was to create a superficial appearance of harmony while driving conflict underground. This created the divergence between the public and private faces of the organization observed by Smircich, and led to a situation where the organization became increasingly unable to deal with real problems. Since the identification of problems or concerns about company operation frequently created controversy which the organization didn't really want to handle, the staff tended to confine their discussion of these issues to private places. In public, the impression that all was well gained the upper hand. When problematic issues were identified, they were always presented in the form of "challenges" to minimize the possibility of upsetting anyone. Driven underground by a style of management that effectively prevented the discussion of differences, genuine concerns were not given the attention they deserved. Not surprisingly, the organization no longer exists as a separate entity; the parent group eventually decided to reabsorb the insurance division into the main company.

In this case study we see how corporate culture develops as an ethos (e.g., "let's bury our differences and keep the peace") created and sustained by social processes, images, symbols, and ritual. Rituals are often embedded in the formal structure of the organization, as in the case of the president's weekly staff meeting, the real function of which was to affirm that senior members of the organization were at some form of peace with each other. The case also illustrates the crucial role played by those in power in shaping the values that guide an organization. In this example, even though the president was perceived by the staff as being relatively weak, he managed to exert a decisive influence on the nature of the organization. The case also shows how historical circumstances, in this case the conflict between inside and outside groups, can shape the present. In addition, we see how the fundamental nature of an organization rests as much in its corporate culture as in the more formal organization chart and codes of procedure. Indeed, it is probably no exaggeration to suggest that, in this case, corporate culture may have been the single most important factor standing between success and failure.

The idea of building a team of integrated players is a powerful one, and the president of the insurance company was probably not at fault in choosing this metaphor. Rather, the problems lay in the way it was coupled with norms favoring passivity. Had the metaphor been linked with an ethos favoring openness and innovation, and team players encouraged to make active contributions, the company's fortunes could have turned out very differently indeed.

Such is the case with Hewlett-Packard (H-P), a recognized leader in the microelectronics business. H-P was started in the 1940s by Bill Hewlett and Dave Packard and has established a corporate culture famed for strong team commitment coupled with a philosophy of innovation through people. The company decided to put the team ethos on the line early in its history, adopting a policy that it would not be "a hire and fire company." This principle was severely tested on a couple of occasions in the 1970s, when declines in business forced the company to adopt the policy of a "nine-day fortnight" whereby staff took a 10 percent pay cut and worked 10 percent fewer hours. Whereas other companies resorted to layoffs, H-P kept its full complement of staff, thus emphasizing that all members of the H-P team shared the same fortune, and that a measure of job security was possible even in unfavorable times.

Being a member of this team, of course, carries a set of obligations. Enthusiasm for work, and an ethos of sharing problems and ideas in an atmosphere of free and open exchange are values which the organization actively encourages. Much of this ethos stems from the day-to-day example set by Hewlett and Packard, the founding heroes who have established a reputation for hands-on management throughout the company. The ethos is also fostered by ritual "beer busts" and "coffee klatches," and by numerous ad hoc meetings that create regular opportunities for informal interaction. Stories, legends, and myths about corporate heroes abound and do much to communicate and sustain the cultural values underlying H-P's success. A new recruit may be treated to a slide presentation which relates how "Bill and Dave" started the company in Bill's garage and used the Hewlett oven for making some of the first products. On another occasion he or she may learn the story that when Bill Hewlett visited a plant one Saturday and found the lab stock area locked, he immediately cut the padlock, leaving a note saying, "Don't ever lock this door again. Thanks, Bill." Along with more formal statements of company philosophy, the message soon hits home: at H-P we trust and value you. You're free to be enthusiastic about your job even if it's Saturday, and to innovate and contribute in whatever way you can.

At International Telephone & Telegraph (ITT) under the tough and uncompromising leadership of Harold Geneen we find an example of another kind of corporate culture. The story here is one of success built on a ruthless style of management that converted a medium-sized communications business with sales of $765 million in 1959 into one of the world's largest and most powerful and diversified conglomerates, operating in over ninety countries, with revenues of almost $12 billion in 1978. Under Geneen's twenty-year reign, the company established a reputation as one of the fastest-growing and most profitable American companies—and, following its role in overseas bribery and the down-fall of the Allende government in Chile, as one of the most corrupt and controversial.

Geneen's managerial style was simple and straightforward. He sought to keep his staff on top of their work by creating an intensely competitive atmosphere based on confrontation and intimidation. The foundation of his approach rested in his quest for what were known as "unshakable facts." He insisted that all managerial reports, decisions, and business plans be based on irrefutable premises, and developed a complete information system, a network of special task forces, and a method of cross-examination that allowed him to check virtually every statement put forward. Geneen possessed an extraordinary memory and an ability to absorb vast amounts of information in a relatively short time. This made it possible for him to keep his executives on their toes by demonstrating that he knew their situations as well as, if not better than, they did. His interrogation sessions at policy review meet-ings have become legendary. These meetings, which have been de-scribed as "show trials," were held around an enormous table capable of seating over fifty people, each executive being provided with a mi-crophone into which to speak. It is reported that Geneen's approach was to pose a question to a specific executive, or to sit back listening to the reports being offered while specially appointed staff people cross-examined what was being said. As soon as the executive being ques-tioned showed evasiveness or lack of certainty, Geneen would move in to probe the weakness. In complete command of the facts, and equipped with a razor-sharp ability to cut to the center of an issue, he would invariably also cut the floundering executive and his argument to shreds. It is said that these experiences were so grueling that many executives were known to break down and cry under the pressure.

Geneen's approach motivated people through fear. If an executive was making a presentation there was every incentive to stay up prepar-ing throughout the night to ensure that all possible questions and an-gles were covered. This intimidating style was set by Geneen from the very beginning of his tenure. For example, it is reported that early in his career with ITT he would call executives at all hours, perhaps in the

middle of the night, to inquire about the validity of some fact or ob-
scure point in a written report. The message was clear: ITT executives
are expected to be company men and women on top of their jobs at all
times. The idea that loyalty to the goals of the organization should take
precedence over loyalty to colleagues or other points of reference was
established as a key principle.

ITT under Geneen was a successful corporate jungle. High executive performance was undoubtedly achieved, but at considerable cost
in terms of staff stress and in terms of the kind of actions that this sometimes produced, such as the company's notorious activities in Chile.
The pressure on ITT executives was above all to perform and deliver
the goods they had promised. Their corporate necks were always on
the line. Geneen's approach typifies the managerial style that psychoanalyst Michael Maccoby has characterized as that of the "jungle
fighter": the power-hungry manager who experiences life and work as
a jungle where it is eat or be eaten, and where winners destroy losers.
The jungle fighter tends to see his peers as accomplices or enemies,
and subordinates as objects to be utilized. The "lions" among these
fighters are conquerers who, like Geneen, build empires. More foxlike
jungle fighters move ahead with more stealth and politicking. Interestingly, the actions of both types help to *create* the dog-eat-dog world that
is implied in their basic philosophy of action.

The "cut and thrust" corporate culture of ITT under Geneen stands
poles apart form the "let's bury our differences" culture of the humble
insurance company considered earlier. It also stands poles apart from
the successful team atmosphere created at Hewlett-Packard. In these
three organizations we find very different cultures being created
through different styles of corporate leadership. Like it or not, the attitudes and visions of top corporate staff tend to have a significant impact on the ethos and meaning system that pervade the whole
organization. In the case of our insurance company the results were
unfavorable, at least insofar as corporate performance was concerned.
At H-P and ITT more successful corporate cultures were produced,
though at ITT this was achieved at great private and public cost.

A focus on the links between leadership style and corporate culture
often provides key insights on why organizations work in the way they
do. However, it is important to realize that formal leaders do not have a
monopoly on the creation of organizational culture. Their position of
power lends them a special advantage in developing value systems and
codes of behavior, since they often have the power to reward or punish
those who follow or ignore their lead. However, others are also able to
influence this process by acting as informal opinion leaders, or simply
by acting as the people they are. Culture is not something that is im-

posed on a social setting. Rather, it develops during the course of social interaction.

In organizations there are often many different and competing value systems that create a mosaic of organizational realities rather than a uniform corporate culture. For example, different professional groups may each have a different view of the world and of the nature of their organization's business. Accountants may subscribe to one kind of philosophy and marketing people to another. The frame of reference guiding development engineers may be different from the perspective of members of the production department. Each group may have developed its own specialized language and set of favored concepts for formulating business priorities. Interestingly, the successful organizations observed by Peters and Waterman seem to have found ways of breaking down these functional divisions so that different professionals can guide their activities with reference to a common and integrated set of norms and priorities. However, for many organizations the divisions are very real, resulting in a set of professional subcultures that have great difficulty in communicating with each other.

Other subcultural divisions within an organization may also be forged along different lines. For example, social or ethnic groupings may give rise to different norms and patterns of behavior with a crucial impact on day-to-day functioning. An excellent example of this has been provided by sociologist W. F. Whyte in his studies of restaurants, where status and other social differences between kitchen staff and those waiting on tables often create many operational problems. When a high-status group interacts with a low-status group, or when groups with very different occupational attitudes are placed in a relation of dependence, organizations often become plagued by this kind of "cultural warfare."

Subcultural divisions may also arise because organization members have divided loyalties. Not everyone is fully committed to the organization in which they work. People may develop specific subcultural practices as a way of adding meaning to their lives, e.g., by getting involved with friendship and other social groupings at work, or by developing norms and values that advance personal rather than organizational ends. For example, the politicking through which organizational members sometimes advance careers or specific interests can result in the development of coalitions sustained by specific sets of values. These coalitions sometimes develop into forms of counterculture, in opposition to the organizational values espoused by those formally in control. Many organizations are characterized by such informal divisions of opinion within the top management group, and sometimes in the organization at large. Typically these divisions usually result in a struggle for control, which in certain important respects can be understood as a struggle for the right to shape corporate culture. As in politics, such struggles are often closely linked to questions of ideology.

Foremost among all organizational countercultures, of course, are those fostered by trade unions. It is here that the battle for ideological control is often most clearly defined, since trade unions are in effect counterorganizations, in the sense that their existence stems from the fact that the interests of employee and employer may not be synonymous. Trade unions have their own specific cultural histories, which vary from industry to industry and from organization to organization within an industry. The philosophy, values, and norms of union culture usually exert an important impact on the mosaic of culture, subculture, and counterculture that characterizes life in any organization.

Creating organizational reality

Shared meaning, shared understanding, and shared sense making are all different ways of describing culture. In talking about culture we are really talking about a process of reality construction that allows people to see and understand particular events, actions, objects, utterances, or situations in distinctive ways. These patterns of understanding also provide a basis for making one's own behavior sensible and meaningful.

How, then, is culture created and sustained? How does reality construction occur? We have already begun to answer these questions in general terms. But let us take a closer and more systematic look at the process involved.

CULTURE: RULE FOLLOWING OR ENACTMENT?

Sociologist Harold Garfinkel has demonstrated that the most routine and taken-for-granted aspects of social reality are in point of fact skillful *accomplishments*. When we travel on a subway car, visit a neighbor, or act as a normal person walking down the street, we employ numerous social skills of which we are only dimly aware. Just as a tightrope walker might think nothing of running across a high wire to collect his or her possessions at the end of rehearsal, oblivious to the skill that this involves, so too in the most mundane accomplishments of daily life.

Garfinkel elucidates our taken-for-granted skills by showing us what happens if we deliberately attempt to disrupt normal patterns of life. Look a fellow subway passenger in the eye for a prolonged period of time. He or she will no doubt look away at first, but get increasingly uncomfortable as your gaze continues, and perhaps eventually inquire what's wrong, change seats, or get off at the next stop. Behave in your neighbor's house as if you live there. Disrupt the smooth and continuous line of your walk down a crowded street with a series of random stops, turns, and starts, or with the shifty manner of a suspicious character. In each case you will gradually discover how life within a given culture flows smoothly only insofar as one's behavior conforms with unwritten codes. Disrupt these norms and the ordered reality of life inevitably breaks down.

In one sense, then, we can say that the nature of a culture is found in its social norms and customs, and that if one adheres to these rules of behavior one will be successful in constructing an appropriate social reality. Thus a business person visiting overseas, or even visiting a client or another organization at home, may be well advised to learn the norms that will allow him or her to "go native." For example, in visiting an Arab state it is important to understand the different roles played by men and women in Arab society and the local rules regarding the flexible nature of time. In general Arabs in their home country have reservations about conducting business with women. Also, they like to take their time in building business trust and sound relationships before they make decisions, refuse to be hurried, and do not necessarily see a 2 p.m. appointment as meaning 2 p.m. People who unwittingly break these rules and attempt to keep a fixed schedule, or to rush their business, will frequently get nowhere. Their actions are likely to be as disruptive as those of the norm-breaking passenger on the subway car.

However, there seems to be more to culture than rule following. This has been illustrated in several important studies conducted by Garfinkel and his colleagues, which show that the ability to apply a rule calls for much more than a knowledge of the rule itself, since rules are invariably incomplete. For example, sociologist David Sudnow has illustrated that even in the administration of justice, an area of human activity where action is supposed to be determined by clearly defined rules, the application of a specific law calls upon background knowledge on the part of the legal officer or judge that goes well beyond what is stated in the law itself. His studies show that cases of child molesting or burglary, for example, are typically assigned to legal categories on the basis of images and judgments as to what constitutes a "normal crime" in these areas. A series of subjective decisions are thus made on the nature of the case before any rule is applied. Lawyers and judges do not follow the rules. Rather, they invoke rules as a means of making a particular activity or particular judgment sensible and meaningful to themselves and to others. In effect, the parties involved in this process are involved in a search for and definition of the rules that are to be applied. This process often involves negotiation, e.g., among the defendant and his or her lawyer, the public prosecutor, and the judge, all of whom may subscribe to competing definitions of the situation being considered.

If we return to consider how we accomplish the everyday realities of riding a subway car, visiting a neighbor, or walking down the street, we will find the same process at work. As in judgments within the legal system, our constructions of the situation influence what rules and codes of behavior are to be summoned as appropriate to the situation. Suppose that we are visiting a neighbor to party and drink beer. Our understanding of the nature of the situation will lead us to invoke certain rules (e.g., that it is OK to go to the refrigerator to fetch another beer, or to search for a corkscrew in the kitchen drawers), even though these rules might be considered quite inappropriate on another occasion. The point is that the norms operating in different situations have to be invoked and defined in the light of our understanding of the context. We implicitly make many decisions and assumptions about a situation before any norm or rule is applied. Many of these decisions and assumptions will be made quite unconsciously, as a result of our previous socialization and taken-for-granted knowledge, so that action appears quite spontaneous. And in most circumstances, the sense-making process or justification for action will occur only if the behavior is challenged.

Organizational psychologist Karl Weick has described the process through which we shape and structure our realities as a process of *enactment*. Like Garfinkel's concept of accomplishment, Weick's concept stresses the proactive role that we unconsciously play in creating our world. Although we often see ourselves as living in a reality with objective characteristics, life demands much more of us than this. It requires that we take an active role in bringing our realities into being through various interpretive schemes, even though these realities may then have a habit of imposing themselves on us as "the way things are."

The point is well illustrated in a wonderful tale related by Charles Hampden-Turner about a man whose wife's portrait was being painted by Picasso. One day the man called at the artist's studio. "What do you think?" asked Picasso, indicating the nearly finished picture. "Well . . ." said the husband, trying to be polite, "it isn't how she really looks." "Oh," said the artist, "and how does she really look?" The husband decided not to be intimidated. "Like this!" said he, producing a photograph from his wallet. Picasso studied the photograph. "Mmm . . ." he said, "small, isn't she?"

In recognizing that we accomplish or enact the reality of our everyday world, we have a powerful way of thinking about culture. For this means that we must attempt to understand culture as an ongoing, proactive process of reality construction. This brings the whole phenomenon of culture alive. When understood in this way, culture can no longer just be viewed as a simple variable that societies or organizations possess. Rather, it must be understood as an active, living phenomenon through which people create and recreate the worlds in which they live.

ORGANIZATION: THE ENACTMENT OF A SHARED REALITY

This enactment view of culture has enormous implications for how we understand organizations as cultural phenomena. For it emphasizes that we must root our understanding of organization in the processes that produce systems of shared meaning.

What are the shared interpretive schemes that make organization possible?
Where do they come from?
How are they created, communicated, and sustained?

These questions now become central to the task of organizational analysis. The enactment view of culture leads us to see that organizations are in essence socially constructed realities that rest as much in the heads and minds of their members as they do in concrete sets of rules and relations.

In order to come to grips with an organization's culture, it is necessary to uncover the mundane as well as the more vivid aspects of the reality-construction process. And sometimes these are so subtle and all-pervasive that they are very difficult to identify. Recall our discussion of how Japanese organizations are shaped by the values of the rice field, or of how some British organizations reproduce attitudes rooted in a long history of class conflict. These values may have very little to do with the actual organizations in which they are found, being imported in an invisible way.

Take again the way in which the dollar may be allowed to shape the reality of an organization through the routine operation of financial information systems. Under their influence people or organizational units, whether they be pupils in schools, patients in hospitals, or work teams in manufacturing plants, become seen as profit centers generating costs and revenues. And where financial considerations become a major issue, the data generated by such systems often exert a decisive influence on the decisions that are made. Many cost-conscious, bottom line-oriented organizational cultures are actually produced through the interpretive schemes that underpin such systems of control.

While it is not usual to regard accountants as "reality constructers" exerting a decisive influence on an organization's culture, this is exactly the role that they play. They can shape the reality of an organization by persuading others that the interpretive lens provided by the dollar should be given priority in determining the way that organization is to be run. This, of course, is not to say that financial considerations are unimportant. The point is that thinking about organization in financial terms is but one way of thinking about that organization. There are always others, and these are usually forced into the background as financial considerations gain a major hold on the definition of organizational reality.

Organizational structure, rules, policies, goals, missions, job descriptions, and standardized operating procedures perform a similar interpretive function. For they act as primary points of reference for the way people think about and make sense of the contexts in which they work. Though typically viewed as among the more objective characteristics of an organization, an enactment view emphasizes that they are cultural artifacts that help shape the ongoing reality within an organization.

Just as a tribal society's values, beliefs, and traditions may be embedded in kinship and other social structures, many aspects of an organization's culture are thus embedded in routine aspects of everyday practice. For these routine aspects define the socially constructed stage on which the current generation of actors lend their culture living form. More mundane than the vivid ritual and ceremony that decorated meetings at the insurance company discussed earlier, the weekly "Rally" at Tupperware, or the gold banana awards at Foxboro, they are incredibly important in understanding the way an organization works when no one is really looking.

As we explore corporate culture with this frame of reference in mind, it is amazing to see the extent to which *every* aspect of organization is rich in symbolic meaning, and how the familiar often appears in a new light. That weekly meeting or annual planning cycle that everyone knows is a waste of time assumes a new significance as a ritual serving various kinds of hidden function. We begin to realize that the everyday language of bureaucracy is one of the means through which the organization actually creates its bureaucratic characteristics. We see that the aggressive character of an organization is sustained by a kind of military mentality that leads it to shape aggressive relations with its environment and the local labor union, or to foster strategies designed to outmaneuver all kinds of opposition. We find that organizations end up being what they think and say, as their ideas and visions realize themselves.

As we look at the everyday relations between people in an organization with an eye on the reality-construction process, new insights on group functioning and leadership also emerge. We find that the formation of a group or the process of becoming a leader ultimately hinges on an ability to create a shared sense of reality. We find that cohesive groups are those that arise around shared understandings, while fragmented groups tend to be those characterized by multiple realities.

"Sell it to the sales staff" (Hewlett Packard).

"Those who *implement* the plans must *make* the plans" (Texas Instruments).

"Forty-eight-hour parts service anywhere in the world or Cat pays" (Caterpillar).

"Ten years' trouble-free operation" (Maytag).

"IBM means service" (IBM).

"Progress is our most important product" (General Electric).

"No surprises" (Holiday Inns).

"Never kill a new product idea" (3M).

All these phrases communicate central values around which these different organizations build, and symbolize important aspects of corporate philosophy. However, an organization's culture always runs much deeper than this. The slogans, evocative language, symbols, stories, myths, ceremonies, rituals, and patterns of tribal behavior that decorate the surface of organizational life merely give clues to the existence of a much deeper and all-pervasive system of meaning. The challenge in understanding organizations as cultures is to understand how this system, in its mundane as well as its more dramatic aspects, is created and sustained.

Strengths and limitations of the culture metaphor

In an essay on the use of statistics as a basis for public policy published in 1954, British economist Ely Devons drew parallels between decision-making processes in formal organizations and magic and divination in tribal societies. He noted that while organizational decision makers would not normally think of examining the entrails of a chicken or of consulting an oracle about the fortunes of their organization or the state of the economy, many of the uses of statistics have much in common with the use of primitive magic. In primitive society magic decides whether hunting should proceed in one direction or another, whether the tribe should go to war, or who should marry whom, giving clear-cut decisions in situations that might otherwise be open to endless wrangling. In formal organizations techniques of quantitative analysis seem to perform a similar role. They are used to forecast the future and analyze the consequences of different courses of action in a way that lends decision making a semblance of rationality and substance. The use of such techniques does not, of course, reduce risks. The uncertainties surrounding a situation still exist, hidden in the assumptions underlying the technical analysis. Hence Devons's point that the function of such analysis is to increase the credibility of action in situations that would otherwise have to be managed through guesswork and hunch. Like the magician who consults entrails, many organizational decision makers insist that the facts and figures be examined before a policy decision is made, even though the statistics provide unreliable guides as to what is likely to happen in the future.

Devons's critique points to the exaggerated faith we often tend to place in such techniques, and hence the lack of reflection and critical awareness that accompanies their use. Like the primitive magicians, all kinds of experts are encouraged to engage in their mysterious calculations, and are allowed to preserve their credibility even when events prove them wrong. If the magician's advice proves misguided, his magic is not discredited. Failure is usually attributed to an imperfection in execution or the unanticipated intervention of some hostile force. In a similar way the technical expert is allowed to blame the model used, or the turn of events, as a means of explaining why forecasts are inaccurate. The analysis is never discredited; the appearance of rationality is preserved.

Modern organizations are sustained by belief systems that emphasize the importance of rationality. Their legitimacy in the public eye often depends on their ability to demonstrate rationality and objectivity in action. It is for this reason that anthropologists often refer to rationality as the myth of modern society. For like primitive myth, it provides us with a comprehensive frame of reference, or structure of belief, through which we can make day-to-day experience intelligible. The myth of rationality helps us to see certain patterns of action as legitimate, credible, and normal, and hence to avoid the wrangling and debate that would arise if we were to recognize the basic uncertainty and ambiguity underlying many of our values and actions.

One of the major strengths of the culture metaphor rests in the fact that it directs attention to the symbolic or even "magical" significance of even the most rational aspects of organizational life. As will be apparent from earlier discussion, numerous organizational structures and practices embody patterns of subjective meaning that are crucial for understanding how organization functions day by day. For example, meetings are more than just meetings. They carry important aspects of organizational culture: norms of passivity in the insurance company; fear and respect for unshakable facts in Geneen's intimidation rituals. Even the nature of an empty meeting room conveys something about the general organizational culture, since these rooms generally reflect and reproduce the structures of interaction expected in the organization. Straight lines of chairs and note pads, each guarded by a water glass as erect as a sentry, communicate a sense of conformity and order. The friendly chaos and casualness of more informal meeting rooms extend a more open invitation to self-organization. In highlighting the symbolic significance of virtually every aspect of organizational life, the culture metaphor thus focuses attention on a human side of organization that other metaphors ignore or gloss over.

A second major strength of the culture metaphor stems from the fact that in showing that organization rests in shared systems of meaning, and hence in the shared interpretive schemes that create and recreate that meaning, the metaphor provides a new focus and avenue for the creation of organized action. Under mechanical and organismic metaphors, primary emphasis tends to be placed upon the process of design: the design of organizational parts or the design of adaptive processes. The culture metaphor points towards another means of creating organized activity: by influencing the language, norms, folklore, ceremonies, and other social practices that communicate the key ideologies, values, and beliefs guiding action. Hence the current enthusiasm for the idea of managing corporate culture as the "normative glue" that holds the organization together. Whereas previously many managers have seen themselves as more or less rational men and women designing structures and job descriptions, coordinating activities, or developing schemes for motivating their employees, they can now see themselves as symbolic actors whose primary function is to foster and develop desirable patterns of meaning. The results of research on organizational culture show how this form of symbolic management can be used to shape the reality of organizational life in a way that enhances the possibility of coordinated action.

The culture metaphor thus opens the way to a reinterpretation of many traditional managerial concepts and processes. For example, we have already mentioned how the metaphor influences our view of leadership. Traditional approaches to leadership have tended to focus on the problems of linking tasks and the people who are to perform those tasks by identifying the *behavioral* styles appropriate for different situations. The culture metaphor encourages us to reinterpret the nature of these styles to recognize the role they play in the social construction of reality. We can see that different leadership styles hinge on a question of how reality is to be defined. Authoritarian leaders "sell" or "tell" a reality, forcing their definition of a situation upon others. More democratic leaders let the reality of a situation evolve from the definitions offered by their colleagues, listening to what is being said, summoning and integrating key themes, and evoking and developing imagery that captures the essence of the emergent system of meaning. Such leaders define the reality of others in a more gentle and subtle way than their authoritarian counterparts, through strategic interventions that communicate key directions and sense of value, rather than by forcing people to follow their lead. Leaders do not have to lead by placing themselves in the forefront of action. They can often play a background role, shaping the all-important stage of action and the general direction that events will take but leaving choice about details to those responsible for their implementation. In viewing leadership as the management of meaning, the culture metaphor leads us to understand old styles in new ways.

The metaphor also helps us to reinterpret the nature and significance of organization-environment relations. We have already hinted at how we can understand familiar organizational concepts, rules, and procedures as interpretive schemes through which we construct and make sense of organizational reality. Equally, we can understand the way an organization makes sense of its environment as a process of social enactment. Organizations choose and structure their environment through a host of interpretive decisions. One's knowledge of and relations with the environment are extensions of one's culture, since we come to know and understand our environment through the belief systems that guide our interpretations and actions. This insight has prompted anthropologist Gregory Bateson to suggest that mind and nature are intertwined: nature renders itself visible through culture. Our understanding of nature is cultural.

This has profound implications for how we understand organization-environment relations and strategic management. For in stressing the fundamental interconnection between these phenomena we recognize that our environments are extensions of ourselves. (This idea is explored in some detail in Chapter 8.) We choose and operate in environmental domains according to how we construct conceptions of what we are and what we are trying to do, e.g., "be an organization in the computer industry," "produce and sell automobiles," "be a leader in our field," "whip the competition." And we act in relation to these domains through the definitions that we impose on them. For example, firms in an industry typically develop a language for making sense of their market, technology, and relations with other segments of the economy, aligning their actions in relation to the pattern of threats and opportunities which this set of interpretations makes visible. Firms organize their environments exactly as they organize their internal operations, enacting the realities with which they have to deal. Of course, the environment is not so easily controlled as internal operations. Other organizations also inhabit this domain, shaping action in accordance with *their* favorite interpretive schemes and thus influencing the environment to which others are trying to adapt and react. Environmental turbulence and change is a product of this ongoing process of enactment. Environments are enacted by hosts of individuals and organizations each acting on the basis of their interpretations of a world that is in effect mutually defined. A competitive ethos produces competitive environments. Visions of recession produce recession. The beliefs and ideas that organizations hold about who they are, what they are trying to do, and what their environment is like, have a much greater tendency to realize themselves than is usually believed.

This has considerable relevance for the way organizations should approach strategy formulation. By appreciating that strategy making is a process of enactment that produces a large element of the future with which the organization will have to deal, it is possible to overcome the false impression that organizations are adapting or reacting to a world that is independent of their own making. This can help empower organizations to appreciate that they themselves often create the constraints, barriers, and situations that cause them problems. For example, in the 1970s the American automobile industry saw the Japanese challenge as lying at the heart of their problems. A closer look at the situation would have led them to see that members of their industry had enacted the conditions that helped to make the Japanese challenge successful, e.g., by ignoring the possibility that the American market might be amenable to the idea of buying smaller cars.

A final strength of the culture metaphor is the contribution that it makes to our understanding of organizational change. Traditionally, the change process has been conceptualized as a problem of changing technologies, structures, and the abilities and motivations of employees. While this is in part correct, effective change also depends on changes in the images and values that are to guide action. Attitudes and values that provide a recipe for success in one situation can prove a positive hindrance in another. Hence change programs must give attention to the kind of corporate ethos required in the new situation and find how this can be developed. In highlighting the fact that organization to a large extent rests in the shared interpretive schemes that inform action, the culture metaphor elevates the importance of attending to changes in corporate culture that can facilitate the required forms of organizational activity. Since organization ultimately resides in the heads of the people involved, effective organizational change implies cultural change.

The insights generated by the culture metaphor have sent many managers and management theorists scurrying to find ways of managing corporate culture. Most are now aware of the symbolic consequences of organizational values, and many organizations have started to explore the pattern of culture and subculture that shapes day-to-day action. On the one hand this can be seen as a positive development, since it recognizes the truly human nature of organizations and the need to build organization around people rather than techniques. However, there are a number of potentially negative consequences.

Persuaded by the ideas that there are good and bad cultures, that a strong organizational culture is essential for success, or that modifications to an existing culture will lead employees to work harder and feel more content, many managers and management consultants have begun to adopt new roles as corporate gurus attempting to create new forms of corporate consciousness. While many managers approach this task on the assumption that what's good for the organization will inevitably be in the interests of its employees, critics feel that this trend is a potentially dangerous one, developing the art of management into a process of ideological control. Of course, management has always been to some extent an ideological practice, promoting appropriate attitudes, values, and norms as means of motivating and controlling employees. What is new in many recent developments is the not-so-subtle way in which ideological manipulation and control is being advocated as an essential managerial strategy. There is a certain ideological blindness in much of the writing about corporate culture, especially by those who advocate that managers attempt to become folk heroes shaping and reshaping the culture of their organizations. The fact that such manipulation may well be accompanied by resistance, resentment, and mistrust, and that employees may react against being manipulated in this way, receives scant attention. To the extent that the insights of the culture metaphor are used to create an Orwellian world of corporate newspeak, where the culture controls rather than expresses human character, the metaphor may thus prove quite manipulative and totalitarian in its influence.

When we observe a culture, whether in an organization or in society at large, we are observing an evolved form of social practice that has been influenced by many complex interactions between people, events, situations, actions, and general circumstance. Culture is always evolving. Though at any given time it can be seen as having a discernible pattern, e.g., reflecting an ethos of competition or cooperation, dominance or equality, seriousness or playfulness, this pattern is an abstraction imposed on the culture from the outside. It is a pattern that helps the observer to make sense of what is happening in the culture by summarizing the sweep of history in retrospect, but it is not synonymous with experience in the culture itself. Our understanding of culture is usually much more fragmented and superficial than the reality.

This is an important point, since many management theorists view culture as a distinct entity with clearly defined attributes. Like organizational structure, culture is often viewed as a set of distinct variables, such as beliefs, stories, norms, and rituals, that somehow form a cultural whole. Such a view is unduly mechanistic, giving rise to the idea that culture can be manipulated in an instrumental way. It is this kind of mechanistic attitude that underlies many perspectives advocating the management of culture. However, from the inside, culture seems more holographic than mechanistic. Where corporate culture is strong and robust a distinctive ethos pervades the whole organization: employees exude the characteristics that define the mission or ethos of the whole; e.g., outstanding commitment to service, perserverance against the odds, a commitment to innovation, or in less fortunate circumstances, lethargy or a sense of helplessness or futility. Corporate culture rests in distinctive capacities and incapacities which, as a result of the evolution of the culture, have become defining features of the way the organization works by being built into the attitudes and approaches of its employees. Managers can influence the evolution of culture by being aware of the symbolic consequences of their actions and by attempting to foster desired values, but they can never control culture in the sense that many management writers advocate. The holographic diffusion of culture means that it pervades activity in a way that is not amenable to direct control by any single group of individuals. An understanding of organizations as cultures opens our eyes to many crucial insights that elude other metaphors, but it is unlikely that these insights will provide the easy recipe for solving managerial problems that many writers hope for.

When anthropologist Franz Boas entertained a Kwakiutl Indian from the Pacific Northwest in New York City earlier in this century, the Indian reserved most of his intellectual curiosity for the brass balls on hotel banisters and the bearded ladies then exhibited in Times Square. His attention was caught by the bizarre rather than the fundamental aspects of the culture he was visiting. His experience contains a valuable caution for those interested in understanding organizational culture, for in this sphere too attention may be captured by the hoopla and ritual that decorate the surface of organizational life, rather than by the more fundamental structures that sustain these visible aspects. In studies of organizational culture, enactment is usually seen as being a voluntary process under the direct influence of the actors involved. This view can be important in empowering people to take greater responsibility for their world by recognizing that they play an important part in the construction of their realities. But it can be misleading to the extent that it ignores the stage on which the enactment occurs. We all construct or enact our realities, but not necessarily under circumstances of our own choosing. There is an important power dimension underlying the enactment process that the culture metaphor does not always highlight to the degree possible. When this is taken into account, the culture metaphor becomes infused with a political flavor that has close links with the perspectives to be explored in subsequent chapters.

6

Interests, Conflict, and Power

Organizations as Political Systems

I live in a democratic society. Why should I have to obey the orders of my boss eight hours a day? He acts like a bloody dictator, ordering us around and telling us what we should be thinking and doing. What right does he have to act in this way? The company pays our wages, but does this mean it has the right to command all our beliefs and feelings? It certainly has no right to reduce us to robots who must obey every command.

This rather angry comment of a factory worker exasperated by the grinding and oppressive experience of daily work life captures an aspect of organization that has escaped us up to now. He recognizes that his rights as a citizen and as a paid employee are in conflict with each other. As a citizen in a democratic society he is theoretically free to hold his own opinions, make his own decisions, and be treated as an equal. As an employee he is denied all these rights. He is expected to keep his mouth shut, do what he is told, and submit to the absolute rule of his superior. For eight hours a day, five days a week, he is expected to forget about democracy and get on with his work. His only democratic right rests in the freedom to find another job and move on. Or as his manager put it, "You can vote with your feet. If you don't like it here, you don't have to stay."

The situation described is an extreme one. Not all organizations are characterized by such entrenched relations between managers and workers, or by such dictatorial modes of rule. But the situation is more common than we often like to think, especially in industrial organizations where battle lines have developed between labor and management. Typical or not, the point of our illustration is that it invites us to understand organizations as political systems.

Managers frequently talk about authority, power, and superior-subordinate relations. It takes but a small leap in imagination to recognize these as political issues involving the activities of rulers and ruled. And if we develop this idea, it is clear that we can understand organizations as systems of government that vary according to the political principles employed.

Some, like the one considered above, may be highly authoritarian while others may be model democracies. By recognizing that organization is intrinsically political, in the sense that ways must be found to create order and direction among people with potentially diverse and conflicting interests, much can be learned about the problems and legitimacy of management as a process of government, and about the relation between organization and society.

The political metaphor can also be used to unravel the politics of day-to-day organizational life. Most people working in an organization readily admit in private that they are surrounded by forms of "wheeling and dealing" through which different people attempt to advance specific interests. However, this kind of activity is rarely discussed in public. The idea that organizations are supposed to be rational enterprises in which their members seek common goals tends to discourage discussion or attribution of political motive. Politics, in short, is seen as a dirty word.

This is unfortunate, since it often prevents us from recognizing that politics and politicking may be an essential aspect of organizational life, and not necessarily an optional and dysfunctional extra. In this regard it is useful to remember that in its original meaning, the idea of politics stems from the view that, where interests are divergent, society should provide a means of allowing individuals to reconcile their differences through consultation and negotiation. For example, in ancient Greece, Aristotle advocated politics as a means of reconciling the need for unity in the Greek *polis* (city-state) with the fact that the *polis* was an "aggregate of many members." Politics, for him, provided a means of creating order out of diversity while avoiding forms of totalitarian rule. Political science and many systems of government have built on this basic idea, advocating politics, and the recognition and interplay of competing interests that politics implies, as a means of creating a non-coercive form of social order.

By attempting to understand organizations as systems of government, and by attempting to unravel the detailed politics of organizational life, we are able to grasp important qualities of organization that
are often glossed over or ignored.

Organizations as systems of government

In April 1979 *Business Week* ran a
cover story on the Ford Motor Company. The cover featured a cartoon
of Henry Ford II sitting in a thronelike driving seat with a driving wheel
between his hands. Behind the throne stands a shadowy figure—we
are left to guess who. The prominent Ford-like nose suggests that it
may be Henry Ford I, founder of the Ford dynasty, scrutinizing the way
his grandson is driving the company. The focus of the story is on the
problem of succession. After thirty-four years as chief executive officer,
Henry II was contemplating retirement, but there was no obvious successor capable of taking the wheel. Up until his demotion and dismissal in the summer of 1978, the popular candidate had been Lee
Iacocca, the highly successful Ford executive who later became head of
Chrysler. The firing of Iacocca added depth to the imagery conveyed in
the cartoon since it symbolized the authoritarian nature of Ford under
the two Henrys. Iacocca's dismissal was merely the most recent and
controversial in a list of firings that had included the names of seven
company presidents since 1960. Iacocca was a popular and powerful
figure at the Ford company, but obviously not popular where it mattered most: his dismissal was solely linked to the fact that he did not
have Henry II's approval. Henry II is reported as having presented an
"it's him or me" ultimatum to his board's Organization Review Committee, and won. The formal reason given by Henry II to *Business Week*
was that Iacocca didn't fit into his way of looking at things. Informally,
it is speculated that Iacocca's fate was sealed by the fact that he had
become too powerful within the company. Though the guiding philosophy of Ford was reported to be towards a General Motors style of
"group management," *Business Week* stated that it believed Henry had
found it difficult to reconcile himself with the loss of personal power
that this kind of decentralization involves. It is speculated that like
Henry I, Henry II will continue as the same kind of blunt, visible, absolute ruler until he is forced to relinquish power.

The story at Ford is by no means unique. Many organizations are
ruled by authoritarian managers who wield considerable power as a
result of their personal characteristics, family ties, or skill in building

influence and prestige within the organization. Obvious examples are the owner-operated firm where the principle that "It's my business and I'll do as I like" holds sway; the family business ruled through "iron hands" that respect family interest and tradition above all else; large corporations such as ITT under Harold Geneen; and business firms, labor unions, and even voluntary organizations or clubs dominated by self-perpetuating oligarchies. The basis of day-to-day order in these organizations tends to be autocratic rather than democratic, in that the ultimate power to shape action rests in the hands of a single individual or group, who typically make all the important decisions. Though it is rare in practice to find an organization that is completely autocratic, many organizations have strong autocratic tendencies and characteristics.

When we summon terms like autocracy and democracy to describe the nature of an organization we are implicitly drawing parallels between organizations and political systems. As indicated in Exhibit 6.1, we do the same when we talk about organizations as bureaucracies or technocracies, because in each case we are characterizing the organization in terms of a particular style of political rule. In each of these words the suffix *cracy*, which derives from the Greek *kratia* meaning power or rule, is coupled with a prefix that indicates the precise nature of the power or rule employed. Thus the word autocracy signifies the kind of absolute and often dictatorial power associated with ruling by oneself. In bureaucracies, rule is associated with use of the written word, and is exercised by bureaucrats who sit behind their *bureaux* or desks making and administering the rules that are to guide organizational activity. Power and accountability in such organizations are intimately connected with one's knowledge and use of the rules, and with the lawlike form of administration that this implies. In technocratic organizations, such as the flexible and ever-changing firms that thrive in the electronics industry and other turbulent environments, power and accountability are directly linked to one's technical knowledge and expertise. Whereas in autocracies and bureaucracies that pattern of power and authority is fairly stable and clearly defined, in technocracies it is often in flux as different individuals and groups rise and decline in power along with the value of their technical contributions. Power and influence often tend to follow the "whiz kids" and other knowledgeable people who seem capable of addressing dominant concerns or of opening new paths to corporate fame and fortune. Finally, in democratic organizations, the power to rule rests with the *demos* or populace. This power may be exercised through representative forms of management, where different stakeholders are formally represented in decision-making processes, as in systems of codetermination or coalition government and in forms of worker or shareholder control. Democratic

Organizations, like governments, employ some system of "rule" as a means of creating and maintaining order among their members. Political analysis can thus make a valuable contribution to organizational analysis. The following are among the most common varieties of political rule found in organizations:

Autocracy: absolute government where power is held by an individual or small group and supported by control of critical resources, property or ownership rights, tradition, charisma, and other claims to personal privilege.

Bureaucracy: rule exercised through use of the written word, which provides the basis for a rational-legal type of authority, or "rule of law."

Technocracy: rule exercised through use of knowledge, expert power, and the ability to solve relevant problems.

Codetermination: the form of rule where opposing parties combine in the joint management of mutual interests, as in coalition government or corporatism, each party drawing on a specific power base.

Representative democracy: rule exercised through the election of officers mandated to act on behalf of the electorate, and who hold office for a specified time period or so long as they command the support of the electorate, as in parliamentary government and forms of worker control and shareholder control in industry.

Direct democracy: the system where everyone has an equal right to rule and is involved in all decision making, as in many communal organizations such as cooperatives and kibbutzim. This political principle encourages self-organization as a key mode of organizing.

It is rare to find organizations that use just one of these different kinds of rule. More often mixed types are found in practice. For example, while some organizations are more autocratic, more bureaucratic, or more democratic than others, they often contain elements of other systems as well. One of the tasks of political analysis is to discover which principles are in evidence, where, when, why and how.

Exhibit 6.1. Organizations and modes of political rule

power may also be exercised directly through participative forms of rule where everyone shares in the management process.

Many people hold the belief that there is a separation between business and politics, and that they should be kept apart. Hence when someone proposes the idea that workers should sit on boards of directors, or that there is a case for employee control of industry, that person is often viewed as taking an unwarranted political stand. However, the foregoing discussion shows that this interpretation is not quite correct. The person advocating the case of employee rights or industrial democracy is not introducing a political issue so much as arguing for a different approach to a situation that is already political. Organizations that are autocratic, bureaucratic, or technocratic have as much political significance as those dominated by systems of worker control. Their political nature is simply of a different kind, drawing on different principles of legitimacy.

The system of industrial codetermination which has developed in West Germany and other European countries since World War II explicitly recognizes the rival claims to legitimate rule that can be advanced by owners of capital on the one hand, and by employees on the other. Under this system, owners and employees codetermine the future of their organizations by sharing power and decision making. The system varies widely in application. In West Germany codetermination systems vary from industry to industry. For example, in the coal and steel industries legislation dating from the 1950s provides for the appointment of supervisory boards comprising eleven members, five to be elected by shareholders and five by employees, the remaining member being appointed by the other ten. The supervisory board is then responsible for appointing a managing board of three members to run the day-to-day affairs of the organization. One member of this board must be a business specialist, another a production specialist, and the other a trade unionist. Elections to these boards are held every three years. The boards are designed to give capital and labor equal rights, though many would argue that this does not always work out in practice. A modification of the codetermination principle in other European and North American countries is found in the appointment of worker directors, as in Denmark, Norway, and Sweden, where a certain number of seats on corporate boards are usually allocated to union representatives. Another application of the principle is found in the forms of corporatism where management, unions, and government join together to consult and collaborate with each other on issues of mutual interest.

Though such developments recognize the rights of labor to participate in the management of an enterprise, they have not always been readily embraced by those in the labor movement. The reason for this is found in another political principle: that in healthy systems of government those in power should be held in check by some form of opposition. Many people concerned with the rights of labor fear that direct involvement in the management process creates a situation that co-opts or incorporates, and hence reduces, the power of dissent. By being a part of a decision-making process one loses one's right to oppose the decisions that are made. Many advocates of labor rights have thus suggested that employee interests can best be protected through associations such as labor unions or professional bodies that adopt an oppositional role in order to shape policy without owning it.

This problem of "incorporation" often accompanies changes in organization favoring increased employee participation in decision making. The fear of many opponents of such changes is that employees will be allowed to exercise their democratic rights in decisions of minor importance while being excluded from major ones. "We're allowed to choose the color of the wallpaper, but little else" is a familiar complaint. As these critics see it, partial movements toward industrial democracy are often motivated by a managerial intent to divert or diffuse potential opposition by sharing the less important aspects of control. For these reasons, advocates of industrial democracy suggest that participation is not enough, and that organizations should move towards styles of management based on fully developed forms of workers' control.

These have been widely employed in countries such as Yugoslavia, where workers elect their managers and where the principle of self-management provides a key organizational value. This kind of system differs from schemes of codetermination, which recognize that owners of capital and labor have equal rights, by dissolving the distinction between capital and labor. In Yugoslavia and other countries where industry is state-owned, this form of self-management is fairly easily achieved, but elsewhere it has run into difficulties from those who wish to protect the rights of owners.

The most obvious large-scale experiments on workers' control in capitalist countries have occurred in ailing firms and industries where changes in fortune have increased the probability of unemployment and plant closures, and prompted the desire of owners to sell their interest in the organization. The employee response has occasionally been to buy and run the company, often with mixed success, partly because the organizations are in "lame duck" industries, and partly because of the problems of co-option that arise when workers become or appoint managers of an organization operating in a capitalist system. Like other managers in nondemocratic organizations they find that survival in the system calls for certain kinds of action that are not always popular with their fellow owner-employees. The system has a logic of its own, and being an owner does not necessarily imply freedom of action. Despite these problems, there have been a number of successful employee-run organizations that have found ways to create new kinds of environment and styles of organization that satisfy many of their employees. The Lucas-Aerospace experiment in England provides an outstanding example.

Whether we are discussing the management of the Ford Motor Company under a member of the Ford dynasty or the management of a worker-controlled cooperative, it is clear that organizational choice always implies political choice. Though the language of organization theory often presents ideas relating to the management and motivation of people at work in relatively neutral terms—for example, as issues of leadership style, autonomy, participation, and employer-employee relations—they are by no means as neutral as they seem. In understanding organizations as political systems we have a means of exploring the political significance of these issues and the general relation between politics and organization.

Organizations as systems of political activity

An analysis of organization from the perspective of comparative government can place our understanding of organizations in a refreshing perspective. However, in order to understand the day-to-day political dynamics of organization, it is also necessary to explore the detailed processes through which people engage in politics. For this purpose, it is useful to return to Aristotle's idea that politics stems from a diversity of interests, and trace how this diversity gives rise to the "wheeling and dealing," negotiation, and other processes of coalition building and mutual influence that shape so much of organizational life.

An organization's politics is most clearly manifest in the conflicts and power plays that sometimes occupy center stage, and in the countless interpersonal intrigues that provide diversions in the flow of organizational activity. More fundamentally, however, politics occurs on an ongoing basis, often in a way that is invisible to all but those directly involved.

We can analyze organizational politics in a systematic way by focusing on relations between *interests, conflict,* and *power.* Organizational politics arise when people think differently and want to act differently. This diversity creates a tension that must be resolved through political means. As we have already seen, there are many ways in which this can be done: autocratically ("We'll do it this way"); bureaucratically ("We're supposed to do it this way"); technocratically ("It's best to do it this way"); or democratically ("How shall we do it?"). In each case the choice between alternative paths of action usually hinges on the power relations between the actors involved. By focusing on how divergent interests give rise to conflicts, visible and invisible, that are resolved or perpetuated by various kinds of power play, we can make the analysis of organizational politics as rigorous as the analysis of any other aspect of organizational life.

ANALYZING INTERESTS

In talking about "interests" we are talking about a complex set of predispositions embracing goals, values, desires, expectations, and other orientations and inclinations that lead a person to act in one direction rather than another. In everyday life we tend to think of interests in a spatial way, as areas of concern that we wish to preserve or enlarge, or as positions that we wish to protect or achieve. We live in the midst of our interests, often see others as "encroaching" on them, and readily engage in defenses or attacks designed to sustain or improve our position. The flow of politics is intimately connected with this way of positioning ourselves.

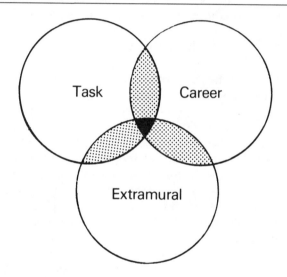

The above diagram illustrates the relationship and tension that often exist between one's job (task), career aspirations, and personal values and life-style (extramural interests). The three domains can interact (the shaded areas) and also remain separate. In working in an organization we try and find or are forced to strike a balance between the three sets of interest. Most often, the balance is an uneasy and ever-changing one, creating tensions that lie at the center of political activity. The fact that the area of complete convergence of interests is often small (the darkest area) is one reason why organizational (or task) rationality is such a rare phenomenon.

Exhibit 6.2. Organizational interests: task, career, and extramural

There are many ways in which we can define and analyze this pursuit and defense of interests. One way that has particular relevance for understanding organizational politics is to conceive interests in terms of three interconnected domains relating to one's organizational task, career, and personal life (Exhibit 6.2). *Task interests* are connected with the work one has to perform. The manager of a production plant has to ensure that products are produced in a timely and efficient manner. A sales person must sell his or her quota of goods and sustain customer relations. An accountant must maintain appropriate records and produce regular accounts. However, work life always involves more than just doing one's job. Employees bring to the workplace aspirations and visions as to what their future may hold, providing the basis for *career interests* that may be independent of the job being performed. They also bring their personalities, private attitudes, values, preferences, and beliefs, and sets of commitments from outside work, allowing these *extramural interests* to shape the way they act in relation to both job and career.

The relations among the three sets of interests are best understood if we examine a specific situation. Consider for example the position of a corporate executive working in a large organization. He may be highly committed to his job, ambitious, and also highly involved with family life. In his work experience he may desire to manage all three: to do a good job, move ahead in the organization, and strike a reasonable balance between work and leisure so that he can spend weekends and most evenings with his family. In some situations all three may coincide, in others two spheres of interest may be compatible, while in others the different interests may have no relation with each other. Life runs very smoothly for the executive in the first case (e.g., he gets a great idea that contributes to his job performance and promotion prospects and gives him more leisure time as well), but gets difficult in the latter cases. His great idea may improve performance and career prospects but mean more work and less leisure. Or it may enable him to reduce his work load, but in a way that makes him less visible and hence a less obvious candidate for promotion. Sometimes the idea will be great for getting on with his job, but have no other significance at all. The executive's attitude and relation to tasks, the ideas that he pursues and attempts to implement, and the way he reacts to the suggestions of others are all likely to be crucially affected by where the tasks, ideas, or suggestions fall on the map of interests depicted in Exhibit 6.2. The tensions existing between the different interests that he wishes to pursue makes his relation to work inherently "political," even before we take into account the existence and actions of other organizational members. These tensions are inherent in work life in Western society because of the latent contradictions between the demands of work and leisure on the one hand, and the demands of present and future on the other.

The orientation of different people toward these tensions varies from situation to situation, producing a great variety in styles of behavior. While some people are committed to doing their job as an end in itself, others are more careerist. Yet others spend most of their energy attempting to make work life less onerous, or as comfortable and consistent with their personal preferences as possible. Many people manage to achieve considerable degrees of overlap between competing aims and aspirations, shaping their general task or mission in a way that allows them to achieve all their aims at once. Others have to content themselves with compromise positions.

This way of understanding different kinds of interests thus provides us with a means of decoding the personal agendas underlying specific actions and activities. We can begin to understand how people relate to their work through their own personal concerns, and detect the motivating factors that underpin the varied styles of careerism, gamesmanship, task commitment, rigidity, "turf protection," zealousness, detachment, and free wheeling that lend the politics of organizational life its detailed character.

By simply following one's personal inclinations one shapes the drama of organizational life in accordance with a political script. However, the political content increases manyfold when we begin to recognize the existence of other players, each with interest-based agendas to pursue. The politicking to which this gives rise becomes particularly visible in situations that present choices between different avenues for future development, and in other transitional contexts such as the influx of new people or the succession of one person by another.

For the purpose of illustration consider the following case example.

Mr. X was the flamboyant marketing vice-president in a medium-sized cosmetics firm. After five years he had a solid reputation within his firm, having steered many successful campaigns designed to establish the firm's products as premier brands available in up-market retail outlets. Though he had encountered difficult times in persuading his colleagues that it was preferable to concentrate on relatively low-volume, high-quality products rather than to go for the mass market, over the years they had come to accept his viewpoint. His marketing philosophy and vision were in keeping with his personality, reflecting an interest and involvement with the social elites with whom he felt at home. The settings and themes of the firm's ads were selected by Mr. X and, as noted by many of his colleagues, were very much a reflection of his personal lifestyle. Crucial to the adoption of this marketing strategy and the line of corporate development it involved was the support of key members of the board who shared family connections and a taste for the style of life symbolized by Mr. X and his marketing philosophy. Other, less well-connected members who were appointed for their professional knowledge and links with the industry at large, along with the chief executive officer and a number of vice-presidents, felt that many opportunities were being lost by the need to preserve an elite image. Whenever possible, they thus tried to mobilize an awareness of the need to consider other policy options, but the success of the company muted their inclination to press their concerns too far. So long as Mr. X's charismatic influence remained an important driving force, the firm was thus committed to preserving and developing its elite status.

An opportunity for change dropped by chance in the letter box of Mr. Y, vice-president for corporate planning and one of those most concerned about the lost opportunities. A friend and former colleague, now chief of a prestigious "head-hunting" firm, had written asking if he could recommend possible candidates for the position of marketing VP in the new North American branch of a European firm dealing in high-society fashion. A vision of Mr. X smiling in the midst of furs, diamonds, and Paris fashions immediately floated into Y's mind. Within the hour he had made an off-the-record call to his friend suggesting that Mr. X might well be approached. Within two months, X had been offered and had accepted the job.

Mr. X's successor at the cosmetics firm, Ms. Z, was a relatively young and ambitious woman with a liking for the glossy life. She had been a compromise selection, the board having been split on two other candidates. Ms. Z seemed to strike the balance between the dashing style to which X's allies had become accustomed, and the promise of new initiative favored by those who had felt constrained by the direction set by X's philosophy. While neither group was delighted with the appointment, they both felt that Ms. Z was eminently capable of handling the job, especially since she would inherit a successful operation.

For Ms. Z the job was a great opportunity. She felt that the time was right to make her mark in the industry and saw in the steady direction steered by X a base on which to launch new initiatives. In her interview discussions with X's former supporters she had made much of the need to conserve what had been achieved. In her discussions with those less committed to this philosophy she had stressed the promise of new markets. Her first year in the new job was spent developing an initiative that would bring these goals together by retaining the up-market image but broadening marketing outlets to include selected chains of retail drug and department stores. She knew that she had to come up with a philosophy that set her apart from X, but that she must retain the support of the board and the senior executives who were essential for ensuring success. Her colleagues ready for a change were willing partners, and excellent working relations soon developed through a give-and-take approach that helped define ideas and opportunities where all seemed to gain. Her task in relation to those who still equated the style and personality of Mr. X with what the company stood for was much more difficult. Resistance and heated exchange became a feature of boardroom discussion. Over a period of three years, however, most came to accept the idea that the broadening of the market was still consistent with the image of a high-status product, particularly since the changing strategy was sweetened by its obvious financial success. As one board member put it while looking at the latest returns, "I think I'll be able to live with even more ads in those dreadful magazines if I think about these figures."

Our case only sketches the dynamics of the situation in broadest outline. However, it does serve to illustrate the politics intrinsic to any situation where people wish to pursue divergent interests. Mr. X had a vision that others were persuaded to share. His charismatic personality allowed him to use the organization to express himself through a strategy that combined task, career, and extramural interests in a coherent way. The colleagues who bought into his strategy did so to the extent that their aims were achieved as well. Those opposed to the strategy had other aspirations. They wanted to see the organization go elsewhere. For this reason Mr. Y took advantage of a chance opportunity to change the situation. The state of transition opened up new opportunities. Rival coalitions formed around the candidates who people thought would be able to advance their interests. Ms. Z, the very able compromise candidate, read and played the situation well. She saw a convergence between personal and corporate opportunity and used her new job to further both. Given her ambitions there was no way that she could accept the status quo. Her personal style and career aspirations required her to "be a mover" and "make her mark." X's philosophy, though solidly successful, thus had to change. Others were prepared to join Z in shaping a new corporate direction in return for prizes of their own. The confidence of the rival coalitions, though doubtful at times, was retained because the new situation resulted in a transformation that most could identify with and thus own. Even though our discussion glosses over the power relations and other aspects of this case, the interactions between these few key actors and their supporters do give a clue to the thick and rich political dynamic of organizational life. The diversity of interests that Aristotle observed in the Greek city-state are evident in every organization, and can be analyzed by tracing how the ideas and actions of people collide or coincide.

In contrast with the view that organizations are integrated rational enterprises pursuing a common goal, the political metaphor encourages us to see organizations as loose networks of people with divergent interests who gather together for the sake of expediency, e.g., in making a living, developing a career, or pursuing a desired goal or objective. Organizations are coalitions and are made up of coalitions, and coalition building is an important dimension of almost all organizational life.

Coalitions arise when groups of individuals get together to cooperate in relation to specific issues, events, or decisions, or to advance specific values and ideologies. Organizations fit this definition of coalitions in the sense that they comprise groups of managers, workers, shareholders, customers, suppliers, lawyers, governmental agents, and other formal and informal groups with an interest or stake in the organization but whose goals and preferences differ. The organization as a coalition of diverse stakeholders is a coalition with multiple goals.

Some organization theorists draw a distinction between cliques that become aware of common goals, and coalitions of two or more such groups who unite to pursue a joint interest, often working against a rival network. Clearly, people in organizations can pursue their interests as individuals, specific interest groups, or more generalized coalitions, so this distinction is often a useful one. In many organizations there is often a dominant coalition that controls important areas of policy. Such coalitions usually build around the chief executive or other key actors in the organization, each participant making demands on and contributions to the coalition as a price of participation. All coalitions have to strike some kind of balance between the rewards and contributions necessary to sustain membership, a balance usually influenced by factors such as age, organizational position, education, time spent in the organization, and values and attitudes.

Most approaches to organization actually foster the development of cliques and coalitions, since functional and other divisions fragment interests—for example, by allocating different goals and activities to subunits such as departments or project teams. The "bounded rationality" discussed in Chapter 4 thus assumes a political dimension as sales people become preoccupied with sales objectives, production people with production, and project teams with their group projects. Given such fragmentation, while there may be a general consensus about overall goals, there is often considerable disagreement about specific objectives, since at this level the interests of individuals and their subunits often become paramount. The organization as a whole is thus often obliged to function with a minimal kind of consensus. This allows the organization to survive while recognizing the diversity of the aims and aspirations of its members. The organization often has to be content with satisfactory rather than optimal solutions to problems, with negotiation and compromise becoming more important than technical rationality.

Coalition development offers a strategy for advancing one's interests in an organization, and organization members often give considerable attention to increasing their power and influence through this means. Sometimes coalitions are initiated by less powerful actors who seek the support of others. At other times they may be developed by the powerful to consolidate their power; e.g., an executive may promote people to key positions where they can serve as loyal lieutenants. Whether formal or informal, confined to the organization or extended to include key interests outside, coalitions and interest groups often provide important means of securing desired ends.

UNDERSTANDING CONFLICT

Conflict arises whenever interests collide. The natural reaction to conflict in organizational contexts is usually to view it as a dysfunctional force that can be attributed to some regrettable set of circumstances or causes. "It's a personality problem." "They're rivals who always meet head on." "Production people and marketing people never get along." "Everyone hates auditors and accountants." Conflict is regarded as an unfortunate state that in more favorable circumstances would disappear.

If our analysis in the previous section is correct, however, then conflict will always be present in organizations. Conflict may be personal, interpersonal, or between rival groups or coalitions. It may be built into organizational structures, roles, attitudes, and stereotypes, or arise over a scarcity of resources. It may be explicit or covert. Whatever the reason, and whatever the form it takes, its source rests in some perceived or real divergence of interests.

As Scottish sociologist Tom Burns has pointed out, most modern organizations promote various kinds of politicking because they are designed as systems of simultaneous competition and collaboration. People must collaborate in pursuit of a common task, yet are often pitted against each other in competition for limited resources, status, and career advancement. These conflicting dimensions of organization are most clearly symbolized in the hierarchical organization chart, which is both a system of cooperation, in that it reflects a rational subdivision of tasks, *and* a career ladder up which people are motivated to climb. The fact that there are more jobs at the bottom than at the top means that competition for the top places is likely to be keen, and that in any career race there are likely to be far fewer winners than losers. Along with the fact that different individuals and groups are mandated to exercise authority and influence over others, the hierarchy more or less ensures the kinds of competitive struggle on which organizational politics thrives. One does not have to be consciously cunning or deviously political to end up playing organizational politics. For political behavior is a fairly natural response to the tensions created between individuals and their organizations. The corporate Machiavellis who systematically wheel and deal their way through organizational affairs merely illustrate the most extreme and fully developed form of a latent tendency present in most aspects of organizational life.

. The literature on organization theory is full of examples that illustrate the competitive system implicit in hierarchy. Some of the most vivid of these are found in reports by sociologists who have infiltrated the workplace in the role of participant observers. The setting of budgets and work standards, the day-to-day supervision and control of work, as well as the pursuit of opportunity and career, are often characterized by sophisticated forms of gamesmanship. Take, for example, the situations reported by W. F. Whyte in his classic study *Money and Motivation*. These reveal the guile with which factory workers are able to control their pace of work and level of earnings, even when under the close eye of their supervisors or of efficiency experts trying to find ways of increasing productivity. The workers know that to maintain their positions they have to find ways of beating the system, and do so with great skill and ingenuity.

For example, Starkey, an experienced factory worker, finds ways of building extra movements into his job when work standards are being set so that the job can be made easier under normal circumstances. He also finds completely new ways of working at high speeds when his supervisor is not around, thus allowing him to create slack time elsewhere in his day. Ray, famed among his fellow workers for his skill in outthinking and outperforming his controllers, finds ways of getting his machine to destroy the product on which he is working when he is asked to work at too fast a pace. He also has a great ability to look as if he is working harder than he is, generating a profuse sweat to impress and deceive his observers. Workers share ideas on how to get better work standards, to restrict output, to cash in on "gravy" jobs, or to land their competitors with the "stinkers." Such collaboration is often used against management, and at other times against other workers or work teams. Management, of course, often know that this is happening, but are frequently powerless to do anything about it, particularly where plants are unionized. Sometimes they gain control of the problem at hand, only to find another one arising elsewhere. For the relationship is essentially combative, the status and self-respect of both groups resting on their ability to outwit or control the other.

Similar relations are found in office settings, where staff manage impressions and schedules in a way that makes them seem busier and more productive than they actually are. And in budget-setting and other decision-making sessions managers often attempt to outwit their own managers by padding their estimates to create slack resources, or by negotiating easy work targets to allow room for error or to allow them to look good when the next salary review comes around.

Politicking is also latent in the horizontal relations between specialist units. As noted earlier, people begin to identify with the responsibilities and objectives associated with their specific role, work group, department, or project team, in a way that often leads them to value achievement of these responsibilities and objectives over and above the achievement of wider organizational goals. This is especially true when reward systems and one's general status, visibility, and sense of success are linked with good performance at the level of one's specialized responsibilities.

Even when people recognize the importance of working together, the nature of any given job often combines contradictory elements that create various kinds of role conflict. For example, the politicized interactions so often observed between production and marketing staff, or between accountants and the users of financial services, often rest in part on the fact that they are being asked to engage in activities which impinge on each other in a negative way. The product modification requested by marketing creates problems in the design and sequencing of production. The accountant's concern for firm control over expenditure proves an unwelcome constraint for executives in the spending department. As the actors in their various roles attempt to do the job for which they have been appointed, interpreting their task interests in a way that seems ideally suited for the achievement of organizational goals, they are set on a collision course. Similar conflicts are often observed between "line" managers responsible for day-to-day results and "staff" people such as planners, lawyers, accountants, and other experts who perform an advisory role; between professionals seeking to extend their sphere of autonomy and bureaucrats seeking to reduce it in the interests of improving control; and so on.

The potential complexity of organizational politics is mind-boggling, even before we take account of the personalities and personality clashes that usually bring roles and their conflicts to life. Sometimes the conflicts generated will be quite explicit and open for all to see, while at other times they will lie beneath the surface of day-to-day events. For example, relations in meetings may be governed by various hidden agendas of which even the participants are unaware. In some organizations disputes may have a long history, decisions and actions in the present being shaped by conflicts, grudges, or differences that others believe long forgotten or settled. The manager of a production department may align with the marketing manager to block a proposal from the production engineer not because he disagrees with the basic ideas, but because of resentments associated with the fact that he and the production engineer have never gotten along. Though such resentments may seem petty, they are often powerful forces in organizational life.

Many organizational conflicts often become institutionalized in the shape of attitudes, stereotypes, values, beliefs, rituals, and other aspects of organizational culture. In this socialized form, the underlying conflicts can be extremely difficult to identify and to break down. Here again history can shape the present in subtle ways. However, by remembering Aristotle's injunction to understand the source of politics in the diversity of interests to which conflicts merely lend visible form, organizational analysts have a means of penetrating beneath the surface of any conflict situation to understand its genesis. We will examine some of the ways in which conflicts can be managed when we discuss the politics of pluralist organizations later in this chapter.

EXPLORING POWER

Power is the medium through which conflicts of interest are ultimately resolved. Power influences who gets what, when, and how.

In recent years organization and management theorists have become increasingly aware of the need to recognize the importance of power in explaining organizational affairs. However, no really clear and consistent definition of power has emerged. While some view power as a resource, i.e., as something one possesses, others view it as a social relation characterized by some kind of dependency, i.e., as an influence *over* something or someone. Most organization theorists tend to take their point of departure from the definition of power offered by American political scientist Robert Dahl, who suggests that power involves an ability to get another person to do something that he or she would not otherwise have done. For some theorists this definition leads to a study of the "here and now" conditions under which one person, group, or organization becomes dependent on another, while for others it leads to an examination of the historical forces that shape the stage of action on which contemporary power relations are set. As listed in Exhibit 6.3, the sources of power are rich and varied, providing those who wish to wheel and deal in the pursuit of their interests with many ways of doing so. In the following discussion we will examine how these sources of power are used to shape the dynamics of organizational life. In so doing we will be creating an analytical frame-

---

The following are among the most important sources of power:

1. FORMAL AUTHORITY
2. CONTROL OF SCARCE RESOURCES
3. USE OF ORGANIZATIONAL STRUCTURE, RULES, AND REGULATIONS
4. CONTROL OF DECISION PROCESSES
5. CONTROL OF KNOWLEDGE AND INFORMATION
6. CONTROL OF BOUNDARIES
7. ABILITY TO COPE WITH UNCERTAINTY
8. CONTROL OF TECHNOLOGY
9. INTERPERSONAL ALLIANCES, NETWORKS, AND CONTROL OF "INFORMAL ORGANIZATION"
10. CONTROL OF COUNTERORGANIZATIONS
11. SYMBOLISM AND THE MANAGEMENT OF MEANING
12. GENDER AND THE MANAGEMENT OF GENDER RELATIONS
13. STRUCTURAL FACTORS THAT DEFINE THE STAGE OF ACTION
14. THE POWER ONE ALREADY HAS

These sources of power provide organizational members with a variety of means for enhancing their interests and resolving or perpetuating organizational conflict.

Exhibit 6.3. Sources of power in organizations

work that can help us to understand the power dynamics within an organization, and to identify the ways in which organizational members can attempt to exert their influence.

Formal authority. The first and most obvious source of power in an organization is formal authority, a form of legitimized power that is respected and acknowledged by those with whom one interacts. As sociologist Max Weber has noted, legitimacy is a form of social approval that is essential for stabilizing power relations, and arises when people recognize that a person has a right to rule some area of human life, and when the ruled consider it their duty to obey. Historically, legitimate authority has been underpinned by one or more of three characteristics: charisma, tradition, or the rule of law (see Exhibit 9.1 for further details). Charismatic authority arises when people respect the special qualities of an individual (charisma means "gift of grace") and see those qualities as defining the right of the individual to act on their behalf. Traditional authority arises when people respect the custom and practices of the past and vest authority in those who symbolize and embody these traditional values. Monarchs and others who rule because of some kind of inherited status acquire their right to rule through this kind of principle. Bureaucratic or rational-legal authority arises when people insist that the exercise of power depends on the correct application of formal rules and procedures. Those that exercise bureaucratic authority must win their rights to power through procedural means, for example by demonstrating ownership or property rights in a corporation, through election in a democratic system, or by demonstrating appropriate professional or technical qualifications in a meritocracy.

Each of these three kinds of formal authority may be found in modern organizations. A hero figure may acquire immense charismatic power that allows him or her to control and direct others as he or she wishes. The owner of a family firm may exercise authority as a result of his or her membership in the founding family. A bureaucrat may exercise power as a result of the formal office that he or she holds. So long as those who are subject to the kind of authority in use respect and accept the nature of that authority, the authority serves as a form of power. If it is not respected, the authority becomes vacuous, and power depends on the other sources named in Exhibit 6.3.

The most obvious type of *formal* authority in most organizations is bureaucratic and is typically associated with the position one holds, whether as sales manager, accountant, project coordinator, secretary, factory supervisor, or machine operator. These different organizational positions are usually defined in terms of rights and obligations, which create a field of influence within which one can legitimately operate with the formal support of those with whom one works. A factory supervisor is given a "right" to instruct those under his or her control. A sales manager is given the "right" to influence policy on sales campaigns—but not on financial accounting. The latter falls within the field of discretion and influence delegated to the accounting manager. The formal positions on an organization chart thus define spheres of delegated authority. To the extent that authority is translated into power through the assent of those falling under the pattern of command, the authority structure is also a power structure. Though the authority is often seen as flowing down from the top of the organization chart, being delegated by one's superior, our discussion of the nature of legitimacy suggests that this is only partly true. For the authority becomes effective only to the extent that it is legitimized from below. The pyramid of power represented in an organization chart thus builds on a base where considerable power belongs to those at the bottom of the pyramid as well as to those at the top. Trade unionization has of course recognized this, channeling the power existing at the lower levels of the pyramid to challenge the power at the top. To the extent that trade-union power is legitimized by the rule of law and the right to unionize, it too represents a type of formal authority. We will have more to say on this later in our discussion of "counterorganizations."

Control of scarce resources. All organizations depend for their continued existence on an adequate flow of resources, such as money, materials, technology, personnel, and support from customers, suppliers, and the community at large. An ability to exercise control over any of these resources can thus provide an important source of power within and between organizations. Access to funds, possession of a crucial skill or raw material, control of access to some valued computer program or new technology, or even access to a special customer or supplier can lend individuals considerable organizational power. If the resource is in scarce supply and someone is dependent on its availability, then it can almost certainly be translated into power. Scarcity and dependence are the keys to resource power!

When we begin to talk about the power associated with resources, attention usually focuses on the role of money. For money is among the most liquid of all resources, and can usually be converted into the others. A person with a valued skill, a supplier with a precious raw material, or a person holding information on a new project opportunity can often be persuaded to exchange their valued resource for an attractive price. Money can also be converted into promotions, patronage, threats, promises, or favors to buy loyalty, service, support, or raw compliance.

No wonder therefore that so much organizational politics surrounds the process of budgeting and the control and allocation of financial resources. As Jeffrey Pfeffer of Stanford University has suggested, the use of such power is critically linked with one's ability to control the *discretionary* use of funds. It is not necessary to have full control over financial decisions. One needs to have just enough control to pull the crucial strings that can create changes at the margin. The reason for this is that most of the financial resources available to an organization are committed to sustain current operations. Changes to these operations are usually incremental, decisions being made to increase or reduce current expenditure. It is the ability to increase or decrease this flow of funds that gives power. Hence if a manager can acquire access to uncommitted resources that he or she can use in a discretionary way, e.g., as a slush fund, he or she can exert a major influence over future organizational development and at the same time buy commitment from those who benefit from this use of funds. Similarly, someone outside an organization who is responsible for deciding whether his or her financial support to that organization should be continued is in a position to exercise considerable influence on the policies and practices of the organization. Often this influence is out of all proportion with the amount actually given, since organizations are often critically dependent on marginal funds to create room to maneuver. Organizations often have a tendency to use their slack in one year in ways that create commitments or expectations for the next year— e.g., by giving a raise in salary that will be expected to be repeated next year, by appointing staff whose appointments will need to be renewed, or by launching a new program that staff will wish to continue—thus lending considerable power to the marginal funder.

The principles that we have discussed in relation to the use of financial power apply to other kinds of resource power as well. The important point is that power rests in controlling resources on which the organization is dependent for current operations or for creating new initiatives. There must be a dependence before one is able to control; and such control always derives its power from there being a scarcity of, or limited access to, the resource in question. Whether we are talking about the control of finance, skills, materials, or personnel, or even the provision of emotional support to a key decision maker who has come to value one's support and friendship, the principles remain the same. The more Machiavellian among us will quickly see how these principles point the way to a strategy for increasing power by *creating* dependence through the planned control of critical resources.

One's power can also be increased by reducing one's dependence on others. This is why many managers and organizational units like to have their own pockets of resources. The seemingly needless duplication of resources in an organization, where each department has the same underemployed machine or set of experts or a stockpile of staff that can be used in rush periods, is often a result of attempts to reduce one's dependence on the resources of others.

Use of organizational structure, rules, and regulations. Most often, organizational structure, rules, regulations, and procedures are viewed as rational instruments intended to aid task performance. A political view of these arrangements, however, suggests that in many situations they are often best understood as products and reflections of a struggle for political control.

Consider the following example drawn from research that I conducted on British "new town" development corporations. The corporation in question was established in the early 1960s to develop a new town in an old industrial area. A functional organization was established with separate departments (finance, law, administration, commercial development, housing, architecture and planning, and engineering services) reporting to a general manager, who reported to the board. In the late 1960s an energetic businessman became chairman of the board. He made the corporation's chief legal officer the new general manager and split the now vacant legal officer's post into two parts, creating the post of corporation secretary and leaving the new legal officer with a narrower range of functions. The secretary's post was filled by a nominee of the chairman who had worked with him in a similar capacity at another organization. The chairman and secretary began to work closely together, and the board eventually agreed that the secretary should have direct access to the board without having to go through the general manager. The chairman involved himself in the day-to-day running of the organization, often bypassing the general manager, whose role became very difficult to perform.

This situation came to a rather abrupt end after just one year, with the surprise resignation of the chairman in response to a controversy over policy issues. With the appointment of a new chairman who was interested in delegating the task of running the organization to the general manager, power relations within the corporation changed dramatically. The general manager gradually established his control over his department heads, many of whom had become quite powerful through the interventions of the former chairman. His approach was to bring many of the functions that had been allocated to the secretary under his own control, and to reorganize other departmental responsibilities. For example, he split the functions of the architecture and planning department, establishing a new planning department and a new department dealing with surveys. This move left the chief architect, who had become a strong executive during the reign of the previous chairman, with but a fraction of the department he once ran. These structural redesigns were later accompanied by further changes that in effect demoted the heads of the functional departments, and it was not long before a number left the organization, including the secretary and the chief architect.

While these structural changes were justified in technical terms, they were also motivated by political considerations relating to issues of control. The initial changes created by the corporation's energetic chairman were designed to enhance his own control of the organization by weakening that of the general manager. The changes introduced after the chairman's resignation were primarily designed to help the general manager regain control over powerful department heads. Structural change was part of a power play to limit the role and influence of other key individuals.

The circumstances of this case may be unique, but the pattern is quite general, since organizational structure is frequently used as a political instrument. Plans for organizational differentiation and integration, designs for centralization and decentralization, and the tensions that can arise in matrix organizations often entail hidden agendas related to the power, autonomy, or interdependence of departments and individuals. The size and status of a group or department within an organization often provides an indication of its power within the overall structure, since one obvious tactic of control is to downgrade the importance of a function or group of individuals, or to adopt a divide-and-rule strategy that fragments potential power bases. This tactic is illustrated in the case study discussed above and was also present in a number of other "new town" corporations included in my research. For example, in one corporation the community-development function, which often achieved departmental status in other corporations, was relegated to a small subdivision under the control of the chief legal officer—someone who had little knowledge of or interest in this kind of work. The community development staff, who usually took radical stands on planning matters, were correct in their perception that their unusual location within the organizational structure reflected the general manager's desire to reduce their influence and exclude them from meetings among department heads. The same general manager attempted to stifle the development of project teams across middle levels of the hierarchy, which would have led the organization toward a matrix rather than bureaucratic structure. The general manager wished to exercise strong authoritarian control through his department heads by discouraging project teams and making his department heads responsible for cross-departmental integration. Many of the middle-rank planning professionals became extremely discouraged by their lack of autonomy and influence and soon left the organization in large numbers.

The tensions surrounding the process of organizational design and redesign thus provide many insights on organizational power structures. And the rigidity and inertia of organizational structures can do the same, since people often preserve existing structures in order to protect the power that they derive from them. For example, people and departments often cling to outdated job descriptions or organizational designs, e.g., by resisting adoption of computer technology, because their power and status within the organization is so closely tied with the old order. One of the ironies of bureaucratic organization is that job and departmental designs that were originally introduced to control the work of employees can also be used by employees to control their superiors.

The same is true in relation to rules, regulations, and other kinds of formal procedures. Just as a job description can be used by an employee to define what he or she is *not* prepared to do ("that's not part of my job," or "I'm not paid to do that"), rules and regulations often prove to be two-edged swords. One outstanding example is found in the case of British Rail, where employees have discovered the power of "working to rule." Rather than going on strike to further a claim or address a grievance, a process that proves costly to employees since they forfeit their pay, the union often declares a "work to rule" whereby employees do exactly what is required by the regulations developed by the railway authorities. The result is that hardly any train leaves on time, schedules go haywire, and the whole railway system quickly slows to a snail's pace if not to a halt. The rules of course were created to control employees, to protect the safety of passengers, and, equally important, to protect the railway authorities, since in the event of a major accident a clear structure of rules and responsibilities can help allocate blame. The only trouble is that there are so many rules that they render the railway system almost inoperable. Normal functioning thus requires that employees find shortcuts or at least streamline procedures. British Rail is of course not unique in this regard. Many organizations have similar rules that, as many employees know, are not routinely applied.

The importance of these rules for their creators is clearly illustrated in the public investigations that follow major accidents, where investigators compare the evidence of events with the norms prescribed in formal regulations to find who is in error. Sometimes gaps in the rules are found. Sometimes gross negligence is discovered. But often the accident is no more than what Charles Perrow of Yale University calls a "normal accident," in the sense that its probability is built into the nature of the system. The broken rules that accompany the accident have often been broken thousands of times before as part of normal work practice, since normal work is impossible without breaking the rules. The railwaymen in Britain, like others who have adopted the "work to rule" practice, have discovered how they can use a weapon designed to control and possibly punish them to control and punish others.

Rules and regulations are thus often created, invoked, and used in either a proactive or retrospective fashion as part of a power play. All bureaucratic regulations, decision-making criteria, plans and schedules, promotion and job-evaluation requirements, and other rules that guide organizational functioning give potential power to both the controllers and those controlled. Rules designed to guide and streamline activities can almost always be used to block activities. Just as lawyers make a profession out of finding a new angle on what appears to be a clear-cut rule, many organizational members are able to invoke rules in ways that no one ever imagined possible. An ability to use the rules to one's advantage is thus an important source of organizational power and, as in the case of organizational structures, defines a contested terrain that is forever being negotiated, preserved, or changed.

Control of decision processes. An ability to influence the outcomes of decision-making processes is a well-recognized source of power, and one that has attracted considerable attention in the organization-theory literature. Since organizations are in large measure decision-making systems, an individual or group that can exert a major influence on decision processes can exert a great influence on the affairs of his or her organization. No wonder, therefore, the time, energy, and meticulous attention that so many power-hungry men and women devote to endless strings of meetings. These "politicos," as they are often known, are wheeling and dealing in terms of agendas that are often hidden to create the decision outcomes that they desire. It is these hidden agendas that allow many of them to emerge triumphant after hours of circular discussion that ends in stalemate. For the politics of organizational decision making often involves preventing crucial decisions from being made, as well as fostering those that one actually desires.

In discussing the kinds of power utilized in decision making it is useful to distinguish between control of three interrelated elements: decision *premises*, decision *processes*, and decision *issues and objectives*. One of the most effective ways of getting a decision is to allow it to be made by default. Hence much of the political activity within an organization hinges on the control of agendas and other decision premises that influence how a particular decision will be approached, perhaps in ways that prevent certain core issues from surfacing at all. By avoiding explicit discussion of an issue, one may be able to get precisely what one wants. For example, in an organization where members wish to form a trade union, or where there is a growing coalition in favor of opening up a new program area, these key decisions can often be avoided or delayed by making marginal though significant changes elsewhere in order to redirect attention. This tactic of preventing certain subjects from becoming hot issues that *must* command attention often proves popular with those who wish to preserve the status quo.

In addition to the conscious manipulation of decision premises there is also often a large unconscious or socialized element of control. As Charles Perrow has noted, much unobtrusive control is built into vocabularies, structures of communication, attitudes, beliefs, rules, and procedures that, though unquestioned, exert a decisive influence on decision outcomes. These factors shape decision premises by shaping the way we think and act. Visions of what the problems and issues are and how they can be tackled often act as mental straitjackets that prevent us from seeing other ways of formulating our basic concerns and the alternative courses of action that are available. Many of these constraints are built into organizational assumptions, beliefs, and practices about "who we are" and "the way we do things around here."

Control of decision-making *processes* is usually more visible than the control of decision premises. How should a decision be made? Who should be involved? When will the decision be made? By determining whether a decision can be taken and then reported to appropriate quarters, whether it must go before a committee, and which committee, whether it must be supported by a full report, whether it will appear on an agenda where it is likely to receive a rough ride (or an easy passage), the order of an agenda, and even whether the decision should be discussed at the beginning or end of a meeting, a manager can have a considerable impact on decision outcomes. The ground rules that are to guide decision making are thus important variables that organization members can manipulate and use to stack the deck in favor of or against a given action.

A final way of controlling decision making is to influence the *issues and objectives* to be addressed and the evaluative criteria to be employed. An individual can shape issues and objectives most directly through preparing the reports and contributing to the discussion on which the decision will be based. By emphasizing the importance of particular constraints, selecting and evaluating the alternatives on which a decision will be made, and highlighting the importance of certain values or outcomes, decision makers can exert considerable influence on the decision that emerges from discussion. Eloquence, command of the facts, passionate commitment, or sheer tenacity or endurance can in the end win the day, adding to a person's power to influence the decisions with which he or she is involved.

Control of knowledge and information. Evident in much of the above discussion, particularly with regard to the control of decision premises, is the idea that power accrues to the person who is able to structure attention to issues in a way that in effect defines the reality of the decision-making process. This draws attention to the key importance of knowledge and information as sources of power. By controlling these key resources a person can systematically influence the definition of organizational situations and can create patterns of dependency. Both these activities deserve attention on their own account.

The American social psychologist W. I. Thomas once observed that if people define situations as real, they are real in their consequences. Many skillful organizational politicians put this dictum into practice on a daily basis by controlling information flows and the knowledge that is made available to different people, thereby influencing their perception of situations and hence the ways they act in relation to those situations. These politicians are often known as "gatekeepers," opening and closing channels of communication and filtering, summarizing, analyzing, and thus shaping knowledge in accordance with a view of the world that favors their interests. Many aspects of organizational structure, especially hierarchy and departmental divisions, influence how information flows and are readily used by unofficial gatekeepers to advance their own ends. Even by the simple process of slowing down or accelerating particular information flows, thus making knowledge available in a timely manner or too late for it to be of use to its recipients, the gatekeeper can wield considerable power.

Often the quest for control of information in an organization is linked to questions of organizational structure. For example, many battles have been fought over the control and use of centralized computer systems, because control of the computer often carried with it control over information flows and the design of information systems. The power of many finance and other information-processing departments is tied up with this fact. Finance staff are important not only because they control resources, but because they also define and control information about the use of resources. By influencing the design of budgeting and cost-control information systems they are able to influence what is perceived as being important within the organization, both on the part of those who use the information as a basis for control and among those who are subject to these controls. Just as decision-making premises influence the kind of decisions that are made, the hidden and sometimes unquestioned assumptions that are built into the design of information systems can be of crucial importance in structuring day-to-day activity.

Many of the hot issues regarding the merits and problems of microprocessing hinge on the question of power. The new information-processing technology creates the possibility of multiple points of access to common data bases and the possibility of local rather than centralized information systems. In principle the technology can be used to increase the power of those at the periphery or local levels of the organization by providing them with more comprehensive, immediate, and relevant data relating to their work, facilitating self-control rather than centralized control. In practice the technology is often used to increase power at the center. The designers and users of such systems have been acutely aware of the power in information, decentralizing certain activities while centralizing ongoing surveillance over their performance. Thus executives in remote parts of the world, airline reservation staff in unsupervised offices, and workers on the factory floor perform under the watchful eye of the computer, which reports almost every move to someone at the heart of the information system.

In addition to shaping definitions of organizational realities or exercising control, knowledge and information can be used to weave patterns of dependency. By possessing the right information at the right time, by having exclusive access to key data, or by simply demonstrating the ability to marshal and synthesize facts in an effective manner, organizational members can increase the power they wield within an organization. Many people develop these skills in a systematic way, and jealously guard or block access to crucial knowledge to enhance their indispensability and "expert" status. Obviously, other organizational members have an interest in breaking such exclusivity and widening access. There is thus usually a tendency in organizations to routinize valued skills and abilities whenever possible. There is also a tendency to break down dependencies on specific individuals and departments by acquiring one's own experts. Thus departments often prefer to have their own specialist skills on hand, even if this involves duplication and some redundancy of specialisms within the organization as a whole.

A final aspect of expert power relates to the use of knowledge and expertise as a means of legitimizing what one wishes to do. "The expert" often carries an aura of authority and power that can add considerable weight to a decision that rests in the balance but that has already been made in the minds of key actors.

Control of boundaries. Any discussion of power in organizations must give attention to what is sometimes known as "boundary management." The notion of boundary is used to refer to the interface between different elements of an organization. Thus we can talk about the boundary between different work groups or departments, or between an organization and its environment. By monitoring and controlling boundary transactions people are able to build up considerable power. For example, it becomes possible to monitor changes occurring outside one's group, department, or organization and initiate timely responses. One acquires knowledge of critical interdependencies over which one may be able to secure a degree of control. Or one gains access to critical information that places one in a particularly powerful position to interpret what is happening in the outside world, and thus to help define the organizational reality that will guide action. One can also control transactions across boundaries by performing a buffering function that allows or even encourages certain transactions while blocking others.

Most people in leadership positions at all levels of an organization can engage in this kind of boundary management in a way that contributes to their power. The process is also an important element of many organizational roles, such as those of a secretary, special assistant, or project coordinator, and of liaison people of all kinds. People in such roles are often able to acquire power that goes well beyond their formal status. For example, many secretaries and special assistants are able to exert a major impact on the way their boss views the reality of a given situation by determining who is given access to the manager and when, and by managing information in a way that highlights or downplays the importance of events and activities occurring elsewhere in the organization. One outstanding example of boundary management is found in the management of the White House under the Nixon administration, where Nixon's top aides Richard Erlichman and Bob Haldeman exercised tight control over access to the president. In doing so it seems that they were able to manage the president's view of what was happening in the White House and elsewhere. One of the main issues in the notorious Watergate affair and the collapse of the presidency was whether Nixon's aides had allowed him to receive the critical information regarding the Watergate burglary. Erlichman and Haldeman were experts at boundary management, and their basic strategy for acquiring power is found in many different kinds of organizations all over the world.

Boundary management can help integrate a unit with the outside world, or it can be used to isolate that unit so that it can function in an autonomous way. The quest for autonomy—by individuals, groups, and even departments—is a powerful feature of organizational life, because many people like to be in full control over their life space. Boundary management aids this quest, since it often shows ways in which a unit can acquire the resources necessary to create autonomy and points to strategies that can be used to fend off threats to autonomy. Groups and departments often attempt to incorporate key skills and resources within their boundaries and to control admissions through selective recruitment. They also often engage in what sociologist Erving Goffman has described as "avoidance rituals," steering clear of issues and potential problems that will threaten their independence.

The quest for autonomy is, however, often countered by opposing strategies initiated by managers elsewhere in the system. They may attempt to break down the cohesiveness of the group by nominating their own representatives or allies to key positions, find ways of minimizing the slack resources available to the group, or encourage organizational redesigns that increase interdependence and minimize the consequences of autonomous actions. Boundary transactions are thus often characterized by competing strategies for control and countercontrol. Many groups and departments are successful in acquiring considerable degrees of autonomy, and in defending their position in a way that makes the organization a system of loosely coupled groups and departments rather than a highly integrated unit.

Ability to cope with uncertainty. One source of power implicit in much that has been discussed above is the ability to cope with the uncertainties that influence the day-to-day operation of an organization. Organization implies a certain degree of interdependence, so that discontinuous or unpredictable situations in one part of an organization have considerable implications for operations elsewhere. An ability to deal with these uncertainties gives an individual, group, or subunit considerable power in the organization as a whole.

The ability to cope with uncertainty is often intimately connected with one's place in the overall division of labor in an organization. Generally speaking, uncertainty is of two kinds. Environmental uncertainties (e.g., with regard to markets, sources of raw materials, or finance) can provide great opportunities for those with the contacts or skills to tackle the problems and thus minimize their effects on the organization as a whole. Operational uncertainties within the organization (such as from the breakdown of critical machinery used in factory production or data processing) can help troubleshooters, maintenance staff, or others with the requisite skills and abilities acquire power and status as a result of their ability to restore normal operations. The degree of power that accrues to people who can tackle both these kinds of uncertainty depends primarily on two factors. First, the degree to which their skills are substitutable, and hence the ease with which they can be replaced. Second, the centrality of their functions to the operations of the organization as a whole.

Organizations generally try to reduce uncertainties whenever possible, usually by "buffering" or through processes of routinization. For example, stocks of critical resources may be built up from different sources, maintenance programs may be developed to minimize technological failures, and people may be trained to deal with environmental contingencies. However, some uncertainty almost always remains, since by nature, uncertain situations cannot always be accurately predicted and forestalled. In addition, those who see the power deriving from their capacity to deal with uncertainty often preserve their power base by ensuring that the uncertainties continue, and sometimes by manipulating situations so that they appear more uncertain than they actually are.

In understanding the impact of uncertainty on the way an organization operates, we thus have an important means of understanding the power relations between different groups and departments. We also get a better understanding of the conditions under which the power of the expert or troubleshooter comes into play, and of the importance of the various kinds of power deriving from the control of resources that we discussed earlier. The existence of uncertainty and an ability to cope with uncertainty are often reasons explaining why and when these other kinds of power become so critical in shaping organizational affairs.

Control of technology. From the beginning of history technology has served as an instrument of power, enhancing the ability of humans to manipulate, control, and impose themselves on their environment. The technology employed in modern organizations performs a similar function. It provides its users with an ability to achieve amazing results in productive activity, and it also provides them with an ability to manipulate this productive power and make it work effectively for their own ends.

Organizations usually become vitally dependent on some form of core technology as a means of converting organizational inputs into outputs. This may be a factory assembly line; a telephone switchboard; a centralized computer or record-keeping system; or perhaps a capital-intensive plant like those used in oil refining, the production of chemicals, or power stations. The kind of technology employed influences the patterns of interdependence within an organization and hence the power relations between different individuals and departments. For example, in organizations where the technology creates patterns of sequential interdependence, as in a mass-production assembly line where task A must be completed before B, which must be completed before C, the people controlling any one part of the technology possess considerable power to disrupt the whole. In organizations where the technology involves more autonomous systems of production, the ability of one individual or group to influence the operation of the whole is much more limited.

The fact that technology has a major impact on power relations is an important reason why attempts to change technology often create major conflicts between managers and employees and between different groups within an organization. For the introduction of a new technology can alter the balance of power. The introduction of assembly-line production into industry, designed to increase managerial control over the work process, also had the unintended effect of increasing the power of factory workers and their unions: in standardizing jobs the technology standardized employee interests in a way that encouraged collective action, and also gave employees the power over the production process to make that action extremely effective. A strike on any part of an assembly line can bring the work of hundreds or even thousands of people to a complete halt. The technology is designed in a way that makes collective action by a small group of people extremely effective. The system of production based on the use of autonomous work groups and other forms of "cellular technology," on the other hand, fragments the interests of workers. Work and rewards accrue to the work team as a primary organizational unit. The interests of an employee thus often become more closely associated with those of his team than with those of a general type of employee or occupational group, making unionization and collective action much more difficult, especially since competitive relations may develop between different work teams. Since under the group system a withdrawal of work does not affect overall operations unless other work groups do the same, the power of workers and their unions over the organization as a whole tends to be reduced quite substantially.

The introduction of new production methods, machines, computing facilities, or any kind of technological change that will increase the power of one group or department at the expense of another thus tends to develop into a hot political issue. Groups of employees usually have a clear understanding of the power relations inherent in current work arrangements and are usually ready to marshal all their resources and ingenuity to fight changes that threaten their position.

The power associated with the control of technology becomes most visible in confrontations and negotiations surrounding organizational change, or when groups are attempting to improve their lot within the organization. However, it also operates in more subtle ways. In working with a particular machine or work system an employee learns the ins and outs of its operation in a way that often lends him or her considerable power. Earlier in this chapter we discussed how machine operators were able to use their knowledge of their machines to outwit the work-study experts attempting to set work standards. They were able to control the use of their technology to improve their wages and control their pace of work. This kind of process is used for many purposes in different kinds of work settings every day. People manipulate and control their technology, just as they twist and turn rules, regulations, and job descriptions. Technology designed to direct and control the work of employees frequently becomes a tool of workers' control!

Interpersonal alliances, networks, and control of "informal organization." Friends in high places; sponsors; mentors; coalitions of people prepared to trade support and favors to further their individual ends; and informal networks for touching base, sounding out, or merely shooting the breeze—all provide a source of power to those involved. Through various kinds of interlocking networks an individual can acquire advance notice of developments that are relevant to his or her interests, exert various forms of interpersonal influence to shape these developments in a manner that he or she desires, and prepare the way for proposals he or she is interested in advancing. The skilled organizational politician systematically builds and cultivates such informal alliances and networks, incorporating whenever possible the help and influence of all those with an important stake in the domain in which he or she is operating. Alliances and coalitions are not necessarily built around an identity of interests; rather, the requirement for these forms of informal organization is that there be a basis for some form of mutually beneficial exchange. Successful networking or coalition building involves an awareness that in addition to winning friends it is necessary to incorporate and pacify potential enemies, and an ability to see beyond immediate issues and find ways of trading help in the present for promises in the future. The successful coalition builder recognizes that the currency of coalition building is one of mutual dependency and exchange.

The coalitions, alliances, and networks built through these processes may remain highly informal and to a degree invisible. The coalition building may occur over the telephone, through old-boy networks and other friendship groups, through the golf club, or through chance contacts. For example, people sharing a meeting on one project may find that they share an interest in relation to another area of their work, and use informal exchanges at the meeting to lay the ground for cooperative action elsewhere. Much of the coalition building found in organizational life occurs through this kind of chance encounter, or through planned informal meetings such as lunches and receptions. Sometimes, however, alliances and networks are forged through various kinds of institutionalized exchange, such as meetings of professional groups and associations, and may themselves eventually become institutionalized in enduring forms such as project teams, advisory boards, joint ventures, or cartellike organizations. As will be clear from the above examples, networks may be internal to an organization or extend to include key people outside. Sometimes they are explicitly interorganizational, such as interlocking directorships where the same people serve on the boards of different organizations. In all networks, some players may take an active central role while others may operate at the fringes. Some will contribute to and derive power from the network more than others, according to the pattern of mutual dependence on which the alliance builds.

In addition to drawing power from networking and coalition building, many members of an organization may draw power from their role in the social networks known as the "informal organization." All organizations have informal networks where people interact in ways that meet various kinds of social needs. Groups of coworkers may make a habit of going to lunch together or drinking on Fridays after work, or may evolve means of enhancing the quality of their life at work. Informal group leaders may become as powerful an influence on their group as any rule, regulation, or manager, and become forces to be recognized and respected for the way their area of the organization operates. The attention currently given to the importance of corporate culture in determining an organization's success highlights the power possessed by leaders and other members of social groups who are in a position to shape the values and attitudes of the particular subculture to which they belong.

One other variant of informal organization arises in situations where one member of an organization develops a psychological or emotional dependency on another. This becomes particularly significant when the dependent party draws considerable power from other sources. The history of corporate and public life is full of examples where a key decision maker has become critically dependent on his or her spouse, lover, secretary, or trusted aide, or even on a self-proclaimed prophet or mystic. In the power-behind-the-throne syndrome that results, the informal collaborator exerts a critical influence on how the decision maker's power is used. While such relations often develop by chance, it is by no means uncommon for people to rise to power by cultivating such dependencies in a Machiavellian way.

Control of counterorganizations. Another route to power in organizations rests in the establishment and control of what can be called "counterorganizations." Trade unions are the most obvious of these. Whenever a group of people manages to build a concentration of power in relatively few hands it is not uncommon for opposing forces to coordinate their actions to create a rival power bloc. Economist John Kenneth Galbraith has described the process as one involving the development of "countervailing power." Thus unions develop as a check on management in industries where there is a high degree of industrial concentration; government and other regulatory agencies develop as a check on the abuse of monopoly power; and the concentration of production is often balanced by the development of large organizations in the field of distributions, e.g., chain stores often develop in ways that balance the power exercised by the large producers and suppliers.

The strategy of exercising countervailing power thus provides a way of influencing organizations where one is not part of the established power structure. By joining and working for a trade union, consumers' association, social movement, cooperative, or lobby group—or by exercising citizen's rights and pressuring the media, one's political representative, or a government agency—one has a way of balancing power relations. Many people make a career out of doing this. Thus a shop-floor worker may spend a major part of his leisure time working for his union, perhaps rising through the ranks of the union bureaucracy to a level at which he deals with senior management face to face. For many people at the lowest levels of an organization the only effective way that they can influence their work life is through this form of counter-vailing power. Consumer advocate Ralph Nader has been able to have a much greater influence on American industry by acting as critic and champion of consumer rights than he would have had as an employee of any of the organizations he has criticized. Many socially conscious lawyers, journalists, academics, and members of other professional groups have also found an effective route to influence by criticizing rather than joining the organizations that are the object of their concern. The principle of countervailing power is also often employed by the leaders of large conglomerates, who in effect play a form of chess with their environment, buying and selling organizations as corporate pawns. More than one multinational has attempted to counter the power of its competitors or bargain with its host government with the principle of countervailing power in mind.

Symbolism and the management of meaning. Another important source of power in organizations rests in one's ability to persuade others to enact realities that further the interests one wishes to pursue. Leadership ultimately involves an ability to define the reality of others. While the authoritarian leader attempts to "sell," "tell," or force a reality on his or her subordinates, more democratic leaders allow definitions of a situation to evolve from the views of others. The democratic leader's influence is far more subtle and symbolic. He or she spends time listening, summarizing, integrating, and guiding what is being said, making key interventions and summoning images, ideas, and values that help those involved to make sense of the situation with which they are dealing. In managing the meanings assigned to a situation, the leader in effect wields a form of symbolic power that exerts a decisive influence on how people perceive their realities and hence the way they act. Charismatic leaders seem to have a natural ability to shape meaning in this way.

We will focus upon three related aspects of symbolic management: the use of imagery, the use of theater, and the use of gamesmanship.

Images, language, symbols, stories, ceremonies, rituals, and all the other attributes of corporate culture discussed in Chapter 5 are tools that can be used in the management of meaning and hence in shaping power relations in organizational life. Many successful managers and leaders are aware of the power of evocative imagery and instinctively give a great deal of attention to the impact their words and actions have on those around them. For example, they often encourage the idea that the organization is a team and the environment a competitive jungle, talk about problems in terms of opportunities and challenges, symbolize the importance of a key activity or function by giving it high priority and visibility on their own personal agenda, or find other ways of creating and massaging the systems of belief deemed necessary to achieve their aims. In managing the meaning of organizational situations in these ways, they can do much to shape patterns of corporate culture and subculture that will help them achieve desired aims and objectives.

Many organizational members are also keenly aware of the way in which theater—including physical settings, appearances, and styles of behavior—can add to their power; and many deserve organizational Oscars for their performances. We have all walked into senior executives' offices that exude power in terms of decor and layout, shouting out that someone of considerable influence works there. An executive's office is the stage on which he or she performs and is often carefully organized in ways that will help that performance. In one area we may find a formal desk with a thronelike chair where the executive plays authoritarian roles. In another we may find casual chairs around a coffee table, setting a more convivial scene. When one is summoned to such an office, one often senses the likely tone of the meeting according to where one is seated. If you are guided to a low-level chair facing a desk where the manager can physically look down and thus dominate you, you can almost be sure that you are in for a hard time. Situations often speak louder than words, and do much to express and reproduce the power relations existing within an organization.

Appearances can also count for a great deal. For example, most people in an organization soon learn the rules of dress and other unwritten requirements for successful progress to higher ranks. In some organizations it is possible to distinguish marketing people, accountants, or even those who work on a certain floor according to their choice of fashion and general demeanor. Many aspiring young executives quickly learn the value of carrying the *Wall Street Journal* to work and ensuring that it is always visible, even if they never actually manage to read it. Some people symbolize their activity with paper-strewn desks, and others demonstrate their control and mastery of their work with a desk where no trace of paper is ever seen. In organizational contexts, there is usually more to appearance than meets the eye.

Style also counts. It's amazing how you can symbolize power by being a couple of minutes late for that all-important meeting where everyone depends on your presence, or how visibility in certain situations can enhance your status. For example, in many organizations senior executives dramatize their presence at high-profile events but fade into the woodwork at low-status functions. It is reported that in the White House people often dramatize their access to the president by making sure that they arrive at least half an hour early so that others can see that they are seeing the president. Access to the president is itself both a reflection and a source of power, but if others know that you have such access, it can usually be used to acquire even more power. Those who are aware of how symbolism can enhance power often spend a great deal of time dramatizing their work, utilizing "impression management" to influence the systems of meaning surrounding them and their activities.

Finally, we must note the skills of "gamesmanship." The organizational game player comes in many forms. Sometimes he is reckless and ruthless, shooting from the hip at targets that he dislikes, engaging in boardroom brawls when he's certain that he's the best around. In doing so, he increases his visibility and asserts his power and superiority over his competitors. Other kinds of gamesmen may be as crafty and low in profile as a fox, making their way through the organization in a more subtle manner, shaping key impressions at every turn. In seeing organization—with its rewards of success, status, power, and influence—as a game to be played according to their own sets of unwritten rules, organizational game players often have a significant influence on the structure of power relations.

Gender and the management of gender relations. It often makes a great deal of difference if you're a man or a woman! Many organizations are dominated by gender-related values that bias organizational life in favor of one sex over another. Thus, as many feminist writers have emphasized, organizations often segment opportunity structures and job markets in ways that enable men to achieve positions of prestige and power more easily than women, and often operate in ways that produce gender-related biases in the way organizational reality is created and sustained on a day-to-day basis. This is most obvious in situations of open discrimination and various forms of sexual harassment, but often pervades the culture of an organization in a way that is much less visible.

Consider, for example, some of the links between gender stereotypes and traditional principles of organization. Exhibit 6.4 counterposes a series of characteristics that are often used to differentiate between male and female. The links between the male stereotype and the values that dominate many ideas about the nature of organization are striking. Organizations are often encouraged to be rational, analytical, strategic, decision-oriented, tough, and aggressive, and so are men. This has important implications for women who wish to operate in this kind of world, for insofar as they attempt to foster these values, they are often seen as breaking the traditional female stereotype in a way that opens them to criticism, e.g., for being "overly assertive" and "trying to play a male role." Of course, in organizations that cultivate values that are closer to those of the female stereotype, women can have an advantage, reversing the traditional imbalance.

These and other gender biases are also found in the language, rituals, myths, stories, and other modes of symbolism that shape an organization's culture. General conversation and day-to-day ritual can serve to include or to exclude and is sometimes constructed to achieve this end. A lone man or woman can quickly feel outnumbered or "out on a limb" when others talk about matters that he or

Relations between men and women are frequently shaped by predefined stereotypes and images as to how they are expected to
behave. Here are some of the more common traits traditionally
associated with being male and female in Western society:

The Male Stereotype	The Female Stereotype
Logical	Intuitive
Rational	Emotional
Aggressive	Submissive
Exploitative	Empathic
Strategic	Spontaneous
Independent	Nurturing
Competitive	Cooperative
"A leader and decision-maker"	"A loyal supporter and follower"

Under the influence of the "gender revolution" these stereotypes
are now in flux and transition.

Exhibit 6.4. Traditional male and female stereotypes

she cannot share, or when language and jokes assume a derogatory
form. He or she can miss important conversation by not being in the
same locker room, and can be subjected to all kinds of subtle degradation through the stories and myths that circulate on the organizational grapevine. All the factors shaping corporate culture discussed
in Chapter 5 are relevant for understanding the gender realities constructed in an organization. They also identify the means through
which a person can begin to counter and reshape the power relations
thus produced.

The subtleties associated with gender often create different experiences of the same organizational situation and present many practical
problems for the way men and women interact on a daily basis. Sometimes the difficulties created are so significant that they give rise to conscious and unconscious strategies for "gender management."

Consider the following situation, drawn from research conducted
by my colleague Deborah Sheppard:

Susan Jones is a marketing research manager in a male-dominated
industry. She frequently has to give presentations to her male colleagues, and feels a need to ensure that she "blends in" by managing
her appearance and behavior so that conventional expectations and

norms relating to sex-roles are maintained. She strives to be "credible," while not overly challenging the status quo, and monitors herself on a continuing basis. She is particularly careful not to act in a malelike way, and much of her "impression management" rests in avoiding giving offense because she is a woman. Thus, in her oral presentations she tries to demonstrate competence while avoiding being assertive. She stands in the same place rather than engaging in the more aggressive act of walking around, even if the presentation lasts three hours. She attempts to get her ideas across gently. She does not raise her voice, finding other ways of emphasizing critical points, e.g., by using over-heads, but being sure never to use a pointer. She avoids wearing pants or three piece suits with a vest, and is always careful to balance her more formal attire with a feminine blouse.

Susan Jones works in a male-dominated reality, and spends a lot of her time living on other people's terms. Ms. Jones knows exactly what she is doing: She feels that to succeed in her organization she must try and fit in as best she can.

Many people would challenge her style of gender management, and suggest that she should be more assertive and confront and change the status quo. And many women in organizations do this very effectively. But the point about the case for present purposes rests in the fact that it shows how life in organizations is often guided by subtle and not so subtle power relations that guide attention and behavior in one direction rather than another. To do a good job Susan Jones has to put a much greater effort into accomplishing everyday reality than her male colleagues.

Exhibit 6.5 presents an evocative illustration of some of the implicit role models that men and women sometimes adopt in dealing with these gender-related issues. Whether or not gender is perceived as a factor shaping power relations, the choice or inclination toward one gender management strategy rather than another can have a major effect on one's success and general influence within an organization. We shall have more to say about the source and nature of gender biases in Chapter 7, when we discuss the role of repressed sexuality, the influence of the patriarchal family, and the general role of ideology in corporate life.

Structural factors that define the stage of action. One of the surprising things one discovers in talking with members of an organization is that hardly anyone will admit to having any real power. Even chief executives often say that they feel highly constrained, that they have few significant options in decision making, and that the power they wield is more apparent than real. Everyone usually feels in some degree hemmed in, either by forces within the organization or in terms of requirements posed by the environment. Given the numerous and varied sources of power already discussed, these attitudes present us with a paradox. How is it that there can be so many sources of power, yet so many feelings of powerlessness?

One possible answer is that access to power is so open, wide, and varied that to a large extent power relations become more or less balanced. While some people may be able to amass considerable personal power, this is offset by the power of others, and even the powerful thus feel constrained. We will give more attention to this "pluralist" view later in the chapter.

Another possible explanation rests in the idea that it is important to distinguish between the surface manifestations and the deep structure of power. This view is linked with perspectives on organization to be explored in Chapters 8 and 9. It suggests that while organizations and society may at any one time comprise a variety of political actors drawing on a variety of power bases, the stage on which they engage in their various kinds of power play is defined by the logic of change shaping the social epoch in which they live. This view summons the idea that organization and society must be understood from a historical perspective. To illustrate let us examine an analogy from the natural world. Suppose that we are considering the ecology of a river valley. We can understand that ecology in terms of the "power relations" between the various species of tree, shrub, fern, and undergrowth and the soil from which they draw sustenance. But these power relations are underpinned by the basic structure of the river valley, as determined by the impact of glaciation millennia before. One species of tree may be more powerful and thus dominate another, but the conditions of this domination are structurally determined.

Applying this analogy to organizational life, we see how underlying structures or logics of change underpin power relations. A manager may control an important budget, have access to key information, and be excellent at impression management, and be a powerful person for all these reasons. But his ability to draw on and use these sources of power is underpinned by various structural factors, such as the invested capital that sustains the organization. Similarly a factory worker may possess considerable power to disrupt production as a result of his or her role on an assembly line. His or her knowledge of the way in which production can be disrupted is the immediate source of power, but the ultimate source is the structure of productive activity that makes such power significant. These considerations encourage us to see people as agents or carriers of power relations embedded in the wider structure of society. As such people may be no more than semi-autonomous pawns moving themselves around in a game where they

As one looks around the organizational world it is possible to identify different ways in which people manage gender relations. Here are a variety of popular strategies. Each can be successful or unsuccessful, according to the persons and situations involved.

Some Female Strategies

Queen Elizabeth I	— Rule with a firm hand, surrounding one-self as far as possible by submissive men. Margaret Thatcher provides a modern example.
The First Lady	— Be content to exercise power behind the throne: a tactic adopted by many "corporate wives" such as executive secretaries and special assistants.
The Invisible Woman	— Adopt a low profile and try and blend with one's surroundings, exercising influence in whatever ways one can.
The Great Mother	— Consolidate power through caring and nurturing.
The Liberationist	— Play rough and give as good as you get; be outspoken and always make a stand in favor of the role of women.
The Amazon	— Be a leader of women. This style is especially successful when one can build a powerful coalition by placing like-minded women in influential positions.
Delilah	— Use the powers of seduction to win over key figures in male-dominated organizations.
Joan of Arc	— Use the power of a shared cause and mission to transcend the fact that you are a woman, and gain widespread male support.
The Daughter	— Find a "father figure" prepared to act as sponsor and mentor.

can learn to understand the rules but have no power to change them. This phenomenon may explain why even the powerful often feel that they have little real choice as to how they should behave. For example, a chief executive may face some of these wider rules of the game in terms of the economic conditions that influence the survival of her organization. Insofar as she wishes the organization to survive, she may perceive herself as having no real options about what must be done to ensure its survival.

Some Male Strategies

The Warrior	— Frequently adopted by busy executives caught up in fighting corporate battles. Often used to bind women into roles as committed supporters.
The Father	— Often used to win the support of younger women searching for a mentor.
King Henry VIII	— Use of absolute power to get what one wants, attracting and discarding female supporters according to their usefulness.
The Playboy	— Use of sex appeal (both real and imagined) to win support and favor from female colleagues. A role often adopted by executives lacking a more stable power base.
The Jock	— Based on various kinds of "display behavior" concerned to attract and convince women of one's corporate prowess. Often used to develop admiration and support from women in subordinate or lateral positions.
The Little Boy	— Often used to try and "get one's way" in difficult situations, especially in relation to female co-workers and subordinates. The role may take many forms, e.g., the "angry little boy" who throws a temper to create a stir and force action; the "frustrated or whining little boy" who tries to cultivate sympathy; and the "cute little boy" who tries to curry favor, especially when he's in a jam.
The Good Friend	— Often used to develop partnerships with female colleagues, either as confidants or as key sources of information and advice.
The Chauvinist Pig	— Often used by men who feel threatened by the presence of women. Characterized by use of various "degradation" rituals, which seek to undermine the status of women and their contributions.

Exhibit 6.5. Some strategies for the management of gender relations

This view of the deep structure of power leads us to recognize the importance of factors such as class relations in determining the role we occupy within organizations and hence the kind of opportunity structure and power to which we have access. It draws attention to the way educational systems and other processes of socialization shape basic elements of culture. It draws attention to the logic of capital accumulation, which shapes the structure of industry, levels of employment, patterns of economic growth, and the ownership and distribution of wealth. We will be considering these underlying factors in some detail in the following chapters. They define the stage on which organizational members act, and moderate the significance and influence of the other sources of power to which one has access.

The power one already has. Power is a route to power, and one can often use power to acquire more. The biographies of many consummate politicians illustrate this fact. For example, politicians within organizations and in public life frequently tie the use of power to informal IOU agreements where help or favor begs its return in kind at a later date. Thus a manager may use his or her power to support X in a struggle with Y, knowing that when X is successful it will be possible to call upon similar (if not more) support from X: "Remember last July. Your future was on the line, and I risked everything to help out. Surely you'll now do a small favor for me?" Often the exchanges are more subtle than this, but the message is essentially the same. Power used in a judicious way takes the form of an investment and, like money, often becomes useful on a rainy day.

It is also possible to take advantage of the honey-pot characteristic of power. The presence of power attracts and sustains people who wish to feed off that power, and actually serves to increase the power holder's power. In the hope of gaining favor, people may begin to lend the power holder uninvited support or buy into his or her way of thinking so that he or she can see that they're on the same side. When the time comes for the power holder to recognize this interest with active support, people then actually become indebted to the power holder, with all kinds of IOUs coming into play. Power, like honey, is a perpetual source of sustenance and attraction among the worker bees.

Finally, there is the empowering aspect of power. When people experience progress or success, they are often energized to achieve further progress and success. In this way a sense of power can actually lead to more power. This kind of potential or transformative power is overlooked in most contemporary discussions of power relations but is vital in understanding the kind of dynamism and energy that can develop from very small and insignificant beginnings. The process is perhaps most evident in those situations in which people who believe that they have absolutely no power fight and win a small victory. Very soon they realize that one victory can lead to another and feel as if they are being carried on the crest of a wave. Action itself can be an empowering force, and many organizations and communities have been transformed by its effects in quite unexpected ways.

The ambiguity of power. While we have identified numerous sources of power, which are probably far

from being exhaustive, it is difficult to tie down exactly what the phenomenon is. We know that it has a great deal to do with asymmetrical
patterns of dependence whereby one person or unit becomes dependent on another in an unbalanced way, and that it also has a great deal
to do with an ability to define the reality of others in ways that lead
them to perceive and enact relations that one desires. However, it is far
from clear whether power should be understood as an interpersonal
behavioral phenomenon or as the manifestation of deep-seated structural factors. It is not clear whether people have and exercise power as
autonomous human beings or are simply carriers of power relations
that are the product of more fundamental forces. These and other
issues—such as whether power is a resource or a relationship, whether
there is a distinction between power and processes of societal domination and control, whether power is ultimately linked to the control of
capital and the structuring of the world economy, or whether it is important to distinguish between actual manifest power and potential
power—continue to be the subject of considerable interest and debate
among those interested in the sociology of organization.

These problems aside, however, it is clear that our discussion of possible sources and uses of power provides us with an inventory of ideas
through which we can begin to decode power plays and political dynamics in organizational contexts. Like our analysis of interests and
our discussion of conflict, it provides us with a working tool through
which we can analyze organizational politics and, if we so wish, orient
our action in a politicized way.

Managing pluralist organizations

The image of organizations devel-
oped above reflects what is sometimes known as a "pluralist" frame of
reference. For it emphasizes the plural nature of the interests, conflicts,
and sources of power that shape organizational life. The term "pluralism" is used in political science to characterize idealized kinds of liberal
democracies where potentially authoritarian tendencies are held in
check by the free interplay of interest groups that have a stake in government. The pluralist vision is of a society where different groups bargain and compete for a share in the balance of power and use their
influence to realize Aristotle's ideal of politics: a negotiated order that
creates unity out of diversity.

This pluralist philosophy stands in contrast with an older organic or
"unitary" frame of reference. The unitary view pictures society as an
integrated whole where the interests of individual and society are syn-

onymous. This unitary view emphasizes the sovereignty of the state and the importance of individuals subordinating themselves in the service of society as a means of realizing and satisfying their true interests and the common good. It is an ideology that has grown in importance along with the development of the nation-state and the idea that individuals should place the interests of the state above all else.

The pluralist view also contrasts with the so-called "radical" frame of reference, which views society as comprising antagonistic class interests, characterized by deep-rooted social and political cleavages, and held together as much by coercion as by consent. This radical view, influenced by a Marxist perspective, suggests that the interests of disadvantaged groups can be furthered in a substantial way only through radical changes in the structure of society that will displace those currently in power.

These three frames of reference (Exhibit 6.6) have considerable relevance for understanding organizations and the ideologies that shape management practice. Some organizations tend to function like unitary teams, others as vibrant political systems with the kind of pluralist politics discussed earlier in this chapter, and others as battlefields where rival groups engage in ongoing warfare. Unitary characteristics are most often found in organizations that have developed a cohesive culture based on respect for management's right to manage, especially those that have a long and continuous history of paternalistic management. Organizations where there are sharp distinctions between different categories of employee, such as the division between blue- and white-collar workers found in many heavy industries, or where there has been a history of conflict between management and labor, tend to reflect the characteristics of the radical model. Organizations primarily made up of white-collar staff, particularly where there is room for employees to acquire considerable autonomy, often tend to fit the pluralist model. Sometimes the three models apply to different parts of the same organization. It is often a salutary experience for a person to ask: "Which frame of reference applies to my organization?" By using the model presented in Exhibit 6.6 to assess the general pattern of interests, conflict, and power one can often gain a useful initial grasp on the character of the political system with which one is dealing.

In addition to serving as analytical tools, the three frames of reference often serve as organizational ideologies. Thus managers or employees may encourage the idea that "we're a team, let's work together," or that "we all want different things, so let's talk about and resolve our differences so we can all gain," or that "we're at war, I don't trust you, so we'll have to fight it out." Clearly, the ideology in use will determine the character of the organization. If a manager believes that he or she is managing a team and can persuade employees to believe that this is the case, harmonious cooperation with a three-musketeers attitude of "all for one and one for all" may gain ground. If the radical frame of reference provides the major context for interpreting organizational events, then a battle-torn organizational life is almost certain. These ideologies may emerge and be used as a means of shaping the organization to conform with the image that best suits specific ends. This, after all, is the role of ideology in organizations, as in society.

Each frame of reference leads to a different approach to management. If one believes that one is managing a team, one tends to expect and demand that people rally around common objectives, and to respect "the right of the manager to manage and the duty of employees to obey." Employees are expected to perform the roles for which they have been appointed. No less, no more. Conflict is seen as a source of trouble and as an unwanted intrusion. Hence the orientation of the unitary manager is usually to eliminate or suppress conflict whenever possible. Given this ideology, there is no room to recognize or accept the kind of organizational politics discussed earlier in this chapter. Unitary managers tend to see formal authority as the only legitimate source of power, and thus rarely acknowledge the right or ability of others to influence the management process. Unions are seen as a scourge, and the pursuit of individual interest through use of different kinds of power is viewed as a form of malpractice.

Though this unitary view may seem somewhat narrow and old-fashioned, it is often extremely pervasive and influential and is supported by many theories of management. For example, theories based on the mechanical and organismic metaphors discussed in Chapters 2 and 3 often encourage this unitary view, emphasizing the importance of designing or adapting the organization to achieve common goals. Hence they provide primary resources for the unitary manager who wishes to believe that an enterprise *ought* to possess the unity and shared sense of direction that we find in carefully designed machines or in organisms in the natural world. The team idea is often much more attractive than the idea of a somewhat chaotic political system that wishes to move in many directions at once. Hence many managers often unconsciously take refuge in this team ideology rather than deal with political realities.

Also, unitary ideology can serve as a resource for a crafty manager who recognizes that in espousing the attitude that "we're a team where conflict has no place," he or she may have a means of creating unity among divergent elements. By identifying conflict itself as a *source* of trouble he or she may be able to unite the rest of the organization against those who are key actors in the trouble. This tactic is often

Organizations can be understood as mini-states where the relationship between individual and society is paralleled by the relationship between individual and organization. The unitary, pluralist, and radical views of organization can be characterized in the following terms:

	Unitary	Pluralist	Radical
Interests	Places emphasis on the achievement of common objectives. The organization is viewed as being united under the umbrella of common goals and striving towards their achievement in the manner of a well-integrated team.	Places emphasis on the diversity of individual and group interests. The organization is regarded as a loose coalition which has just a passing interest in the formal goals of the organization.	Places emphasis on the oppositional nature of contradictory "class" interests. Organization is viewed as a battleground where rival forces (e.g. management and unions), strive for the achievement of largely incompatible ends.
Conflict	Regards conflict as a rare and transient phenomenon that can be removed through appropriate managerial action. Where it does arise it is usually attributed to the activities of deviants and troublemakers.	Regards conflict as an inherent and ineradicable characteristic of organizational affairs and stresses its potentially positive or functional aspects.	Regards organizational conflict as inevitable and as part of a wider class conflict that will eventually change the whole structure of society. It is recognized that conflict may be suppressed and thus often exists as a latent rather than manifest characteristic of both organizations and society.

| **Power** | Largely ignores the role of power in organizational life. Concepts such as authority, leadership, and control tend to be preferred means of describing the managerial prerogative of guiding the organization towards the achievement of common interests. | Regards power as a crucial variable. Power is the medium through which conflicts of interest are alleviated and resolved. The organization is viewed as a plurality of power holders drawing their power from a plurality of sources. | Regards power as a key feature of organization, but a phenomenon that is unequally distributed and follows class divisions. Power relations in organizations are viewed as reflections of power relations in society at large, and as closely linked to wider processes of social control, e.g., control of economic power, the legal system, and education. |

Exhibit 6.6. Unitary, pluralist and radical frames of reference
SOURCE: Based on Burrell and Morgan (1979: 204-388).

used to unite employees and, through the media, the public in general against a group of workers or a union leader who are seen as disruptive elements in an otherwise harmonious and rational enterprise. The unitary frame of reference is a powerful ideology among the public at large, and managers can often use this public ideology as a strategy for mobilizing support and achieving control in the pluralist or radical power plays that characterize their organization. The fact that managers who at times espouse the unitary ideology may not actually believe in that ideology themselves, can make it difficult to determine which ideology has a controlling influence in an organization. However, the person who has an awareness of the role played by rhetoric and espoused ideology has a means of understanding when this form of power play is occurring. The unitary manager is often a pluralist in unitary clothing!

The hallmark of the pluralist manager is that he or she accepts the inevitability of organizational politics. He or she recognizes that since individuals have different interests, aims, and objectives, employees are likely to use their membership in the organization for their own ends. Management is thus focused on balancing and coordinating the interests of organizational members so that they can work together within the constraints set by the organization's formal goals, which really reflect the interests of shareholders and others with ultimate control over the fate of the organization. The pluralist manager recognizes that conflict and power plays can serve both positive and negative functions; hence the main concern is to manage conflict in ways that will benefit the overall organization or, more selfishly, in ways that will promote his or her own interests within the organization. The pluralist manager is, after all, not politically neutral. He or she recognizes the politics of organization and accepts his or her role as an organizational power broker and conflict manager.

For example, the pluralist manager seeks ways to use conflict as a means of promoting desired ends. He or she recognizes that various kinds of conflict can energize an organization. Conflict counters tendencies towards lethargy, staleness, apathetic compliance, and similar organizational pathologies by creating a "keep on your toes" atmosphere where it is dangerous to take things for granted. In addition, conflicts can encourage forms of self-evaluation that can challenge conventional wisdom and theories in use. Such conflict may cause a certain degree of pain within the organization, but can also do much to stimulate learning and change, helping to keep the organization in touch with what is going on in the environment. Conflicts can thus be an important source of innovation in that they encourage the parties involved to search for solutions to underlying problems, often to the benefit of all. This is particularly true in group decision-making situations, where the absence of conflict often produces conformity and "groupthink." The existence of rival points of view and of different aims and objectives can do much to improve the quality of decision making. Conflict can also serve as an important release valve that gets rid of pent-up pressures. It facilitates processes of mutual accommodation through the exploration and resolution of differences, often in a way that preempts more subversive or explosive resolutions. Somewhat paradoxically, conflict can thus at times serve to stimulate change, and at other times help to maintain the status quo.

One of the main tasks of the pluralist manager, then, is to find ways of maintaining just the right level of conflict. While too much conflict can immobilize an organization by channeling the efforts of its members into unproductive activities, too little conflict may encourage complacency and lethargy. In the former case, the manager may need to employ conflict-resolution techniques or reorient conflict in more productive directions. In the latter case he or she may need to find ways of promoting appropriate conflicts, often by making hidden conflicts overt, or perhaps by actually creating conflict. While this may at times help to enliven the atmosphere and performance of an organization, it can also be perceived as a form of unwarranted manipulation, with disastrous results for relations between managers and their employees.

In approaching the task of conflict management, the pluralist manager is faced with a choice of styles, which hinge on the extent to which he or she wishes to engage in assertive or cooperative behavior (Exhibit 6.7). Though a manager may have a preferred style, all the different styles are likely to be appropriate at one time or another (Exhibit 6.8). Even in the realm of politics, contingency theory thus has an important place. On some occasions the manager may wish to buy time through various kinds of avoidance behavior. On others, head-on competition, collaboration, accommodation, or compromise may prove more effective. While some managers prefer to battle it out in a way that all can see, others prefer more subtle fly-fishing techniques that depend on an intimate knowledge of the situation and the skillful use of the right bait at the right time for the right people. The choice of the style and tactics to be used in a given situation is crucial, but unfortunately cannot be explored in detail here.

Regardless of style, successful pluralist management always depends on an ability to read developing situations. The manager must be able to analyze interests, understand conflicts, and explore power relations, so that situations can be brought under a measure of control. This requires a keen ability to be aware of conflict-prone areas, to read the latent tendencies and pressures beneath the manifest actions of or-

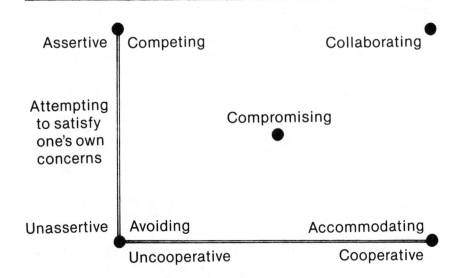

Attempting to satisfy others' concerns

The five styles can be characterized in terms of the following kinds of behavior:

Avoiding
- Ignoring conflicts and hoping that they'll go away.
- Putting problems under consideration or on hold.
- Invoking slow procedures to stifle the conflict.
- Use of secrecy to avoid confrontation.
- Appeal to bureaucratic rules as a source of conflict resolution.

Compromise:
- Negotiation.
- Looking for deals and trade-offs.
- Finding satisfactory or acceptable solutions.

Competition:
- Creation of win-lose situations.
- Use of rivalry.
- Use of power plays to get one's ends.
- Forcing submission.

Accommodation:
- Giving way.
- Submission and compliance.

Collaboration:
- Problem-solving stance.
- Confronting differences and sharing ideas and information.
- Search for integrative solutions.
- Finding situations where all can win.
- Seeing problems and conflicts as challenging.

Exhibit 6.7. Conflict management: a question of style
SOURCE: Adapted from Thomas (1976: 900). Reprinted by permission of John Wiley & Sons, Inc.

Situations in which to use the five conflict-handling modes, as reported by twenty-eight chief executives

Conflict mode	Situation	Conflict mode	Situation

Competing
1. When quick, decisive action is vital—e.g., emergencies.
2. On important issues where unpopular actions need implementing—e.g., cost cutting, enforcing unpopular rules, discipline.
3. On issues vital to company welfare when you know you're right
4. Against people who take advantage of noncompetitive behavior.

Collaborating
1. To find an integrative solution when both sets of concerns are too important to be compromised.
2. When your objective is to learn.
3. To merge insights from people with different perspectives.
4. To gain commitment by incorporating concerns into a consensus.
5. To work through feelings which have interfered with a relationship.

Compromising
1. When goals are important, but not worth the effort or potential disruption of more assertive modes.
2. When opponents with equal power are committed to mutually exclusive goals.
3. To achieve temporary settlements to complex issues.
4. To arrive at expedient solutions under time pressure.
5. As a backup when collaboration or competition is unsuccessful.

Avoiding
1. When an issue is trivial, or more important issues are pressing.
2. When you perceive no chance of satisfying your concerns.
3. When potential disruption outweighs the benefits of resolution.
4. To let people cool down and regain perspective.
5. When gathering information supersedes immediate decision.
6. When others can resolve the conflict more effectively.
7. When issues seem tangential or symptomatic of other issues.

Accommodating
1. When you find you are wrong— to allow a better position to be heard, to learn, and to show your reasonableness.
2. When issues are more important to others than to yourself— to satisfy others and maintain cooperation.
3. To build social credits for later issues.
4. To minimize loss when you are outmatched and losing.
5. When harmony and stability are especially important.
6. To allow subordinates to develop by learning from mistakes.

Exhibit 6.8. When to use the five conflict-handling styles
SOURCE: Thomas (1977: 487). Copyright 1977 *Academy of Management Review*. Reprinted with permission of the *Academy of Management Review* and the author.

ganizational life, and to initiate appropriate responses. In general, the manager can intervene to change perceptions, behaviors, and structures in ways that will help redefine or redirect conflicts to serve constructive ends.

Many organizational conflicts can be fruitfully resolved through pluralist means, but not all. This is particularly true in radicalized organizations where conflicts between managers and employees run deep. Here, issues often have to be negotiated in fairly formal terms if progress is to be made, or else grind their way to a bitter end through the raw interplay of structural forces embedded in the economic and industrial structure of society itself. Disputes leading to head-on clashes between management and unions, such as those relating to the replacement of skilled employees by automation or the closing and relocation of plants, are obvious examples. The underlying power relations and bitterness between the parties involved often encourage a winner-take-all or fight-to-the-death attitude that makes compromise extremely difficult, often leading to painful outcomes such as unemployment or bankruptcy of the organizations involved. Though the intransigence that often accompanies such disputes can seem senseless to outside observers, it is intelligible in terms of the basic premises on which the radical frame of reference builds. We will examine these in Chapter 9.

Strengths and limitations of the political metaphor

One of the curious features of organizational life is the fact that though many people know that they are surrounded by organizational politics, they rarely come out and say so. One ponders politics in private moments or discusses it off the record with close confidants and friends, or in the context of one's own political maneuverings with members of one's coalition. One knows that manager A is pushing for a particular project because it will serve her own aims, or that B got a particular job because of his associations with C, but one can rarely say so. It breaks all the rules of organizational etiquette to impute private motive to organizational acts, which are supposed to serve the organization's interests above all else. For these and other reasons, including the fact that privatization and secrecy can serve political ends, organizational politics becomes a taboo subject, which at times makes it extremely difficult for organization members to deal with this crucially important aspect of organizational reality.

The discussion presented in this chapter helps us to accept the reality of politics as an inevitable feature of organizational life, and following the Aristotelian view, to recognize its constructive role in the creation of social order. The political metaphor encourages us to see how *all* organizational activity is interest-based and to evaluate all aspects of organizational functioning with this in mind. Organizational goals, structure, technology, job design, leadership style, and other seemingly formal aspects of organizational functioning have a political dimension, as well as the more obvious political power plays and conflicts. The model of interests, conflict, and power developed in this chapter provides a practical and systematic means of understanding the relationship between politics and organization and emphasizes the key role of power in determining political outcomes. The metaphors considered in earlier chapters tend to underplay the relation between power and organization. The political metaphor overcomes this deficiency, placing a knowledge of the role and use of power at the center of organizational analysis.

The metaphor also helps to explode the myth of organizational rationality. Organizations may pursue goals and stress the importance of rational, efficient, and effective management. But rational, efficient, and effective for whom? Whose goals are being pursued? What interests are being served? Who benefits? The political metaphor emphasizes that organizational goals may be rational for some people's interests, but not for others. An organization embraces many rationalities, since rationality is always interest-based and thus changes according to the perspective from which it is viewed. Rationality is always political. No one is neutral in the management of organizations—even managers! They, like others, use the organization as a legitimizing umbrella under which to pursue a variety of task, career, and extramural interests. And like others, they often use the idea of rationality as a resource for pursuing political agendas—justifying actions that suit their personal aspirations in terms that appear rational from an organizational standpoint. The idea of rationality is as much a resource to be used in organizational politics as a descriptive term describing the aims of organization.

These considerations suggest a reevaluation of the ideological significance of the concept of rationality. Above all else, the idea of rationality seems to be invoked as a myth to overcome the contradictions inherent in the fact that an organization is simultaneously a system of competition and a system of cooperation. The emphasis on rationality attempts to bind together a political system which, because of the diversity of interests on which it builds, always has a latent tendency to move in diverse directions, and sometimes to fall apart.

This leads us to another strength of the political metaphor: that it helps us to find a way of overcoming the limitations of the idea that organizations are functionally integrated systems. As will be recalled from discussion in Chapter 3, much organization theory has built on the assumption that organizations, like machines or organisms, are unified systems that bind part and whole in a quest for survival. The political metaphor suggests otherwise, pointing to the disintegrative strains and tensions that stem from the diverse sets of interests on which organization builds. Because of these tensions, the possibility of a high degree of integration and commitment to the survival of the whole is highly problematic, depending on the degree of reciprocal dependence between the people and units that form the organization. Many organizations have the characteristics of loosely coupled systems, where semiautonomous parts strive to maintain a degree of independence while working under the name and framework provided by the organization. Universities, with their various departments all tied together under general goals relating to education and research, are good examples. In organizations where the quest for autonomy or private sectional or subunit goals take priority over those of the wider organization, the schismatic tendencies may in point of fact destroy or transform the organization. For example, key members may leave to set up organizations of their own, or an industrial dispute may put a company out of business. An analysis of organizational politics in terms of the interplay among rival interests, conflicts, and sources of power can help us understand these forces of endogenous change.

Another strength of the metaphor is the fact that it politicizes our understanding of human behavior in organizations. We may not agree with Nietzsche that humans have a will to power, mastery, and control, or with writers who suggest that politics and game playing are fundamental to human nature, but we are obliged to recognize that tensions between private and organizational interests provide an incentive for individuals to act politically. Whereas some people view such action as a manifestation of the selfish or "dark" side of human personality, the analysis presented here suggests that there is usually a structural as well as a motivational basis. Even the most altruistic persons may find their action following a political script in the sense that their orientation to organizational life is influenced by the conflicting sets of interests that they bring to issues of immediate concern. While some people are no doubt more political in orientation than others, employing gamesmanship and other forms of wheeling and dealing as a basic strategy, the enactments of everyone are, at least in part, of a political nature. The political metaphor encourages us to recognize how and why the organizational actor is a political actor, and to understand the political significance of the patterns of meaning enacted in corporate culture and subculture.

Finally, the metaphor also encourages us to recognize the sociopolitical implications of different kinds of organization and the roles that organizations play in society. Recall the quotation that opened this chapter. Should people be prepared to surrender their democratic rights when they begin work each morning? Is it possible to have a democratic society if the majority of the population spend their working lives obeying the commands of others? Should organizations be allowed to play politics by lobbying in an attempt to influence legislation and other government policies? Should there be closer or more distant relations between business and government? The political metaphor brings questions such as these to the center of our attention. Though it is common to draw strict divisions between organization theory and political science, it is clear that business and organization is always to some extent political, and that the political implications of organization need to be systematically explored.

Against these strengths of the metaphor, it is necessary to identify a number of important limitations. The first can be framed as a potential danger. When we analyze organizations in terms of the political metaphor it is almost always possible to see signs of political activity, confirming the relevance of the metaphor. However, this mode of understanding often leads to an increased politicization of the organization. For when we understand organizations as political systems we are more likely to behave politically in relation to what we see. We begin to see politics everywhere, and to look for hidden agendas even where there are none. For this reason, the metaphor must be used with caution. There is a very real danger that its use may generate cynicism and mistrust in situations where there were none before. In a course that I teach on the nature of organizational politics I usually begin by warning my students that by the second or third week there is a danger that they will be looking for hidden motives everywhere, even wondering whether a colleague's innocent offer to buy the coffees is really a political act. Though at first my warning is seen as a joke, by week two or three its gravity and significance usually hit home. Under the influence of a political mode of understanding everything becomes political. The analysis of interests, conflicts, and power easily gives rise to a Machiavellian interpretation that suggests that everyone is trying to outwit and outmaneuver everyone else. Rather than use the political metaphor to generate new insights and understandings that can help us deal with divergent interests, we often reduce the metaphor to a tool to be used to advance our own personal interests.

This kind of manipulative stance is reflected in many contemporary writings on the politics of organization, which have a tendency to emphasize the cynical, selfish, ruthless, get-ahead-at-all-costs mentality that so often turns organizations into corporate jungles. These writings "sell" the insights of the metaphor through statements such as: "Find out where the real power is and use it," "Understand and harvest the grapevine," "Win through intimidation," "Protect your job by knowing your enemies and retaliation devices," or "Seize power and wield clout." This use of the metaphor breeds mistrust and encourages the idea that organization involves a zero-sum game where there must be winners and losers. While there may be a measure of truth in this, in that many organizations are dominated by competitive relations, the effect is to reduce the scope for genuine openness and collaboration. This kind of thinking loses sight of the more general implications of the political metaphor, such as the Aristotelian vision of politics as a constructive force in the creation of social order, and the possibility of using political principles to examine and restructure the relationship between organization and society.

A final potential limitation of the metaphor, and one to which I have already briefly alluded, relates to the question of whether the applications of pluralism are merely superficial. Is it realistic to presume a plurality of interests and a plurality of power holders, or are more radical organization theorists correct in seeing fundamental class antagonisms between structures of interest and power? A strong case can be made for the idea that the interests of individuals or small coalitions may best be served if they recognize affinities of a "class" kind and act in a unified manner. Such is the logic of trade unionism, though the trade-union movement has fragmented along sectionalist rather than class lines. A strong case can also be made for the idea that though everyone has access to sources of power, ultimate power rests with those who are able to define the stage of action, as discussed earlier in this chapter. From a radical standpoint, pluralist power may be more apparent than real. Ultimately, some people have much more power than others. These considerations, which will be examined in more detail in Chapters 8 and 9, suggest that pluralist politics may be restricted to the resolution of marginal, narrow, and superficial issues and may fail to take account of the structural forces that shape the nature of those issues. As a result, the political metaphor may overstate the power and importance of the individual and underplay the system dynamics that determine what becomes political and how politics occurs.

7

Exploring Plato's Cave

Organizations as Psychic Prisons

$\mathbf{H}$uman beings have a knack of getting trapped in webs of their own creation. In this chapter we will examine some of the ways this occurs by exploring the idea of organizations as psychic prisons. This metaphor joins the idea that organizations are psychic phenomena, in the sense that they are ultimately created and sustained by conscious and unconscious processes, with the notion that people can actually become imprisoned or confined by the images, ideas, thoughts, and actions to which these processes give rise. The metaphor encourages us to understand that while organizations may be socially constructed realities, these constructions are often attributed an existence and power of their own that allow them to exercise a measure of control over their creators.

The idea of a psychic prison was first explored in Plato's *Republic* in the famous allegory of the cave where Socrates addresses the relations among appearance, reality, and knowledge. The allegory pictures an underground cave with its mouth open toward the light of a blazing fire. Within the cave are people chained so that they cannot move. They can see only the cave wall directly in front of them. This is illuminated by the light of the fire, which throws shadows of people and objects onto the wall. The cave dwellers equate the shadows with reality, naming them, talking about them, and even linking sounds from outside the cave with the movements on the wall. Truth and reality for the prisoners rest in this shadowy world, because they have no knowledge of any other.

However, as Socrates relates, if one of the inhabitants were allowed to leave the cave, he would realize that the shadows are but dark reflections of a more complex reality, and that the knowledge and perceptions of his fellow cave dwellers are distorted and flawed. If he were then to return to the cave, he would never be able to live in the old way, since for him the world would be a very different place. No doubt he would find difficulty in accepting his confinement, and would pity the plight of his fellows. However, if he were to try and share his new knowledge with them, he would probably be ridiculed for his views. For the cave prisoners, the familiar images of the cave would be much more meaningful than any story about a world they had never seen. Moreover, since the person espousing this new knowledge would now no longer be able to function in the old way, since he would no longer be able to act with conviction in relation to the shadows, his fellow inmates would no doubt view his knowledge as being extremely dangerous. They would probably regard the world outside the cave as a potential source of danger, to be avoided rather than embraced as a source of wisdom and insight. The experience of the person who left the cave could thus actually lead the cave dwellers to tighten their grip on their familiar way of seeing.

The cave stands for the world of appearances and the journey outside stands for the ascent to knowledge. People in everyday life are trapped by illusions, hence the way they understand reality is limited and flawed. By appreciating this, and by making a determined effort to see beyond the superficial, people have an ability to free themselves from imperfect ways of seeing. However, as the allegory suggests, many of us often resist or ridicule efforts at enlightenment, preferring to remain in the dark rather than to risk exposure to a new world and its threat to the old ways.

In this chapter we will use the image of a psychic prison to explore some of the ways in which organizations and their members become trapped by constructions of reality that, at best, give but an imperfect grasp on the world. We will start by examining how people in organizations can become trapped by favored ways of thinking. We will then explore how organizations can become trapped by unconscious processes that lend organization a hidden significance.

The trap of favored ways of thinking

Consider the following examples:

Trapped by success: Following the OPEC oil crisis of 1973 the Japanese automobile industry began to make massive inroads on the North American market. Caught up in the mind-set of the American way of producing cars, the large U.S. manufacturers were completely ill equipped to meet the Japanese challenge. For years they had taken their superior resources, technical competence, and skills in engineering and marketing as a given. Oriented to the large-car market and kept alive by annual model changes, the large firms ignored the potential of small, fuel-efficient cars. Because of its feeling of technical superiority and confidence in its product, the American industry devoted much of its engineering competence to the development of solar-battery- and gas-turbine-driven cars, leaving the Japanese to devote their more modest resources to redesign of the established product, and opening the way for the massive breakthrough this created. The American auto industry in the early 1970s was a prisoner of its early success. And numerous firms in other industries have shared a similar experience, declining and decaying as a result of policies that made them world leaders in earlier stages of development.

Trapped by organizational slack: "Create certainty." "Build in margins for error." These ideas have been guiding principles in the design of thousands of manufacturing and other organizational systems. The result: institutionalized inefficiency. Buffer stocks of inventory and work in progress allow systems of production to absorb uncertainties in the production process. But they can be extremely expensive, and they provide leeway for people to engage in sloppy work and to hide their mistakes. Many quality-control systems do the same, institutionalizing error and inefficiency by accepting a certain percentage of damaged products as the norm. Many progressive firms are now challenging the wisdom of such organized inefficiencies, looking to policies of "zero inventory" and "zero defects" as means of revolutionizing the workplace.

These policies, which often have an enormous positive effect on cost efficiency and product quality, require modes of organization that attempt to cope with rather than avoid uncertainty and interdependence. When there are no buffer stocks to absorb error, people can no longer work as if they are isolated. They have to recognize their dependence on one another, and ensure that they make a full and timely contribution to the work process. Thus under the "just in time" systems of management that eliminate inventories, all activities have to be completely synchronized. Under zero-defects policies, root problems must be spotted and solved on the spot, rather than after they have resulted in wasted products. These examples illustrate how a change in key operating assumptions can transform the way one organizes and does business. Interestingly, the ideas of zero inventory and zero defects were never really considered as practical possibilities until the Japanese showed that it was feasible to organize in this way: the need for inventory and buffered forms of organization were treated as a given.

Trapped by group processes: On April 17, 1961 the Kennedy administration launched an abortive invasion of Cuba at the Bay of Pigs by 1,200 anti-Castro Cuban exiles. "How could we have been so stupid?" President Kennedy later remarked. In retrospect the plan looked completely misguided. Yet the plan had never seriously been questioned or challenged, being carried along by the process that psychologist Irving Janis has characterized as "groupthink." Kennedy and his advisers had unwittingly developed shared illusions and operating norms that interfered with their ability to think critically and to engage in the required reality testing. The president's charisma and a sense of invulnerability set the momentum for all kinds of self-affirming processes that produced conformity among key decision makers and advisers. Strong rationalizing tendencies mobilized support for favored opinions. A strong sense of "assumed consensus" inhibited people from expressing their doubts. Self-appointed people worked informally to protect the president from information that might damage his confidence. As a result, the CIA-planned invasion went ahead with a minimum of debate about the core assumptions on which its success depended.

This kind of "groupthink" has been reproduced in thousands of decision-making situations in organizations of all kinds.

Each of the above examples illustrates how organizations and their members can become enmeshed in cognitive traps. False assumptions, taken-for-granted beliefs, unquestioned operating rules, and numerous other premises and practices can combine to create self-contained views of the world that provide both a resource for and a constraint on organized action. While they create a way of seeing and suggest a way of acting, they also tend to create ways of not seeing, and eliminate the possibility of actions associated with alternative views of the world.

Perhaps the image of organizations as psychic prisons is a little too dramatic to capture this self-confining quality. Certainly, many people would prefer the image of corporate culture built around patterns of shared belief and meaning. But there is great merit in recognizing the prisonlike qualities of culture. We may seem a long way from Plato's cave in discussing the nature of modern organizations, but there are remarkable parallels between Socrates's allegory and many of the ways we enact the reality of our world. Numerous organizations develop corporate cultures that prevent them from dealing with their environments in an effective manner. And as has been shown in every chapter of this book, the metaphors we use to shape and understand organization are invariably partial and one-sided. To the extent that organizations and their members become trapped by favored metaphors or aspects of their corporate culture, there is always a tendency for them to imprison themselves.

In thinking about organization in this way, we are thus alerted to the pathologies that may accompany our ways of thinking. And we are encouraged to recognize the importance of probing the strengths and weaknesses of the assumptions that shape how organizations view and deal with their world.

Organization and the unconscious

The metaphor of a psychic prison may overdramatize how we become trapped by favored ways of thinking. But it certainly does not overdramatize the way organizations and their members can become trapped by the unconscious. For, if the psychoanalysts are correct, much of the rational and taken-for-granted reality of everyday life gives "real" form to preoccupations and concerns that lie beneath the level of conscious awareness. In their view, a full understanding of the significance of what we do and say in going about our daily business must always take account of the hidden structure and dynamics of the human psyche.

The basis for this kind of thinking was laid by Sigmund Freud, who argued that the unconscious is created as humans repress their innermost desires and private thoughts. He believed that in order to live in harmony with one another humans must moderate and control their impulses, and that the unconscious and culture were thus really two sides of the same coin, giving hidden and manifest form to the "repression" that accompanied the development of human sociability. It was in this sense that he talked about the essence of society being the repression of the individual, and about the essence of the individual as being the repression of him or herself.

This view of civilization has interesting consequences, for in stressing the link between psychic repression, culture, and the unconscious, it suggests that we must search for the hidden meaning and significance of our organizational cultures in the unconscious concerns and preoccupations of those who create and sustain them.

Since Freud's early work, the whole field of psychoanalysis has become a battleground between rival theories of the origin and nature of the unconscious. While Freud placed importance on its links with various forms of repressed sexuality, others have stressed its links with the structure of the patriarchal family, with fear of death, with anxieties associated with breast-feeding and early infancy, with the collective unconscious, and so on.

Common to all these different interpretations is the idea that humans live their lives as prisoners of their own personal history. And psychoanalysts led by Freud, Jung, and others see freedom as lying in an awareness of how the past influences the present through the unconscious. Thus whereas Plato saw the route to enlightenment in the pursuit of objective knowledge and the activities of philosopher kings, the psychoanalysts have sought ways for humans to liberate themselves through forms of self-understanding that show how in their encounters with the external world, they are really meeting hidden dimensions of themselves.

In the following pages we will explore the relevance of this kind of thinking for our understanding of organization.

ORGANIZATION AND REPRESSED SEXUALITY

Frederick Taylor, the creator of "scientific management," was a man totally preoccupied with control. He was an obsessive, compulsive character, driven by a relentless need to tie down and master almost every aspect of his life. His activities at home, in the garden, and on the golf course, as well as at work, were dominated by programs and schedules, planned in detail and rigidly followed. Even his afternoon walks were carefully laid out in advance. And it was not unknown for him to observe his motions, to measure the time taken over different phases, and even to count his steps.

These traits were evident in Taylor's personality from an early age. Living in a well-to-do household dominated by strong puritan values (emphasizing work, discipline, and the ability to keep one's emotions decently in check), Taylor quickly learned how to regiment himself. Childhood friends described the meticulous "scientific" approach that he brought to their games. Taylor insisted that all be subjected to strict rules and exact formulas. Before playing a game of baseball he would insist that accurate measurements be made of the field, so that everything would be in perfect relation, even though most of a sunny morning was spent ensuring that measurements were correct to the inch. Even a game of croquet was subject to careful analysis, with Fred working on the angles of the various strokes, calculating the force of impact and the advantages and disadvantages of understroke and overstroke. On cross-country walks the young Fred would constantly experiment with his legs to discover how to cover the greatest distance with a minimum of energy, or the easiest method of vaulting a fence, or the ideal length of a walking stick. And as an adolescent, before going to a dance, he would be sure to make lists of the attractive and unattractive girls likely to be present, so that he could spend equal time with each.

Even during sleep this same meticulous regulation was brought into operation. From about the age of twelve Taylor suffered from fearful nightmares and insomnia. Noticing that his worst dreams occurred while he was lying on his back, he constructed a harness of straps and wooden points that would wake him whenever he was in danger of getting into this position. He experimented with other means of overcoming his nightmares as well, constructing a canvas sheet hung between two poles so that he could keep his brain cool. The insomnia and sleeping devices stayed with him in one way or another throughout his life. In later years he preferred to sleep in an upright position, propped by numerous pillows. This made spending nights away from home a rather difficult business, and in hotels where pillows were in short supply he would sometimes spend the night propped up by bureau drawers.

Taylor's life provides a splendid illustration of how unconscious concerns and preoccupations can have an effect on organization. For it is clear that his whole theory of scientific management was the product of the inner struggles of a disturbed and neurotic personality. His attempt to organize and control the world, whether in childhood games or in systems of scientific management, was really an attempt to organize and control himself.

From a Freudian perspective, Taylor's case presents a classic illustration of the anal-compulsive type of personality. As is well known, Freud's theory of human personality emphasizes that character traits in adult life emerge from childhood experience, and in particular from the way the child manages to reconcile the demands of his or her sexuality and the forces of external control and constraint. Freud's view of sexuality was a very broad one, embracing all kinds of libidinal desires and gratifications, whether oral, anal, phallic, or genital. He believed that children typically developed through these different phases of sexuality, and that difficult experiences could lead to various kinds of repression that resurface in disguised forms in later life. As illustrated in Exhibit 7.1, repression may set the basis for all kinds of defense mechanisms that displace and redirect these unconscious strivings, so that they appear in other less threatening and more controlled forms.

Freudian psychology emphasizes how human personality is shaped as the human mind learns to cope with raw impulses and desires. Freud believed that in the process of maturation these are brought under control or banished to the unconscious. The unconscious thus becomes a reservoir of repressed impulses and painful memories and traumas that can threaten to erupt at any time. The adult person deals with this reservoir in a variety of ways, engaging in various defense mechanisms to keep them in check. Here are some of the important defenses that have been identified by Freud and his followers:

Repression:	"pushing down" unwanted impulses and ideas into the unconscious.
Denial:	refusal to acknowledge an impulse-evoking fact, feeling, or memory.
Displacement:	shifting impulses aroused by one person or situation to a safer target.
Fixation:	rigid commitment to a particular attitude or behavior.
Projection:	attribution of one's own feelings and impulses to others.
Introjection:	internalizing aspects of the external world in one's psyche.
Rationalization:	creation of elaborate schemes of justification that disguise underlying motives and intentions.
Reaction formation:	converting an attitude or feeling into its opposite.
Regression:	adoption of behavior patterns found satisfying in childhood in order to reduce present demands on one's ego.
Sublimation:	channeling basic impulses into socially acceptable forms.
Idealization:	playing up the good aspects of a situation to protect oneself from the bad.
Splitting:	isolating different elements of experience, often to protect the good from the bad.

Exhibit 7.1. A glossary of some Freudian and neo-Freudian defense mechanisms
SOURCE: Hampden-Turner (1981: 40-42) and Klein (1980: 1-24).

Taylor's relentless attempt to control his world and his preoccupation with meticulously planned, neat, and efficient arrangements have clear roots in the puritanical discipline of the Taylor family. From a Freudian standpoint, excessive concerns with parsimony, order, regularity, correctness, tidiness, obedience, duty, and punctuality are direct corollaries of what is learned and repressed as the child copes with early anal experiences. Taylor's life is permeated with many of these preoccupations and with "reaction formations" that manifest the opposite.

For example, much of Taylor's life reflects an inner struggle with the discipline and authority relations of his childhood. There is good reason to believe that the relations that his scientific management struck between managers and working men were rooted in the disciplinary structure under which he grew up, while his relish in the dirt and grime of factories and his identification with the workers (he always claimed that he was one of them) were reactions against this very same family situation. His aggressive authoritarian relationship with the worker was accompanied in his own mind by the idea that he was a friend. Amid all the conflict surrounding the introduction of scientific management, including direct insults, threats on his life, and his appearance before a special U.S. House of Representatives subcommittee on Taylorism where he was presented as the "enemy of the working man," Taylor clung to the view that he had the friendship of those whom he sought to control. In Taylor's mind the aggression of scientific management was turned into its opposite, the idea that it was a scheme for promoting harmony. It was this view that allowed him to see himself as an industrial peacemaker at the very same time that scientific management was one of the major forces creating industrial unrest.

In suggesting that Taylorism was the manifestation of a deeply disturbed personality the intention is not to suggest that Taylor's personality was the causal force behind the massive changes in organization created by scientific management. Taylorism had such an effect because the ideas that he promoted had a ready market: they dovetailed perfectly with the concerns of the organizations of his day. Hence rather than be dismissed as a crank, he became a kind of infamous hero. The resolution of his own internal struggle resulted in productive innovations that had a much wider social impact.

However, this said, there is clearly more than a coincidental relationship between Taylor's anal-compulsive approach to life and the mode of organization embraced by scientific management. And this raises a number of intriguing questions about this and other modes of organization. To what extent is it possible to understand organization as an external manifestation of unconscious strivings, as suggested by Freud's theory of the links between culture and the unconscious? To what extent do our modes of organization institutionalize defense mechanisms relating to repressed sexuality? To what extent can we understand the bureaucratic form of organization generally as a manifestation of anal-compulsive preoccupations? To what extent do bureaucratic organizations attract and promote anal-compulsive personalities? To what extent do other more flexible, organic, dynamic organizational forms institutionalize preoccupations concerned with other modes of repressed sexuality?

These questions may seem rather farfetched, but if we wish to push this perspective far enough, a good case can be made for the idea that organization *is* a form of repressed sexuality. We have already mentioned the Freudian view emphasizing how social order develops alongside libidinal repression, but there are other arguments as well. For example, if we go back to the Middle Ages we find that few distinctions were drawn between public and private life, and that open displays of sexual behavior were quite common. My colleague Gibson Burrell at Lancaster University has identified writings which show that even in medieval monasteries, convents, and churches, outrageous sexual behaviors presented a major problem. Manuscripts from the seventh and eighth centuries reveal that punishments for different classes of sexual misconduct were calculated in elaborate detail. Some of the most extreme offenses called for castration, while others required extensive penitentials. Thus a monk found guilty of simple fornication with unmarried persons could expect to fast for a year on bread and water, while a nun could expect three to seven years of fasting and a bishop twelve years. The punishment for masturbation in church was forty days' fasting (sixty days' psalm singing for monks and nuns), while a bishop caught fornicating with cattle could expect eight years' fasting for a first offense and ten years' fasting for each subsequent offense.

The very fact that these schedules existed indicates the extent to which these behaviors posed an ever-present problem to the order and routine of these early forms of organization. And it is more than interesting that some of the earliest examples of organizational rules and regulations of which we are aware give such close attention to the control of sexuality.

However, in the view of the French historian Michel Foucault this conflict between organization and sexuality should come as no surprise, for mastery and control of the body is fundamental for control over social and political life. Foucault thus encourages us to note the parallels between the rise of formal organization and the routinization and regimentation of the human body. This is evident in a vivid way in how Frederick the Great made a disciplined Prussian army out of an unruly mob (discussed in Chapter 2), and it is also very evident in early forms of industrial organization. For example, the British "Factory Acts" of 1833 gave much attention to the problem of controlling sexual behavior at work, while the early industrial masters espoused the virtues of abstinence, restraint, and clean living. In this regard, it is interesting to note the Quaker and puritanical affiliations of many of the early industrialists in Europe and North America, the background against which Frederick Taylor was later to emerge.

In Freudian terms this process of acquiring control over the body hinges on a social process in which the kind of organization and discipline of the anal personality becomes dominant. In effect, this control institutionalizes a redirection of sexual energies, repressing explicit genital sexuality while allowing and encouraging the expression of anal eroticism in sublimated form. This sublimated anal sexuality has provided much of the energy underlying the development of industrial society.

As we examine the bureaucratic form of organization, therefore, we should be alert to the hidden meaning of the close regulation and supervision of human activity, the relentless planning and scheduling of work, and the emphasis on productivity, rule following, discipline, duty, and obedience. The bureaucracy is a mechanistic form of organization, but an anal one too. And not surprisingly, we find that some people are able to work in this kind of organization more effectively than others. If bureaucracies are anal phenomena encouraging an anal style of life, then such organizations will probably operate most smoothly when employees fit the anal character type and can derive various hidden satisfactions from working in this context.

Historically, a strong case can be made for the idea that anality has been the major form of repressed sexuality shaping the nature of organizations. However, as we look around the organizational world, it is easy to see signs of other forms. For example, in many organizations employees find work an outlet for repressed genital sexuality. This kind of sublimation often underlies the energy behind the workaholism on which so many modern organizations depend. We also find repressed sexual drives shaping the aggressive cut-and-thrust policies governing numerous aspects of organizational functioning, especially between an organization and its environment, in many relations with competitors, or between firms in merger or takeover situations. Much boardroom discussion and policy making may have links with various kinds of sexual fantasy.

These hidden forces may also be important in understanding the more flamboyant, flexible, organic, innovative firms now making such an impact on the corporate world. These organizations often call for a creative looseness of style that is quite alien to the bureaucratic personality. Freudian theory would suggest that the corporate cultures of these organizations often institutionalize various combinations of oral, phallic, and genital sexuality. For example, in aggressive, individualistic organizations the corporate culture is often characterized by what Wilhelm Reich would describe as a phallic-narcissistic ethos. Phallic-narcissistic individuals subconsciously identify their ego with their phallus and engage in self-confident, exhibitionistic behaviors, where satisfaction is derived from being visible and "a winner." Such organizations often reward and encourage this behavior, institutionalizing this form of repressed sexuality exactly as the bureaucracy institutionalizes anality. Freudian theory thus provides an interesting twist to the kind of exhibitionistic behavior that Gregory Bateson saw as rooted in child-rearing practices, and which is discussed in Chapter 5.

Many organizations have a narcissistic character rooted in sublimated forms of oral eroticism geared to the satisfaction of individual needs. For some, this is expressed in an aggressive individualism where the main corporate and individual values hinge on an ability to gain personal success and to win recognition from others. Yet others translate this love of self or "me orientation" into more communal environments where ethics of mutual support become dominant.

As we look around the organizational world it is thus possible to see many ways in which repressed sexuality may shape day-to-day activity. Sexual drives and fantasies shape corporate policy; neurotic behaviors shape compulsive, paranoiac, masochistic, and other enactments of the environment and work relations. And repressed sexuality underlies many of the most difficult and entrenched corporate problems. These unconscious influences are often closely connected with the personalities of individual members. Much can thus often be done to resolve problems at the personal and interpersonal level. But it is important to recognize that the significance of repressed sexuality goes beyond individual personalities. For organizations institutionalize unconscious concerns and preoccupations in organizational design and the wider corporate culture. A full understanding of the significance of repressed sexuality thus leads us to a new kind of contingency theory of organization. Organizations are not just shaped by their environments; they are also shaped by the unconscious concerns of their members and the unconscious forces shaping the societies in which they exist.

ORGANIZATION AND THE PATRIARCHAL FAMILY

While the Freudian perspective creates many novel interpretations of organizational life, in the view of many critics Freud was too hung up on sexuality and took the argument too far. Notable among these critics are members of the contemporary women's movement who see Freud as a man espousing male values and trapped in his own unconscious sexual preoccupations, especially as they interacted with the Victorian morality of his day. Rather than place emphasis on repressed sexuality as a driving force behind modern organization, these critics suggest that we ought to try and understand organization as an expression of partriarchy. From their standpoint, patriarchy operates as a kind of conceptual prison, producing and reproducing organizational structures that give dominance to males and traditional male values.

The evidence for a patriarchal view of organization is easy to see. Formal organizations typically build upon characteristics associated with the male sex in Western society, and historically have been dominated by males, except in those jobs where the function is to support, serve, flatter, please, and entertain. Thus men have tended to dominate organizational roles and functions where there is a need for aggressive and forthright behavior, whereas women have until fairly recently been confined to roles that tend to place them in a subordinate position, as in nursing, clerical, and secretarial work, or roles designed to satisfy various kinds of male narcissism. The bureaucratic approach to organization tends to foster the rational, analytic, and instrumental characteristics associated with the Western stereotype of maleness, while downplaying abilities traditionally viewed as "female," such as intuition, nurturing, and empathic support. In the process it has created organizations that in more ways than one define "a man's world," where men, and the women who have entered the fray, joust and jostle for positions of dominance like stags contesting the leadership of their herd.

In the view of many writers on the relationship between gender and organization, the dominant influence of the male is rooted in the hierarchical relations found in the patriarchal family, which, as Wilhelm Reich has observed, serves as a factory for authoritarian ideologies. In many formal organizations one person defers to the authority of another exactly as the child defers to parental rule. The prolonged dependency of the child upon the parents facilitates the kind of dependency institutionalized in the relationship between leaders and followers, and in the practice where people look to others to initiate action in response to problematic issues. In organizations, as in the patriarchal family, fortitude, courage, and heroism, flavored by narcissistic self-admiration, are often valued qualities, as is the determination and sense of duty that a father expects from his son. Key organizational members also often cultivate fatherly roles by acting as mentors to those in need of help and protection.

Critics of patriarchy suggest that in contrast with matriarchal values, which emphasize unconditional love, optimism, trust, compassion, and a capacity for intuition, creativity, and happiness, the psychic structure of the male-dominated family tends to create a feeling of impotence accompanied by a fear of and dependence on authority. These critics argue that under the influence of matriarchal values, organizational life would be far less hierarchical, be more compassionate and holistic, value means over ends, and be far more tolerant of diversity and open to creativity. Many of these traditionally female values are evident in nonbureaucratic forms of organization where nurturing and networking replace authority and hierarchy as the dominant modes of integration.

In viewing organizations as unconscious extensions of family relations we thus have a powerful means of understanding key features of the corporate world. We are also given a clue as to how organizations are likely to change along with contemporary changes in family structure and parenting relations. And we see the major role that women and gender-related values can play in transforming the corporate world. So long as organizations are dominated by patriarchal values and structures the roles of women in organizations will always be played out on "male" terms. Hence, the view of many feminist critics of the modern corporation: that the real challenge facing women who want to succeed in the organizational world is to change organizational values in the most fundamental sense.

ORGANIZATION, DEATH, AND IMMORTALITY

In his book *The Denial of Death* Ernest Becker suggests that human beings are "Gods with anuses." Among all the animals we alone are conscious of the fact that we will die, and we are obliged to spend our lives with knowledge of the paradox that while we may be capable of God-like spiritual transcendence beyond our bodies, our existence is dependent on a finite structure of flesh and bone that will ultimately wither away and disappear. In Becker's view humans spend much of their life attempting to deny the oncoming reality of death by pushing their morbid fears deep into the recesses of their unconscious. He in effect reinterprets the Freudian theory of repressed sexuality, linking childhood fears associated with birth and the development of sexuality with fears relating to our own inadequacies, vulnerability, and mortality.

These views lead us to understand culture and organization in a novel way. For example, they encourage us to understand many of our symbolic acts and constructions as flights from our own mortality. In joining with others in the creation of culture as a set of shared norms, beliefs, ideas, and social practices, we attempt to locate ourselves in something larger and more enduring than ourselves. In creating a world that can be perceived as objective and real, we reaffirm the concrete and real nature of our own existence. In creating symbol systems that allow us to engage in meaningful exchanges with others, we also help to find meaning in our own lives. Though we may in quiet times confront the fact that we are going to die, much of our daily life is lived in the artificial realness created through culture. This illusion of realness helps to disguise our unconscious fear that everything is highly vulnerable and transitory.

Thus, as Becker shows, when viewed from the perspective of our own impending death, the artifacts of culture can be understood as defense systems that help to create the illusion that we are greater and more powerful than we actually are. The continuity and development that we find in systems of religion, ideology, national history, and shared values help us to believe that we are part of a pattern that continues well beyond the bounds of our own life. No wonder, therefore, that people are so quick to defend their basic beliefs, even if it means going to war and confronting the reality of death. For in doing so, they can help preserve the myth of immortality when they are alive.

This perspective suggests that we can understand organizations and much of the behavior within organizations in terms of a quest for immortality. In creating organizations we create structures of activity that are larger than life and that often survive for generations. And in becoming identified with such organizations we ourselves find meaning and permanence. As we invest ourselves in our work, our roles become our realities. And as we objectify ourselves in the goods we produce or the money we make, we make ourselves visible and real to ourselves. No wonder that questions of survival are such a high priority in organizations, for there is much more than the survival of the organization at stake.

In decoding the unconscious significance of the relationship between immortality and organization, we realize that in attempting to manage and organize our world we are really attempting to manage and organize ourselves. Of particular importance here is the fact that many of our most basic conceptions of organization hinge on the idea of making the complex simple. Thus the bureaucratic approach to organization emphasizes the virtue of breaking activities and functions into clearly defined component parts. In much of science and in everyday life we manage our world by simplifying it, because in making it simple we make it amenable to control. And in doing so, we create the myth that we are actually in control and that we are more powerful than we really are. Much of the knowledge through which we organize our world can thus be seen as protecting us from the idea that, ultimately, we probably understand and control very little. Arrogance often hides weakness, and the idea that human beings, so small, puny, and transient, can organize and boast mastery of nature, is, in many respects, a sign of their own vulnerability.

People use detailed myths, rituals, and modes of involvement in everyday life to defend themselves against consciousness of their vulnerability. A splendid illustration of this has been presented by Richard Boland and Raymond Hoffman in a study of the operation of a machine shop producing custom-tooled parts, where jokes and humor are used to cope with difficult working conditions. The jobs on which the men are involved are often hazardous, yet are made even more dangerous by practical jokes. The study illustrates how jokes help the men to deal with a difficult work situation and questions of self-identity, and allow them to exert a measure of control. In other organizational contexts, processes of goal setting, planning, and other kinds of ritual activity perform similar functions. In setting personal or organizational goals we reassert confidence in our future. In investing our time and energy in a favored project, we convert the flight of time into something concrete and enduring. While Freudian analysis would view excessive concerns with productivity, planning, and control as expressions of sublimated anal eroticism, the work of Becker leads us to understand them as an attempt to preserve and tie down life in the face of death.

ORGANIZATION AND ANXIETY

In his later work, particularly in his book *Beyond the Pleasure Principle,* Freud came to place increasing emphasis on the struggle between life and death instincts within the individual. This relationship became a special focus for study by Melanie Klein and the so-called English school of psychoanalysis based at the Tavistock Institute in London, who have spent a great deal of time tracing the impact of childhood defenses against anxiety on the adult personality. The Kleinian school has placed great emphasis on the role of the mother and on relationships between the child and its mother's breast in identifying the links between the conscious and unconscious. Klein's work thus helps to rectify a great bias in Freud's research, which in being overly concerned with the role of the father as the key figure in early childhood experience, had tended to ignore or underplay the importance of the nurturing role of the mother.

Klein's work builds on the premise that from the beginning of life, the human child experiences unease associated with the death instinct and fear of annihilation, and that this fear becomes internalized in the form of "persecutory anxiety." In order to cope with this anxiety, the child develops defense mechanisms, including splitting, introjection, and projection (see Exhibit 7.1). In Klein's view this first occurs in relation to the mother's breast or surrogate, which becomes identified with good and bad experiences, resulting in severance between feelings of love and hate. While experiences of the "good breast" provide a focus for affirmation and integration of the child's existence, experiences of the "bad breast" (where feeding is frustrating, slow, or difficult) become the focus of persecutory anxieties within the child. These anxieties are projected onto the "bad breast," which is often attacked with anger. Although the split between the good and bad breast occurs in the unconscious fantasy life of the child, it is real in its effects: it gets translated into specific patterns of feelings, object relations, and thought processes that have a significant impact on later life.

In Klein's view, the formation of the ego begins in these very early experiences, the "good breast" providing an integrative focus that helps to fight the destructive forces projected onto the "bad breast." The child splits the good feelings from the bad, internalizing, idealizing, and enjoying the good, often as a means of denying the existence of threatening states, while attacking the bad, often by projecting them onto the outside world. The life of the infant thus tends to be a world of extremes, in which ego characteristics associated with idealization, projection, and denial are all visible. In Klein's view these characteristics are associated with normal as well as maladapted development, the infant passing through a persecutory (paranoid-schizoid) phase during the first few months of life, then into a "depressive position" where the child begins to appreciate that the good and bad breast are one and the same, and that he or she has hated and attacked what is also loved. Klein believed that the necessary synthesis between loved and hated aspects of the breast gives rise to mourning and guilt, which represent vital advances in the child's emotional and intellectual life. She believed that if the persecutory fears within the child remain strong, the infant has great difficulty leaving the paranoid-schizoid position and working through the necessary depressive phase. Then these early experiences may become the focus for fear, hate, envy, greed, anger, sadism, frustration, guilt, paranoia, obsession, depression, fantasy, and other feelings that are carried in the unconscious and transferred to other objects and relations. Klein's theory of human development thus suggests that many of the disorders that Freud attributed to human sexuality have their origins in earlier patterns of "object relations."

Klein's approach to the analysis of object relations suggests that adult experience reproduces defenses against anxiety originally formed in early childhood, the techniques of splitting, projection, introjection, idealization, and denial shaping the way we forge relations with our outside world. From this perspective, it is possible to understand the structure, process, culture, and even the environment of an organization in terms of the unconscious defense mechanisms developed by its members to cope with individual and collective anxiety.

This approach to organizational analysis has been systematically developed by many members of the Tavistock Institute. For example, in his analysis of group behavior, Wilfred Bion has shown that groups often regress to childhood patterns of behavior to protect themselves from uncomfortable aspects of the real world. When a group is fully engaged with a task, its energies tend to be occupied and directed in ways that keep the group in touch with an external reality of some kind. However, when problems that challenge the group's functioning arise, the group tends to withdraw its energies from task performance and use them to defend itself against the anxieties associated with the new situation. We have all experienced this in one way or another in our personal lives, and in countless organizational situations where we become so anxious about the dynamics of a situation that we lose sight of the tasks that are supposed to be performed. Concerns about group functioning obliterate concerns relating to the role of the group in the wider world. Bion has shown that in such anxiety-provoking situations groups tend to revert to one of three styles of operation that employ different kinds of defense against anxiety.

In some groups a *dependency* mode is adopted. It is assumed that the group needs some form of leadership to resolve its predicament. The group's attention is split from the problems at hand and projected onto a particular individual. Group members often proclaim helplessness in coping with the situation, and idealize the characteristics of the chosen leader. Sometimes the group projects its energies onto an attractive symbol of its past, celebrating the way things used to be instead of coping with the current reality. Such a climate makes it easy for a potential leader to step in and take charge of the group's affairs. However, he or she often inherits an extremely difficult situation, since the very existence of a leader will provide an excuse for personal inaction on the part of others. The leader will also have to embody traits fantasized by people in the group who project desired aspects of their own egos onto the leader figure. As a result, the leader often fails to live up to expectations and is soon replaced by another person, often one of the least able members of the group. He or she in turn usually fails, and so the problems continue, perhaps leading to fragmentation and infighting within the group. Group functioning thus tends to become immobilized as all kinds of petty wrangling and divisionary issues serve as substitutes for real action.

In another pattern of response, a group may attempt to deal with its problems through what Bion calls *pairing*. This involves a fantasy where members of the group come to believe that a messiah figure will emerge to deliver the group from its fear and anxiety. The group's dependence on the emergence of such a figure again paralyzes its ability to take effective action.

A third pattern of response is what Bion describes as *fight-flight*, in which the group tends to project its fears on an enemy of some kind. This enemy embodies the unconscious persecutory anxiety experienced by the group. The enemy may take the form of a competitor in the environment, a government regulation, a public attitude, or a particular person or organization that appears to be "out to get us." While uniting the group and making a strong form of leadership possible, the fight-flight process tends to distort the group's appreciation of reality and hence its ability to cope. Time and energy tend to be devoted to fighting or protecting the group from the perceived danger, rather than to taking a more balanced look at the problems that are evident in the situation.

A good example of this process is the way automobile manufacturers and many other branches of manufacturing industry in North America first reacted to the challenge posed by the import of goods from Japan and other parts of Asia. While this new source of competition was very real in its effects, preoccupation with "the enemy" and the need to fight or protect oneself through legislation and import quotas diverted attention from an equally important aspect of the situation: the need to reexamine the nature of one's own products to find how they might be modified or improved to compete in the new market conditions. The fight-flight response illustrated in this example tapped an unconscious paranoia that is common to many group situations.

The relevance of these ideas for understanding the dynamics of leadership, group processes, the enactment of organizational culture, relations between organization and environment, and other day-to-day aspects of organizational functioning is clear. The defense mechanisms elucidated by Klein and Bion pervade almost every aspect of organizational activity. People construct realities wherein threats and concerns within the unconscious mind become embodied in structures for coping with anxiety in the outside world. People may project these unconscious concerns as individuals, or through patterns of unconscious collusion that tap shared fears, concerns, and general anxiety.

These ideas can also help explain many of the more formal aspects of organization. For example, Eliott Jaques and Isobel Menzies, former members of the Tavistock Institute, have shown how aspects of organizational structure can be understood as social defenses against anxiety. Jaques has shown that many organizational roles are the focus of various kinds of paranoid or persecutory anxiety in that people project bad objects and bad impulses onto the occupant of the role, who, more often than not, will introject these projections or deflect them elsewhere. Thus the first officer on a ship is typically held responsible for many things that go wrong, even if he is not responsible for them. By common unconscious consent, he is usually the source of all trouble, allowing the crew to find relief from their own internal persecutors. The process also allows the captain to be more easily idealized as a good protective figure. All kinds of organizational scapegoats serve similar functions—people in roles everyone "loves to hate," convenient "troublemakers" and "misfits," and people who are "just not playing the game." They provide a focus for unconscious anger and sadistic tendencies, relieving tension in the wider organization and binding it together.

Jaques has shown that this kind of defense against paranoid anxiety is often a feature of labor-management relations, bad impulses being projected onto different groups who are then perceived as villains or sources of trouble and who become the objects of vengeful attitudes and actions. The process also occurs in many patterns of interorganizational relations. For example, Robert Chatov characterizes many of the relations between government and business as "regulatory sadism," where regulators inflict burdensome and superfluous requirements on regulatees. The process can also be observed in the way organizations in competitive environments may attempt to dominate, punish, and control their rivals or other organizations with whom they work, and in the way some organizations punish themselves. For example, one part of an organization may set out to create punishing problems for another, or build various kinds of punishment into its general policies and procedures. This was very much in evidence in the recession of the early 1980s when key people in many organizations took great pleasure in "tightening up" on organizational practices and privileges that had developed in the preceding "fat" years. Similar attitudes can be found in the field of labor-management relations, where the weakened position of many trade unions has opened the door to "union-bashing" policies that often are motivated as much by desires to take revenge and punish unions for the power they exercised in the 1960s and 1970s, as by the genuine rationalization of work practices.

Isobel Menzies developed related insights in a pioneering study on nursing staff in hospitals, showing how defenses against anxiety underpin many aspects of the way nursing work is organized. As is well known, nurses often have to deal with distressing tasks that can arouse mixed feelings of pity, compassion, love, guilt, fear, hatred, envy, and resentment. Hence, in the nursing profession the splitting up of the nurse-patient relation into discrete tasks distributed among different nurses, the depersonalization, categorization, and denial of the significance of the patient as an individual in favor of the patient as a "case," and the detachment and denial of personal feelings, often have unconscious as well as bureaucratic significance. For they are coping mechanisms. Sometimes they may contribute to the efficient achievement of the substantive tasks for which they have been rationally designed, while at other times they may actually block effective task achievement. However, they may be extremely difficult to remove or change.

In yet another area of research, Abraham Zaleznik of the Harvard Business School has shown that patterns of unconscious anxiety often exert a decisive influence on coalition building and the politics of organizational life. In some situations leaders are unable to develop close relations with their colleagues and subordinates because of unconscious fears, or because some form of unconscious anger or envy leads them to resent any trace of rivalry. Such concerns may motivate the leader to maintain control by dividing and ruling subordinates in ways that ensure that they are "kept in place." Often the unconscious fears prevent the leader from being able to accept genuine help and advice. For example, policy suggestions put forward by subordinates may be interpreted as rivalry and hence dismissed or suppressed regardless of their substantive merit. Very often the relations between a leader and his or her subordinates are also the focus of unconscious projections of an Oedipal nature, with subordinates projecting their fantasy of replacing their parent onto the leader, a factor which may reinforce the leader's anxiety. When relations are dominated by this kind of unconscious competition, the leader frequently becomes isolated, providing an ideal situation for subordinates to club together in a way that may actually lead to his or her demise. In this manner, unconscious projections often have self-realizing effects.

It is easy to see that the patterns of meaning that shape corporate culture and subculture may also have unconscious significance. The common values that bind an organization often have their origin in shared concerns that lurk below the surface of conscious awareness. For example, in organizations that project a team image, various kinds of splitting mechanisms are often in operation, idealizing the qualities of team members while projecting fears, anger, envy, and other bad impulses onto persons and objects that are not part of the team. As in war, the ability to create unity and a feeling of purpose often depends upon the ability to deflect destructive impulses onto the enemy. These impulses then confront the team as "real" threats.

In organizations characterized by internal strife or an ethos of cut-throat competition, these destructive impulses are often unleashed within, creating a culture that thrives on various kinds of sadism rather than by projecting its sadism elsewhere. For example, deep-seated envy may lead people to block the success of their colleagues, because they fear that they will be unable to match that success. This hidden process may undermine the ability to develop teamlike cooperation, which requires organizational members to enjoy success through affiliation with successful others as well as through their own achievements. Again, unresolved persecutory anxieties, which invariably inhibit learning because they prevent people from accepting criticism and correcting their mistakes, may lead to a culture characterized by all kinds of tension and defensiveness.

Considerations such as these suggest that there may be much more to corporate culture than is evident in the popular idea that it is possible to "manage culture." Culture, like organization, may not be what it seems to be. Culture may be of as much significance in helping us to avoid an inner reality as in helping us to cope with the external reality of our day-to-day lives.

ORGANIZATION, DOLLS, AND TEDDY BEARS

As children, most of us had a favorite soft toy, blanket, piece of clothing, or other special object on which we lavished attention and from which we were virtually inseparable. Psychoanalyst Donald Winnicott has developed the Kleinian theory of object relations in a way that emphasizes the key role of such "transitional objects" in human development. He suggests that they are critical in developing distinctions between the "me" and the "not-me," creating what he calls an "area of illusion" that helps the child develop relations with the outside world. In effect these objects provide a bridge between the child's internal and external worlds. If the favored object or phenomenon is modified (e.g., Teddy is washed or cleaned), then the child may feel that his or her own existence is being threatened in some way.

In Winnicott's view the relationship with such objects continues throughout life, the doll, teddy bear, or blanket gradually being replaced by other objects and experiences that mediate one's relations with one's world and help one maintain a sense of identity. In later life a valued possession, a collection of letters, a cherished dream, or perhaps a valued attribute, skill, or ability may come to act as a substitute for our lost doll or teddy, symbolizing for us and reassuring us about who we actually are and where we stand in the wider world. While playing a crucial role in linking us with our reality, on occasion these objects and experiences may also acquire the status of a fetish or fixation that we are unable to relinquish. In such cases adult development becomes stuck and distorted, a rigid commitment to a particular aspect of our world making it difficult for us to move on and deal with the changing nature of our surroundings. In other words, adults, like children, can become overly committed to the comfort and security provided by their new teddy bears in disguise!

If Winnicott is correct, the theories of transitional phenomena and associated areas of illusion explain yet another aspect of how we engage and construct organizational reality, and of the role of the unconscious in shaping and resisting change.

This idea has been studied in depth by Harold Bridger of the Tavistock Institute, who has run numerous seminars exploring the unconscious significance of transitional phenomena in organizational life. His perspective leads us to understand that many organizational arrangements can themselves serve as transitional phenomena: they play a critical role in defining the nature and identity of organizations and their members, and in shaping attitudes that can block creativity, innovation, and change. For example, in many organizations a particular aspect of organizational structure or corporate culture may come to assume special significance and be preserved and retained even in the face of great pressure to change. A family firm may cling to a particular aspect of its history and mission, even though it is now operating in new conditions where this aspect is no longer relevant. Trade-union officials may want to fight to the death to defend a particular principle or a set of concessions won in previous battles, even though they are no longer of any real value to their members. A manager or work group may insist that they have the right and discretion to make particular decisions, or that work must be performed in a specific manner, even though when pressed they recognize that their requirements are ritualistic rather than substantive in nature.

In each of these cases the phenomenon to be preserved may be of transitional significance to those involved. Just as a child may rely on the presence of his or her doll or teddy bear as a means of reaffirming who and where they are, managers and workers may rely on equivalent phenomena for defining their sense of identity. When these phenomena are challenged, basic identities are challenged. The fear of loss which this entails thus often generates a reaction that may be out of all proportion to the importance of the issue when viewed from a more detached point of view. This unconscious dynamic may help explain why some organizations have been unable to cope with the changing demands of their environment, and why there is often so much unconscious resistance to change in organizations.

The general principles are well illustrated in the case of an engineering company which, like many others in its industry, experienced difficulties in adapting to changes being created by new developments in computer technology. One of the interesting features of the culture of the company was its commitment to the use of slide rules. While the new computer technology in effect offered a more efficient way of making engineering calculations, many of the engineers insisted on continuing to use their "slides." The theory of transitional phenomena leads us to understand this in terms of an unconscious process where the use of slide rules was associated with a past that was fast disappearing and a reluctance to relinquish an old identity and move on with the changing times. As might be expected, the firm lost their position in the industry and eventually got taken over by another firm.

The theory of transitional phenomena contributes important insights to the practice of organizational change and development, for it suggests that change will occur spontaneously only when people are prepared to relinquish what they hold dear for the purpose of acquiring something new. The engineering firm in the above example was committed to a symbolic object that could not perform transitional functions in the current situation. Some new object or phenomenon was needed to aid in the transition to microprocessing. Interestingly, consultants and other change agents often become transitional objects for their client firms: The client refuses to "let go," and becomes crucially dependent on the change agent's advice in relation to every move.

In helping to facilitate any kind of social change it may thus be necessary for the change agent to create transitional phenomena when they do not exist naturally. Just as a father or mother may have to help their child find a substitute for Teddy, a change agent—whether a social revolutionary or a paid consultant—must usually help his or her target group to relinquish what is held dear before they can move on. Significantly, this can rarely be done effectively by "selling" or imposing a "change package," an ideology or a set of techniques. The theory of transitional phenomena suggests that in situations of voluntary change, the person doing the changing must be in control of the process. For change ultimately hinges on questions of identity and the problematic relation between the "me and not-me." In order to create transitional situations a change agent must help create that area of illusion identified by Winnicott, which, in his terms, is "good enough" for people to explore their situations and the options they face. People frequently need time to reflect, think over, feel out, and mull through action if a change is to be effective and long lasting. If the change agent tries to bypass or suppress what is valued, it is almost sure to resurface at a later date.

The theory of transitional phenomena thus provides a way of understanding the dynamics of change and prescribes a method for the design of change. As yet, the perspective has not been widely applied to our understanding of organization, but is one that offers considerable promise for the future.

ORGANIZATION, SHADOW, AND ARCHETYPE

In the above analysis we have focused on Freudian and neo-Freudian interpretations of the unconscious. It is now time to turn to the implications of the work of Carl Jung.

Whereas Freud was in many ways preoccupied with the demands that the body, as carrier of the psyche, placed on the unconscious, Jung cut loose from this constraint, viewing the psyche as part of a universal and transcendental reality. As his thinking developed, he came to place increasing emphasis on the idea that the human psyche is part of a "collective unconscious" that transcends the limits of space and time. Many criticize this aspect of Jung's work as bordering on the occult. However, a more informed interpretation encourages us to see how this concept links with developments in modern physics. Jung dematerialized our understanding of the psyche just as Einstein, whom Jung knew well, dematerialized our understanding of the physical world. In the light of evidence on premonitions and other psychic phenomena, Jung came to see matter and psyche as two different aspects of one and the same thing. The physical energy that Einstein saw as underlying all matter came to be paralleled in Jung's work by a conception of psychic energy, which, like physical energy, was open to many kinds of transformation through conscious and unconscious activity. Hence Jung's holistic view of the psyche as a universal phenomenon that is ultimately part of a transcendental reality linking mind to mind and mind to nature.

One of the most distinctive features of Jung's analysis is his emphasis on the role of archetypes. "Archetype," which literally means "original pattern," is defined by Jung in a variety of ways, and plays a critical role in linking the individual to the collective unconscious. At the most basic level archetypes are defined as patterns that structure thought and hence give order to the world. Jung's use of archetypes was inspired by Plato's view of images or schemata, and he talks about them in various ways, for example, as "living ideas" that constantly produce new interpretations, and as "ground plans" that give the stuff of experience a specific configuration. He also speaks of them as "organs of the prerational psyche" and as "inherited forms and ideas" that acquire content in the course of an individual's life as personal experience is taken up in these forms. In other words, archetypes are structures of thought and experience, perhaps embodied in the structure of the psyche or inherited experience, which lead us to mold our understanding of our world in a patterned way. Jung devoted great time and energy to demonstrating the universal and timeless character of these archetypal structures, showing how they are found in the dreams, myths, and ideas of primitive, ancient, and modern man. Though the empirical contents may vary in detail, the principles that lend them shape and order seem to be one and the same. For Jung these archetypes shape the way we "meet ourselves" in encounters with the external world, and are crucial for understanding links between conscious and unconscious aspects of the psyche.

Jung's work thus has major implications for understanding how people enact organizational reality. We will focus here on two of the more important: the way Jung encourages us to understand the general relations between internal and external life, and the role which archetypes play in shaping our understanding of the external world.

The first theme has been explored in some detail by Robert Denhardt of the University of Kansas. In his book *In The Shadow of Organization* he invites us to examine the repressed human side of organization lying beneath the surface of formal rationality. Jung used the term "shadow" to refer to unrecognized or unwanted drives and desires, the other side of the conscious ego, standing in relation to the ego as a kind of submerged opposite that at the same time strives for completeness with the ego. For Jung, the development of the ego always tended to be two-sided. He thus placed particular emphasis on understanding conscious and unconscious life in terms of an interplay between opposing tendencies. He believed that full development of self-knowledge and human personality, a process which he described as individuation, rested on a person's ability to recognize the rival elements within his or her personality and to deal with their contradictions in a unified manner. In his view, neurosis and human maladaption stemmed from an inability to recognize and deal with the repressed shadow, which typically contained both constructive and destructive forces. Like the other theorists we have considered in this chapter, he also believed that many of these unresolved tensions in ourselves were projected onto other people and external situations, and that to understand our external reality we must first understand what he called "the other within."

Thus, in the shadow of organization we find all the repressed opposites of rationality struggling to surface and change the nature of rationality in practice. Sociologist Max Weber noted that the more the bureaucratic form of organization advances the more perfectly it succeeds in eliminating all human qualities that escape technical calculation. However, Jung's work suggests that these can never be eliminated, only banished. His work also leads us to understand that these irrational qualities never accept their banishment idly, and are always looking for a way to modify their rational other side. We see this in much of the unofficial politicking that shapes organizational life, and also in stress, lying, cheating, depression, and acts of sabotage. From a Jungian standpoint, such factors reflect inevitable yet neglected or suppressed tensions in a two-sided process. Just as the unconscious of the individual strives to achieve completeness with the ego, the shadowy unconscious in an organization can also be seen as crying for recognition, warning us that the development of one side of our humanness, e.g., the capacity to exercise technical reason, often does violence to other sides. The pathologies and alienations we find in organizational contexts can, from a Jungian standpoint, be interpreted as a manifestation of this essential wholeness of the psyche.

The theme of the unity in opposites is a powerful one running throughout Jung's work. It has been constructively used by many organization theorists interested in understanding how people relate to their realities and in improving organizational decision making. Jung distinguished two ways of perceiving reality (through sensation and intuition), and two ways of judging reality (thinking and feeling). These two dimensions are often combined to identify different personality types (Exhibit 7.2) and to demonstrate styles of decision making. This scheme provides a nice illustration of how repressed elements of the psyche may signify unused skill and potential within the human which, if tapped, could contribute much to an individual's ability to cope with the problems he or she faces. Jung's work shows that the repressed shadow of organization acts as a reservoir not only of forces that are unwanted and hence repressed but of forces that have been lost or undervalued. By recognizing and coming to grips with the resources of this reservoir, Jungian organization theorists are at one in suggesting that we can tap new sources of energy and creativity and make our institutions much more human, vibrant, and morally responsive and responsible than they are now.

Jung's analysis of personality in terms of the way people relate to their world conveniently brings us to consider the role of archetypes in shaping the details of our reality. As noted earlier, archetypes are recurring themes of thought and experience that seem to have universal significance. For example, as Northrop Frye of the University of Toronto has shown, mythology and literature are dominated by a small number of basic themes—apocalyptic, demonic, romantic, tragic, comic, and ironic. While the characters, situations, and actions change, the stories remain pretty well the same. In other aspects of life, too, powerful

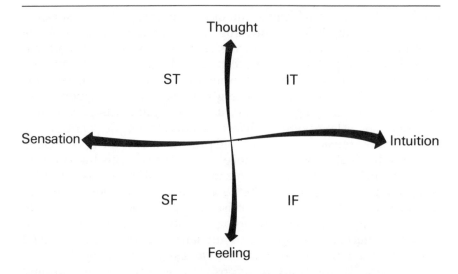

Jung suggests that people tend to process data about the world in terms of sense or intuition, and to make judgments in terms of thought or feeling. According to which functions are dominant (or in the shadow), we can identify four ways of dealing with the world and of shaping one's reality: *ST* individuals tend to be empiricists who sense and think their way through life, making judgments and interpretations on the basis of "hard facts" and logical analysis; *SF* individuals also tend to pay a great deal of attention to data derived from the senses, but arrive at judgments in terms of "what feels right" rather than in terms of analysis; *IT* individuals tend to work their way through life by thinking about the possibilities inherent in a situation. Their actions tend to be shaped by ideas and insight rather than facts; *IF* individuals tend to be guided by a combination of insight and feeling which pays much more attention to values than to facts. When one style of action is dominant, then the other styles occupy background roles. Clearly, since each style presents an alternative way of understanding the same situation, opportunities are lost in this imbalance.

This scheme has been used by Ian Mitroff and various colleagues (Mitroff and Kilmann 1978, Mason and Mitroff 1981, and Mitroff 1984) to analyze managerial and decision-making styles, and to develop dialectical approaches to planning and decision making that attempt to take rival points of view into account. The scheme has been used by Ingalls (1979) as the foundation for a Jungian analysis of the use and direction of human energy in organizations, and by Myers and Briggs (1962) to develop a personality test that has many managerial applications. A variation of the scheme has also been developed by McWhinney (1982) as a means of tackling complex problems.

Exhibit 7.2. The Jungian interplay of opposites

themes that help people make sense of their experience are used time and again to create patterns of meaning. These archetypal structures give people a sense of place in their own lives and in history and thus help them to make sense of who and where they are in the grand order of things.

If Jung's theory of archetypes is correct, then we would expect the pattern of organizational life to be created and recreated in accordance with the structures found in the history of myth and literature. Unfortunately very little research has, as yet, been conducted on this topic. Ian Mitroff of the University of Southern California has made an important theoretical contribution to our understanding of the links between archetype and organization and has suggested that organizational life can be understood in terms of the relations between fools, magicians, warriors, high priests, lovers, and other symbolic characters. His analysis suggests that we may be able to understand the unconscious significance of much organizational behavior in terms of the great themes that have shaped history. It appears that even though we may use the latest electronic technology and management technique to plan and execute our affairs, we do so in ancient ways. For we are all primitives at heart, reproducing archetypal relations to make sense of the basic dilemmas of life.

Our exploration of organization and the unconscious has drawn on many images of the psychic prison, tracing relations between our conscious and unconscious life in terms of repressed sexuality, patriarchy, fear of death, mother's breast, teddy bears, and shadows and archetypes. And the list is by no means exhaustive. These metaphors encourage us to become more sensitive about the hidden meaning of our everyday actions and preoccupations, and to learn how we can process and transform our unconscious energy in constructive ways. They lead us to see how aggression, envy, anger, resentment, sexual sublimations, and numerous other dimensions of our hidden life may be built into work and organization. These hidden concerns influence whether we attempt to design work to avoid or to deal with problematic aspects of our reality, and how we enact our organizational world. They lie at the center of many issues associated with group dynamics, effective leadership, and innovation and change.

The overall significance of these ways of understanding organizations has been vividly grasped by Delahanty and Gemmill of Syracuse University, who suggest that we should understand the role of the unconscious in organizational life as a kind of "black hole." As is well known, this metaphor has been used in physics to characterize invisible yet intense gravitational fields that capture all passing matter. In a similar way, the invisible dimension of organization that we have described as the unconscious can swallow and trap the rich energies of people involved in the organizing process.

The challenge of understanding the significance of the unconscious in organization carries with it a promise: that it is possible to release trapped energy in ways that may promote creative transformation and change and create more integrated relations among individuals, groups, organizations, and their environments. And this promise is in perfect harmony with the metaphor of the psychic prison. For a vision of confinement is invariably accompanied by a vision of freedom. For Plato, this freedom rested in the pursuit of knowledge about the world. For the psychoanalysts, it has rested in knowledge of the unconscious, and in the capacity of humans to create a better world through an improved understanding of how we construct and interpret our realities, and hence an enhanced ability to change them.

Strengths and limitations of the psychic prison metaphor

The insights generated by this metaphor provide the basis for a thorough critique of the nature and significance of organization as a distinctively human phenomenon. The metaphor directs attention to the fact that human beings can and do create social worlds that many may experience as problematic and confining, and helps identify ways out of these self-created traps. As such, the metaphor has much to offer in an age where so many people feel enmeshed in problems that, at least in part, are of their own making.

In terms of specific contributions, the psychic prison metaphor presents a set of perspectives for exploring the hidden meaning of our taken-for-granted worlds. The metaphor encourages us to dig below the surface to uncover the unconscious processes and related patterns of control that trap people in unsatisfactory modes of existence. In showing how there is a close and interactive link between factors as diverse as the unconscious and the structure of organizations and their environments, repressed sexuality and the design of work, and teddy bears and organizational consultants, the implications of the metaphor challenge us to stand back and question what is really happening in the world around us. As such, the metaphor provides the impetus for a critical analysis of organization and society that may allow us to understand and cope with the significance and consequences of our actions in a more informed way.

The metaphor also shows us that we have overrationalized our understanding of organization. Both in our behavior in organizations and in our explanations of organizations, factors such as aggression, greed, fear, hate, and sexual desire have no official status. And when they do break into the open, they are usually quickly banished through apologies, rationalizations, and punishments designed to restore a more neutered state of affairs. An outburst of anger may be interpreted as a sign that someone is under pressure, an emotional breakdown treated with a few days' leave, and an act of sabotage punished with further controls. Yet apologize, rationalize, punish, and control as we may, we do not rid organization of these repressed forces lurking in the shadow of rationality. For if the ideas of Freud and other theorists are correct, rationality is often irrationality in disguise. Thus the rationality of a Frederick Taylor may disguise an extreme form of compulsiveness, just as a manager's excessive concern for clear-cut targets and goals may disguise a basic insecurity in life. Rationality and irrationality (a term for human forces that we cannot order and control) appear to be central to the human condition. We tend to fear the irrational and to use reason to bring its manifestations under control. In celebrating the rational aspects of organization and rationalizing the irrational we may make ourselves feel more secure, but we won't necessarily understand the hidden meaning and significance of the actions that shape organization. The ideas presented in this chapter provide a means of overcoming this deficiency through a recognition of the close interplay between the celebrated and repressed sides of human life.

The metaphor also draws specific attention to the ethical basis of organization by reinforcing the view that organization is human in the fullest sense. In encouraging us to scrutinize the nature and consequences of organizational actions with this in mind, the metaphor encourages increased awareness of the human significance of almost every aspect of organizational life.

The metaphor also encourages us to recognize and deal with the power relations shaping the enactment of organizational life. The metaphor recognizes that certain individuals and groups may be able to evoke archetypal feelings, shape subconscious languages of control, placing our understanding of the management of meaning discussed in Chapters 5 and 6 in a new light. However, the metaphor also shows how we *all* play a role in the construction of these unconscious power relations and how this knowledge can have an empowering effect.

Finally, the metaphor identifies many of the barriers standing in the path of innovation and change. As we have seen, many aspects of social and organizational culture and structure serve conscious and unconscious purposes that are invisible to the human eye. This means that they can be changed only if the underlying concerns and preoccupations are modified in some way. This explains why it is often so difficult to change organizational situations, even when the change seems logical and beneficial to all concerned. An excellent illustration of this is found in a study of coal mines conducted by Eric Trist. He found that the habit of working in "bad systems" had the compensation of allowing many of the workers to leave some of their own sense of "badness" in the system. Hence while hating their work, they could not change it: the system had a strange way of tying them in. In a similar way, people may build a dependency on some aspect of culture or social life that leads them to resist innovations that would undermine this dependency. In drawing attention to the deep structure of forces that sustain the status quo, the ideas discussed in this chapter thus contribute much to our understanding of the dynamics of change.

Against these strengths and insights, it is necessary to register a number of limitations. First, our discussion has placed emphasis on understanding unconscious patterns of behavior and control. A fuller treatment of the psychic prison metaphor requires that we also take into account the more explicit ideologies that control and shape organizational life. People are often locked into cognitive traps because it is in the interests of certain individuals and groups to sustain one pattern of belief rather than another. This aspect of the management of meaning was discussed briefly in Chapter 6, but as highlighted in the bibliographic notes to this chapter, is worthy of much more detailed attention. Our understanding of the psychic prison metaphor could thus be extended to embrace all the ideological processes through which we create and sustain meaning, not just the unconscious.

Second, the metaphor can be criticized for placing too much emphasis on the role of cognitive processes in creating, sustaining, and changing organizations and society. For many, it may seem more appropriate to talk about organizations as prisons rather than as psychic prisons, since the exploitation and domination of people is often grounded as much in control over the material basis of life as in control over ideas, thoughts, and feelings. This view builds on a long-standing debate between humanists and materialists, and will be placed in better perspective in the following two chapters, where we will give more attention to the idea that organizations and society may be shaped by forces that have a logic and momentum of their own. In the meantime, we must note the important point that a change in consciousness or an appreciation of the role of the unconscious may not itself be enough to effect major change in the basic structure of organization and society.

Another limitation of the metaphor is that it often encourages utopian speculation and critique. While it does contribute certain insights on how to improve the conduct of day-to-day affairs, particularly in showing how we can challenge taken-for-granted mind-sets or achieve a better understanding of the psychodynamics of change, many of its implications ignore the realities of power and the force of vested interests in sustaining the status quo. Of course, the fact that reform may be dismissed as utopian adds power to the argument that our imprisoned state prevents us from imagining and realizing alternative modes of existence. For claims that proposals for change must be feasible and realistic inevitably confine change to modifications of the status quo. However, the criticism of utopianism still remains.

A final limitation of the metaphor is that it raises the specter of an Orwellian world where we attempt to manage each other's minds. We noted in Chapter 5 how an awareness of the importance of corporate culture has sent many managers and management theorists scurrying to find ways of managing culture. In highlighting the role of the unconscious in organization, there is a danger that many will now want to find ways of managing the unconscious as well. This, of course, is impossible, because the unconscious is by nature uncontrollable.

While it is possible to act in a way that is sensitive to the existence and role of the unconscious in everyday life, knowledge of the unconscious does not produce blueprints for reform. The psychic prison metaphor promotes a very useful style of critical thinking that can help us penetrate many of the complexities of organizational life, but it does not always provide the easy answers and solutions to problems that many may wish to find.

8

Unfolding Logics of Change

Organization as Flux and Transformation

Around the year 500 B.C. the Greek philosopher Heraclitus noted that "you cannot step twice into the same river, for other waters are continually flowing on." He was one of the first Western philosophers to address the idea that the universe is in a constant state of flux embodying characteristics of both permanence *and* change. As he noted, "Everything flows and nothing abides; everything gives way and nothing stays fixed. . . . Cool things become warm, the warm grows cool; the moist dries, the parched becomes moist. . . . It is in changing that things find repose." For Heraclitus, the secrets of the universe were to be found in hidden tensions and connections that simultaneously create patterns of unity and change.

In our own time, David Bohm (a theoretical physicist at the University of London) has developed a remarkable theory that invites us to understand the universe as a flowing and unbroken wholeness. Like Heraclitus, he views process, flux, and change as fundamental, arguing that the state of the universe at any point in time reflects a more basic reality. He calls this reality the *implicate* (or *enfolded*) order, and distinguishes it from the *explicate* (or *unfolded*) order manifested in the world around us. Bohm argues that the latter realizes and expresses potentialities existing within the former.

The implicate order is viewed as a creative process, which like a hologram has everything enfolded in everything else. Bohm uses the terms *holomovement* or *holoflux* to express the undivided and flowing nature of this implicate order, which provides the generative source of explicate forms. These forms, like the river described by Heraclitus, have the appearance of stability while being underpinned by flux and change. Imagine a whirlpool in the river. While possessing relatively constant, recurrent, and stable form, it has no existence other than in the movement of the river in which it exists. The analogy illustrates how an explicate order flows out of the implicate order in accordance with a coherent process of transformation. Bohm believes that the world unfolds and enfolds from moment to moment (the word moment derives from movement) as a kind of pulsating wholeness. Each moment of existence has similarities with, yet differs from, its predecessors, creating the appearance of continuity in the midst of change.

This theory, which has provided a means of resolving many problems in modern physics, has remarkable consequences. For it suggests that in order to understand the secrets of the universe we have to understand the generative processes that link implicate and explicate orders. Up to now, much of science has confined its attention to understanding relations *within* the explicate order. If Bohm is correct, the explicate world is but a particular case or expression of the holomovement. We can study relations between objects and processes in this world and attempt to explain them in causal terms, but, in Bohm's view, we will not discover the all-important "laws of the whole" embedded in the implicate order. To discover these, we have to understand the movement, flux, and change that *produce* the world we experience and study.

Bohm's theory, like that of Heraclitus, reverses the usual relationship between reality and change. While in science and everyday life we tend to view change as an attribute of reality and see the world as changing, Bohm's theory encourages us to understand that the world is itself but a moment in a more fundamental process of change. His theory suggests that underlying the surface of our reality there are hidden processes—I call them "logics of change"—that help to explain the concrete form of the world at any given point in time.

In this chapter we will explore some of these logics of change.

Implicate and explicate aspects of organization

What relevance can these ideas have for understanding organization and organizations? In what conceivable ways can the image of a pulsating, changing universe, or a whirling river, inform our understanding of the way we organize in social life? Taking Bohm's work as a point of departure, it is clear that if the world of organization is an unfolded empirical reality, then we can best understand the nature of organization by decoding the logics of transformation and change through which this reality unfolds. Such imagery invites us to search for the basic dynamics that generate and sustain organizations and their environments as concrete social forms.

In searching for these hidden dynamics our attention can move in many directions. For example, we could return to a consideration of the unconscious as the implicate source of organizational life, and pay more attention to how unconscious energy is transformed into patterns of organization. In this regard, Jung's theory of the role and significance of the collective unconscious has many parallels with Bohm's theory of the implicate order and provides an obvious framework for understanding relations between implicate and explicate aspects of organization. We could also give closer attention to the processes that generate the patterns of meaning and symbolic action that create and change organizations as cultural phenomena. These and other perspectives considered in earlier chapters are amenable to examination in terms of deep processes of transformation and change that produce surface phenomena.

Rather than pursue these directions here, however, our aim will be to explore three different images of change that each provide a way of explaining how the reality of organization may be embedded in the logic of change itself. The first draws upon some of the latest insights in biology to explain how organizations may be understood as self-producing systems. The second draws on related cybernetic ideas that suggest that the logic of change is enfolded in the strains and tensions found in circular relations. The third suggests that change is the product of dialectical relations between opposites. Each provides a means of explaining how the explicate reality of organizational life is formed and transformed by underlying processes with a logic of their own.

Autopoiesis: the logic of self-producing systems

Traditional approaches to organization theory have been dominated by the idea that change originates in the environment. As we saw in Chapter 3, the organization is typically viewed as an open system in constant interaction with its context, transforming inputs into outputs as a means of creating the conditions

necessary for survival. Changes in the environment are viewed as presenting challenges to which the organization must respond. While
there is great debate as to whether adaptation or selection is the primary factor influencing survival, both contingency theorists and
population ecologists are at one in believing that the major problems
facing modern organizations stem from changes in the environment.

This basic idea is challenged by the implications of a new approach
to systems theory developed by two Chilean scientists, Humberto Maturana and Francisco Varela. They argue that all living systems are or-
ganizationally closed, autonomous systems of interaction that make
reference only to themselves. The idea that living systems are open to
an environment is, in their view, the product of an attempt to make
sense of such systems from the standpoint of an external observer.
Their theory challenges the validity of distinctions drawn between a
system and its environment, and offers a new perspective for understanding the logic through which living systems change.

Maturana and Varela base their argument on the idea that living systems are characterized by three principal features: autonomy, circu-
larity, and self-reference. These lend them the ability to self-create or
self-renew. Maturana and Varela have coined the term *autopoiesis* to refer to this capacity for self-production through a closed system of relations. They contend that the aim of such systems is ultimately to
produce themselves: their own organization and identity is their most
important product.

How is it possible to say that living systems such as organisms are
autonomous, closed systems? Maturana and Varela argue that this is
the case because living systems strive to maintain an identity by subordinating all changes to the maintenance of their own organization as a
given set of relations. They do so by engaging in circular patterns of
interaction whereby change in one element of the system is coupled
with changes elsewhere, setting up continuous patterns of interaction
that are always self-referential. They are self-referential because a system cannot enter into interactions that are not specified in the pattern
of relations that define its organization. Thus a system's interaction
with its "environment" is really a reflection and part of its own organization. It interacts with its environment in a way that facilitates its own
self-production, and in this sense we can see that its environment is
really a part of itself.

In saying that living systems are closed and autonomous Maturana
and Varela are not saying that systems are completely isolated. The closure and autonomy to which they refer is organizational. They are saying that living systems close in on themselves to maintain stable
patterns of relations, and that it is this process of closure or self-

reference that ultimately distinguishes a system as a system. In order to discover the nature of the total system it is necessary to interact with it and trace the circular pattern of interaction through which it is defined. In doing so we encounter the problematic question of where the system begins and ends. Maturana and Varela recognize that in any systems analysis one will usually have to stop unwinding the pattern of circular relations at some point, because systems, like Chinese boxes, can be seen as being made up of wholes within wholes. However they believe that this kind of self-referential paradox is fundamental. There is no beginning and no end to the system because it is a closed loop of interaction.

Thus, to take an example, in the organization of a biological organism such as the honeybee we find self-referring systems within self-referring systems. The bee as an organism comprises a chain of self-referring biological systems with their own circular organization, and lives within a society of bees where relations are also circular. In turn, the relationship between the society of bees and the wider ecology is also circular. Eliminate the bees and the whole ecology will change, for the bee system is linked with the botanical system, which is linked with insect, animal, agricultural, human, and social systems. All these systems are self-referential and turn back on each other. A change in any one system, e.g., a decision to use an insecticide which eliminates bees as a side effect, can transform all the others.

We could attempt to understand such systems by drawing an artificial boundary between system and environment, e.g., around the individual bee, or the society of bees, or the bee-flora-fauna system, but in doing so we would break the circular chain of interaction. An understanding of the autopoietic nature of systems requires that we understand how each element simultaneously combines the maintenance of itself with the maintenance of the others. It is simply not good enough to dismiss a large part of the circular chain of interaction as "the environment." The environment is part of the bee system, and the different levels are in effect coproduced.

To provide a further illustration of these ideas it is useful to consider how Maturana and Varela reinterpret the way the human brain and nervous system operate. As will be recalled from Chapter 4, one of the most familiar images of the brain is that of an information-processing system, importing information from the environment and initiating appropriate responses. The brain is viewed as making representations of the environment, recording these in memory, and modifying the information thus stored through experience and learning. In contrast, Maturana and Varela argue that the brain is closed, autonomous, circular, and self-referential. They argue that the brain does not process information from an environment, and does not represent the environment in memory. Rather, it establishes and assigns patterns of variation and points of reference as expressions of its own mode of organization. The system thus organizes its environment as part of itself. If one thinks about it, the idea that the brain can make representations of its environment presumes some external point of reference from which it is possible to judge the degree of correspondence between the representation and the reality. This implicitly presumes that the brain must have a capacity to see and understand its world from a point of reference outside itself. Clearly this cannot be so, thus the idea that the brain represents reality is open to serious question. Maturana and Varela's work identifies this paradox and suggests that the brain creates images of reality as expressions or descriptions of its own organization and interacts with these images, modifying them in the light of actual experience.

To those of us who have become used to thinking about organisms and organizations as open systems this kind of circular reasoning may seem very strange indeed. We have learned to see living systems as distinct entities characterized by numerous patterns of interdependence, both internally and in relation to their environment. As noted earlier, Maturana and Varela argue that this is because we insist on understanding these systems from *our* point of view as observers, rather than attempting to understand their inner logic. As my colleague Peter Harries-Jones has put it, in doing this we tend to confuse and mix the domain of organization with that of explanation. If we put ourselves "inside" such systems we come to realize that we are within a closed system of interaction and that the environment is *part of* the system's organization because it is part of its domain of essential interaction.

The theory of autopoiesis thus recognizes that systems can be recognized as having "environments," but insists that relations with any environment are *internally* determined. While there may be countless chains of interaction within and between systems, A being linked to B, to C, D, E, and so forth, there is no independent pattern of causation. Changes in A do not cause changes in B, C, D, or E, since the whole chain of relations is part of the same self-determining pattern. Gregory Bateson and other theorists who have interested themselves in the ecological aspects of systems have made a similar point in emphasizing that "wholes" evolve as complete fields of relations that are mutually determining and determined. The system's pattern has to be understood as a whole, and as possessing a logic of its own. It cannot be understood as a network of separate parts. This is ultimately why it makes no sense to say that a system interacts with an external environment. For a system's transactions with an environment are really transactions within itself.

These theoretical insights have important implications. For if systems are geared to maintaining their own identity, and if relations with the environment are internally determined, then systems can evolve and change only along with self-generated changes in identity. How then does this occur?

When we recognize that identity involves the maintenance of a recurring set of relations, we quickly see that the problem of change hinges on the way systems deal with variations that influence their current mode of operation. Our attention is thus drawn to system processes that try to maintain identity by ignoring or counteracting threatening fluctuations, and to the way variations can lead to the emergence of new modes of organization. As will be recalled from discussion in Chapter 4, these issues have received considerable attention from cyberneticians. Their work emphasizes that systems can maintain stable identities by sustaining processes of negative feedback that allow them to detect and correct deviations from operating norms, and can evolve by developing capacities for double-loop learning that allow them to modify these norms to take account of new circumstances.

But where do the variations in system operation come from? What is the source of potential change? The theory of autopoiesis locates the source of change in random variations occurring *within* the total system. These may stem from random modifications introduced through processes of reproduction, or through the combination of chance interactions and connections that give rise to the development of new system relations.

In this insight the theory of autopoiesis has much in common with recent developments in a variety of scientific disciplines. For example, in 1978 Illya Prigogine of Brussels received a Nobel prize for his work on "dissipative structures" in chemical reaction systems, which shows that random changes in a system can lead to new patterns of order and stability. The same insights have been found to apply in other living systems. Termites and bees engage in random behaviors that increase the variety of the systems to which they belong. If these random behaviors attract a critical level of support, they then often become incorporated in the ongoing organization of the system. For example, termites build elaborate arches and tunnels by making random deposits of earth, which, after they attain a certain size, become a focus of attention for other termites, and thereafter a focus of deliberate activity. Random piles of dirt thus become transformed into coherent structures. In these and numerous other living systems order and self-organization emerge from randomness, large fluctuations triggering instabilities and quantum jumps capable of transforming the whole system of activity. Human ideas and practices seem to develop in a similar manner, exerting a major transformational effect once they acquire a critical level of support.

From an autopoietic standpoint random variation provides the seed of possibility that allows the emergence and evolution of new system identities. Random changes can trigger interactions that reverberate throughout the system, the final consequences being determined by whether or not the current identity of the system will dampen the effects of the new disturbance through compensatory changes elsewhere, or whether a new configuration of relations will be allowed to emerge.

The theory of autopoiesis thus encourages us to understand the transformation or evolution of living systems as the result of internally generated change. Rather than suggesting that the system adapts to an environment or that the environment selects the system configuration that survives, autopoiesis places principal emphasis on the way the total system of interactions shapes its own future. It is the pattern, or whole, that evolves. In providing this kind of explanation, autopoiesis presents an alternative to Darwinian theory. While recognizing the importance of system variation and the retention of "selected" features in the process of evolution, the theory offers different explanations as to how this occurs.

Organizations as self-producing systems

Maturana and Varela developed their theory primarily as a new interpretation of biological phenomena, and they have strong reservations about applying it to the social world. However, used as metaphor, the theory of autopoiesis has intriguing implications for our understanding of organizations.

First, a creative interpretation of the theory helps us to see that organizations are always attempting to achieve a form of self-referential closure in relation to their environments, enacting their environments as projections of their own identity or self-image. Second, it helps us to understand that many of the problems that organizations encounter in dealing with their environments are intimately connected with the kind of identity that they try to maintain. And third, it helps us to see that explanations of the evolution, change, and development of organizations must give primary attention to the factors that shape an organization's self-identity, and hence its relations with the wider world.

ENACTMENT AS A FORM OF NARCISSISM: ORGANIZATIONS INTERACT WITH PROJECTIONS OF THEMSELVES

In Chapter 5 we gave attention to the idea that organizations enact their environments: they assign patterns of variation and significance to the world in which they operate. The ideas on autopoiesis add to our understanding of this enactment, in that they encourage us to view organizational enactments as part of the self-referential process through which an organization attempts to tie down and reproduce its identity. For in enacting an environment an organization is attempting to achieve the kind of closure that is necessary for it to reproduce itself in its own image.

Consider, for example, the cartoon in Exhibit 8.1. We find here a typical process of organizational self-reference. An organization has convened a meeting to discuss certain policy issues and to take a general look at its environment.

Where do we stand?

What's happening in the environment?

Why are our sales people having so much trouble this month?

What scope is there for penetration of new markets?

What business are we in?

Are we in the right business?

Questions such as these allow those asking them to make representations of themselves, their organization, and the environment, in a way that helps orient action to create or maintain a desirable identity. The charts that decorate the walls of the meeting room are really mirrors. Like the reflecting globe in Escher's lithograph they allow members of the organization to see themselves within the context of their ongoing activity. The figures and pictures that an organization produces on market trends, competitive position, sales forecasts, raw-material availability, and so forth are really projections of the organization's own interests and concerns. They reflect the organization's understanding of itself. It is through this process of self-reference that organizational members can intervene in their own functioning, and thus participate in creating and maintaining their identity.

When we view the enactment process as an attempt to achieve a form of closure in relation to the environment, the whole idea of enactment assumes new significance. For we come to realize that enactment

Autopoietic systems are closed loops: self-referential systems that strive to shape themselves in their own image.

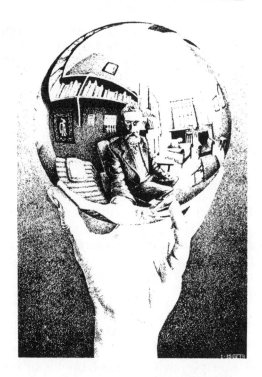

Hand with reflecting globe. Self-portrait by M.C. Escher (lithograph, 1935).

Well Jack, where do we stand ?

Exhibit 8.1. Systems that look at themselves
SOURCE: Escher self-portrait reprinted by permission of Haags Gemeentemuseum, The Hague, and courtesy of Vorpal Gallery, San Francisco and New York City, by permission of the heirs of M. C. Escher, © M. C. Escher heirs c/o Cordon Arts-Baarn-Holland. Boardroom cartoon reproduced by permission of the artist.

is not just a mode of perception whereby we see or emphasize certain things while ignoring or downplaying others, but is a much more active process. By projecting itself onto its environment and thereby organizing its environment, an organization sets the basis for acting in relation to that environment in a way that actually allows it to produce itself.

IDENTITY AND CLOSURE: EGOCENTRICISM VERSUS SYSTEMIC WISDOM

Nowadays many organizations are preoccupied with understanding their environment as a kind of "world out there" that has an existence of its own. The ideas discussed above show the dangers in this kind of thinking, and suggest that if one really wants to understand one's environment, one must begin by understanding oneself, for one's understanding of the environment is always a projection of oneself. As an organization "looks at" its environment, or makes exploratory probes to test its nature, it should thus appreciate that it is really creating an opportunity to understand itself and its relation with the wider world.

Many organizations encounter great problems in dealing with the wider world, because they do not recognize how they are a part of their environment. They see themselves as discrete entities that are faced with the problem of surviving *against* the vagaries of the outside world, which is often constructed as a domain of threat and opportunity. This is most evident in the practices of what I call *egocentric organizations*, which have a rather fixed notion of who they are, or what they can be, and are determined to impose or sustain that identity at all costs.

This kind of egocentricism leads organizations to become preoccupied with and to overemphasize the importance of themselves, while underplaying the significance of the wider system of relations in which they exist. When we look at ourselves in a mirror we create a relation between "figure," the face that we see, and "ground," the context in which our face is located. When we focus on our face, our context is pretty well eliminated from view. The egocentric enactments through which organizations attempt to structure and understand their environments often manifest a similar imbalance. In their quest to see and promote their own self-interest against that of the wider context, they create an overassertive relation between figure and ground. Just as a face in a mirror is dependent on a host of conditions for its existence, such as the biological processes that create and sustain the face and the physical and cultural conditions required for the existence of the mirror, the defining features of organizations are dependent on a host of less obvious contextual relations that must be maintained if the organization is to continue to exist. The figure and its ground are part of the same system of relations, and exist only in relation with each other. In enacting and dealing with their environment in a egocentric way, organizations often do not understand their own complexity and the numerous recursive loops on which they depend for their very existence.

As a result of this kind of egocentricism, many organizations end up trying to sustain unrealistic identities, or to produce identities that ultimately destroy the contexts of which they are part.

A good example of the former is found in those firms making watches and typewriters that failed to take account of developments in digital and microprocessing technology. Seeing themselves as "watchmakers" or "typewriter firms," they continued in the production of traditional products with traditional technologies, failing to understand that these identities were no longer relevant or realistic. As a result, many were obliterated by new forms of competition. We can correctly say in retrospect that all firms serving the traditional markets *should have* seen and included the new developments as part of their environment. But this misses the important point: that their understanding of the environment was a product of their identity as watchmakers or typewriter manufacturers. To be successful they needed very different conceptions of themselves and of what their future might entail.

Good examples of how egocentricism can destroy the context on which an organization depends are found in many modern industries. For example, producers of toxic chemicals create all kinds of environmental and social hazards as a side effect of their interest in making profits. They implicitly treat the physical and social environment as a kind of external dumping ground, setting the basis for long-run problems that challenge their future viability. The pollution and health problems created by toxins are likely to eliminate or severely constrain the operations of this industry in the long term. Similarly, in agriculture the use of fertilizers, pesticides, fungicides, and other chemicals, and mechanized methods of farming, are bringing short-term profits while destroying the soil and other aspects of the ecology on which farming ultimately depends.

Egocentric organizations draw boundaries around a narrow definition of themselves, and attempt to advance the self-interest of this narrow domain. In the process, they truncate and distort their understanding of the wider context in which they operate, and surrender their future to the way the context evolves. Because of their truncated and distorted understanding, they cannot be proactive in a systemic sense. Their fate thus often rests in "seeing what happens" rather than in attempting to shape what happens. For example, the future of many firms in agriculture or the chemical business will depend on how government, consumers, and citizens will react to and punish their activities, rather than on systematic attempts to change themselves.

One of the strengths of the theory of autopoiesis is that it shows us that while the preservation of an identity is fundamental for all living systems, there are different ways in which closure in relation to the environment can be achieved. When we recognize that the environment is not an independent domain, and that we don't necessarily have to compete or struggle against the environment, a completely new relationship becomes possible. For example, an organization can explore possible identities and the conditions under which they can be realized. Organizations committed to this kind of self-discovery are able to develop a kind of systemic wisdom. They become more aware of their role and significance within the whole, and of their ability to facilitate patterns of change and development that will allow their identity to evolve *along with* that of the wider system.

TOWARD A NEW VIEW OF ORGANIZATIONAL EVOLUTION AND CHANGE

These ideas have important implications for how we understand the process of organizational evolution. For we see organizations as playing an active role in constructing their environment along with their own identities. All organizations are successful in creating identities of one kind or another, for in many respects the whole process of organizing is the realization of an identity. But some identities are likely to be more robust and enduring than others.

As organizations assert their identities they can initiate major transformations in the social ecology to which they belong. They can set the basis for their own destruction. Or they can create the conditions that will allow them to evolve along with the environment. For example, a chemical industry that has a systemic sense of identity could attempt to transform itself to eliminate the threat of toxics to the environment. As it is, however, many organizations eat away their future livelihood, creating the opportunity for new patterns of relations to emerge, but at the expense of their own future existence. Egocentric organizations see survival as hinging on the preservation of their own fixed and narrowly defined identity rather than on the evolution of the more fluid and open identity of the system to which they belong. It is often difficult for them to relinquish identities and strategies that have brought them into being or provided the basis for past success, yet this is what survival and evolution often requires. As in nature, many lines of organizational development can prove to be dead ends. While viable and considerably successful for a while, particular organizations or industries may experience a change in fortune as a result of who they are, and as a result of the actions and inactions this sense of identity encourages. In the long run, survival can only be survival *with*, never survival against the environment or context in which one is operating. Less egocentric conceptions of identity facilitate this process by requiring organizations to appreciate that they are always more than themselves. In seeing how one's suppliers, one's market, one's labor force, one's local, national, and worldwide community, and even one's competition are really parts of the same system of organization, it becomes possible to move towards an appreciation of systemic interdependence.

The challenge presented by the theory of autopoiesis is to understand how organizations change and transform themselves along with their environment, and to develop approaches to organization that can foster the kind of open-ended evolution discussed above.

If one wished to summarize the implications of the above argument in a kind of motto it might read, "Think and act systemically: more self-reflection, less self-centredness." An organization's self-image is critical in shaping almost every aspect of its functioning and in particular its impact on the context of which it is part, and thus organizations should give considerable attention to discovering and developing an appropriate sense of identity.

Recent interest in corporate culture has begun to grasp this. However, our discussion shows that the kind of self-image that an organization develops is crucial. While an egocentric image may lend an organization a clear and strong identity, and even considerable short-run success, in the long run it is likely to have many unfortunate effects. Indeed, it is important to put the issue more strongly than this. Egocentric corporate cultures that are strong and successful in the short run often achieve their success at the expense of their wider context, and in advancing themselves they are capable of destroying the whole. Our development of corporate culture should always be approached with this important point in mind.

The ideas discussed above highlight the key role of corporate strategy. However, it is in certain respects a more modest role than that advocated in much conventional theory. The corporate strategist is usually seen as someone in command, directing the path of corporate development. But the ideas presented here suggest that successful strategic development can never be unilateral. An individual or organization can influence or shape change, but the process is always dependent on complex patterns of reciprocal connectivity that can never be predicted or controlled. As in nature, significant combinations of chance circumstances can transform social systems in ways that were never dreamed possible. Robotization introduced to reduce costs of manufacturing can reverberate in its effects in completely unpredictable ways; a strategy for achieving one competitive advantage or competence can generate repercussions that eventually transform the system in other ways as well. The theory of autopoiesis suggests that the pattern of organization that unfolds over time does so in an open-ended and evolving way. Some forms disappear and others survive through transformations controlled by the self-referential processes that define the total system. Individuals and organizations have an ability to influence this process by choosing the kind of self-image that is to guide their actions and thus to help shape their future.

Loops not lines: the logic of mutual causality

The theory of autopoiesis encourages us to understand how change unfolds through circular patterns of interaction. Organizations evolve or disappear along with changes occurring in their context, and their strategic management calls for an understanding of this context. This requires that organizational members acquire a new way of thinking about the circular systems of relations to which they belong, and that they understand how these relations are formed and transformed through processes that are mutually determining and determined. In other words we are encouraged to think about change in terms of loops rather than lines, and to replace the idea of mechanical causality—e.g., that A causes B—with the idea of mutual causality, which suggests that A and B may be codefined as a consequence of belonging to the same system of circular relations.

Numerous cyberneticians have attempted to develop methodologies for studying this kind of mutual causality, and hence how systems engage in their own transformation. One of the most notable methodologies is found in the work of Magorah Maruyama, who focuses on positive and negative feedback in shaping system dynamics. Processes of negative feedback, where a change in a variable initiates changes in the opposite direction, are important in accounting for the stability of systems. Processes characterized by positive feedback, on the other hand, where more leads to more, and less to less, are important in accounting for system change. Together, these feedback mechanisms can explain why systems gain or preserve a given form, and how this form can be elaborated and transformed over time.

The power of this kind of thinking was dramatically illustrated in the Club of Rome's project on the predicament of mankind, which pioneered the idea that we should understand world economics as a system of loops. Their report *Limits to Growth* focused on trends in world population, pollution, food production, and resource depletion, suggesting that these are driven by loops of positive feedback. Their analysis demonstrated how systems of positive feedback that do not have stabilizing loops can result in exponential change that cannot be sustained in the long run.

The characteristics of this kind of change are beautifully illustrated in the story of an ancient Persian courtier who presented a chessboard to his king. In return he asked to receive 1 grain of rice for the first square on the board, 2 for the second, 4 for the third, and so on. The king readily agreed, ordering rice to be brought from his store. The fourth square required 8 grains, the tenth 512, the fifteenth 16,384, and the twenty-first topped the million mark. By the fortieth square a million million grains had to be brought forth. The entire rice supply was exhausted long before the sixty-fourth square was reached!

Exponential change is change that *increases* at a constant rate, in this case doubling at each stage. And the moral is easy to see. The change seems fine for a while, but soon runs completely out of control, just as a constantly increasing rate of pollution that begins by killing a few fish will soon kill them all. Many aspects of our socioeconomic system seem to be changing in this way, as attempts to maximize the rate of growth of specific economic and social variables generate changes that transform the whole system of relations in which the activity takes place.

Magorah Maruyama has developed this kind of loop analysis, showing how positive feedback accounts for the differentiation of complex systems. For example, a small crack in a rock may collect water, which freezes and makes the crack larger, permitting more water to collect and the crack to get bigger and bigger, allowing small organisms and earth to collect, a seed to grow, and the rock to be transformed by the growth of vegetation and perhaps even a tree. The runaway process creates differentiation, which may then be sustained in a given form by processes of negative feedback. Or, to take another of Maruyama's examples, a large homogeneous plain attracts a farmer, who settles on a given spot. Other farmers follow, and one of them opens a tool shop. The shop becomes a meeting place, and a food stand is established next to the shop. Gradually a village grows as merchants, suppliers, farmhands, and others are attracted. The village facilitates the marketing of agricultural products, and more farms develop around the village. Increased agricultural activity encourages the development of industry, and the village gradually becomes a city. In the process, the homogeneous plain has been transformed by a series of positive-feedback loops that amplify the effects of the initial differentiation.

The secret of the growth of the city, like the growth of the crack that collects water and vegetation, does not rest in any simple cause but in the deviation-amplifying *process*. Maruyama argues that this kind of process explains the evolution of both nature and society, processes of positive feedback producing changes that are quite out of proportion with the initial "kick" or incident that activates them. Initial kicks of high probability, e.g., that water will collect in a crack, or that a farmer will settle on a plain, escalate to produce deviations that have a very low probability, e.g., that a particular tree will grow in a particular crack, or that a city will develop at a particular point on a homogeneous plain. Random mutations in nature and accidental events and connections in social life, given favorable circumstances, initiate open-ended processes of self-organization in which positive and negative feedback interact to produce changing patterns that may at some point assume relatively stable forms.

The relevance of this kind of analysis for understanding the events and processes that shape organizations and their contexts is obvious. As illustrated in Exhibits 8.2, 8.3, and 8.4, the approach can be used to understand the dynamics of many different classes of organizational problems.

For example, Exhibit 8.2 presents a contextual analysis of some of the relations contributing to price inflation. Most analyses of this problem tend to fall into the trap of "thinking in lines," searching for simple causes that lie at the root of the problem. The level of employment, money supply, trade-union power, wage rates, interest rates, and government spending have all at one time or another been identified as the root cause. This linear thinking then sets the basis for linear solutions: e.g., create unemployment, reduce the money supply, reduce trade-union power, introduce wage restrictions, increase interest rates, or reduce government spending. The kind of contextual analysis diagramed in Exhibit 8.2 offers an alternative way of thinking about the problem by revealing the *pattern of relations* that create and sustain inflation. Our attention now is directed toward an understanding of how the network of positive-feedback loops that amplify price rises can be stabilized through negative feedback. Hence we are encouraged to find ways of redefining the total system to strengthen the pattern of relations that we wish to maintain.

Exhibit 8.3 illustrates how this kind of analysis can be used to understand some of the relations shaping a specific industrial sector—the power industry. As the diagram shows, a network of positive and negative feedback loops links the fortunes of many seemingly discrete elements of the industry. Quite often energy plans, even at a national

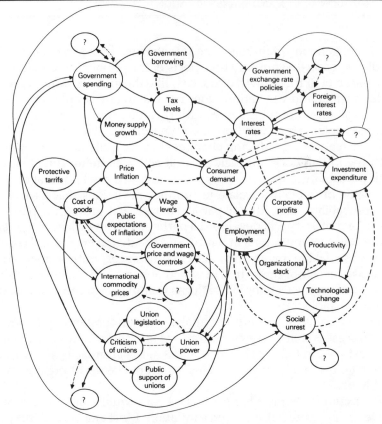

———— signifies positive feedback relations where more leads to more and less leads to less

◄---- signifies negative feedback relations where changes in one direction are associated with changes in the opposite direction.

When we understand the problem of price inflation as a system of mutual causality defined by many interacting forces, we are encouraged to think in loops rather than in lines. No single factor is the cause of the problem. Price inflation is enfolded in the nature of the relations that define the total system. Many of the links represented in this diagram are deviation-amplifying (heavy lines); negative-feedback relations (dotted lines) are more sparse. Positive feedback thus gains the upper hand. The system can be stabilized by strengthening existing negative-feedback loops and by creating others. Many government policies implicitly attempt to have this effect. For example, wage and price controls introduce negative-feedback loops that attempt to moderate the wage-price spiral. Government or media criticism of trade unions as unreasonable, greedy "villains" attempts to weaken the positive-feedback loop between public support and union power, in the hope that it will moderate the power of trade unions to negotiate higher wages.

In understanding this kind of mutual causality, we recognize that it is not possible to exert unilateral control over any set of variables. Interventions are likely to reverberate throughout the whole. It is thus necessary to adjust interventions to achieve the kind of *system* transformation that one desires.

Exhibit 8.2. Price inflation as a system of mutual causality

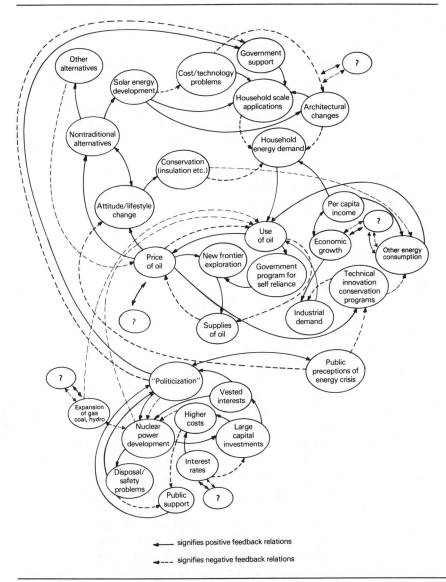

signifies positive feedback relations

signifies negative feedback relations

Exhibit 8.3. Positive and negative feedback in the power industry

level, are based on the capacities and responses of individual industries—coal, hydro, oil, nuclear power, gas. The demand for energy is often treated as an autonomous factor, the function of the various industries being to respond in an economic way. The kind of contextual analysis presented in Exhibit 8.3 allows one to arrive at a different way of formulating the dynamics through which the total system is evolving, and to formulate different corporate responses. It is possible to influence the pattern of relations generating demand as well as supply, and to design interventions that take advantage of the scope for collaborative action in the solution of shared problems.

Exhibit 8.4 applies the same kind of analysis to a set of more detailed organizational and interorganizational relations. The focus here is on how an initial kick, in this case the Watergate burglary, can reverberate in a way that transforms the wider context of relations, in this case the Nixon White House and the scene of American politics. The example chosen is rather an extreme one, but does serve to illustrate how organizational processes are shaped by negative and positive feedback. Sometimes the overall system of relations achieves a state of balance or orderly change, while in other instances positive-feedback relations can dominate and lead to the complete breakdown in existing configurations of relations. Such was the case of the Nixon White House. Examples of such transformation are more common than we realize, and are often the product of very ordinary kinds of behavior. For example, competitive behavior where rivals attempt to outmatch each other—as when aggressive acts evoke further aggressive acts—often sends the situation out of control unless systems of negative feedback intervene. Hostilities between individuals, departments, organizations, and nations often result in this kind of breakdown.

When we analyze situations as loops rather than lines we invariably arrive at a much richer picture of the system under consideration. There are many levels at which a system can be analyzed, and the choice of perspective will very much depend on the nature of the problem with which one is dealing. As noted earlier, systems always contain wholes within wholes, and one often finds that the problem with which one starts quickly becomes part of a larger problem requiring a broader focus. It is thus often necessary to supplement analysis conducted at one level (e.g., of socioeconomic trends at a macro level) with a richer picture of the dynamics of a set of relations that seem particularly important (e.g., organizational and interorganizational relations among a specific set of institutions). This broadening or deepening of analysis adds to the complexity of the overall picture, but often brings benefits in that it may identify new ways of solving the problems of specific concern. For when the problem is reframed, new opportunities often come into view.

In conducting this kind of analysis it may not always be possible to map the loops defining a system with the degree of certainty and completeness that one might desire. In complex systems the degree of differentiation is high, and there are usually numerous intervening processes shaping any given set of actions. However, the mode of thinking involved in this kind of analysis can itself be of considerable

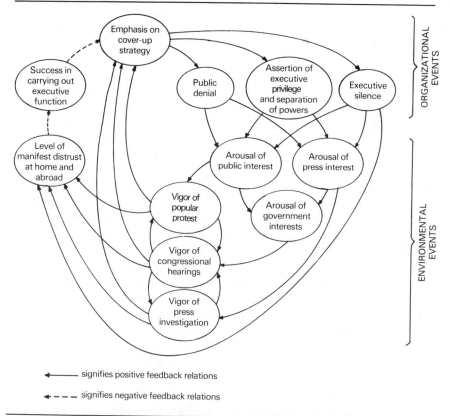

Exhibit 8.4. The Watergate affair: positive and negative feedback in the Nixon White House
SOURCE: Miles (1980: 214).

benefit. We have here a new epistemology for the management of complex systems that shows how we can grasp a better understanding of the processes shaping organizational life. Even though this understanding is neither complete nor perfect, it provides a powerful tool for guiding decisions and interventions.

Relations are always in flux, and stability (if there is indeed such a phenomenon in complex systems) always exists in the midst of flux. Complex systems, like the river described by Heraclitus, are always flowing on, and must be understood as process. The logic of such systems rests in the network of *relations* that define and sustain patterns of causality. Though it is often possible to spot an initial "kick" that sets a system moving in a particular direction, it is important to realize that such kicks are not really the cause of the end result. They merely trigger transformations embedded in the logic of the system. Thus we could say that the Watergate burglary caused the downfall of the Nixon presidency only in the sense that it set in motion processes and problems already embedded in the system.

One of the features of complex systems of mutual causality that include random components is that any given set of starting conditions can lead to different end points. Given other patterns of chance connection, the Watergate burglary might have come to nothing. Or some other trigger might have led to equally large problems for the presidency. As we have seen, random kicks combine with systemic relations to transform the system in unpredictable ways. Systems frequently move from kick to kick, one pattern of transformation being kicked into another. Thus a system like the nuclear power industry unfolds along one line of development until kicked by an incident like the Three Mile Island episode. The transformations stemming from this kick settle into a new pattern of relations that is eventually kicked by another incident or pattern of chance connections.

Our discussion again emphasizes the difficulties associated with contextual analysis, but also reaffirms the power of this kind of thinking. Conceptions of simple causality are just inadequate for understanding the dynamics of complex systems. As Anthony Wilden has noted, in complex systems there are always causes that cause causes to cause causes. By attempting to map system relations and identifying their principal tendencies, it is possible to acquire the appreciative understanding that Gregory Bateson has described as "systemic wisdom" and to frame interventions that attempt to influence the pattern of relations defining a system, rather than attempting to manipulate artificial "causes" and "effects." The best approach is often to (a) attempt to identify the principal subsystems or nests of loops that hang together, (b) modify their relations when necessary by reducing or increasing the strengths of existing linkages and adding or removing loops, and (c) give particular attention to the loops joining different subsystems. The latter are particularly important for understanding how local action can reverberate throughout the whole, and how one can restrict or amplify those effects when necessary. The quest for systemic wisdom thus carries concrete and important implications for the management of complex systems.

The development and practice of this kind of systemic wisdom requires an organizational capacity for appreciation and learning, and for the process of self-organization discussed in Chapter 4. An understanding of mutual causality in complex systems shows that it is extremely difficult to halt change, to eliminate all positive feedback, or to preserve a given mode of organization interminably. A more appropriate strategy is to learn to change with change, influencing and shaping the process when possible, but being sensitive to the idea that in changing times new forms of system organization must be allowed to emerge. This process often hinges on an ability to detect and avoid destructive system tendencies, which often lie in the vicious circles created by positive-feedback relations, to create space in which learning and patterns of coevolution can occur. In particular, attention needs to be given to the scope for collaborative action, to reduce the independent lines of activity that contribute to the complexity and turbulence of a system, and thus to broaden the opportunities for learning and mutual adjustment.

In understanding the logic of mutual causality we have a means of appreciating how the explicate reality of organizational life unfolds and is transformed on an ongoing basis. We also have a means of influencing that unfolding. However, as noted, that influence is never unilateral. It is always circumscribed by the wider system of relations in which it occurs.

Contradiction and crisis: the logic of dialectical change

Let's now move from the study of circular loops to the study of opposites.

Any phenomenon implies and generates its opposite. Day and night, hot and cold, good and evil, life and death, figure and ground, positive and negative are pairs of self-defining opposites. In each case the existence of one side depends on the existence of the other. We cannot know what is cold without knowing what is hot. We cannot conceive of day without knowing night. Good defines evil and life defines death. Opposites are intertwined in a state of tension that also defines a state of harmony and wholeness. Could this tension lie at the basis of all change? Could flux and transformation be a manifestation of contradictory tendencies through which phenomena change themselves?

This idea has a long history. For example, Taoist philosophy, which originated in ancient China, has long emphasized how the way of nature (the word *Tao* means Way) is characterized by a continuous flux and wholeness shaped by the dynamic interplay of *yin* and *yang* (Exhibit 8.5). These words, which originally denoted the dark and sunny sides of a hill, symbolize how the *Tao* is underpinned by a flow of complementary yet opposite energies through which all trends eventually reverse themselves. As the ancient sage Lao-tzu put it, "reversion is the movement of the *Tao*." Whenever a situation develops extreme qualities it invariably turns around and assumes opposite qualities, just as the brightest light of day begins to pass into the pitchest dark of

The dynamic character of *yin* and *yang* is illustrated by the ancient Chinese symbol called *T'ai-chi T'u*, or "Diagram of the Supreme Ultimate."

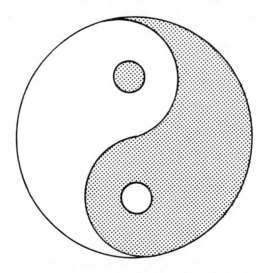

This diagram is a symmetric arrangement of the dark *yin* and the bright *yang*, but the symmetry is not static. It is a rotational symmetry suggesting, very forcefully, a continuous cyclic movement: The *yang* returns cyclically to its beginning, the *yin* attains its maximum and gives place to the *yang*. The two dots in the diagram symbolize the idea that each time one of the two forces reaches its extreme, it contains in itself already the seed of its opposite. From the very early times, the two archetypal poles of nature were represented not only by bright and dark, but also by male and female, firm and yielding, above and below. *Yang*, the strong, male, creative power, was associated with Heaven, whereas *yin*, the dark, receptive, female and maternal element, was represented by the Earth. Heaven is above and full of movement, the Earth —in the old geocentric view —is below and resting, and thus *yang* came to symbolize movement and *yin* rest. In the realm of thought, *yin* is the complex, female, intuitive mind, *yang* the clear and rational male intellect. *Yin* is the quiet, contemplative stillness of the sage, *yang* the strong, creative action of the king.

Exhibit 8.5. Yin and yang: the primordial opposites guiding all change
SOURCE: Capra (1975: 113-114).

---

night. Taoist philosophy emphasizes that all of natural and human life is shaped by this cycle of coming and going, growth and decay, everything being in the process of becoming something else.

The Taoists believed that the disposition or tendency of any situation could be understood in terms of *yin* and *yang*. And they believed that many human situations could be balanced and improved by influencing the relationship between these opposing elements. For example, a healthy and tasty diet attempts to reconcile *ying* and *yang*, and principles of acupuncture address disrupted flows between the *yin* and *yang* of the human body. The Taoist *I Ching* (meaning Book of Changes) formulates a way of thinking in terms of opposites, codifying archetypal patterns of the *Tao* found in the natural and social worlds. Although the *I Ching* is now often viewed as the equivalent of a crystal ball, to be used for predicting the future, its true function was to provide a means of understanding the tendencies inherent in the present. As such, it is a document that has much in common with modern attempts to understand the dynamics of transformation and change.

Many of these Taoist notions were brought into Western thought through the work of Heraclitus, and have been developed and expressed in different ways by generations of social theorists and scientists subscribing to what is now known as a dialectical view of reality. For example, they have had a strong influence on the work of Hegel, a nineteenth-century German philosopher who did much to advance the dialectical method, and on the work of social theorists like Karl Marx and Mao Tse-tung. These theorists developed the dialectical view that the world evolves as a result of internal tensions between opposites into a powerful theory of social change. For example, in the four large volumes of *Capital* Marx used the dialectical method to reveal how economic and social contradictions within a society provide a basis for its self-transformation.

It will be useful to focus on some of the work of Marx as an example of dialectical thinking. Since Marx was analyzing the society of his day, much of our attention will focus on the strains and tensions found under capitalism. But the method can be applied to the analysis of all kinds of societies and organizations, since the principle of dialectical opposition is a universal one.

DIALECTICAL ANALYSIS: UNDERSTANDING HOW SOCIETIES AND ORGANIZATIONS CHANGE THEMSELVES

At the risk of some oversimplification, the thrust of Marx's analysis and the nature of his conclusions can be understood as the expression of three dialectical principles. As Exhibit 8.6 suggests, these combine to provide a complex explanation of the processes that set the basis for both gradual and revolutionary kinds of change. Marx's method was to search for the primary tensions or contradictions shaping a given society, and to trace their repercussions on the detailed pattern of social life. In so doing, he identified the

Marx never wrote about the dialectical method employed in his work, preferring to demonstrate it in the concrete analysis of specific situations. Not surprisingly, his view of dialectical analysis has thus been subject to a wide range of interpretation. One of the clearest and most influential statements is found in Frederick Engels's *Dialectics of Nature*, which, despite its rather deterministic flavor, provides a useful perspective on how Marx's theory of social change relfects three principles:

1. The mutual interpenetration (struggle, or unity) of opposites.
2. The negation of the negation.
3. The transformation of quantity into quality.

The first principle accounts for processes of self-generated change whereby phenomena change themselves as a result of tension with their opposite. This principle underpins the idea of contradiction, and is used by Marx to explain how one social arrangement inevitably gives way to another. For example, an act whereby one person attempts to rule or control another tends to set up a process of resistance or countercontrol that undermines the initial attempt at control. The act of control *itself* sets up consequences that work against its effectiveness.

The second principle explains how change may become developmental in the sense that each negation rejects a previous form, yet also retains something from that form. Thus an act of control may be negated by an act of countercontrol, which is in turn negated by a further act of control (the negation of the negation) and so on. Each successive pattern of control will retain an element of the previous negation.

The third principle accounts for processes of revolutionary change whereby one form of social organization gives way to another. Marxists call them "totality shifts." In nature there are many processes where changes in quantity eventually lead to a catastrophic event leading to a change in quality. Water will absorb increases in temperature until the boiling point, when it changes into steam. A camel can be loaded with more and more weight until the final straw breaks its back. Similar processes can be observed in patterns of social organization. A process of control and countercontrol may continue until control is no longer possible, leading to a new phase of collaborative or destructive activity. Cumulative changes in society may thus provide the platform for a revolution that changes the underlying basis of that society.

When we combine these three dialectical principles we arrive at a rich and complex picture of the nature of change. Marx's analysis of society stresses that social arrangements generate inner contradictions that defeat the purposes for which they were set up, leading to a continuing pattern of negation and counternegation. The negation of the negation allows for the progressive development of the system until a limit is reached where its inner contradictions can no longer be contained.

These three principles help to explain the transformation of *all* social systems.

Exhibit 8.6. Three principles of dialectical change

"laws of movement" of a society, documenting how one stage of social organization inevitably passes into another.

Marx worked on the premise that one must begin by understanding the material conditions of life through which humans produce and reproduce their existence. Under the capitalist mode of production these conditions are found in the system of work organization where certain individuals employ others for the purpose of making a profit and accumulating capital. Marx thus analyzed the nature and implications of the process of capital accumulation as a means of revealing the basic contradictions and laws of movement that it generated.

To do this he examined the most elementary form of capitalist wealth, the simple commodity, tracing an inner contradiction between its "use value" (its value in terms of satisfying one's own needs) and its "exchange value" (its value as a product in the marketplace). In analyzing this contradiction Marx gave considerable attention to the concept of "surplus value," which arises when someone profits from discrepancies between use and exchange values. The acquisition of surplus value is the source of capital and wealth. Nowadays we typically view capital as a possession or entity, and view profit as a return for initiative and enterprise. Marx offers a different perspective, preferring to focus on how the making of a profit and the accumulation of capital place people in conflict with each other. He views these phenomena dialectically, in terms of the forces that pit buyers against sellers, emphasizing that the generation of surplus value always rests in an ability to pay less than one can get elsewhere, and thus always occurs at the expense of another partner in the relationship. As the Marxian economist Ernest Mandel has suggested, this dialectical appreciation of the nature of capital and wealth is captured in the ancient belief that Mercury, the god of trade (and etymological source of the word merchant), is also the king of thieves; and in the old anarchist slogan that "property is theft." Dialectically, capital, wealth, and profit are based on antagonisms that have a momentum of their own.

Marx's *Capital* illustrates these antagonisms in operation. For example, he shows how the generation of surplus value creates an opposition between the interests of capitalists and the work force. One of the distinctive features of industrial capitalism is that it attempts to increase surplus value through the use of labor power. This can only occur when the use value of labor to the employer, i.e., the value that can be generated by employing labor, exceeds the exchange value that has to be paid in the form of wages. Marx argues that the quest for surplus value thus naturally leads the capitalist to try to reduce the cost of labor. Historically, capitalists have done this in many ways: by increasing the length of the working day for the same wages; by attempting to reduce wage levels; by increasing the productivity of labor through better organization of work or through use of machines; by increasing the degree of control exercised over the use of labor time, e.g., through supervision; by using cheaper forms of labor whenever possible, such as women, children, migrant workers, or people in countries now known as the Third World; and by replacing labor by machines whenever profitable. The whole thrust of Marx's analysis is to show that an inner conflict is inherent in the nature of surplus value. He argues that the fact that capitalist production depends for its very existence on a difference between the use and exchange value of labor means that there will always be a struggle between capitalists intent on making a profit, and labor seeking better wages. The conflicts featured in Marxist theory—between capitalists and workers, management and unions, ruling class and working class, bourgeoisie and proletariat, producers and nonproducers, the economic base or "substructure" of a society and its political-ideological "superstructure"—all stem from the contradiction between use and exchange values inherent in surplus value and the nature of the simple commodity. For Marx, social life in capitalist society unfolds as a result of these basic contradictions.

Marx argues that the crises of capitalism are logical extensions of the same basic contradiction. For example, under conditions of market competition surplus value can be increased only by outperforming one's competitors. This often means that the goods one is producing must be sold at a lower price, leading firms to strive for economies in production or to enter or find new markets, for in itself a price reduction tends to reduce the rate at which surplus value is acquired, and if followed by one's competitors can remove surplus value altogether. Market competition thus tends to set firms in competition to find ways of reducing labor and other costs of production. Very often this will entail the use of new machinery, which often calls for extensive new capital investment. The attempt to increase surplus value thus often compels a firm to grow, and to place old capital at risk in the generation of new capital. However, the larger the capital investment, the smaller the average rate of profit, which always has a tendency to decline. In situations of high average profit new firms appear, leading to a lower rate of profit. The profitability of a firm's own expansion also eventually becomes subject to diminishing returns. The excess capacity and unprofitable nature of many sectors of advanced industrial economies are products of this harsh logic. The system adjusts by eliminating marginal firms and forcing reorganizations among the more successful. Very often it is the small enterprise that suffers most, for it does not usually have the resources to weather the storm. The crises of the capitalist system thus often leave their most obvious mark in the bankruptcy of small firms. Although the fates of individual firms may seem quite separate, they are in point of fact closely interlinked.

These crises are often accompanied by sharp conflicts with the labor force, since the efficiencies needed to achieve and sustain the required competitive advantage often have to be gained by increasing the productivity of labor by an amount greater than any increase in wages, or by replacing labor with machines. In both cases, the changes can often be achieved only through some form of struggle with the work force, especially when it is unionized. These struggles are intensified by the fact that the logic of capitalist production creates instability within the system. For example, in times of increasing business activity the demand for labor increases, often bidding up wage rates. However, the increase in wage rates tends to reduce the rate of surplus value. This makes labor less attractive and increases the profitability of labor-saving investments. The demand for labor declines, often creating a downturn in the business cycle. In this way, the quest for surplus value *produces* economic crises where boom times are followed by recession and stagnation. Marx thus suggests that the logic of the business cycle is enfolded in the logic of the capitalist system, and offers his own explanation of the origin of the inflationary processes illustrated in Exhibit 8.2.

Many of the conflicts that arise between capital and labor are thus not autonomous conflicts generated by the attitudes or actions of any single party, but products of the *relations* created by a system geared to the generation of surplus value. By and large the interests of capital are favored by processes and pressures that keep wage rates as low as possible, even though it is the relation between wages and prices that is most important, i.e., the relative rather than the absolute level of wages. The logic of the system makes employers feel that they have to keep wages low in order to stay in business, since without new efficiencies firms tend to lose their competitive advantage. But unless unions resist efficiencies that result in absolute or relative wage cuts, or unemployment, their membership will be moved around and bought and sold at will like any other commodity in the marketplace. No wonder therefore that management and workers so often become embroiled in bitter struggle; for the struggle on both sides is often a struggle for existence. Most often each sees the other as the enemy or villain in the plot. Thus employers attempt to undermine and control the power of unions whenever possible; unions tend to fight management at every turn, feeling that wage raises, even in response to increases in productivity, have to be extracted from the employer since they are rarely freely given.

We now see why Marx envisaged ongoing class conflict as a defining feature of the capitalist mode of production and argued that this antagonism would end only when the working class acquired control over the means of production. Marx saw this occurring gradually as the working class, a class organized and united by the capitalist process itself, acquired the capacity to move to communal organization, replacing exploitation based on a quest for surplus value with a mode of life emphasizing the expression and development of human capacities. His analysis of this process consistently emphasizes how the capitalist system produces its own downfall as a result of its own inner nature. The centralization of the ownership of capital and the means of production in fewer and fewer hands, a logical consequence of the drive to increase surplus value, centralizes and unites the work force. The system thus produces the "fetters" or countercontrols that make it stumble from crisis to crisis, and which, in Marx's view, ultimately provide the foundation for a transformation or "totality shift" whereby communal ownership of the means of production replaces capitalist private property. Marx's vision of the new society is shaped by the dialectical idea that the system of capitalist property, which negated the system of individual property (produced through the direct labor of its owner), will itself be negated by a system that retains certain achievements of the capitalist era, namely cooperation among people and concentration of the means of production (in a form of common ownership). This, of course, is the negation of the negation (Exhibit 8.6).

As we all know, this qualitative change in society has not occurred. (The USSR and similar state-dominated regimes do not fit the Marxist model, for like their capitalist neighbors, they too are based on the extraction of surplus value from their work force. They differ in terms of ideology and politics rather than basic economics.) From the point of view of Marx's critics this proves that Marx's analysis was wrong. From the point of view of his defenders, it shows only that Marx, who died in 1883, died too soon to take account of the sophisticated and resilient way in which the capitalist system would unfold, or of its ingenuity in managing its inner contradictions, at least temporarily. In support of their view they argue that many of his most important predictions have indeed stood the test of time—for example, his predictions with regard to the increased accumulation of capital, an increasing rate of technological progress, accelerating gains in the productivity of labor, the increased concentration and centralization of capital in fewer and fewer hands, the transformation of labor into wage labor and the decline of private entrepreneurship, the declining rate of profit, the increased rate of surplus value, a trade cycle fluctuating from boom to slump, and ongoing conflict between capital and labor, management and unions. This is quite remarkable when we realize that Marx wrote *Capital* at the dawn of the industrial age, when most modern economies were dominated by agriculture and small-scale enterprise, and before the age of large trade unions, multinational corporations, the radio, telephone, automobile, airplane, and significant automation. Marx failed to anticipate the rising standard of living among the majority of the Western working class, the development of the mixed economy, and the extent to which the state would intervene in the regulation of economic and social life, though he always argued that the role of the state was to serve the interests of capital.

In the view of Marx's defenders these omissions are minor compared with his achievements, and in any case do not negate the validity of his approach, since they merely call for an extension of his basic mode of analysis. Marx concentrated on analyzing the *major* contradictions enfolded in the logic of capital accumulation. This analysis is perfectly consistent with the idea that there may be many levels or nests of contradictions within the major contradictions, producing numerous sets of dialectical oppositions shaping the detailed patterns of development that unfold. Thus in a society shaped by the pursuit of surplus value, which pits labor against capital, we also find labor pitted against labor, capital against capital, men against women, white people against black, nation against nation, and so on. The dominant contradiction between labor and capital creates a framework within which other oppositions occur.

As we examine the detailed development of capitalism we see that its rich and developing texture is the product of this kind of dialectical logic. Thus in times of economic crisis and high unemployment it is not uncommon for the unemployed to see their particular condition as being produced by other elements of the labor force, e.g., by "immigrants who take our jobs," "labor unions who have made us too expensive," "women workers who are putting men out of work," rather than by contradictions within the economic system itself. In times of prosperity, developments that improve the well-being and status of the labor force emerge dialectically from oppositions nested within the dominant opposition between labor and capital. For example, union power creates political power, which establishes minimum wages and consolidates programs in the fields of education, health, and welfare, all of which may later act as fetters on the process of capital accumulation, creating fiscal and other crises within the system. To take another example, the contradictions of capitalism in Western societies have often been resolved by exporting them. Many of the old tensions between capital and labor, between ruling class and working class, are now reflected in an internationalized division of labor and internationalized class structure. The working class supporting many Western countries is now overseas in the Third World.

The refinement and resilience of the capitalist system owes much to this kind of dialectical development. Marx's analysis did not capture this richness, though its existence is perfectly consistent with his view of the nature of change. Historical experience leads us to see that Marx overestimated the ease with which the capitalist system would be replaced by a qualitatively different form of social organization, and it now seems more likely that the primary negation of capitalism will come from irreversible pollution of the planet, from pressures in the Third World, or from nuclear holocaust, rather than from a revolution initiated by the Western working class. Our society continues to evolve through dialectical processes, and the dialectical method of analysis pioneered by Marx remains a crucially important one, even though the precise pattern of social change is now unlikely to take the form he predicted.

LIVING WITH CONTRADICTION
AND MANAGING FLUX

The idea that Marx's writings belong to the realm of political ideology has become so ingrained in popular belief that it is often difficult for people to take a dispassionate view of his basic work. Yet when we strip away the crude sloganizing that characterizes so many views about Marxism, remembering that Marx himself declared that he was not a Marxist in order to emphasize how his work was being misinterpreted and abused, we can see that his mode of analysis is of immense power. Like the ancient Taoists, he was ultimately endeavoring to understand the ever-present dynamic through which the world changes itself, and like the Taoists, he developed a system of thought that invites us to see all change as the product of tensions between opposites. By analyzing these tensions we have a powerful means of understanding how our world unfolds, and can appreciate contemporary events and phenomena in a completely different light.

As we examine the broad sweep of industrial development in these terms we can see how the growing industrialization and urbanization of the nineteenth century in effect produced the unionized and militant labor force that then began to shape future industrial development. We can see how the dehumanization of work that accompanied industrialization produced the human-relations movement. We can see how the success and power of unions produced the internationalization of the labor force and the substitution of robots for labor. We can see how the success of these strategies in reducing costs of production produces unemployment in Western countries that removes the primary markets for which the products are manufactured. We can see how unemployment and the need to sustain consumption produces the welfare state, which, because it consumes surplus value, has to live off surplus value produced elsewhere, creating fiscal and other crises which reverberate in their effects throughout society. We can see how the wealth of the advanced countries produces the poverty and industrialized ghettos of the Third World. We can see how the pressure of industry in the Third World produces the demise of local agriculture as people leave the land to move to urban areas. We can see how the prosperity of the West may produce its own downfall with the rise of a Third World working class capable of taking ownership of the local means of production used in creating that prosperity. We can see how man's mastery of nature turns back on man, as problems of pollution, resource depletion, and general degradation of the environment threaten to dominate man himself.

In all these illustrations we are not talking about linear processes where A's cause B's. Rather, we are looking at self-generating oppositions where one side of the phenomenon tends to produce the existence of the other. Thus industrialization tends to produce unionization as a force opposing the process of industrialization. Wealth tends to produce poverty, which produces forces that undermine wealth. All phenomena generate latent tendencies and contradictions that tend to change themselves. Our habit of "thinking in lines," discussed earlier, tends to hamper our ability to think dialectically. We thus fail to appreciate how the seeds of the future are always enfolded in the oppositions shaping the present.

A dialectical imagination invites us to embrace contradiction and flux as defining features of reality. As with the theory of mutual causality, this leads us to think in terms of loops, but loops of a special kind in which we recognize that every action has a tendency to produce a movement in the opposite direction. This has important consequences for the way we organize in all spheres of life, encouraging us to recognize that the parameters of organization define the rallying points for disorganization, that control always generates forces of countercontrol, and that every success is the basis for a potential downfall.

In this kind of dialectical analysis it is important to consider which tensions and oppositions are primary and which are subsidiary, since, as we have already noted, oppositions tend to arise within oppositions, creating patterns of change where the importance of the primary opposition may be masked by a variety of more superficial differences. The successful analysis of change, and of the dispositions and tendencies inherent in the present, thus requires that we come to grips with the basic forces shaping organization and society. If Marx's analysis is correct, we may well find that these lie in the structures through which we produce and sustain our material conditions of existence, i.e., in our economics. Interestingly, many business men and women will readily agree with this. Marx's approach to social analysis is thoroughly consistent with many contemporary points of view. However, it urges us to go farther than just accepting the rules of contemporary economics as "facts of life," to analyze and understand the generative oppositions and tendencies enfolded in these rules.

When we begin to understand our world in these terms we inevitably raise a question regarding the extent to which our lives are determined by the logic of unfolding oppositions. Clearly, much experience in everyday life is shaped by forces over which we feel we have little control. A manager may feel that he or she has no option but to follow the rules of the market and general environment in shaping corporate policy. A worker may feel that job opportunities and career prospects are predetermined by his or her education or social background. In each case, the logic of "the system" or "the environment" is seen as being in the driving seat, those involved viewing themselves as players acting in accordance with a script determined elsewhere. This, of course, is the classic view presented in many interpretations of Marx's work. A truly dialectical understanding of the Marxist logic of change, however, offers a more optimistic scenario. While recognizing that if a passive attitude to social reality is adopted we are indeed likely to remain prisoners of the system in which we live, it also recognizes that, in principle, we may be able to exercise some influence over the logic shaping our actions. We can do this by attempting to reframe the tensions and oppositions underlying the forces shaping the system, and thereby influencing their direction. Here again, the distinction between primary and subsidiary oppositions becomes important. So long as our activities are geared to reframing the latter, then we have power only to make relatively superficial changes in our world. As Marx himself and other dialecticians have shown, significant and lasting change ultimately depends on an ability to reframe the primary oppositions within which the other surface opposites are set.

Dialectical analysis has major implications for the practice of social and organizational change. It invites us to think of ways in which oppositions between capital and labor, men and women, black and white, business and government, capitalism and communism, rich and poor nations, employed and unemployed, young and old, organization X and organization Y, and even production and sales can be reframed so that the energies generated by traditional tensions are expressed in a new way. Dialectical analysis thus shows us that the management of organization, of society, and of personal life ultimately involves the management of contradiction. This becomes most evident in times of crisis, when competing values and logics force their way to center stage, highlighting the contradictory tendencies shaping social reality. The resolution of such crisis invariably rests in the dominance of one or the other side or in some kind or reframing whereby differences find a new unity in relation to another opposition, e.g., when management and labor join forces to compete with a rival firm. Though many dream of a conflict-free existence, such a vision is unrealistic. A dialectical view of reality suggests that tension and contradiction will always be present, though they will vary in their degrees of explicitness and will take different forms according to the oppositions that are drawn. The choice that individuals and societies ultimately have before them is thus really a choice about the kind of contradiction that is to shape the pattern of daily life.

Strengths and limitations of the flux metaphor

We now often take change for granted, viewing it as an external force transforming the world around us and presenting us with all kinds of novel problems with which we have to cope. One of the major strengths of the images examined in this chapter is that they attempt to fathom the nature and source of change, so that we can understand its logic. This has immense significance for the way we understand and manage organizations. For if there is an inner logic to the changes that shape our world, it becomes possible to understand and manage change at a new and higher level of thought and action.

If we examine contemporary ideas about the management of change in writings on organization theory, we find that change is addressed on two levels. The first is mainly descriptive and attempts to identify and catalogue manifestations of change, e.g., in terms of discrete events influencing the nature, pace, and direction of technological, market, demographic, and other socioeconomic fluctuations. The second is more analytical and attempts to characterize change in terms of more abstract concepts such as its degree of uncertainty or turbulence. These efforts succeed in producing descriptions and classifications of the nature of change, but do not really explain its basic dynamic. They allow us to develop theories about how organizations can respond to different types of change, but they provide no indication as to how organizations can begin to influence the nature of the change that they encounter. To do this we need to move to the new level of thinking provided by the flux metaphor. We need to try and understand how the discrete events that make up our experience of change, and which we use in our classifications of the certainty or uncertainty of our environments, are generated by a logic enfolded in the process of change itself.

In understanding this logic we create new means of thinking about change and of dealing with change. For rather than attempting to deal with the manifestations of this logic, i.e., the discrete events that contribute to uncertainty, we can attempt to deal with the logic itself. In doing so, we begin to shape and guide the forces that we now often experience as belonging to an objective reality that appears independent of our own making.

The three images of change examined in this chapter provide alternative ways of thinking about the process and logic of change. As metaphors, they grasp different aspects of the flux shaping everyday life and encourage us to understand that flux in different ways: as an autopoietic manifestation of our own actions, as a network of mutual causality shaped by processes of positive and negative feedback, and as a dialectical process of unfolding contradiction. And they provide us with different ways of managing change. The autopoietic viewpoint suggests that we can best manage change by being more aware of the self-referential processes through which we organize and produce our environments, and that we may be able to *change the nature of change* by replacing egocentric images with ones that recognize our interdependence with others. The perspective of mutual causality develops a related viewpoint, encouraging us to give particular attention to the nature of relations and interconnections and to manage and reshape those relations to influence patterns of stability and change. The dialectical viewpoint encourages us to understand the generative oppositions that shape our world and to manage change by reframing these oppositions. Despite their differences, these three strategies have many complementary features and can no doubt be integrated to provide an extremely powerful means of influencing the logic through which we produce and reproduce the world in which we live.

The images explored in this chapter provide a means of examining what can be described as the "deep structure" of everyday reality. They invite us to understand our world as the manifestation of a deeper generative process, or, in David Bohm's terms, as the explicate or unfolded order of a more basic implicate reality. In this regard, there is a parallel with the ideas explored in Chapter 7, where it was argued that the everyday world can be understood as a manifestation of the unconscious. The distinctive contribution of the present chapter is to suggest that the hidden processes that ultimately shape reality are enfolded in the logics of change that create the totality of our existence. While this may sound somewhat metaphysical, as we have seen, this idea has very concrete implications.

For example, in much of science and everyday life we traditionally focus on explaining what is tangible and visible. In organizations managers have a similar frame of reference, formulating problems and solutions on the basis of the obvious empirical dimensions of the situations with which they are dealing. If the ideas explored in this chapter have substance, these traditional modes of understanding will fail to gain a full and effective appreciation of the situation they address unless they also grasp how these surface features of reality are shaped by the logic of change that produces them. To take a simple example, we might attempt to understand a conflict between labor unions and management over a decision to close an industrial plant as simply a clash of interests. Management wishes to close the plant for economic reasons. The union wishes the plant to remain open to preserve jobs for its members and to preserve the local community for which the firm provides a primary source of income. At a surface level we can say that they are in opposition because they seek different and perhaps incompatible ends. However, at a deeper level of analysis they may be found to be in opposition because of the interplay of hidden forces that create this sort of crisis.

In the 1970s and 1980s many industrial firms in traditional sectors of Western economies such as coal, steel, shipping, and heavy manufacturing have found themselves in this kind of crisis situation. As a result, management and unions in these industries have often been locked in fierce battle. By understanding the battle in terms of the forces shaping the stage of action on which it is fought, rather than in terms of the political maneuvering of those involved, we are encouraged to formulate the problem of plant closure as a symptom of a fundamental process enfolded in the logic of the industrial system. We see similar crises in other situations, for example, in health care and judicial services where fiscal crises create attempts to rationalize and streamline operations in ways that create other kinds of crises. For example, in hospitals the crisis takes the form of conflict between the requirements of efficiency and humanitarian and professional concerns, and in the courts there is obvious conflict between the requirements of efficiency and the equitable administration of justice and the rights and principles advocated by both citizens and the judiciary. As in the case of the closing of the industrial plant, we can see the problem as a simple clash of interests, or as a manifestation of the basic logic that drives the system.

The way one formulates basic problems is critical in determining the way they will be solved. To the extent that we focus on problems as clashes of interests we can only find solutions where there are winners and losers. Thus the firm closes its plant, leaving the community and government to deal with the unemployment. The drive for efficiency in health and legal services produces crises and anomalies in health-care and the administration of justice that are passed on to the community rather than solved by the services concerned. An understanding of a problem in terms of the logics of change that produce it, on the other hand, opens many different scenarios, often involving possible change in the logic of the system itself. Often this will lead to a new under-

standing of the interests represented in the problem, and a reformulation of the relations between those involved.

Typically such reformulation has to begin locally, through an examination of specific problems that may then be found to be connected
with wider systemic issues. These wider issues may need to be addressed on a broader front with others sharing the same concerns.
Thus local labor-management committees, established to find innovative responses to the decline of local industries, may eventually link up
with other similar groups interested in effecting some kind of structural change in the industrial system through broad-based community
and political action. Similarly, local legal groups dealing with local
problems may combine to influence the funding and structure of the
services with which they are concerned.

In thinking about logics of change we are encouraged to reflect on
the most fundamental assumptions influencing organization and society. Very often these assumptions are rooted in layers of ideology that
encourage us to accept them at face value. Under capitalism, various
kinds of social Darwinism endorse competition between individuals
and organizations as the most effective way of organizing society. In
communist states, various misinterpretations of Marxist theory are
used to legitimate systems of centrally based economic and social planning. Since the principles underpinning these different systems are
usually presented as a matter of ideological or political choice, the detailed consequences and inner logic of the alternative systems are
rarely subjected to critical analysis. One is encouraged to believe in the
virtues of one or the other. The ideas considered in this chapter suggest
that the deep structures of different ideologies imply and support different logics of change that can be analyzed in a systematic and rigorous way. Thus rather than merely accept Adam Smith's famous
assertion that capitalist systems are guided by an "invisible hand"
whereby the pursuit of individual interest is also advantageous to society as a whole, we can subject the logic of the capitalist system to detailed analysis. Rather than accept the beliefs of a Trotsky, Lenin, or
Stalin as recipes for making a good communist society, we can analyze
the logic and fundamental tendencies of such societies. The ideas examined in this chapter provide a concrete means through which this
can be done.

Finally, the overall thrust of this chapter leads us to see that many
social and organizational problems are unlikely to be solved in a piecemeal way. The reasons are implicit in what has been said above, but the
point is so important that it justifies further emphasis. Put simply, the
basic ideas discussed in this chapter all suggest that since problems
may be a natural consequence of the logic of the system in which they
are found, we may be able to deal with the problems only by restruc-

turing the logic. Thus, to take a simple example, the kind of egocentric and fragmented thinking whereby people implicitly view themselves as separate from their environment and externalize problems they do not wish to handle often has pathological consequences. A paper mill produces waste products as a consequence of its manufacturing process and is faced with a disposal problem. Rather than incur the costs of this disposal directly (which might be financially crippling), it dumps the products in a waste site. The wastes pollute the water supply, but it's someone else's problem to ensure that the water is made clean again. Though we may try to deal with this kind of problem through legislation that imposes fines upon the mill and through moral appeals for greater social responsibility, the basic problem rests in the logic that inclines the firm to think and act in this fragmented way. Given this kind of thinking, it is certain that new problems of a similar kind will appear, even if the immediate issue is resolved. There is a self-generating aspect to many contemporary problems, which we can tackle only by addressing the logic that produces them as problems. And this is precisely what the ideas explored in this chapter encourage us to do.

The flux metaphor does have some limitations. First, it can be argued that the approaches generated by this kind of thinking are far too idealistic. For example, any problem solutions that require a radical reframing of the logic of a social system are likely to encounter the resistance of the system. The ideology supporting a particular logic of change may eliminate the possibility of adopting others. If this is the case then our lot may be to remain prisoners of our underlying logics of change, even though they have pathological consequences that may ultimately destroy the viability of society itself. It is difficult to counter this determinism in an effective way. For even though humans in theory have an ability to choose the logics through which they are to produce and reproduce themselves, this does not mean that they always have the ability to make this choice effective in practice. The criticism is perhaps a pessimistic one, but contains a valuable warning in that the logic of certain lines of development may ultimately lead to dead ends, or more correctly, to patterns of change where the old forms of life are no longer recognizable.

A second potential criticism of the metaphor is that a full understanding of logics of change always depends on hindsight. However, this probably does not carry as much weight as the first weakness. While it is undoubtedly true that the logics of change explored in this chapter are much more powerful in explaining the past than in predicting the future, their successes in prediction are noteworthy. For example, as we have already discussed, many of the predictions in Marx's analysis of capitalist development have stood the test of time extremely well, despite some errors and omissions. Nevertheless, it is a mistake to place too much emphasis on a theory's ability to predict the future. We often forget that since we can judge a theory's predictive ability only in hindsight, its success in predicting the future is *always* unknown. In any case, as so many "futurists" now remind us, there is no such thing as *the* future; for in talking about futures, we are talking about possibilities. As human beings who are able to make choices, we have in principle the ability to shape and influence the future, at least to some degree. The ideas explored in this chapter help us to do this by showing how the characteristics of possible futures may be enfolded in the dispositions and tendencies of the present.

9

The Ugly Face

Organizations as Instruments of Domination

Our organizations are killing us!

Ramparts magazine noted many years ago that the Western world is slowly eating itself to death. Our food is often adulterated with thousands of different synthetic flavors, colors, thickeners, acidifiers, bleaches, preservatives, package contaminants, antibiotics, and poison pesticides. Food and tobacco companies spend billions of dollars each year promoting health-damaging products, thereby contributing to the high incidence of cancer and various forms of liver, kidney, heart, and lung disease. While many argue that the scientific evidence is not conclusive enough to ban other than the most obvious hazards, many scientists believe that we are dealing with a human time bomb, since the most damaging effects are likely to be long-term. Ingested toxins may well have an influence on mutations of the human gene pool, producing irreversible damage in generations to come.

Similar threats stem from environmental pollution. Every day industrial organizations spew millions of tons of toxic waste into our waterways or the atmosphere, or bury them in leaky containers underground. The economics of waste disposal are such that many organizations feel that they have no choice but to continue in these damaging practices so long as they remain legal. As a result, it is now estimated that as many as 2,000 toxins pollute the Great Lakes, and there are thousands of dangerous toxic-waste sites adding pollution to the groundwater. For example, over 160 such sites have been identified within three miles of the Niagara River, which feeds into Lake Ontario. The fish have cancer, and in areas of concentrated pollution such as the infamous Love Canal near the Niagara River, concern about pollution-related diseases among the local population is growing at a rapid rate. As in the case of food and tobacco production, human health is adversely affected by corporate practices that place profits before human welfare.

Working in many organizations can be dangerous too. Each year hundreds of thousands of workers throughout the world die of work-related accidents and illnesses. Over one hundred thousand deaths occur in North America alone. Hundreds of thousands more workers suffer from occupational diseases of varying severity, such as heart disease, eye strain, back pain, or lung ailments. And only the worst hazards are closely monitored or controlled. Others occur within the law, and are frequently treated as "inevitable" aspects of the lines of business in which they occur. Accidents and occupational disease, like pollution, are often viewed in a way that places more emphasis on the dollar than on the health of employees.

Throughout the Third World large multinational corporations often ride roughshod over the interests of local people. As in the early industrial revolution in Europe, people are legally and illegally dispossessed of their land and traditional ways of life, and transformed into an urban poor working for subsistence wages in sweatshops and factories. In the view of many analysts, the multinationals virtually rob their host countries of resources and labor power. At the same time they engage in modes of strategic management that increase the dependence of these countries on their continued presence. Industrial accidents, occupational disease, pollution, and general degradation of the people and the land continue to occur at a level that vividly reproduces the conditions of raw exploitation and human despair experienced in the worst industrial centers of England in the late eighteenth and nineteenth centuries. Again, the logic of economics and the imperative of making large profits tend to be the dominant concerns.

In all these illustrations we are talking about what former British Prime Minister Edward Heath once described as the "ugly face" of organizational life. Whether by design or by default, organizations do often have a large negative impact on our world. Our purpose in this chapter is to gain insight on this aspect of organization by exploring how organizations can be understood as instruments of domination. Though we are usually encouraged to think about organizations as rational enterprises pursuing goals that aspire to satisfy the interests of all, there is much evidence to suggest that this view is more an ideology than a reality. Organizations are often used as instruments of domination that further the selfish interests of elites at the expense of others. And there is often an element of domination in *all* organizations.

Organization as domination

Throughout history organization has been associated with processes of social domination where individuals or groups find ways of imposing their will on others. This becomes clearly evident when we trace the lineage of the modern organization from its roots in ancient society, through the growth and development of military enterprise and empire, to its role in the modern world.

Consider, for example, the incredible feat of organization, planning, and control required to build the Great Pyramid at Giza. It is estimated that its construction involved work by perhaps ten thousand persons over a period of twenty years. The pyramid is built from over 2,300,000 blocks of stone, each weighing two and one-half tons. These had to be quarried, cut to size, and transported over many miles, usually by water when the Nile was in flood. When we admire this and other pyramids today it is the incredible ingenuity and skill of the early Egyptians that probably strikes us, both from an aesthetic and from an organizational standpoint. From another standpoint, however, the pyramid is a metaphor of exploitation, symbolizing how the lives and hard labor of thousands of people were used to serve and glorify a privileged few.

In the view of some organization theorists this combination of achievement and exploitation is a feature of organization throughout the ages. Whether we are talking about the building of the pyramids, the running of an army, a multinational corporation, or even a family business, we find asymmetrical power relations that result in the majority working in the interests of the few. Of course, important differences in practice can be observed, and over the ages much has changed. The conscription and slavery that provided much of the labor power required to build pyramids and empires has given way to use of paid employment where employees have the right to leave. Slave drivers have given way to managers. And employees now typically work in the interests of shareholders rather than of pharaohs, emperors, or absolute monarchs. However, in all cases, pursuit of the goals of the few through the work and labor of the many continues. Organization, in this view, is best understood as a process of domination. And the varied organizations observed in history and the modern world are best understood as instruments that reflect variations in the *mode* of domination employed.

This aspect of organization has been made a special focus of study by radical organization theorists inspired by the insights of Karl Marx and two other very famous sociologists: Max Weber and Robert Michels. As was discussed in Chapter 2, Weber is famous among organization theorists for his work on the nature of bureaucracy. But his main concern was to understand how different societies and epochs are characterized by different forms of social domination. He viewed bureaucracy as a special mode of social domination, and was interested in the role of bureaucratic organizations in creating and sustaining structures of domination.

For Weber, domination can occur in several ways. First and most obviously, domination arises when one or more persons coerce others through the direct use of threat or force. However, domination also occurs in more subtle ways, as when a ruler can impose his or her will on others while being *perceived as having a right to do so*. This is the kind of domination that most interested Weber, and much of his effort was devoted to understanding the process through which forms of domination become legitimized as normal, socially acceptable power relations: patterns of formal authority in which rulers see themselves as having the *right* to rule, and those subject to this rule see it as their *duty* to obey.

As a result of his historical studies Weber identified three types of social domination that could become legitimate forms of authority or power. He called these the charismatic, the traditional, and the rational-legal (Exhibit 9.1). He believed that a ruler's ability to use one or another of these kinds of authority depended on his or her ability to find support or legitimation in the ideologies or beliefs of those being ruled. And the ability to place this authority on a firm base depended on an ability to develop an appropriate administrative apparatus to provide a bridge between the ruler and the ruled. Thus, he believed that each mode of domination was accompanied by a particular kind of legitimacy and by a specific form of administrative organization.

Weber recognized that these three types of domination are rarely found in their pure form, and that when the different kinds of authority impinge on one another, the result is often an uneasy tension. Weber was much concerned by the trend towards increasing bureaucratization and rationalization. For him, the process of bureaucratization presented a very great threat to the freedom of the human spirit and the values of liberal democracy, since those in control have a means of subordinating the interests and welfare of the masses. Hence his view that bureaucracy could all too easily turn into an iron cage. He

---

Charismatic domination occurs when a leader rules by virtue of his or her personal qualities. Legitimacy of rule is grounded in the faith that the ruled vest in the leader, e.g., as a prophet, hero, heroine, or demagogue. The administrative apparatus under this mode of domination is very loose, unstructured, and unstable, usually working through the activities of a few disciples or intermediaries.

Traditional domination occurs when the power to rule is underwritten by a respect for tradition and the past. Legitimacy is vested in custom and in a feeling of the "rightness" of traditional ways of doing things. People thus often command power as a result of inherited status, as in systems of monarchy or family succession. The administrative apparatus under this mode of domination typically takes two forms— *patriarchal* or *feudal*. In the former the officials or administrators are usually personal retainers—servants, relatives, or favorites—dependent on and remunerated by the ruler. In the latter the officials retain a measure of independence. In return for giving their allegiance to the ruler they are usually allowed autonomy within a specified sphere of influence, and are not directly dependent on the ruler for remuneration or subsistence.

Under the mode of *rational-legal domination*, power is legitimized by laws, rules, regulations, and procedures. The ruler can thus only attain legitimate power by following the legal procedures that specify how the ruler is to be appointed. The power is also formally bounded by rules. The typical administrative apparatus is the bureaucracy, a rational-legal framework in which formal authority is concentrated at the top of the organizational hierarchy. In contrast with the feudal case, the means of administration do not belong to the bureaucrat: his or her position can neither be inherited nor sold. There is a strict separation between private and official income, fortune, and life generally.

Exhibit 9.1. Weber's typology of domination
SOURCE: Mouzelis (1979: 16-18).

---

saw bureaucracy as a power instrument of the first order and believed that where the bureaucratization of administration is completely carried through, a form of power relation is established that is "practically unshatterable."

Similar concerns have been voiced by the French sociologist Robert Michels, who saw in the politics of bureaucratic organization distinct oligarchic tendencies. In his famous "iron law of oligarchy" he developed the view that modern organizations typically end up under the control of narrow groups, even when this runs against the desires of the leaders as well as the led. In his study of supposedly democratic organizations, such as trade unions and political parties, he found that the democracy was often no more than window dressing. Despite the best intentions these organizations seemed to develop tendencies that gave their leaders a near monopoly of power. As leaders rise to power they tend to become preoccupied with their own way of looking at things, and it seems that the most that can be hoped for is that they will attempt to keep the interests of their members in mind. But in Michels's view, even democratically elected leaders with the best intentions have a tendency to become part of an elite furthering their own interests, and to hang onto their power at all costs. Hence he was very pessimistic with regard to the domineering character of modern organization, in a way that parallels the pessimism of Weber.

The real value of these perspectives is that they show how even the most rational and democratic forms of organization can result in modes of domination where certain people acquire and sustain a commanding influence over others, often through subtle processes of socialization and belief. To take Weber's ideas as an illustration, we can become dominated by such basic and hidden forces as those underpinning the quest for rationality. Indeed, for Weber the process of rationalization is itself a mode of domination. As we become increasingly subject to administration through rules and engage in strict calculations relating means and ends and costs and benefits, we become increasingly dominated by the process itself. Impersonal principles and the quest for efficiency tend to become our new slave drivers.

These ideas resonate with those of Karl Marx, especially those discussed in Chapter 8. For Weber the logic driving modern society is found in the process of domination through rationalization. For Marx it is found in the domination generated by the quest for surplus value and the accumulation of capital. In recent years, many "radical" theorists and researchers have become very interested in the links between these different insights and in the way the process of rationalization is often used to serve the interests of capital accumulation. Collectively, their work brings the ideas of Marx and Weber right up to date, showing how organization in the modern world is based on processes of domination and exploitation of many kinds. In the remainder of this chapter we will explore the ideas of these radical organization theorists, focusing on how the forces of domination embedded in the ways we organize often lead organizations to exploit their employees and the social and economic contexts in which they operate.

How organizations use and exploit their employees

Arthur Miller's well-known play *Death of a Salesman* explores the tragic life and death of Willy Loman.

Willy has been a salesman with the Wagner company for thirty-four years, traveling through New England year after year as Wagner's "New England man." However, at the age of sixty Willy feels that he can no longer cope with the demands of life on the road. After a number of nervous breakdowns he reluctantly decides to ask for a posting in New York City, so that he can work at his home base. His family has grown up, and his financial needs are modest. He thus feels confident that Wagner's will be able to find a niche for him, even though his sales performance is nowhere near what it once was.

However, on raising the subject with Howard Wagner, Willy is rudely disappointed. Howard has little time for Willy's plight. Willy talks about his time with the firm, his close association with Howard's father, and the promises that had been made. But it has no effect on Howard. Within a matter of minutes Willy finds himself suggesting that his wages could be reduced from sixty-five dollars per week to fifty and finally to forty since he only needs to earn enough to get by.

Howard is uncomfortable with Willy's pleading but insists that there's no room for favors. After various attempts at escaping the situation by claiming that he has no more time and must move on to his next appointment, Howard finally ends the conversation by telling Willy that the company no longer needs him. Willy is shattered. He feels like "an empty orange peel." The company has eaten thirty-four years of his life as if it were a piece of fruit, and is now throwing the rest of him away.

He ends up committing suicide.

Miller's play stands as a metaphor for the way organizations often consume and exploit their employees, taking and using what they need while throwing the rest away. Of course, there are exceptions. But many workers and managers at all levels of organization find their health and personal lives being sacrificed on the altars created by modern organizations. Willy's story, though extreme in its end result, is not necessarily extreme in substance. In the world today, individuals and even whole communities find themselves being thrown away like empty orange peels when the organizations they serve have no further use for them. Individuals find themselves permanently unemployed even though they feel that they have many good years of useful work ahead of them. Communities find that they are unable to survive once the organizations on which they have depended for their economic livelihood decide to move their capital elsewhere. Increasingly, many managers find themselves ending lives of workaholic involvement with their employer as the victims of cutbacks or "early retirement plans." Even though cushioned by "golden handshakes" and comfortable pension plans, the blow to their ego and self-confidence can be shattering. Somewhat ironically, those with the most privileged access to important information or with pivotal positions in their companies are often those who receive the hardest blow. Many important executives, on being told that they are no longer needed, are also told that their termination is immediate. They will not be required to turn up at work ever again, because, despite their glowing reputation, the organization fears that resentment may lead them to carry away documents that could be used to help competitors or to damage the organization in some way. In these cases, insult is added to injury.

In the opinion of many radical organization theorists, while we have advanced a long way from the naked exploitation found in slavery and in the developing years of the industrial revolution, the same pattern of exploitation continues today in a more subtle form. They find particularly striking evidence of this in the way organizations structure job opportunities to produce and reproduce the class structure of modern societies; in the way organizations approach the problems of hazardous work situations, industrial accidents, and occupational disease; and in the way organizations perpetuate structures and practices that promote workaholism and associated forms of social and mental stress.

ORGANIZATION, CLASS, AND CONTROL

A strong case can be made for the idea that organization has always been class-based. The first types of formal organization probably arose in hierarchical societies where one social group imposed themselves on another, often through conquest. Such societies became further stratified as certain individuals placed themselves in the service of the ruling class as priests, scribes, bookkeepers, traders, and merchants. Since these people were not involved in producing the goods necessary to sustain their livelihood, they formed an intermediate class of people between the ruling class and the peasants or slaves involved in the actual production of goods. We find the same system reproduced in modern organization in terms of the distinctions between owners, managers, and workers.

Thousands of years intervene between the emergence of the first formal organizations and the corporations that we see around us today. These embrace many major social epochs in different parts of the world. We can pick up the story in the period of the industrial revolution in Britain around the 1760s, and in the industrialization of the United States from the early 1800s. Though the two countries began the process of industrialization in very different circumstances, there are many common links in the way growing industrialization develops and extends the tripartite class system handed down from earlier times.

As is well known, the industrial revolution in Britain was set against the background of an agrarian society with a "domestic" or "cottage" system of production, supplemented by a small amount of mining and construction and a system of industrial workshops run by merchant-craftsmen organized in craft guilds. These workshops were typically stratified according to skill and status, in terms of masters, journeymen, and apprentices. The guilds controlled entry and working conditions and managed to secure a reasonable livelihood for their members, especially when compared with the poor farmers or landless poor who had lost their source of livelihood as a result of the enclosure of land during the sixteenth century. The industrial revolution changed this picture as capitalist producers sought to overcome the uncertainties of output and quality associated with domestic production; to serve the new markets created by expanding world trade and a growing population (certain privileged sectors of which had a rising standard of living); and most important of all, to take advantage of mechanical systems of production. The development of factory production transformed the structure of the work force and intensified the growth of urban areas. Increasing numbers of people who had formerly been self-employed in workshops and cottage industry, often on a subcontracting basis, assumed new roles as part of an emerging wage-earning class. Labor increasingly became viewed as a commodity to be bought and sold. And since these changes eliminated earlier systems of production, for the new wage earners the process was irreversible, making them dependent on the wage system.

Similar developments occurred in the United States, though the emergence of a class of wage earners was hampered by the availability of land. At the beginning of the nineteenth century capitalist production for profit using wage labor was insignificant outside the major cities. Most of the population lived in rural areas, and over 80 percent of the labor force was employed in agriculture, over 20 percent being slaves and indentured laborers. About 80 percent of the nonslave work force were property holders and professionals—farmers, merchants, craftsmen, small manufacturers, doctors, lawyers, and others. Slavery remained important in agriculture for most of the century—there were almost four and one-half million slaves in 1860—and even after emancipation many continued in feudal servitude under sharecropping and other systems of farming. In manufacturing, however, systems of capitalist production had an increasing impact throughout the nineteenth century, replacing cottage industry and small business with a system of wage labor. Immigrants, Indians, women and children, and displaced artisans and agricultural workers swelled a labor force which, as in Britain, found it increasingly difficult to find alternative sources of livelihood. Thus, as the figures in Exhibit 9.2 demonstrate, historically the growth of capitalist organization has always been accompanied by a decline in the number of self-employed persons and an increase in the number of wage and salary earners.

The growth of a capitalist system of production depends on the existence of a supply of wage labor, unless it is to rely on slaves or on some system of subcontracting, both of which have problems. Slavery often runs against important social norms and can be inefficient, and subcontracting can be highly unpredictable from the capitalist's standpoint. Early capitalism in North America combined elements of these different systems, but as the century progressed, a consistent trend toward the use of wage labor occurred—and with it the rise of the profession and activities of management as we know it today.

In many respects, it is possible to say that the system of wage labor created modern management, since for the first time outside systems of slave labor, profits depended on efficiency in the use of labor time. Under the systems of domestic manufacture and subcontracting, the

Year	% wage and salaried employees (b)	% self-employed (c)	% salaried managers and administrators	Total labor force (a)
1780(d)	20.0	80.0	---	100.0
1880	62.0	36.9	1.1	100.0
1890	65.0	33.9	1.2	100.0
1900	67.9	30.8	1.3	100.0
1910	71.9	26.3	1.8	100.0
1920	72.9	23.5	2.6	100.0
1930	76.8	20.3	2.9	100.0
1939	78.2	18.8	3.0	100.0
1950	77.7	17.9	4.4	100.0
1960	80.6	14.1	5.3	100.0
1969	83.6	9.2	7.2	100.0
1974	83.0	8.2	8.8	100.0

(a) Defined as all income recipients who participate directly in economic activity; unpaid family workers have been excluded.
(b) Excluding salaried managers and administrators.
(c) Business entrepreneurs, professional practitioners, farmers, and other property owners.
(d) Figures for 1780 are rough estimates. Slaves, who comprised one-fifth of the population, are excluded; white indentured servants are included in the wage and salaried employees category.

Exhibit 9.2. The changing structure of the U.S. labor force
SOURCE: Reich (1978: 180). Reprinted by permission.

profit of the merchant-capitalist who bought and sold the goods produced did not necessarily depend on how the goods were produced. The merchant paid an appropriate price and lived off the profit margin. Great inconvenience arose when private producers failed to deliver the appropriate quantity or quality on time, but the problems involved were outside the merchant's direct sphere of interest. With the appearance of the factory system, however, every second of wasted time or inefficient use of time represented a loss of profit. The employment of wage labor thus led the capitalist to place primary emphasis on the efficiency of labor time, and to seek increasing control over the process of production. The establishment of a wage system thus carried with it implications for the organization of the labor process, and as a corollary, institutionalized class divisions in the workplace, particularly between managers involved in the design and control of work (who may themselves be controlled by other managers) and the work force directly engaged in productive activity.

The radical organization theorist thus emphasizes the close links that exist between organization, class, and control. If we examine the history of work organization since the beginning of the industrial revolution, we find a common pattern in both Europe and North America. The development of a system of wage labor tends to be followed by increasingly strict and precise organization, close supervision, and increasingly standardized jobs. Skilled and semiskilled workers are increasingly replaced by cheaper unskilled workers, leading to what is sometimes described as a "degradation" or "deskilling" of work and a "homogenization" of the labor market.

As was discussed in Chapter 2, mechanical systems of production operate most efficiently when there is a plentiful supply of standardized, easily designed, replaceable parts. The deskilling and routinization of jobs that accompanied the development of the factory system throughout the nineteenth and early twentieth centuries was an essential aspect of the mechanization process. It served to increase managerial control over the work force, to reduce labor costs, and to facilitate centralization of the planning and control of work. The effects of this homogenization and deskilling are still very much evident. Taylorism and the mechanization of production have produced vast numbers of jobs of very uniform skill levels, the special characteristics of which can be quickly learned. One recent estimate suggests that in some modern organizations 87 percent of manual workers exercise less skill in their jobs than they use in driving to work, and that most jobs could easily be performed by most workers.

This homogenization of work, however, created its own problems in the form of an indispensible work force with a strong sense of shared interests. This quickly set the basis for a militant class consciousness expressing itself through strong unions. As time advanced, therefore, new strategies of control became necessary. In the view of many radical organization theorists these strategies effectively fragmented class consciousness by creating and emphasizing differences and institutional divisions among various kinds of workers. The divisions are most clearly reflected in the distinction labor economists now draw between "primary" and "secondary" labor markets, and in the segmentation of labor markets into different occupational groups. The result has been to construct organizations with unequal levels of privilege and opportunity, and to fragment a work force that might otherwise be united.

To understand the radical theorists' arguments, it is necessary to understand how the growth in the size of organizations, particularly from 1890 on, changed capitalism in Europe and North America from a competitive to an oligopolistic structure dominated by a few large bureaucratic organizations surrounded by many smaller ones. These organizations typically had large capital investments in factories and many fixed costs, leaving expenditure on labor as the main variable item. Therefore, there was a great incentive for organizations to develop a system that would allow labor to bear the vagaries of the business cycle and other changing circumstances by adjusting the size and cost of the work force to suit the organizations' immediate needs. The existence of a homogenized labor market with a pool of interchangeable workers helped in this. However, from the corporate standpoint much more was needed. All labor does not have the same value, since that employed in some roles requires more training and development than that in others. In this sense some labor is like capital: it calls for an investment which, once made, becomes a fixed cost. The dualism between capital and labor reflected in the distinction between fixed and variable costs thus highlights a distinction *within* the labor force between what are known as "primary" and "secondary" labor markets.

The primary labor market is a market for career-type jobs that are especially crucial, or which call for a high degree of skill and detailed knowledge, often of a corporation-specific nature. This market has grown along with the proliferation of bureaucratic and technocratic enterprises whose members are enticed to work not only for money but for nonmonetary rewards such as job satisfaction, the promise of career advancement, and security of employment. Very often members of such labor markets are expected to become committed and loyal to their employer, who has an investment in such people. Corporations often develop distinctive means of fostering commitment and loyalty, and often use extensive and rigorous selection mechanisms to eliminate high-risk candidates. The selection practices of firms such as IBM provide obvious examples. If you can pass the IBM recruitment and training programs, the firm can be pretty certain that you will remain an "IBMer."

The secondary labor market, on the other hand, is a market for lower-skilled and lower-paid workers in offices, factories, and open-air work. It calls for little capital investment in the form of training and education, and workers can be hired and fired along with the vagaries of the business cycle. This type of labor provides a "buffer" that allows the organization to expand output in good times and to contract in bad, leaving the organization's operating core and elite primary labor force unaffected by many fluctuations occurring in the world at large. The existence of the two categories of labor gives an organization a great deal more control over its internal and external environment than it would otherwise have. The fact that primary workers are committed to the firm increases the predictability of its internal operations, while the existence of the secondary buffer facilitates its general ability to adapt. However, this means of control creates a differential system of status and privilege within the organization that parallels and sustains broader class divisions outside. It means that the vagaries of the business cycle have the harshest effects on the poorer sections of society who belong to the secondary sector, and on special groups such as women, ethnic minorities, the handicapped, and poorly educated youth, who form a large part of this labor market.

While the distinctions between primary and secondary markets are clear for all to see, their structure has been complicated by various kinds of segmentation. First, both markets are segmented by numerous occupational divisions within professional, trade, and unionized groupings. Many of these divisions are highly arbitrary in substantive terms, being maintained by institutional boundaries that limit entry to people with specific credentials or qualifications. Second, important distinctions have appeared in the primary market between jobs that are relatively independent, in that the holder has a great deal of autonomy and scope for exercising initiative, and jobs that place people in subordinate and dependent roles. These different types of jobs are frequently subject to different types of control. With the growing sophistication of bureaucratic and computerized controls, many people in the primary labor market have become more and more subject to the kinds of close control originally developed to monitor workers in the secondary market. For example, managers and many office workers increasingly find themselves constrained by job requirements, management-by-objective schemes, and performance ratings that make them no more than functionaries in a wider system of tasks.

The common principle underlying all these kinds of labor-market segmentation seems to be that of control. In order to enhance the predictability of internal operations organizations have found it increasingly necessary to specify the characteristics of different jobs and the qualifications that are required, creating separate patterns of opportunity for different groups of people. Many radical organization theorists see this as a deliberate policy of "divide and rule" that gained ground after the labor militancy of the 1930s. Others argue that the fragmentation is due as much to the activities of professions and unions as to management policy, in that these groups have been eager to advance their own interests by emphasizing their distinctive qualities. Thus professions and unions have promoted artificial barriers to entry into different types of work, and have created hierarchical patterns that identify seniority within their ranks. For example, it is not uncommon for professions to splinter or to create a group of lower-qualified professions below them so that their own status and sense of exclusivity is advanced. Unions also make much of their differences and insist on periods of apprenticeship before admission to full membership. While there can be little doubt that much of the drive towards segmentation has been fueled by these activities, the radical theorists argue that this is still consistent with a deliberate corporate strategy that has encouraged unions and other groups to buy into a structure of corporate control. For example, since the 1930s corporations have allowed unions and professional groups to have an influence on the definition of occupations and the qualifications that are appropriate. In the process these groups have been able to serve their own interests, but at the expense of the possibility of presenting a united front on behalf of labor against the interests of capital. As unions have become coopted into the structure of control they have reduced their ability to shape corporate strategy, contenting themselves with regulating changes in their working conditions and with advancing monetary interests and fringe benefits.

Whatever position one takes on the "divide and rule" issue, segmentation has had a decisive influence on opportunity structures in society, creating or at least perpetuating the class divisions referred to earlier. People in different labor markets often find themselves fighting each other to protect their own interests, rather than seeing their situations as being produced by the system that places them in opposition. This fragmentation has undoubtedly had an important impact on political consciousness, in terms of the concerns and aspirations of different occupational groups and the perception of class relations. On the one hand, segmentation has reduced class consciousness in favor of occupational, professional, trade, or even factory consciousness. Many people increasingly understand their place in society in relation to their occupational roles rather than in terms of class. On the other hand segmentation, especially that between primary and secondary workers, has emphasized class divisions, because the distinction often emphasizes the difference between the so-called middle class and disadvantaged groups of poor whites and ethnic minorities.

For example, if we examine the occupational structures of many Western societies we find that on average people with dark skins have a greater chance of having to perform dirty work for relatively low wages, with little security of employment and few fringe benefits. Secondary-sector jobs are usually left for those who can't get any other. Employment patterns in this sector of the economy thus end up reflecting social attitudes and patterns of prejudice and discrimination in society as a whole. Discrimination often operates by blocking access to desirable jobs, thus forcing minority groups such as blacks, Hispanics, native people (such as American Indians or Eskimos), or immigrant workers into the secondary sector. Some European countries have institutionalized this pattern by allowing migrant or "guest" workers from other countries to enter the work force on temporary visas to perform the jobs that no one else wants. It is estimated that as many as ten million migrant workers are employed in Europe, making up as much as 11 percent of the work force in Germany and 27 percent in Switzerland. Historically, the ranks of the British working class have always been swelled by immigrants, most recently by immigrants from the West Indies, India, Pakistan, and other European and Commonwealth countries. In the United States it is estimated that anywhere between 2 and 12 percent of the labor force consists of undocumented workers from Mexico, the Caribbean, and elsewhere. And, of course, black workers have formed a substantial part of the working class ever since the days of slavery. Since the 1920s they have become increasingly involved in manufacturing and service-sector jobs, and despite affirmative action programs, still remain overrepresented in the secondary labor market.

Institutionalized discrimination? Or an unintended consequence of industrial development? The debate continues. It is clear that even though the domination and exploitation of disadvantaged groups may not be a stated aim of the modern corporation, many corporate policies and practices have this effect. Despite many major advances, the implicit or explicit exploitation of employees persists. Modern organizations play an important part in creating and sustaining a working class of "secondary" labor, in the deskilling of work, in the systematic production of inequality, in the segmentation of labor markets, and in the institutionalization of discrimination. In creating and reinforcing the market system for labor they inevitably reinforce a power structure that encourages people with certain attributes while disadvantaging others. And in developing differential patterns of control for employees from different sectors, they produce patterns of favor and privilege that symbolize, and hence reinforce underlying socioeconomic divisions. No wonder, therefore, that the radical organization theorist is so critical of the domineering role of modern corporations in producing the ills and inequities of modern society.

WORK HAZARDS, OCCUPATIONAL DISEASE, AND INDUSTRIAL ACCIDENTS

In one of the most vivid and moving chapters of *Capital* Karl Marx gives detailed attention to how many capitalist employers of his day were working their employees to death in horrific conditions. Quoting from the reports of factory inspectors and magistrates, his account bristles with incredible detail. In the lace industry in Nottingham, "children of nine or ten years were dragged from their squalid beds at two, three, or four o'clock in the morning, and forced to work for subsistence wages until ten, eleven, or twelve at night, their frames dwindling, their faces whitening, and their humanity sinking into a stone-like torpor, utterly horrible to contemplate." Mr. Broughton Charlton, the county magistrate whose words are quoted above, castigated the system as one of "unmitigated slavery, socially, physically, morally, and spiritually." "We declaim against the Virginian and Carolinian cotton planters. Is their lash, and the barter of human flesh more detestable than this slow sacrifice of humanity which takes place in order that veils and collars may be fabricated for the benefit of capitalists?"

In quoting reports on the pottery industry in Staffordshire, Marx produces similar facts, relating, for example, the story of William Wood, nine years old, who had been working for over a year from 6 a.m. until 9 p.m., six days a week. Quoting from health reports on how potters were dying from pulmonary diseases at an alarming rate, he notes the observations of three physicians who had reported how each successive generation of potters was more dwarfed and less robust than the previous one. For example, Dr. J. T. Arledge reported in 1863 how the potters as a class of both men and women represent a "degenerated population . . . stunted in growth, ill-shaped, and frequently ill-formed in the chest . . . prematurely old, and . . . short lived . . . [dogged by] disorders of the liver and kidneys, and by rheumatism . . . [and] especially prone to pneumonia, phthisis, bronchitis, and asthma."

Reports on match factories in the large cities documented how half the workers were children and young persons under eighteen, and how tetanus, a disease long associated with match making, was rife. Reports on the wallpaper industry tell how young girls and children were obliged to work from 6 a.m. until at least 10 p.m., with no stoppage for meals. Working seventy or eighty hours a week, they were often fed at their machines.

Reports on the baking industry document how bakers often worked from 11 p.m. until 7 p.m. the following evening, with just one or two short intervals of rest. They were among the most short-lived workers, rarely reaching the age of forty-two.

Reports on the clothing industry document how girls and young women were being worked to death on sixteen-hour shifts, and on shifts of up to thirty hours in peak seasons. They often worked without a break, being kept awake by occasional supplies of sherry, port, or coffee. On the railways men often worked fourteen to twenty hours a day, forty or fifty hours of continuous work being common in peak travel periods. And in the steel mills boys nine to fifteen years old were reported working continuous twelve-hour shifts in high temperatures, often at night, and not seeing daylight for months on end. It was Marx's opinion that capital lived "vampire-like . . . sucking living labor," and that in general, capital took no account of the health or length of life of the worker unless society forced it to do so.

Many people conducting research on health and safety at work today believe that, though the working conditions in the majority of organizations are much better than those described above, many basic problems remain. Many employers take account of work hazards only when legislation requires them to do so, and even in the developed Western countries, accidents and occupational diseases continue to take an alarming toll on human life.

For example, in the United States it is estimated that around fourteen thousand people are killed in industrial accidents each year. That's one every forty minutes. Conservative estimates suggest that a further 2.2 million people become disabled, many seriously, and some experts suggest that the figures are much higher. For example, in his book *Crisis in the Workplace*, Dr. Nicholas Ashford suggests that the figure may be as high as 11 million. According to which figure one chooses to take, that means that anywhere between four and twenty industrial accidents occur every minute in the United States alone.

Deaths from occupational disease occur at an even more alarming rate. For example, in 1980 the U.S. Department of Labor reported that one hundred thousand Americans die each year as a result of work-related illness. And a report produced by the U.S. Department of Health, Education, and Welfare suggests that anywhere between 23 and 38 percent of cancer deaths may be work-related. Annual occupation-related deaths outnumber those from automobile accidents, and during the years 1966-1970 more Americans died on the job than were killed in the Vietnam War. But while the war has stopped, the industrial fatalities continue. All this amounts to an incredible rate of human suffering. And suffering aside, the economic costs are staggering. For example, over 50 million days of work are lost to accidents and occupational disease each year, at a cost of billions of dollars.

We're a long way from the industrial revolution in terms of general working conditions, but these figures speak for themselves. The question of efficiency versus safety looms large in many corporate decisions, with primary emphasis being placed on the former. Thus as one safety officer in an automobile factory described it, while the explicit policy is "safety first," the reality is "safety when convenient." Many industrial accidents occur because of problems unintentionally built into the structure of plant and buildings, because of poor maintenance, or because it is easier or more efficient to work without using safety equipment. Because it is either expensive or inconvenient to remedy such problems, nothing tends to get done until someone gets hurt, or until the organization is forced to introduce changes by government regulation.

Similar problems arise in relation to the hazards underlying much occupational disease. Here, the problems are so pervasive that it is often difficult to know where to begin dealing with them. It is estimated that industry at present creates and uses over sixty-three thousand chemicals, perhaps twenty-five thousand of which would be classified as toxic. Many of these are new, and their long-term effects are unknown. And the effects of their interaction are impossible to predict in a comprehensive manner, because of the number of possible permutations. In the view of some safety experts the approach commonly adopted is a kind of trial and error using people in the workplace as human guinea pigs until concrete risks are identified.

It is often the most gruesome problems that are brought to our attention, such as the dangers presented to coal miners by black lung, the hazards of brown lung for those exposed to cotton dust, the dangers of working with asbestos, or the risks of radiation from nuclear power plants and uranium mining. However, toxic substances of one sort or another affect the majority of occupational groups. In a recent survey of production workers conducted by the Survey Research Center at the University of Michigan, 78 percent reported some exposure to work hazards. Occupational groups such as carpenters, construction workers, laboratory technicians, agricultural workers, dry cleaners, fire fighters, hospital staff, and even hair stylists increasingly work with chemical substances whose long-term effects are unknown. Even in the modern office building poor ventilation or exposure to radiation from video display terminals can add to the risk of occupationally induced illness of one kind or another.

In the view of many such risk is an inevitable side effect of industrialization. In the view of those directly involved with the promotion of health and safety at work, however, there has long been a reluctance for employers to admit to well-known hazards, even though plenty of early warnings were provided.

As a case in point examine the problems associated with asbestos, which is estimated to account for approximately fifty thousand deaths annually in the United States alone. The risks have been long known. As early as 1918 insurance companies in both the United States and Canada stopped selling life policies to asbestos workers. Yet the industry has continued to allow employees to operate without respirators, sometimes in dust so thick that it is possible to see only a few yards. And the industry has also systematically overlooked the tragic consequences.

For example, in his book *Death on the Job*, Daniel Berman tells the story of asbestos worker Marco Vela. Vela began working in the Johns-Manville asbestos factory in Pittsburg, California, around 1935. In 1959 the company started a policy of conducting medical examinations to detect lung disease. That year a physician paid by the company obtained a chest X ray on Vela and noted the existence of an occupation-related disease. The report contained no recommendation about changing the work environment, and Vela was not informed he was developing asbestosis.

In 1962 Vela was examined by another company-paid physician. A chest X ray again showed the presence of lung disease. The patient was told nothing. The same physician saw Vela again in 1965 and ordered another chest X ray. A diagnosis of work-related pneumoconiosis was made. Vela was told nothing.

In 1968 Vela was given another routine physical. Though he had a cough and was short of breath, and though his X ray showed a "ground glass appearance," Vela was told by the company nurse that everything was fine and received no information to the contrary from the physician. Later that year he was hospitalized, and he never returned to work.

For ten years doctors under contract to the Johns-Manville Corporation, the world's largest private producer of asbestos, knew that Vela was developing asbestosis, refused to tell him, and took no measures to prevent further exposure. The same company had known since 1931, from research that it had sponsored, that asbestos caused lung disease.

The case is only one of many. For example, a recent Ontario Royal Commission on the health dangers of asbestos reported that operations of Johns-Manville in Canada had resulted in more deaths than the whole Ontario mining industry, which employs over thirty thousand. As of 1983 the death toll from asbestos exposure in a Toronto plant was 68, according to claims awarded by the Ontario Workers Compensation Board, even though annual employment at the plant between 1948 and 1980 never exceeded 714 people. No doubt these figures underestimate the gravity of the situation, since in Canada no workers' compensation was awarded for asbestosis until 1979.

Documents in product liability suits against the asbestos industry in the United States suggest that the Johns-Manville Corporation, Raybestos-Manhattan Incorporated, and other companies were involved in an organized cover-up of the ill effects of asbestos. A 1980 report on corporate crime by a subcommittee of the U.S. House of Representatives notes that a number of firms in the asbestos industry made out-of-court settlements to asbestos workers who had registered claims, many in the 1930s, well before they admit to having recognized the hazard presented by asbestos. And the problems continue in the Third World, where international corporations engage in the same dangerous practices, free from the health regulations now imposed in the West. For example, a recent report on the export of hazardous factories to developing countries identifies British- and American-owned factories that are fifty years behind standard practice at home. Workers work in thick clouds of dust and are not told of the findings of their medical examinations. Waste asbestos is also often dumped along the roads and surrounding lots where children play.

The history of the modern asbestos industry is every bit as bad as that of the lace and pottery industries in the mid-nineteenth century. Asbestos-related deaths among shipyard and insulation workers continue at high rates; it is estimated that 20 to 25 percent die from lung cancer, 10 to 18 percent from asbestosis, and 10 percent from gastrointestinal cancer. Additional asbestos-related deaths in industries as diverse as steel, automotive-parts manufacture, construction, and building maintenance also continue at high levels.

While this case history is one of the more extreme and serious ones, it is by no means untypical. For example, similar studies and facts abound in the textile industry. Even today some textile executives deny the reality of brown-lung disease (byssinosis), despite the fact that it is estimated that the disease may strike 8 to 12 percent of mill workers. For example, the *Washington Post* reported in 1980 that manufacturers still insist that the lung disease affecting their workers is produced by smoking, and that there is no evidence to believe that brown lung exists. In the meantime thousands of mill workers are forced into early retirement, their lungs and bodies wasting away, often without any compensation because no liability is admitted by their employers.

We are back to the economics of health and safety. This theme lies at the basis of all the problems. Just as the early manufacturers of the nineteenth century often worked their employees to death because of losses associated with idle machines, modern industrialists feel compelled to keep their plants in operation despite gruesome statistics that suggest all is not well. While workers may prove careless, and while bad management and negligence often occur, many of the problems are systemic. If accidents are built into the structure of a plant, or if the use of toxic chemicals is essential for continued productivity or for gaining a competitive edge, the welfare of the worker frequently takes second place to the economics of the situation. Despite an early start in Britain with the Factory Acts of 1833, legislation has often appeared too late to deal with critical problems and is often difficult to enforce, especially in relation to the threat presented by exposure to toxics. The effect of these is often difficult to prove in a conclusive way, thus many employees bringing compensation claims often find it hard to show employer liability. Of the estimated 581,000 people in the United States severely disabled as a result of occupational disease, less than 5 percent receive formal compensation. The problem is compounded by the fact that the legal and financial consequences of recognizing any liability lead many organizations to marshal their resources to demonstrate that no risk exists. When accidents do occur, organizational prudence suggests that it is much better for the injured worker to sue for compensation than for the organization to acknowledge any responsibility.

Since the passage of the 1970 Occupational Safety and Health Act in the United States and similar legislation in Canada, the situation has improved. But problems still abound. The fact that it is often cheaper to pay accident compensation than to eliminate accidents by making work safe, and that penalties on firms that continue to operate high-risk plants are not stiff enough to close them down, perpetuate the underlying problem. Many safety officers in organizations end up performing a role designed merely to make their organization look good in the eyes of government inspectors, rather than to make substantive improvements. As a result, the relations between safety officers and inspectors often become an elaborate organizational game, reminiscent of those played between time-and-motion staff and production workers in the setting of work standards. As a safety officer in a manufacturing plant tells it, "The tactics employed depend on the government inspector. There's one who usually likes to issue a few minor directives. He's nearing retirement, does not want a fuss, and wants to avoid the paperwork that stems from issuing serious directives . . . in this case the tactic is to create obvious minor infractions so that the inspector does not have to search for problems. . . . [Thus] items such as exit signs with burnt-out bulbs, or guard rails that are not high enough, are left unrepaired near inspection time. . . . In the case of another younger inspector, renowned to be thorough, and wishing to make a name for himself as having promotion potential, everything must be up to scratch. Thus, in this case, a particular machine or process which is known to be in marginal condition is examined before the inspection so that modifications can be planned and budgeted. Then, when the inspection occurs, the inspector, indirectly, is encouraged to shut down the machine, and thus satisfy his own requirements. The approach is successful in minimizing inconvenience and projecting a good image in that we get few instructions for improvement."

Organizations work hard to look good in official records by reducing the number or severity of potential hazards *identified* through various kinds of window dressing. They may do this by influencing the way accidents or hazards are classified, or by reducing the number of days lost to injury by encouraging injured employees to turn up for work in return for assignments to easy jobs. The attempt to control accidents through legislation often encourages this type of response, leaving underlying attitudes and hazards unchanged. Of course, while there are many employers who do not take health and safety seriously, there are also many who do. And there are many workers who no doubt take advantage of the rules, regulations, and compensation schemes. The idea that the majority of employers are unscrupulous "vampires" that willfully suck the blood of labor is no doubt an exaggeration, as is the widespread idea that the majority of workers are fakers and scroungers. While there are many cases at the extremes, the truth stands somewhere in between, but in a place consistent with the general idea that in many situations efficiency tends to come first and safety second. The radical critics of modern organization appear to be correct in asserting that many organizations continue to advance their interests by exploiting and dominating the health and welfare of employees.

WORKAHOLISM AND SOCIAL AND MENTAL STRESS

Our discussion up to now has placed principal emphasis on work-related hazards of a physical kind. As such, many of the victims belong to the "secondary" labor market, a fact that again emphasizes the differential impact of organizations on different sections of the working population. However, those in the "primary" labor market also become victims of certain hazards, especially those producing various kinds of stress. While white-collar workers are, on average, less likely than blue-collar workers to be killed or seriously injured by accidents while working on the job or to be directly exposed to toxic hazards, they are often far more likely to suffer from work-related coronary disease, ulcers, and mental breakdown.

Coronary disease, often labeled the "management killer," is being increasingly recognized as a problem affecting many people in stressful work situations. Not only white-collar workers but also blue-collar workers and women faced with the problem of managing a family as well as holding down a part- or full-time job often suffer coronary disorders. The problem is endemic to stressful situations of all kinds, and seems to be the product of a complex network of factors. One's working conditions, role, career aspirations, and quality of relations at work interact with one's personality to influence personal stress levels and physical and mental well-being. The "Type A" personality, driven by the compulsion to control his or her work environment, ambitious, achievement-oriented, competitive, impatient, and perfectionistic, is always a good candidate for coronary problems. And those who work with such a person also run risks as well, since the Type A personality often creates considerable tension for others in the workplace. The tension, frustration, and anger that often accompany a sense of powerlessness, such as that experienced by people in dead-end blue-collar and clerical jobs, also increases the risk of physical and mental breakdown.

While much can be done to modify the levels of stress and tension experienced at work—for example, through appropriate design of jobs and the attempt to develop balanced relations between work and outside life—it seems that a certain amount of stress is endemic. Indeed, organizations thrive on and at times actively create stress as a means of promoting organizational effectiveness. While in the view of many experts a certain amount of stress may be beneficial, undue stress has a costly long-term impact on organizations because of illness and lost working time. In order to get ahead in many organizations executives and trainees often feel that they must achieve a complete identification with what the organization stands for and comply with organizational norms that demand rushed or missed meals and long hours of work six or seven days a week. The product, of course, is the workaholic. Work becomes an addiction and a crutch, leading to unbalanced personal development and creating many problems for family life. The workaholic tends to be always under pressure, to have little spare time for his or her spouse and children, and to be frequently absent from home. Very often, progress on the organization's career ladder requires frequent change in jobs, often involving moves from one anonymous city to another. The negative impact on home life and the incidence of marital and family breakdown is of course enormous. And in the case of dual-career families, the strains and tensions are often amplified many times. While the individuals involved ultimately make the choices that shape these events, they are in many cases driven by their desire to comply with the norms and values of the corporate world where they're hell-bent on making their mark.

The demands of many executive and professional roles are such that it is often difficult to find the balance in work life that many health experts suggest is desirable. The corporate way of life tends to require that deadlines be met, and that work loads at times be unevenly spread. In this sense many organizations need their share of workaholics and actively develop organizational cultures that sustain the breed. As was discussed in Chapter 5, some organizations specialize in the creation of stress and exploit their executives and other employees in a very deliberate way. Recall for example the intimidation rituals practiced by Harold Geneen at ITT. His executives were expected to be on top of their work even when they were at home asleep! Most organizations need and demand that their executives be organization men and women, living and dreaming about organizational life. And of course many executives learn to like this. In the view of the radical critic of organization, however, this phenomenon reflects yet another aspect of the way organizations exploit employees and their families for corporate ends.

ORGANIZATIONAL POLITICS AND THE RADICALIZED ORGANIZATION

The idea that organizations use and exploit their employees commands a great deal of support, and accounts for important attitudes, beliefs, and practices in many organizations. In Chapter 6 we referred to the "radical frame of reference" built on the principle that organizations are class-based phenomena characterized by deep-rooted divisions between the interests of capital and labor. (See Exhibit 6.6 and related discussion.) The ideas discussed in this chapter help to make the rationale of this perspective clearer, and help us to understand why labor and management often find themselves in such bitter conflict. From the point of view of a member of the "secondary" labor market who suffers periodic unemployment with the ups and downs of the business cycle, or who is engaged in a low-status job that values and uses few of his abilities, or who has suffered from a work-related accident or toxic hazard without compensation, it may make much more sense to understand organizations as battlegrounds than as united "teams" or friendly pluralist coalitions. How can one feel one belongs to a team if one is uncertain whether one will still be employed next week? How can one believe that one is part of a community of shared interests when differences in status and privilege are obvious and rife? It seems quite reasonable in these circumstances to see oneself as part of an exploited and disadvantaged group of people, and to band together with one's fellows to see what gains and benefits can be extracted from one's employers. And it seems reasonable to operate on the principle that any improvement in one's position will probably be the product of a long and arduous fight. Under these circumstances organizations frequently become divided worlds characterized by political behaviors that reflect and entrench class divisions found in the wider society. In extreme cases the separation between the interests of capital and labor, or management and unions, becomes as sharp as that between warring factions. In other words, we arrive at what may be called "the radicalized organization."

More often than not, these organizations are found in sectors of the economy with entrenched organizational divisions between primary and secondary labor. For example, in mining, heavy manufacturing, shipbuilding, steel, and numerous other industries, the difference in privilege between white- and blue-collar workers is often marked. While each group may be fragmented in terms of hierarchical and occupational structures, managers being distinguished from clerical workers, foremen from shop-floor workers, and skilled workers from unskilled, it is "white" and "blue" that often divide the organization. On average, white-collar workers enjoy cleaner and safer work conditions, more regular work hours, more fringe benefits, longer vacations, and higher wages. The imbalance is symbolized time and again in the most routine aspects of work experience, as when the oil-smeared production worker shares an exchange or meeting with a neat executive or has an occasion to interact with other office staff. Because of the differences, various categories of workers are often kept apart. And in some cases, the separation and distance between groups are emphasized by practices that allow new inequities to emerge.

For example, in one British vehicle assembly firm, separate dining rooms are provided for shop-floor workers and white-collar staff. The rooms are next to each other but are worlds apart. In the "staff" dining room one can enjoy lunch and a glass of wine served by uniformed waitresses at an attractive table of one's choice. In the "plant" dining room one has to line up for self-service food to be eaten at long bare tables with the aid of plastic knives and forks. If one wishes to use proper cutlery one must hire it by paying a deposit. As might be expected, the organization is characterized by a strong division between "them" and "us," and management and unions are constantly engaged in a battle where each side is trying to get the better of the other.

But there is no simple rule saying that organizations that combine primary and secondary labor will end up this way—or that the process of radicalization is confined to such organizations. For example, where a cohesive corporate culture reframes the differences between primary and secondary groups within a set of shared values, such radicalized divisions may be absent. And in organizations once unified, radicalized divisions can appear. A highly stratified yet "unitary" organization hard hit by economic recession and obliged to lay off labor is rarely the same again afterwards. And organizations that reflect few marked divisions in relation to social class, such as educational organizations and service-oriented bureaucracies, often end up becoming extremely polarized when put under pressure. For example, in the late 1970s and early 1980s faculty at many educational institutions responded to cutbacks in their work force, salary restrictions, and other measures of restraint by going on strike for the first time. There is often a deep sense of resentment in these polarized situations, and even when work is resumed relations are often strained and hostile. Such organizations often end up at least temporarily as battlefields where people fight on the premise that they are, or are in danger of being, exploited in some way.

As we look around the organizational world we can begin to identify the radicalized organizations where at least one major section of the work force experiences a sense of exploitation and responds in a solidaristic way. This kind of solidarity underpins labor movements that strive for transformations of the workplace to realize some of the more democratic varieties of organization described in Exhibit 6.1. When this democratization is not realized the deep sense of exploitation may atrophy into a form of seething resentment where workers block and fight management, and management blocks and fights workers. This kind of traditional labor-management warfare, as in the case of the 1984 coal miners' strike in Britain, often turns out to be a fight where both sides pay a heavy price. Specific political tactics usually come into play. On the management side the main strategy usually hinges on attempting to ensure that confrontation occurs at a good time (i.e., when there are stockpiles of finished goods and a reduced need for labor, or when labor is perceived to be in a generally weak position) and to proceed on a principle of "divide and rule." Management attempts to break the solidarity of the work force and, through the media, to undermine its support from the community. On the labor side, "united we stand" tends to be the favored principle. Solid collective action thus meets the challenge of divisive strategies until one side gets the better of the other, or until a face-saving deal can be negotiated.

As with the unitary and pluralist frames of reference, the radical perspective may describe the harsh political reality of an organization, and also may be used as an ideological tool. Thus while a pluralist manager may use the idea that "we're a team" to build unity and obtain a measure of compliance on the part of his or her subordinates, a unionist or other radical employee may cultivate belief in the radical ideology as a means of uniting the work force against management. Under certain circumstances unitary and pluralist managers also adopt the radical ideology, shaping relations with their work force as a battle where they must demonstrate their superiority and strength. In doing so they often set the basis for a future radicalization of the work force. Indeed, in the view of many unionists this managerial attitude is an extremely common one, though often veiled by unitary or pluralistic rhetoric. From the standpoint of exploited employees the idea that organizations are instruments of domination may make perfect sense, and provides a powerful metaphor for understanding the organizational world.

Perhaps enough has been said to make a case for the domination metaphor. However, there is another dimension to the radical critique to which we must now turn. This hinges on how many organizations, especially the multinationals, use and exploit the international economy for their own selfish ends.

Multinationals and the world economy

The operation of the world economy is dominated by the activities of giant companies, usually called "multinationals" or "transnational corporations." In 1982 there were 380 corporations with sales of over two billion dollars per annum. The fifty largest corporations each had annual sales ranging from twelve to one hundred and eight billion dollars. Nineteen of these corporations had sales over twenty billion. The largest corporations, including names such as Exxon, Texaco, Mobil, Royal Dutch/Shell, General Motors, General Electric, Ford, IBM, Fiat, Unilever, and ITT, have annual sales figures that exceed the gross national products of many nations (Exhibit 9.3). No wonder, therefore, that they have been described as sovereign states that have a major impact on international politics and the world economy. Indeed, in the late 1960s Jean-Jacques Servan-Schreiber went so far as to suggest that the third greatest industrial power in the world was not Europe, but United States industry in Europe.

Multinational corporations with headquarters in the United States dominate the list of the largest companies. Up until the early 1970s hegemony of the United States was undisputed, but recently corporations from other countries have become of growing importance. Corporations from thirty different countries are now represented among the 380 largest, and increasing numbers have home bases in the Third World. Japanese and West German corporations have the fastest rate of growth, having surpassed that of the American multinationals, whose rate of growth has slowed since the late 1960s.

Rank		GNP or sales (billion dollars)	Rank		GNP or sales (billion dollars)
1	United States	2946.0	51	Chile	28.9
2	USSR	N.A.	52**Gulf		28.3
3	Japan	1186.4	53	Egypt	28.2
4	West Germany	829.6	54	Libya	28.1
5	France	657.6	55**Atlantic Richfield		27.8
6	United Kingdom	510.3	56**General Electric		27.2
7	Italy	391.4	57	United Arab Emirates	26.9
8	China	300.0	58	Hong Kong	26.3
9	Canada	276.2	59	Malaysia	26.1
10	Brazil	267.7	60	New Zealand	25.5
11	Spain	214.3	61	Portugal	24.8
12	India	176.7	62**Unilever		24.1
13	Netherlands	168.0	63**Dupont		22.8
14	Australia	165.5	64**Francaise/Petroles		22.8
15	Mexico	160.2	65	Hungary	22.6
16	Sweden	123.8	66**Shell		21.6
17	Belgium	117.5	67**Kuwait Petroleum		20.6
18	Saudi Arabia	117.2	68	Israel	20.4
19	Switzerland	112.9	69	Peru	20.0
20**Exxon		108.1	70**Elf-Aquitaine		19.7
21**Royal Dutch/Shell Group		82.3	71**Petroleos/Venezuela		19.7
22	South Africa	81.8	72**Fiat		19.6
23	Indonesia	78.8	73**Petrobas		18.9
24	Austria	77.1	74**Pemex		18.8
25	Nigeria	76.2	75	Ireland	18.0
26	Argentina	72.1	76	Morocco	18.0
27	Turkey	70.2	77**ITT		17.3
28	Denmark	67.2	78**Phillips		17.1
29	Korea, Republic	66.1	79**Volkswagenwerk		16.8
30	Venezuela	65.1	80**Daimler-Benz		16.3
31**Mobil		64.5	81**Nissan Motor		16.2
32	Yugoslavia	62.9	82**Renault		16.2
33**General Motors		62.7	83**Siemens		16.0
34**Texaco		57.6	84**Phillips Petroleum		16.0
35	Norway	57.6	85**Matsushita		15.7
36	Romania	57.0	86**Toyota		15.7
37**British Petroleum		52.2	87**Hitachi		15.5
38	Finland	51.3	88**Tenneco		15.5
39**Standard Oil (CA)		44.2	89**Hoechst		15.3
40	Greece	42.9	90**Nippon Steel		15.2
41	Algeria	42.0	91**Sun		15.0
42	Philippines	39.0	92**Bayer		15.0
43**Ford		38.2	93**Occidental Petroleum		14.7
44	Thailand	36.9	94	Syrian Arab Rep.	14.7
45	Colombia	36.4	95**BAT Industries		14.3
46	Kuwait	30.6	96**Nestle		14.2
47**Standard Oil (IN)		29.9	97**U.S. Steel		13.9
48	Pakistan	29.8	98**BASF		13.7
49**ENI		29.4	99**United Technologies		13.7
50**IBM		29.1	100**Standard Oil (OH)		13.5

**Multinational Corporation

Exhibit 9.3. A 1981 Comparison of Country GNPs and Annual Sales of the Largest Multinationals
SOURCE: 1983 *World Bank Atlas* and *Fortune* (August 23, 1982).

Many of the largest multinational corporations are oil companies, with automobile manufacturers, electrical and electronics firms, chemical producers, food companies, and glass and steel manufacturers also represented. They typically operate in countries throughout the world, including many of the state-communist nations. Most multinationals have diversified interests. Most are controlled by shareholders; but a significant number, including firms such as Renault, British Leyland, ENI, and Petroleos de Venezuela, are fully or partly government-owned.

Of course, transnational corporations have been with us for a long time. The Venetian city-state in the fifteenth century was heavily involved in international finance, and large international trading companies such as the Dutch East India Company and the Hudson Bay Company developed commercial operations on many continents as early as the seventeenth century. However, it is in the late ninteenth and early twentieth centuries that we witness the growth and proliferation of multinationals, along with developments in the capitalist world economy. Large, specialized corporations were among the first to appear, amassing a great concentration of economic resources and near-monopoly power with operations in many countries. Around the middle of this century a new development emerged along with antitrust legislation designed to curb the influence of such organizations, namely the emergence of diversified conglomerates. Diversified conglomerate multinationals developed as firms attempted to control supplies of crucial raw materials, to develop a portfolio of different types of investment, to hedge the risks associated with location by operating in many places at once, to engage in defensive foreign investment that protected them from the vagaries of the business cycle or the policies of any single host government, and to open up new markets for products that were reaching a stage of maturity in older markets.

Some of the conglomerates developed as large firms acquired interests in new areas of activity, while others developed very rapidly through series of financial transactions that built giant conglomerates from humble beginnings. The latter development occurred with amazing speed during the 1960s as financiers took advantage of the stock-exchange boom accompanying the Vietnam War, acquiring or merging with company after company. To take one very spectacular example, in just ten years Harold Geneen transformed ITT from a loosely knit group of international telephone companies into a centralized conglomerate with 331 subsidiaries and another 771 subsidiaries of subsidiaries, with operations in seventy countries. During the eleven-year period to 1970 ITT climbed from fifty-second to ninth place on the *Fortune* list of top companies. And as journalist Anthony Sampson reports in his analysis of the affairs of ITT, Geneen's spectacular success was paralleled in many other corporations. Gulf and Western was quickly built up from a small firm making car fenders into a conglomerate with 92 companies in a range of industries as diverse as mining, sugar production, publishing, and show business. Litton Industries developed from a million-dollar electronics firm into a conglomerate of over 100 companies in less than ten years.

The overall trend toward larger and more diversified organizations that dominated the 1960s is reflected in the figures on industrial concentration. In 1948 the two hundred biggest industrial corporations in the United States controlled 48 percent of the manufacturing assets, but by 1969 they controlled 58 percent. In 1983 the top one hundred manufacturing companies controlled 48 percent of total manufacturing assets. While the economic slump that followed the boom years of the sixties has made many investments turn sour, the tendency towards concentration has remained in the United States and in Europe as well. As Anthony Sampson put it: "Giants on one continent provoked rival giants on another. . . . The sixties, all over the world, was the decade of the giants."

THE MULTINATIONALS AS WORLD POWERS

These developments have had major repercussions on power structures throughout the world. Many modern organizations are larger and more powerful than nation-states; but, unlike nation-states, they are often not accountable to anyone but themselves. For example, recent research has suggested that the activities of many multinationals, particularly those operated from the United States, are highly centralized, their foreign subsidiaries being tightly controlled through policies, rules, and regulations set by headquarters. The subsidiaries have to report on a regular basis (often weekly), and their staff are often allowed very little influence on key decisions affecting the subsidiary. The resources of the multinationals are also usually managed in a way that creates dependency rather than local autonomy.

This high degree of centralization is a product of the fact that the corporation's extensive and diverse activities are interpreted as needing strong central direction. While Japanese corporations often develop looser forms of control that rely on familiarity with shared values and norms as a means of guiding local decisions (see Exhibit 4.3), other multinationals tend to favor closer supervision. Indeed, the degree of central planning and direction appears to have closer links with Soviet-style planned economies than with competitive free enterprise. Centralized administration tends to replace the interplay of market forces. Or, as business historian Alfred Chandler has put it, the "visible hand" of management replaces the "invisible hand" that Adam Smith saw as guiding competitive market economies.

Whenever we examine the multinationals, therefore, we are quickly brought face to face with their monolithic power. Of all organizations, they come closest to realizing Max Weber's worst fears with regard to how bureaucratic organizations can become totalitarian regimes serving the interests of elites, where those in control are able to exercise power that is "practically unshatterable." Simply put, the name of the multinational game frequently becomes control, control, control. The multinationals readily engage in forms of vertical integration to acquire ownership or control of critical raw materials and other supplies, and engage in extensive research and marketing to shape consumer preferences. In doing so they make their source of supplies and the markets for their goods a kind of internally administered domain. They also often engage in official and unofficial collusion, developing informal cartels that regulate relations between affiliated organizations, thereby helping to stabilize and control aspects of their environment that would otherwise prove uncertain and threatening.

Thus as Kurt Mirow and Harry Maurer have shown in their book *Webs of Power*, international cartels pervade the world economy, even though their operations are illegal in many countries. Their members reduce competition by entering into home-market protection agreements that establish exclusive territories that competitors will avoid, or where competitors will content themselves with existing market shares, leaving the dominant firm with no competition except from small domestic firms outside the cartel. "Hunting ground" agreements often define the degree of competition that is to be allowed in foreign markets, with preference usually being given to patterns of traditional market dominance. Thus United States firms are usually left to dominate the Caribbean, British and French firms their former colonies, the Germans Northern and Eastern Europe, and Japan East and Southeast Asia. Other territories are usually left for open competition, though even in these markets price fixing and quotas are often the rule. The cartels also frequently make agreements relating to the exchange and transfer of technology and patent rights, thus reducing competition in this sphere as well. Such practices are found in industries such as electrical equipment, oil, pharmaceuticals, industrial chemicals, steel, aluminum, fibers, uranium, and shipping. The cartels tend to establish their headquarters in countries that do not have antitrust laws, such as Switzerland, and find ways of avoiding the legislation in countries that do. These practices add to the already immense power of the multinationals in a very important way, since they help to prevent possibly fateful battles between the giants.

The efforts of multinationals to control their environment also often extend into the realm of politics itself. As is well known, big corporations often use their immense lobbying power to shape the political agenda and to create political outcomes favorable to themselves. In this, perhaps more than any other single activity, the political significance of multinationals as world powers comes to the fore, for they are often in a position to exert major influence on host governments, especially when a nation is critically dependent on their presence or on some aspect of their operations. While the issues on which a multinational wishes to exert its influence are usually economic, the corporation often becomes directly and sometimes illegally involved in the political process. For example, when the economic aims and objectives of a multinational are in conflict with the line of development favored by a host government, it is very easy for the multinational to become embroiled in activities designed to shape the economic and social policies of the government. As a result, it may be drawn into the political arena and become explicitly political and ideological in its activities, though usually acting behind the scenes. The classic and infamous case is ITT's involvement in the affairs of Chile, where it plotted in 1970 to stop the election of Marxist president Salvador Allende. Conspiring with the CIA, ITT sought to create economic chaos within Chile, and thus to encourage a military coup, with the company offering to contribute "up to seven figures" to the White House to stop Allende coming to power.

The multinationals are a major political force in the world economy and, for the most part, a political force without political accountability. The Chilean episode, though extreme in its characteristics, highlights a much more general set of problems relating to the contradictions that arise when strong authoritarian powers like the multinationals are allowed to exist in democratic states. For they are in a position to make complete nonsense of the democratic process, obliging governments to be more responsive to corporate interests than to those of the people who elected them. We can see now why advocates of the radical frame of reference point to the existence of the multinationals as yet further evidence of the general antagonism of interests between people and corporations. The sheer power of the multinationals, the cartels that reduce competition between them, and the interlocking patterns of ownership and control that bind them together, all combine to create a world economy dominated by organizations where the power of the corporate official often dwarfs that of the elected politician and that of the people whom the organization is ostensibly intended to serve.

MULTINATIONALS: A RECORD OF EXPLOITATION?

Advocates of the multinationals often see them as positive forces in economic development, creating jobs and bringing capital, technology, and expertise to communities or countries that might have difficulty developing these resources on their own account. Their critics, on the other hand, tend to see them as authoritarian juggernauts that are ultimately out to exploit their hosts for all they can get. The argument identifies the horns of a major dilemma, in that the policies that serve the interests of a multinational firm may not be in the best interests of the community or nation in which the firm is located. Hence, given the immense power of the multinational firm, its hosts often find themselves having to rely on a benevolent social reponsibility on the part of the multinational.

The record of the multinationals in this regard, however, leaves a great deal to be desired. The highly centralized systems of decision making frequently mean that centralized corporate interests relating to the profitability, growth, or strategic development of the multinational as a whole take first place in decision making, while localized community or national interests take second. Thus when strategic considerations lead the executive staff of a multinational to divest its holdings in a particular industry, to close down a particular plant, or to restructure its operations internationally, the consequences can be devastating for the communities and countries involved. The bitter irony is often that many of these decisions are not made because a particular plant or set of operations is unprofitable, but because the corporation believes that it is possible to earn a greater profit elsewhere.

For example, the decisions of large organizations to relocate manufacturing operations in search of cheaper and nonunionized labor or better operating conditions have fostered urban decay in the cities of the northern United States. As firms have moved from the northern cities to southern states, or to Third World countries such as Taiwan and Korea, the effect has been to divide the United States into the decaying "rust belt" and the prosperous "sun belt." The effect is particularly marked in small communities, where the decision of the multinational to close down the operations of a major plant can remove the economic lifeblood of the community. While such moves make splendid economic sense from a corporate standpoint, they usually spell socioeconomic disaster from the community point of view. Similar developments are found in the decaying industrial and mining centers of Europe, where the closure of coal mines and steel mills leads to the economic and social decline of whole regions. As in the case of

Willy Loman in Arthur Miller's play, these communities often feel that they have been used and sucked dry and are now being thrown away because they are no longer needed. The feelings of resentment and exploitation are particularly severe when the plants or mines being closed are profitable, but not profitable enough from a corporate standpoint.

That corporate and community interests are not always synonymous is a truism common to all organizations, not just the multinationals. But the scale of operations among the latter is so enormous that it makes the consequences of their decisions especially great. We have illustrated the point by focusing on how changes in corporate strategy, even if only to *increase* rates of profit, can set the basis for widespread socioeconomic change. In a similar way, the decisions of multinationals to move their liquid capital from one country to another to take advantage of interest-rate differentials can have a major effect on the international balance of payments of the countries concerned. Or a decision to pursue a particular line of corporate development can have a major effect on national and regional economic planning, distorting the pattern of relations that the host region or nation wishes to encourage. For these and many other reasons, communities and nations often find themselves wishing to attract multinationals while also fearing the consequences, because they know that the underlying sets of interests may be in fundamental conflict. Some nations, such as Canada, where foreign ownership in many sectors of industry runs at levels well over 50 percent, have formally recognized that such conflicts exist, and have tried to codify the conditions under which the multinationals will be allowed to operate within their domains (Exhibit 9.4). However, there is a dilemma in that the more a host government attempts to control the practices of the multinationals, the less attractive investment in that country becomes. Hence multinational and nation-state often end up in a relation of dominance and dependency, or as rival power blocs, each attempting to shape the conditions under which the other is to operate.

While the impact of multinationals on Western countries may be damaging, their impact on the Third World has undoubtedly been much worse. Critics see them as modern plunderers, exploiting natural and other resources for their own ends. Of course the multinationals do not see themselves in this way. They see their activities as helping develop the underdeveloped world amidst the difficulties created by unfavorable publicity about the wrongdoings of a socially irresponsible minority, by propaganda against big business leveled by critics on the "left," and sometimes by hostile and ungrateful foreign governments who fail to honor contracts. While recognizing that multinationals must operate in line with appropriate rules of conduct, they argue that their influence is for better than for worse, and that multinationals and host nations can operate in a way that benefits both. The debate is a hot one, and arguments can be made on either side.

Let us start by examining the main criticisms of multinational operations in the Third World. The first of these hinges on the idea that their effect on the economies of host nations, like that of the colonial empires on whose legacy they build, is basically an exploitative one. If we examine the role of multinationals in Third World countries we find that traditionally they have been heavily involved in the extraction of raw materials and foodstuffs. More recently they have become involved in manufacturing. But in both cases control of operations, technology, and revenues rests with the multinationals and their parent nations, the end result being that the Third World countries are *more* dependent on them than when the process first started.

Consider how multinationals have dealt with Third World mining and agriculture. In both cases, they have used the resources of their host countries to enhance profits and standards of living in the West. For example, in 1970 the International Labor Organization (ILO) reported that the Western industrialized countries got 85 percent of their bauxite, 100 percent of their chrome, 17 percent of their copper, 95 percent of their tin, and almost all tropical crops from the Third World. Until pressured by host governments to do so, multinational corporations conducted little refining or processing of raw products in the country of extraction. The materials were exported in a raw state, often at considerable profit but with little benefit to the host country. A United Nations document of 1972 reported that copper-producing U.S. multinationals in Chile, which controlled more than 90 percent of Chilean copper deposits, were showing a $4 billion profit on a $30 million investment, Chile having signed away its rights to these valuable resources. And the same story is repeated numerous times elsewhere. The dominance of the multinationals in the extractive industries has often proved an effective barrier to the industrialization of the Third World and to local control of economic development.

The story in relation to agriculture is even worse, since producing for export to the West has often made local populations completely dependent on foreign employers and foreign markets for even the most basic subsistence. Consider, for example, how agriculture in many Latin American and Caribbean countries has been restructured towards the production of cash crops such as sugar, coffee, tropical fruits, nuts, and carnations. Under the influence of the small number of multinationals that dominate these and other areas of agriculture,

In 1974 the Canadian government established the Foreign Investment Review Agency and adopted guidelines for good corporate behavior. They serve to highlight areas in which conflicts of interest between government and multinationals may arise.

Canada's Twelve Good Corporate Behavior Principles (as They Relate to Alleged Objectionable U.S. Subsidiary Policies)

Guiding principle	Alleged objectionable practices
1. Full realization of the company's growth and operating potential in Canada.	1. U.S.-based corporate planners institute expansion and cutback plans without regard for Canada's plans and aspirations.
2. Make Canadian subsidiary a self-contained, vertically integrated entity with total responsibility for at least one productive function.	2. The Canadian subsidiary is primarily an assembler of imported parts or distributor of goods produced elsewhere so operations can be easily shut down or transferred.
3. Maximum development of export markets from Canada.	3. Filling export orders to third-country markets from the U.S. stock earns credits for U.S. balance of payments rather than Canada's.
4. Extend processing of Canada's raw materials through maximum number of stages.	4. Have as few as possible materials-processing stages in Canada to minimize political leverage.
5. Equitable pricing policies for international and intracompany sales.	5. Negotiated or spurious prices by Canadian U.S. subsidiaries are designed to get around Canadian income taxes.

the Third World, despite widespread hunger, has become a net exporter of foodstuffs. Even Africa is currently a net exporter of barley, beans, peanuts, fresh vegetables, and cattle. The production of cash crops has meant that the best land is used to produce crops for export rather than for local consumption. Hence poverty in the Third World has often been *produced* by the process of "development," as small farmers dispossessed of land requisitioned by colonialists or bought by the multinationals become laborers working for subsistence wages on large plantations rather than earning a living in their old way. Cash crops are useless for local purposes. One can't survive by eating sugar,

6. Develop sources of supply in Canada.	6. Preference for U.S. or third-country sources for purposes of corporate convenience or political leverage.
7. Inclusion of R&D and product development.	7. The concentration of R&D and product design in the United States means Canada can never develop these capabilities.
8. Retain substantial earnings for growth.	8. Profits earned in Canada do not remain to finance Canadian expansion.
9. Appointment of Canadian officers and directors.	9. Use of U.S. officers and directors to prevent development of local outlook in planning and execution.
10. Equity participation by Canadian investing public.	10. Creation of wholly owned subsidiaries denies policy determination and earnings to Canadians.
11. Publication of financial reports.	11. Consolidation of Canadian operating results into parent company statement or failure to publish any relevant information.
12. Support of Canadian cultural and charitable institutions.	12. Failure locally to support such causes as the United Appeal, while parent corporations give generously to comparable U.S. campaigns.

These guidelines were abandoned in 1984 to make Canada more attractive to foreign investors. The dilemma posed by the presence of multinationals is thus by no means easy to solve. Many governments want multinationals within their boundaries, but are concerned about the consequences.

Exhibit 9.4. Potential conflicts of interest between multinationals and nation-states
SOURCE: Based on Ashton (1968: 57).

coffee, rubber, strawberries, or carnations—the crops that have replaced the more traditional produce. One can survive only by selling one's labor, earning wages, and buying food. But because local food production has largely been replaced by the cash crops, it is extremely expensive. Thus people even in agriculturally fertile countries are often forced into poverty. Many critics of the multinationals see them as actually creating and sustaining many of the problems now being experienced in the Third World. Even liberal economists recognize the way multinationals widen rather than close the gap between rich and poor. As Teresa Hayter has put it, they are involved in "the creation of world poverty."

The way the populations of Third World countries have become dependent on wage labor as a source of livelihood parallels what occurred in the industrial revolution in Europe, when the creation of a dependent working class arose along with the disappearance of traditional means of livelihood. Exactly the same process is still occurring in the Third World today. The introduction of multinational enterprise tends to eliminate local agriculture and traditional craft and industry, creating a dispossessed labor force and a market for unskilled labor. Skilled artisans and farmers go to work on plantations and in factories for subsistence wages, exactly as they did in Europe and North America centuries before. And just as the factory owners in the industrial revolution exploited this work force, so too in the Third World today.

Hence a second criticism of the multinationals: that they exploit local populations, using them as wage slaves, often as a substitute for unionized Western labor. In multinational-owned Third World factories men, women, and children sometimes work ten, twelve, or more hours for less than one dollar a day. No wonder that industry drifts from Western cities to Third World factories at an incredible rate. For example, the AFL-CIO has estimated that the United States alone loses around one million jobs every five years to these sources of cheap and exploited labor.

Other criticisms of multinationals in the Third World hinge on the fact that while they claim to be taking capital and technology to underdeveloped countries, they in fact extract a net outflow of capital and ensure that they always retain control of the technology that they introduce. It has been estimated that multinationals sometimes raise as much as 80 percent of their capital from local sources. Their own direct investment is thus often relatively small, boosting the return generated by overall profits on their own capital to quite staggering heights. In certain industries the estimated rate of return on capital invested by the multinationals sometimes runs as high as 400 percent per annum. Given that it is usual to repatriate a major proportion of profits to headquarters, and hence the parent nation, it is thus easy to see how a net outflow of capital from the host nation can arise. It becomes extremely difficult for the Third World countries to derive any long-term benefit from the presence of the multinationals, since host governments usually do not build any real equity in their industry.

The severity of this problem has been exacerbated by the kinds of foreign aid extended by agencies such as the World Bank, the IMF, and the United States Agency for International Development. Frequently, this aid is tied in ways that promote links with multinational enterprises, and in the long run thus contributes to the net outflow of capital. This problem is vividly illustrated by the fact that the outstanding interest on the international debt of Third World countries is now greater than the capital originally borrowed, and that their annual interest payments often exceed the amount of incoming aid. In other words, international aid has resulted in their paying to the West much more than they have received.

Similar criticisms apply to the export of technology. Though much is often made of how multinationals bring valuable expertise to the Third World, they bring only what they want and ensure that they retain control. Much of the technology exported to the Third World is Western technology that is often not appropriate to local conditions, and much is well-established technology that is no longer at the cutting edge. Technology reaching maturity in the West often finds a ready market in the Third World, especially when supported by foreign aid. Western technology also makes the Third World user dependent on the Western supplier for spare parts, modernization, and often the expertise necessary to maintain and develop the technology. Thus, critics argue that multinationals are doing no more than a form of intelligent marketing that ultimately serves their own interests. For example, most research and development continues to be done in the parent country, so no real opportunity is created for Third World country to build technological expertise of its own. The export of technology thus really exports a new form of dependency.

Another criticism of multinational operations relates to the way they often disguise excess profits and avoid paying appropriate taxes in their host nations through creative "transfer pricing." It has been estimated that a staggering one-third of world trade is intracompany trade. In terms of value, each multinational corporation is often its own most important customer, with one subsidiary buying from another. Such trading gives the corporation great scope for manipulating profit figures for a subsidiary in a given country. By buying materials from one fellow subsidiary at high prices and selling its products to another at low prices, a subsidiary can make an operating loss or a high profit according to the impression it wishes to give to the outside world. Thus the profits of subsidiaries in high-tax countries may be kept artificially low, and those in low-tax countries inflated. Or profits can be switched from one industry to another to take advantage of special incentives offered by host governments. Such transactions often play a big part in the politics of organization, especially in relation to negotiations with trade unions, and in producing rationales for plant closure. The simple statement that a plant is "unprofitable" is often backed by creative accounting that deceives all but the most discerning members of trade unions, investors, and members of the general public. Multinationals, like other organizations, use accounting to shape perceptions of reality to further their own ends.

Finally, the multinationals are heavily criticized for driving unduly hard bargains with their host nations and communities, often playing one group or country against another to achieve exceptional concessions. These may take the form of rights to retain a controlling interest for a set period of time, of excessive rates of return, of local tax concessions or access to subsidies and other forms of host-government support, of freedom from government regulation, or of negotiated regulations of reduced stringency. The multinational often achieves a position where it can do pretty well as it wishes. Some of the most obvious examples of abuses are found in the field of occupational health and safety and in the general conduct of multinationals in relation to the safety of the communities and markets they serve. Free of government regulations, they often end up operating hazardous factories or dumping hazardous products onto unsuspecting publics. It has been suggested that safety standards in some multinational plants in the Third World are decades behind those in the West. The ever-present danger posed by such plants is vividly illustrated by the 1984 tragedy at the Union Carbide plant in Bhopal, India, which took over two thousand five hundred lives and maimed thousands more.

For all these reasons critics of multinational operations tend to stress that these organizations can create economic, political, and social havoc, distorting rather than benefiting the development of their host country. Of course, the blame is not seen as lying entirely with the multinationals, since they are usually invited into the countries where they operate, and often do so with the active cooperation and encouragement of ruling governments, dictatorships, or powerful elites. The critics thus also place a heavy measure of blame on the ruling classes within those countries for participating in the domination and exploitation of their nation's human and material resources. Sometimes, the multinationals engage in explicit or implicit agreements with ruling authorities regarding the conditions under which they will operate, as in the Philippines, where they enjoyed guarantees of a nonunionized labor force from the Marcos dictatorship. Elsewhere the arrangements tend to be more subtle, and the result of careful and continuous political lobbying.

The radical critique thus emphasizes that the modern state and multinational corporations act as partners in systematic domination. The defenders of modern practice, however, tend to see such activities in a more favorable light. State and multinationals are viewed as partners in progress, modernization, and development, and, in the view of advocates of this partnership, the majority of multinationals usually behave in an exemplary way. These advocates would argue that it is necessary to focus on the exemplary behavior as a model of what overall practice could look like. Codes of conduct such as those developed by the United Nations in relation to the dumping of hazardous products, and by the ILO in relation to good corporate citizenship, in this view, define frameworks within which multinationals can offer much to world development. Whereas the radical critic tends to place most of the blame for poor relations with host nations on the multinationals, their advocates contend that governments or ruling elites often fail to honor their contractual obligations or to recognize the need for the multinationals to receive a reasonable reward for their risk and effort.

As an example of these problems viewed from a multinational standpoint, we might take Dow Chemical's experience in Chile in the 1960s and early 1970s, as reported by the chairman of the Dow board. The company was invited to participate in the production of two plastics in a joint venture with the Chilean government in 1965. At first Dow had little interest, since other than having an independent local distributor they had no operations in Chile, had no experience of working with governments in this way, and looked unfavorably on joint enterprises. However, they eventually agreed to go ahead on condition that they received a controlling interest to protect their technology and to ensure the efficient management of the business. The need to make a profit was emphasized throughout the negotiations, recognized by the Chilean government, and written into the master agreement. And the deal eventually went ahead with Dow receiving 70 percent interest in the venture, the Chilean authorities 30 percent. Dow invested $8 million in cash and $2 million by transferring expertise and technology. The remaining $21 million came in the form of $4 million cash from the Chilean government and $17 million in guaranteed loans from the Export-Import Bank and Bank of America. Under the agreement Dow was to receive royalties and other payments while the Chilean government guaranteed availability of raw materials at competitive prices and provided various other protective arrangements. Construction began in 1968, and production in what was described as "the finest petrochemical complex in the Andes" began in 1970. The plant seemed set for success, and Dow began to make arrangements for further investments in Chile.

However, after the election of the Allende government in October 1970, relations with the Chilean authorities began to deteriorate. The first hint of changes to come was the news that the Allende government wanted a controlling 51 percent ownership in the venture, a proposal that Dow, for obvious reasons, did not welcome, especially given that the government was $2 million dollars in arrears on its royalties and other payments to Dow. Discussions took place over a number of months, without resolution; and after a series of labor disputes and work stoppages that Dow now believes were designed to pressure them into a settlement, the plant was eventually "requisitioned" along with several hundred other Chilean companies after widespread economic chaos in the country as a whole.

In Dow's opinion their behavior had been exemplary—a model of how a multinational company should conduct itself in a developing country. They were thus shocked and offended at the unprovoked takeover. They had honored their commitments and received an enthusiastic response from a wide variety of Chilean business, media, and government sources, yet found themselves losing their plant through action that was even ruled illegal by the Chilean courts.

The Dow case thus presents a counterpoint to the radical critique, suggesting that the problems may not be inherent in the nature of multinational enterprise, but in the quality of relations between these organizations and their host country or community. The case supports the arguments that *if* multinationals behave in a socially responsible way, and *if* appropriate relations are struck with their hosts, the partnership may be able to benefit all. This defense of multinational enterprise suggests that the beneficial aspects of partnership can be destroyed on both sides, thus turning a mutually beneficial situation into a zero-sum game where one side wins and the other loses. In the Dow case the Allende government tried to be the winner, "exploiting" the multinational by robbing it of its technology and the energy, time, and money that it had invested in Chile, just as other multinationals elsewhere attempt to exploit their hosts. Defenders of the multinationals frequently emphasize the host's role in the problem, pointing to how the squeeze put on Dow is not untypical of what tends to happen in a less extreme form to multinationals throughout the world. Once a company's operations become really successful, host governments frequently try to get a slice of the action by attempting to renegotiate basic contracts, or even by breaking contracts and promises. From a multinational standpoint there is thus as much a need to teach hosts that organizations that take risks are entitled to earn adequate returns, and to enjoy bonanzas when they are spectacularly successful, as there is a need to educate multinationals about social responsibility.

The arguments in favor of or against the multinationals continue. And much evidence and many case studies can be gathered in support of either side. There can be little doubt that there is a need to improve current practices, for the record of multinational exploitation is often gross, as is the way governments and elites have supported that exploitation. On the other hand, the tendency of hosts to want to have their cake and eat it too, attempting to attract multinationals, then to control them, is also prevalent. The solutions to the basic problems, however, are by no means clear. Reformists call for greater social responsibility and for more shared understanding; but for the radical, greater social responsibility will only result in "affordable reforms," leaving the more fundamental abuses and structured inequalities unchanged. While the reformist encourages us to recognize the plurality of interests affected by multinationals and to change the rules of the game to achieve a more equitable relationship, the radicals encourage us to question the assumptions that allow the game to be played in the first place.

Strengths and limitations of the domination metaphor

Most of what has been discussed in this chapter under the label of domination can, from another standpoint, be seen as but a dysfunctional or unintended consequence of an otherwise rational system of activity. The negative impact which organizations often have on their employees or their environment, or which multinationals have on patterns of inequality and world economic development, are not necessarily intended impacts. They are usually consequences of rational actions through which a group of individuals seek to advance a particular set of aims, such as increased profitability or corporate growth. The overwhelming strength of the domination metaphor is that it draws our attention to this double-edged nature of rational action, illustrating that when we talk about rationality we are always speaking from a partial point of view. Actions that are rational for increasing profitability may have a damaging effect on employees' health. Actions designed to spread an organization's portfolio of risks, e.g., by divesting interests in a particular industry, may spell economic and urban decay for whole communities of people who have built their lives around that industry. What is rational from one organizational standpoint may be catastrophic from another. Viewing organization as a mode of domination that advances certain interests at the expense of others forces this important aspect of organizational reality into the center of our attention. It leads us to appreciate the wisdom of Max Weber's insight that the pursuit of rationality can itself be a mode of domination, and to remember that, as discussed in the conclusions to Chapter 6, in talking about rationality we should always be asking the question *"Rational for whom?"*

The metaphor thus provides a useful counterweight to much of traditional organizational theory, which for the most part has ignored values or ideological premises. Most discussions of organization attempt to be ideologically neutral, often by presenting theories of organization as theories that can be used to serve many different ends, and by identifying questions of business ethics as topics for special and isolated study. Through such means it is possible to talk or write about how one can design a bureaucratic or matrix organization, or create or manage an organizational culture, or play organizational politics, without paying too much attention to the way the ideas will be used. The fact that they may be used to improve the production of food or of bombs, and that in improving the rationality and efficiency of an organization one may be providing the basis for action that is profoundly irrational for many other groups of people, is not addressed. One of the major strengths of the domination metaphor is that it forces us to recognize that domination may be intrinsic to the way we organize and not just an unintended side effect. It shows us that there is often a "seamy" side to otherwise excellent organizations, and suggests that this should be a mainstream concern of managers and organization theorists.

Used in an even more proactive mode, the domination metaphor shows us a way of creating an organization theory *for* the exploited. In exposing the seamy side of organizational life, whether in terms of structured inequality, occupational accidents and disease, or exploitation in the Third World, and in attempting to develop theories to account for these phenomena, the organization theorist has a means of using organization theory as an instrument for social change. Those interested in pursuing this agenda thus make much of the possibility of developing a radical organization theory to counter the influence of more conventional theory, which they see as serving and reinforcing vested interests embodied in the status quo.

Another strength of the domination metaphor is that it helps us to appreciate the issues that fuel this radical frame of reference in practice. As we have discussed, many organizations become radicalized in ways that stress "them and us" attitudes. In understanding how organizations foster dual labor markets, symbolized and extended in differential systems of privilege, or how these operate as opportunity structures that open the doors to success for some employees while closing them to others, we catch a glimpse of the kinds of segregation and division that millions of people experience on a daily basis. As we begin to appreciate the reality of factory workers who see no future in their organization other than an extension of their dingy present, or the sense of exploitation experienced by those who are forced to work under oppressive conditions because they have no other means of survival, we can begin to understand that industrial unrest is not necessarily the work of troublemakers or of unions that have outlived their usefulness.

Many organizations are literally divided societies that perpetuate class warfare in the workplace. And they are societies that naturally generate "radical" leaders hell-bent on changing the circumstances of their followers, even if this means a long and arduous battle that may ultimately be lost. Hence employees may frequently engage in what their employers see as senseless or futile struggle for wage increases they feel they deserve, or may even put a company out of business rather than return to work on unfair terms. The popular notion that organizations serve the interests of all often blinds us to the fact that the radical ideology is not just ideology, but an accurate description of the reality of masses of people. The domination metaphor encourages us to recognize and deal with perceived and actual exploitation in the workplace, rather than merely to dismiss it as a "radical" distortion of the way things are. Clearly, if those managing organizations were to attempt to deal with the radical frame of reference by accepting rather than denying its legitimacy, as tends to be the situation at present, this would help initiate a new era of labor-management relations and conceptions of corporate responsibility. A new and aggressive form of social consciousness would oblige corporate decision makers to take personal responsibility for the inhuman consequences of so many of their conventional practices.

The strengths of the domination metaphor thus provide the basis for a truly radical critique of organization and organization theory. But in the view of many it goes too far and has a number of serious limitations. The first and most important of these arises when the perspective is linked to a crude conspiracy theory of organization and society. Though there is much evidence to suggest that patterns of domination are class-based; that there is a tendency for the interests of ruling elites to converge in centralized ownership and control; and that government policies often work in ways that sustain and serve the interests of dominant social groups, this does not necessarily support the idea that there is a conspiracy in the way one group or social class is pitted against another. Return to a question that has been raised implicitly throughout this chapter: does organizational domination occur by default or by design? A conspiracy theory tends to imply the latter, suggesting that the process of domination in society is rooted in some callous structure of motivation, or in a conscious policy of exploitation. However, this is not necessarily the case. For example, if we return and consider the ideas discussed in Chapter 8, it is easy to see that domination may be encoded in the logics of change through which social life is unfolding: organizational actions that promote structured inequalities, industrial accidents, occupational disease, environmental pollution, or exploitation in the Third World, may all result from the way systemic forces dictate that business be done.

For many this explanation is far too deterministic, serving to remove all responsibility from the powerful decision makers who are actively engaged in producing the organizational world, and who in principle have the power to change things. However, it does serve to raise a very real dilemma. For many top-level decision makers often feel caught "between a rock and a hard place," recognizing the social consequences of their actions while knowing that a sensitive social conscience or undue concern for people may prove economically paralyzing and prevent their organizations from operating in a decisive and efficient way.

To the extent that domination is seen as part of a social conspiracy or the responsibility of a few individuals, the latent consequence is to assign blame, arouse defenses, and entrench the fundamental problems. At best, it mobilizes social and political opposition to the problem, aiming for revolutionary change but usually achieving no more than marginal change. While such mobilization may be appropriate, a more systemic understanding would help to create a greater sense of collective responsibility and to find ways of reframing the problems to create new kinds of remedial actions. For example, such reframing may show that domination is embedded in processes of mutual causality or in dialectical logics of change that can be reshaped by giving attention to special system pathologies, new codes of social responsibility, new concepts of social accounting, and the like. Approached in this manner, the insights of the metaphor transcend the limitations imposed by interpretations grounded in any conspiracy theory.

A second potential limitation of the metaphor stems from the danger that in asserting an equivalence between domination and organization we may blind ourselves to the idea that nondominating forms of organization are possible. With this in mind, it is sometimes argued that the real thrust of the domination metaphor should be to critique the values that guide organization and that the focus of analysis should be to distinguish between exploitive and nonexploitive forms, rather than to engage in critique in a broader sense.

Finally, it is often said that the metaphor merely articulates an extreme form of left-wing ideology, serving to fan the flames of the radical frame of reference and thus adding to the difficulties of managers in an already turbulent world. The criticism has merit in that the perspective is ideological, but it is certainly no more ideological than any other. The chapters in this book show that all theories of organization are inherently ideological in that they tend to give us rather one-sided views. Thus although the domination metaphor may lead us to focus on the negative side of organization in an extreme way, it is really no more extreme than any other viewpoint, including the highly orthodox.

10

Developing the Art of Organizational Analysis

In the preceding chapters we have examined some different ways of thinking about organization. This chapter will show how these ways of thinking can be used in a practical way to read and understand specific situations, and to shape the management and design of organization generally.

Using metaphor to read and understand organization

Any realistic approach to organizational analysis must start from the premise that organizations can be many things at one and the same time. A machinelike organization designed to achieve specific goals can simultaneously be: a species of organization that is able to survive in certain environments but not others; an information-processing system that is skilled in certain kinds of learning but not in others; a cultural milieu characterized by distinctive values, beliefs, and social practices; a political system where people jostle to further their own ends; an arena where various subconscious or ideological struggles take place; an artifact or manifestation of a deeper process of social change; an instrument used by one group of people to exploit and dominate others; and so on. Though managers and organization theorists often attempt to override this complexity by assuming that organizations are ultimately rational phenomena that must be understood with reference to their goals or objectives, this assumption often gets in the way of realistic analysis. If one truly wishes to understand an organization it is much wiser to start from the premise that organizations are complex, ambiguous, and paradoxical.

Fortunately, the kind of metaphorical analysis developed in earlier chapters provides us with an effective means of dealing with this complexity. For it shows us how we can open our thought processes so that we can read the same situation from multiple perspectives in a critical and informed way.

To apply this method of analysis in practice, two steps are necessary. The first is to produce *a diagnostic reading* of the situation being investigated, using different metaphors to identify or highlight key aspects of the situation. The second step is to make a *critical evaluation* of the significance of the different interpretations thus produced. Through these two steps it is possible to explore the complexity of organizations in both a descriptive and prescriptive manner. The following sections of this chapter illustrate this approach in the analysis of an organization we will call Multicom.

THE MULTICOM CASE

Multicom is a small firm employing 150 people in the public-relations field. It was started in 1979 by Jim Walsh, a marketing specialist, and Wendy Bridges, a public-relations expert. They had worked together for several years at a medium-sized communications firm, and decided to branch out on their own to realize their own ideas as to what a good PR firm could and should be. They felt that their combined expertise and extensive contacts provided an excellent base on which to do this.

Before submitting their resignations at their old firm they persuaded two colleagues, Marie Beaumont and Frank Rossi, to join them as minority shareholders. While Walsh and Bridges each held 40 percent of the equity in the new venture, Beaumont and Rossi were each given 10 percent. Rossi was an editor and writer with an excellent reputation, and Beaumont was a well-regarded film and video person.

At first business was difficult, and they were glad of the corporate clients that they had taken with them from their old firm. Competition was keen, and their old firm seemed subtly to be doing everything it could to block their progress. However, they worked hard, and their reputation steadily grew, along with the size of their staff and their earnings. By the end of their second year the four partners were each earning almost double their previous salaries and building a significant capital investment as well. They felt that they were well on the way to achieving the kind of top-notch outfit on which they had set their sights.

These early years were exciting ones.

When they established Multicom the four partners adopted a client-centered mode of organization. They each had certain clients for whom they felt a special responsibility, and in effect became project managers for these clients. Each developed a reasonable competence in all aspects of the agency's work so that they could substitute for each other when necessary. And new staff were encouraged to develop the same all-around skills and capacities in addition to their specializations. While this was often time-consuming and expensive, it created great flexibility. The search for new business and continuing contacts with clients took a significant proportion of staff away from the office most of the time, so the existence of a number of good "all-arounders" was a real asset. Besides that, it often made work more interesting and enjoyable, and added to the general team spirit of the office.

The staff at Multicom worked hard, often starting early in the morning and working late at night. They also played hard, throwing regular parties to celebrate the completion of major projects or the acquisition of new clients. These helped to keep morale high and to project Multicom's image as an excellent and exciting place to work. The firm's clients often attended these parties, and were usually impressed by the vitality and quality of interpersonal relations.

During the company's third year, however, things began to change. The long hours and pace of life at Multicom were getting to Walsh and Bridges. Each had heavy family commitments and wanted more leisure time. They increasingly talked about the need to "get more organized" so that they could exercise a closer control over staff and office activities, which, in their view, at times verged on the chaotic. Beaumont and Rossi, on the other hand, who were both single, and at thirty and thirty-one almost ten years younger than the senior partners, relished the lifestyle and were keen to maintain the firm's present character. They would have been happy to shoulder a greater share of the work and responsibility in return for a greater equity in the company, but Walsh and Bridges were reluctant to hand them this sort of control.

As time went on, it became clear that there were important philosophical differences with regard to the way the office should be run. While Walsh and Bridges regarded the ad hoc style of organization that had developed during the first two years as temporary—"necessary until we've sorted out our ideas as to how we want to put this organization together"—Beaumont and Rossi saw it as a desirable way of doing business in the longer term. While Walsh and Bridges complained about the frequent absence of staff from the office and the lack of clear systems of responsibility and office protocol, Beaumont and Rossi relished what they often described as their "creative chaos." To them, the firm was producing excellent results, clients were happy and knocking at the door, and this was all that mattered.

By the fourth year tensions were close to the breaking point. The four principals frequently found themselves in long meetings about office organization, and the differences were as deep as ever. Walsh and Bridges argued for "more system," and Beaumont and Rossi argued for the status quo. The differences were straining personal relations and were having an unfavorable impact on life in the office generally. Many staff felt that Multicom was in danger of losing its special character and was no longer quite the same "fun place" at which to work.

All four principals sensed this change, and they talked about it frequently. However, there was simply no consensus as to what should be done. And as a result of a general frustration, they began to break an unwritten but golden rule set in the early days of Multicom: that all four would always be involved in major policy decisions. Walsh and Bridges began to meet together, and resolved that the only way forward was for them to exercise their authority and to insist that a reorganization of the office be initiated. They agreed to propose this at a meeting with Beaumont and Rossi the following day.

Walsh and Bridges were surprised. The idea produced little resistance from their two colleagues. It was almost as if it was expected. Beaumont and Rossi insisted that the decision should not be taken without a lot of thought, since it represented a major departure. And they reiterated their view that no change in office organization was necessary, other than a streamlining of a few financial procedures. They were by no means happy with the proposal, but it was clear that they weren't going to fight it.

The following week Walsh and Bridges called a meeting of all staff to outline their plans. In operational terms these involved a clearer definition of job responsibilities, a more formalized procedure governing the exchange of staff between projects, and a closer control over the conditions under which staff were to be away from the office during business hours. A number of other office procedures were also introduced.

The meeting was unique in Multicom's history in tone and nature. For weeks there was talk about a rift among the four principals, and about how winds of change were blowing through the firm. While some members of staff welcomed the greater degree of structure, others resented the new developments. Staff continued to work hard at their jobs with the professionalism they knew Multicom demanded. But everyone knew that things were not quite the same; Multicom was no longer working—or playing—the Multicom way.

Walsh and Bridges, however, were well pleased. They felt a lot more secure with the way things stood, and could see the time ahead when they would be able to take a lot of pressure off themselves and let the office run itself within the framework they had begun to develop.

Beaumont and Rossi continued to work hard as usual, and their project teams were least affected by the new developments. Within a year, however, they had left Multicom and set up a new company of their own, taking a number of key staff and clients with them.

Thanks to a large number of faithful clients, Multicom continued to produce sound financial results, but it gradually lost its reputation as a leading-edge agency. It could be relied on to produce good solid work but was, in the eyes of a number of disaffected clients, "uninspiring."

Beaumont and Rossi's new firm, Media 2000, picked up many of these clients and, adopting the organizational style pioneered at Multicom, recreated a "fun business" employing eighty people. The firm quickly established itself as a talented and innovative agency. Beaumont and Rossi take satisfaction in the firm's reputation and financial success and look back on their days with Multicom as "a great learning experience." In retrospect, they view their differences with Walsh and Bridges as part of a "lucky break" that spurred them to find an even more lucrative and satisfying work situation.

ANALYZING MULTICOM: A DIAGNOSTIC READING

How are we to interpret this case? What metaphors help us to make sense of the developments described?

Let's start with the machine metaphor. In what ways is Multicom like a machine? How does this metaphor help us to explain the case? There is little evidence of mechanistic organization in Multicom's early years. But the changes initiated by Walsh and Bridges definitely have this character. Is their conception of the need "to get more organized" shaped by mechanistic principles? Certainly the changes introduced make the organization more bureaucratic, but it is still a long way from the extreme forms of bureaucratic organization described by Henri Fayol or Max Weber, and there will probably be few signs of Frederick Taylor's scientific management. Exploring the organization through the lens of the machine metaphor, therefore, we could conclude that this is an organization that is being mildly bureaucratized, and is likely to manifest increasingly bureaucratic behavior in the years ahead if the concern for tighter organization takes hold.

Viewing Multicom within the frame of reference provided by the organismic metaphor, we encounter a different set of issues. What is the nature of the organization's environment? What are the critical tasks influencing the organization's ability to survive? Has it secured a niche in the environment? Is it able to defend this niche adequately, or should it be searching for a new one? Has it adopted appropriate organizational and managerial styles for dealing with its environment? Does it have an appropriate strategy? Is it satisfying the needs and aspirations of its employees? We can perform a contingency analysis on this organization, using the framework offered in Exhibit 3.7 to find the degree of congruence of detailed relations. We might arrive at the conclusion that since Multicom is occupying a highly competitive environment where there are few barriers to entry, ongoing creativity and the ability to manage relations with clients are critical. We might conclude that the loose organic or matrix structure that Multicom had in its early years was appropriate, and see the trend toward increasing bureaucratization as a potentially dangerous one that could take the organization out of alignment with its environment. Analyzing the organization as part of an ecology comprising collaborative and competitive relations between similar and dissimilar organizations, we might also note the different lines of strategic development that remain open to the organization.

Using the metaphor of a holographic brain, we could see how Multicom in its early years stumbled on some of the principles of holographic design. Its early mode of operation reflects the principle of redundant functions, and the team-based, client-centered approach allows the organization to build requisite abilities into its various parts. The teams are microcosms of the whole. Learning and development are encouraged, and the organization tends to be open-ended and self-organizing. Beaumont and Rossi have used the same principles in the design and management of Media 2000. We might conclude that familiarity with the holographic metaphor could well allow Multicom to reincorporate these principles in a highly effective and creative mode of organization.

Viewing Multicom from the perspective of the culture metaphor, we may be impressed by the case as an illustration of the dynamics of cultural change. Multicom starts off with a highly cohesive corporate culture built around the values shared by the four principals. There is a corporate philosophy of working hard and playing hard, and a commitment to quality work and good client relations. Regular parties ritualize and affirm corporate identity. And as we probe the corporate culture even further, we might expect to discover detailed mechanisms through which these and other aspects of the culture are created, sustained, and communicated to newcomers. In the latter part of the case the divisions between the four principals gradually reduce the strength of spirit and unity of the organization. As a bureaucratic philosophy becomes institutionalized, the old ethos becomes weaker, because the climate and tone of the office change along with the new structures and routines. We might expect Multicom to become less and less like its old self after the departure of Beaumont and Rossi. We might expect the old culture to take root and grow in a new form in Media 2000 as Beaumont and Rossi recreate the ethos of the old Multicom.

From the standpoint of the political metaphor we might easily convince ourselves that we have here a good old case of organizational politics. Multicom is born politically as the four principals break away from their old firm, taking key clients with them. The seeds of subsequent developments are set in the unequal structure of ownership. While consensus decision making is a favored style during the early years, this breaks down when real differences and divisions appear, and old-fashioned autocracy takes over. Those with majority ownership insist that their opinions carry more weight than those of their colleagues. The fact that Beaumont and Rossi create Media 2000 in exactly the same way that Multicom was created illustrates the force of the basic divisions at work. We can use the model developed in Chapter 6 to trace the competing interests shaping the firm's history. We might try and understand how the conflicting aims, aspirations, and desired lifestyles of the four founders help to precipitate the schism, and note the power relations shaping events and the processes through which key decisions are made and implemented.

Examining the case from the perspective of the psychic prison metaphor, we might choose to investigate the hidden and unconscious aspects of interpersonal relations within the firm. We are not given any in-depth evidence in the material presented, but as we explore the real situation we could well find that unconscious factors may be shaping Walsh's or Bridges's desire for more control, or the other partners' commitment to looser forms of organization. We may well find that the political divisions are ultimately built on these unconscious processes. Or, as we explore the systems of personal ideology and belief that bind Multicom together, we may find interesting cognitive traps and double binds exerting a major influence on organizational dynamics.

From the perspective of the flux and transformation metaphor we may acquire interesting insights on the logics of change shaping Multicom and its environment. We may be able to appreciate the autopoietic loops linking Multicom's self-image to its understanding and enactment of its environment, or to use ideas about mutual causality or the dialectical nature of change to understand the dynamics shaping the organization and its industry. Here again, however, the case as presented does not give us any real information with which to pursue this line of inquiry.

Finally, we could examine the case from the perspective of the domination metaphor. As presented, Multicom, like most firms in its industry, seems to be a cohesive firm whose members are relatively well placed in the overall structure of society. It is a long way from the dichotomized kind of organization where clear divisions are drawn between blue and white collar and where organizational politics become radicalized. While in terms of Max Weber's typology of domination the organization is moving towards a bureaucratized administration, it hardly seems to be managed in an exploitative way. If we probe the internal dynamics we may well find that certain members of staff are being controlled and exploited, but there is no obvious evidence of this in the material presented. If we use the domination metaphor to explore the firm's role in society, however, we may find that indeed it forms part of a wider structure of domination. For example, one or more of the firm's clients may be engaged in activities that are having a negative impact on the environment or on particular social groups, with Multicom being paid to help them disguise the seamy sides of their operations. In revealing this, the metaphor may be of great use, especially if our wish is to improve social responsibility in business.

The above *diagnostic reading* highlights different aspects of the organization. It is diagnostic not in the medical sense of attempting to identify diseases (or, in the case of organizations, problems) but in the old Greek sense of attempting to discern the character of a situation. The images generated by different metaphors are idealized points of reference against which the situation at Multicom can be compared. Each metaphor raises a host of different questions about the nature of the organization. The answers to these questions "fill in" our diagnostic reading.

Thus, to make a partial summary, the machine metaphor is useful in identifying emergent bureaucratic characteristics even though the organization is a long way from being a formal bureaucracy. The organismic metaphor allows us to arrive at some preliminary judgments as to whether the organizational changes are appropriate, given the nature of the organization's environment and the key tasks that it must perform to survive. The holographic metaphor highlights significant organizational characteristics that are important in sustaining its vigor and innovativeness, even though the organization may not be consciously organized around holographic principles. The culture metaphor highlights the fact that key corporate values are in transition. And so on.

This analysis of Multicom is by no means exhaustive, since we have investigated the relevance of the different metaphors only in a partial way. If we were to apply the ideas brought out in previous chapters in more detail, or in a more systematic way, many more insights could well emerge. And it may well be that there are other metaphors that could help us diagnose the situation. For example, members of an organization often have their own metaphors for understanding or expressing what they're doing or what their organization is like. In an actual study of an organization like Multicom (as opposed to an analysis of a case study or other secondary account) these favored metaphors may well emerge, and may need to be given prominent attention.

A *diagnostic reading* thus unfolds as we attempt to judge and document the extent to which different metaphors can help us to read the character of a situation. As our experience in this diagnostic process develops, so does our skill. As we become familiar with the images explored in the previous chapters, and as we learn how a particular image leads us to a way of thinking about the subject under study, the process becomes a very natural ability. Indeed, it becomes part of the intuitive process through which we judge the character of organizational life.

ANALYZING MULTICOM: THE PROCESS OF CRITICAL EVALUATION

Once a diagnostic reading of a situation has been obtained certain questions arise. Are all the insights generated by the different metaphors equally helpful and useful? How can we reconcile the various pieces of information and interpretations? These and related questions point toward the need to make some kind of *critical evaluation* of the general analysis.

Clearly, this evaluation will depend on the viewpoint we bring to our analysis. For example, if we wish to adopt a managerial viewpoint, perhaps that of a consultant wishing to advise Multicom about what has happened, we will find certain insights more useful and certain metaphors more evocative than others. If we approach the analysis from the viewpoint of a social critic writing about the role of communications firms in the world of big business, other metaphors may be deemed more powerful. The usefulness of a metaphor usually depends on the purposes the analysis is to serve.

To illustrate, let us put ourselves in the role of the management consultant wishing to advise Multicom on the future management of the firm. Our immediate task, having completed the diagnostic reading, will be to identify which insights are most useful and to integrate them to produce what I call "the most effective story line." The diagnostic reading allows us the luxury of being able to jump from one position to another and merely describe or document what we see. The process lets us avoid committing ourselves to a point of view, and this is important if we are to remain open to creative interpretations of the situation. However, a time always arrives when we need to move from description to evaluation and arrive at an opinion. This is the story line; it incorporates the metaphorical analyses but is not confined by them. In other words, the metaphor framework is allowed to fade into the background as the story line takes the foreground.

In the Multicom situation the story line would minimally need to integrate

(a) the trend towards bureaucratization;
(b) the potential incongruency with the environment;
(c) the loss of holographic character;
(d) the change in corporate culture;
(e) the politics driving the change; and
(f) the unconscious forces shaping relations within the organization.

And it will need to judge the relative significance of these factors and integrate the insights that they generate. This will usually require that the analyst take a closer look at certain aspects of the organization.

For example, let us assume that in summarizing our diagnostic reading we feel that the driving force underlying the change stems from the divisions between the four principals. As we explore these we may find that their source is the unease of one of the two senior partners about the looseness of organization. Or we may find that the divisions stem from the divergence in aspirations of the two senior and two junior partners. Either explanation would lead us to see factors (a), (b), (c), and (d) as secondary but important consequences of changes initiated by (e) or (f). Or to take another possible scenario, detailed investigation may reveal that (a) is the key factor—in that one of the senior partners was convinced that the firm's recent growth now demanded more bureaucratic control. Under this scenario the drive to "get organized" (which may have had a psychodynamic/unconscious base) may have precipitated the politicking, change in corporate culture, potential incongruency with the environment, and so on.

It is vitally important to be able to investigate these different kinds of explanation, because different story lines emerge in each case. And different ways of dealing with the basic problems are suggested by the different story lines. Indeed, each story line changes the definition of the basic problem. For example, if the changes at Multicom are generated by the unconscious need for control of one of the partners, then we cannot solve the underlying problems by addressing the issue of corporate culture. If the basic problem rests in corporate politics (and is not resolved by the departure of the two junior principals), it may make little sense to see the main problems as resting in the relations between organization and environment. These secondary consequences may be of considerable importance for the future of the organization; that is, Multicom may be getting out of line with its environment and may need to explore its strategic alternatives, or Multicom may be developing a corporate culture that will stifle its vitality. But if these are secondary problems it is doubtful whether they can be remedied in isolation.

The process of *critical evaluation* thus requires that we explore competing explanations and arrive at judgments regarding the way that they fit together. Rather than attempt to make the facts of a situation fit a given theoretical scheme (as happens in much conventional organizational analysis), the method developed here takes account of the complexity of a situation by playing one interpretation against another and, when necessary, choosing between them. Again, in contrast with many conventional approaches, the process does not hinge on spotting isolated problems and finding piecemeal solutions. Rather it is an open-ended mode of inquiry that allows problem definitions and possible solutions to emerge from the readings on which the analysis is based.

Using metaphor to manage and design organization

The images or metaphors through which we read organizational situations help us to describe the way organizations are, and offer clear ideas and options as to how they could be. The processes of *diagnostic reading* and *critical evaluation* combine to create a mode of understanding—the story line—that suggests an approach or, if one prefers, a *prescription*, for dealing with the issues that are of concern.

It is now appropriate to give more attention to how the insights of different metaphors can be used prescriptively. We will do this in two steps. First, by exploring how metaphors give us systematic ways of thinking about how we can or should act in a given situation—what I call *the injunction of metaphor*. And second, by exploring how many organizational problems rest in our ways of thinking.

USING METAPHOR TO INFORM ACTION

To illustrate this first point, let us return to Multicom. Suppose that our detailed reading of the organization leads us to one of the story lines suggested earlier, namely, that the changes in the firm were precipitated by a conscious desire on the part of Jim Walsh to "get organized." Let us further suppose that our detailed investigations have revealed that there was no hidden agenda (such as the attempt to exercise closer control over the junior partners or other staff), and that Walsh's desire was a consequence of his implicit belief that organization means bureaucratization. He was genuinely anxious to arrive at a clear specification of duties and procedures. The decision by Walsh and Bridges to exercise their seniority was taken as an exceptional measure, to hurdle what seemed to be an unbridgeable philosophical difference between the senior and junior partners.

How can the different metaphors help us to frame an appropriate course of action in this case? Clearly, the situation in certain respects is irreversible in that Beaumont and Rossi have now left the agency and established a successful firm of their own. Multicom has to work without them (and some other good staff), has a new competitor, has lost certain clients, and will inevitably be affected in day-to-day operations by the changes that have occurred. But there is a lot that they can learn from the experience. And there is a lot that the firm can do to be effective in the current situation.

As far as learning is concerned, Walsh and Bridges could no doubt benefit from an understanding of the political dynamics that unfolded as a result of what they probably regarded as a perfectly rational decision. Assuming that they wanted to keep Beaumont and Rossi, their behavior was politically inept. At a stroke they changed the basis of decision making among the four partners from democratic to quasi-autocratic, and they underestimated the potential for the schism that eventually developed. Given that Multicom was itself created by breaking away from another firm, the potential for a recurrence is obvious with hindsight, and probably should have been anticipated. By being aware of Multicom as a political system, Walsh and Bridges would have been much better equipped to manage the crisis precipitated by the decision to bureaucratize. If they desired the firm to continue as a partnership involving the four principals, there are many ways in which they could have achieved this purpose. For example, the evidence suggests that there might have been room for an exploration of underlying differences. A longer-term solution might have given symbolic and substantive recognition of the partnership as a relationship among four equals by moving to a more equalized set of power relations in terms of *formal* control, perhaps through a change in the structure of share holdings. Given the potential for schism and the senior partners' desire to avoid it, this option should have been actively explored. In these and other ways, many aspects of the framework for political analysis offered in Chapter 6 could have been used *proactively*, to read what was happening and to develop strategies for dealing with the situation thus revealed.

As to shaping action in the current situation, there is also much that can be done. The basic problem is deciding where to start. Assuming that our diagnostic analysis has discounted any hidden motive in the trend toward increasing bureaucratization, one strategy would be to assess the overall position of Multicom in relation to its environment, then develop prescriptions with this in mind. For example, marshaling the insights of the organismic metaphor, we could appraise Multicom's environment and the niche it occupies, and attempt to determine whether the organization has an appropriate strategy, structure, managerial style, and corporate culture. Almost all the ideas discussed in Chapter 3 can now come into play. Our environmental analysis will help us determine whether Multicom can survive by defending its present niche, or whether it needs to go in search of a new one. This, in turn, will help us decide whether Multicom should be attempting to sustain existing competencies or developing new ones that will allow it to attract new clients or even to move into new areas of activity. A contingency analysis (Exhibit 3.7) could be used to determine whether present organizational arrangements are appropriate. If our conclusion is that Multicom needs to sustain a competitive edge by developing a greater capacity for ongoing creativity and good client relations, Walsh and Bridges will need to recognize that they have been moving the organization in an inappropriate direction. In rectifying this while satisfying their concerns, good use could be made of Lawrence and Lorsch's ideas about differentiation and integration, bureaucratizing only those aspects of the firm where routinization may improve efficiency, while preserving looser organizational arrangements elsewhere.

Other metaphors could also help us in implementing this strategy. For example, the ideas about holographic organization discussed in Chapter 4 could be used to fine-tune the organization so that the organizational requirements for creativity and good client relations are enhanced and sustained. And the ideas on corporate culture discussed in Chapter 5 could help recapture an ethos, spirit, and sense of identity and direction that would enhance these desired capacities.

Our prescriptive action plan conveniently illustrates how the insights of three metaphors combine to suggest an appropriate future for the organization. While the organismic metaphor is used to assess the general direction in which the organization needs to move, the holographic and culture metaphors help to show how this can be put into practice. Other metaphors may also be needed to provide other insights and prescriptions. For example, the proposed changes may mobilize a new set of political tensions within the organization. Here again the ideas discussed in Chapter 6 may become relevant, either to help the prinicipals unblock the situation or, if this is not possible, at least to help them confront the political reality that there is resistance to the proposed changes.

In discussing the above prescription it is as well to remember that analysis is always shaped by the perspective brought to the analysis. We have adopted a managerial point of view, and certain metaphors have proved very useful from that viewpoint. Clearly, if we adopt another perspective—such as that of the social critic referred to earlier—the above analysis could be described as one-sided and as having many undesirable consequences. For example, if the analysis and prescription succeed in making Multicom more effective, this could mean that they are now more effective in helping to cover the unscrupulous side of business that the critic wishes to expose. From the critic's perspective, the domination metaphor discussed in Chapter 9 may be the most useful for understanding Multicom, and the rest judged as dangerous or misleading.

Whether by critic or by consultant, the important point is that the insights of all the metaphors *can* be used prescriptively. As we understand an organization through the lens provided by a particular metaphor we are shown a way of managing and designing the organization in accordance with a particular image. The machine metaphor suggests a mechanistic approach. The organismic metaphor suggests how we can best organize to meet environmental demands. The brain metaphor helps us to organize for learning and innovation. The culture metaphor shows us how we can manage meaning. The political metaphor teaches us how to act politically. The psychic prison metaphor shows a way of escaping from cognitive traps. The flux metaphor shows how we can influence change. The domination metaphor shows us a way of highlighting and marshaling resistance to processes of societal domination. And so on. Each metaphor has its own injunction or directive: a mode of understanding suggests a mode of action.

These different metaphors come into their own in different situations and according to the perspective from which we wish to understand and act in relation to those situations.

MANY ORGANIZATIONAL PROBLEMS REST IN OUR WAYS OF THINKING

Our discussion brings us to a very important point: that there is a close relationship between the way we think and the way we act, and that many organizational problems are embedded in our thinking. This has very important consequences. First, it encourages us to take ownership of the part we play in shaping the problems that we have to solve. For example, Jim Walsh and Wendy Bridges at Multicom could blame the change in the company's situation on the values, behaviors, and intransigence of Beaumont and Rossi. Or they could accept the situation as something that their ideas and actions have, at least in part, helped to create. This kind of acceptance can have an empowering effect, since it brings partial responsibility for many problems to one's own doorstep. And this often opens lines of action that were otherwise closed.

Second, an appreciation of the close relationship between thoughts and actions can help to create new ways of organizing. To illustrate, let's go back to the conception of "getting organized" that shaped the changes within Multicom. The bureaucratic conception to which Jim Walsh subscribed disguised the fact that Multicom was already organized. True, as far as he and Bridges were concerned the present arrangements had undesirable consequences, but Multicom had found a way of tying itself together in a coherent manner. For example, the corporate culture played an important role. If Jim Walsh had been able to understand organization in a different way there might well have been other means of dealing with the problematic situation.

One of the major strengths of the different metaphors explored in this book is that they open numerous avenues for the way we attempt to organize in practice. Take for example the holographic metaphor. To the bureaucratic mind an organization that is organized holographically will appear disorganized and chaotic. Yet, as has been shown in Chapter 4, there may be very clear organizing principles at work, producing a self-organizing process. The holographic metaphor reverses bureaucratic principles. Unless we are familiar with the holographic idea, either consciously or unconsciously, we have difficulty in seeing how to organize in this way.

Take again the culture metaphor. This points to a way of organizing through shared norms, values, ideas, and beliefs, and thus shared visions and directions for future development. Organization rests *in* the system of meaning. It does not depend on the existence of bureaucratic structures or rules.

Similarly, if we think about organization through political meta-phor, we see how it may be possible to organize around the interplay of competing interests, forging unity through negotiation, wheeling and dealing, or perhaps even through raw coercion. Here, of course, the domination metaphor comes into play, offering its own distinctive view of the nature of organization. And so on.

These brief examples serve to illustrate the point that our thinking about organization influences how we organize. We can overcome many familiar problems by learning to see and understand organization and organizations in new ways, so that new courses of action emerge.

Reading as theory in practice

In the previous sections of this chapter, I have shown how the theoretical ideas discussed earlier in this book can be used in a practical way to understand, manage, and design organizations. One of the beauties of the approach is that it builds on what many people already do quite naturally. As was mentioned in Chapter 1, effective managers and professionals in all walks of life are implicitly aware that new insights about a situation emerge as one reads a situation from new angles, and that a wide and varied reading can create a wide and varied range of action possibilities.

The method of analysis developed in this book thus makes explicit a process that is basic to our way of thinking and how we understand all facets of life. In using metaphor to understand organization we are not required to memorize complex theories or long lists of abstract con-cepts. We are simply encouraged to learn how to think about situations from different standpoints. We are invited to do what we do naturally, but to do so more consciously and broadly. The metaphors explored in earlier chapters illustrate how we can follow the implications of a pow-erful image to its logical conclusion. Thus in addition to providing a host of specific insights and ideas, the chapters provide a valuable re-source for learning *how* we can develop and extend our own ability to read organization.

Many practical people believe that theory gets in the way of practice and that, by and large, theorizing is a waste of time. But there is a great fallacy in this way of thinking. For in recognizing how taken-for-granted images or metaphors shape understanding and action, we are recognizing the role of theory. Our images or metaphors *are* theories or conceptual frameworks. Practice is never theory-free, for it is always guided by an image of what one is trying to do. The real issue is whether or not we are aware of the theory guiding our action.

One of the main messages of this book is that we can enhance our ability to organize and to solve organizational problems by understanding the link between theory and practice and by appreciating Kurt Lewin's famous dictum that "there is nothing so practical as a good theory." People who learn to read situations from different (theoretical) points of view have an advantage over those committed to a fixed position. For they are better able to recognize the limitations of a given perspective. They can see how situations and problems can be framed and reframed in different ways, allowing new kinds of solutions to emerge.

As shown, the trick is to learn how to engage in a kind of conversation with the situation one is trying to understand. Rather than impose a viewpoint on a situation, one should allow the situation to reveal how it can be understood from other vantage points. In a way we can say that one should always be sensitive to the fact that a situation "has its own opinion" in that it invites understanding through a frame of reference other than the one being applied. The art of analysis described above allows one to probe a situation through the reading process, gradually moving to some judgment or *critical evaluation* of the situation at hand.

The only way to arrive at balanced judgments is to let this kind of inquiry take its course. But this does not mean that the process must take a long time. For as one develops the art of reading situations, critical analysis and evaluation become a way of thinking. One quickly learns to recognize important cues and to uncover crucial insights.

In developing this style of organizational analysis we have a means of linking theory and practice to deal with the complex and paradoxical nature of organizational life in a very realistic way.

11

Imaginization

A Direction for the Future

Organizations are many things at once!

It is this intriguing idea that provided the inspiration for this book. I believe that some of the most fundamental problems that we face stem from the fact that the complexity and sophistication of our thinking do not match the complexity and sophistication of the realities with which we have to deal. This seems to be true in the world of organization as well as in social life more generally. The result is that our actions are often simplistic, and at times downright harmful. I have written this book in an attempt to make some small contribution to our understanding of the way we oversimplify, and to identify a possible means through which we might begin to develop a capacity for doing a little better than we do now.

My overall approach has been to foster a kind of critical thinking that encourages us to understand and grasp the multiple meanings of situations and to confront and manage contradiction and paradox, rather than to pretend that they do not exist. I have chosen to do this through metaphor, which I believe is central to the way we organize and understand our world. But one does not have to accept this thesis. The much more important general point is that our ways of seeing the world are always bounded ones, and that much can be learned by appreciating the partial nature of our understandings and how they can be broadened. I have used metaphors to show how we can frame and reframe our understanding of the same situation, in the belief that new kinds of understanding can emerge from the process.

When we look at our world with our two eyes we get a different view from that gained by using each eye independently. Each eye sees the same reality in a different way, and when working together, the two combine to produce yet another way. Try it and see. I believe that the same process occurs when we learn to interpret the world through different metaphors. The process of framing and reframing itself produces a qualitatively different kind of understanding that parallels the quality of binocular vision. As we try and understand phenomena like organizations as machines, organisms, cultures, political systems, instruments of domination, and so on, a new depth of insight emerges. The way of seeing itself transforms our understanding of the nature of the phenomenon.

On elephants and organizations

At first sight, much of what I have tried to say has a great deal in common with the old Indian tale of the six blind men and the elephant. The first man feels a tusk, claiming the animal to be like a spear. The second, feeling the elephant's side, proclaims that it is more like a wall. Feeling a leg, the third describes it as a tree; and a fourth, feeling the elephant's trunk, is inclined to think it like a snake. The fifth, who has seized the elephant's ear, thinks it remarkably like a fan; and the sixth, grabbing the tail, says it is much more like a rope. Their understandings would be even further complicated, as Peter Vaill has noted, if the elephant were set in motion. For the man clinging to the elephant's leg would experience an elliptical forward motion. The man holding the tail would be whipped in random fashion, while the others would be jerked and jolted, and perhaps splashed and splattered with water and manure. The elephant's motion would probably destroy all their previous understandings and further complicate the task of arriving at a consensus.

There can be little doubt that, as with the blind men, our actual experiences of organizations are often different and hence we make sense of our experiences in different ways. Thus a person in a dingy factory may find obvious credibility in the idea that organizations are instruments of domination, while a manager in a comfortable office may be more enthusiastic about understanding the organization as a kind of organism faced with the problem of survival, or as a pattern of culture and subculture.

However, the parallels with the Indian tale break down in some important ways. First, as we look at the plight of the blind men we do so with the privilege of sight. We know that they are dealing with an elephant, and that if they were able to get together and share their experiences they might arrive at a much better consensus with regard to what the elephant is really like. However, the problem of understanding organization is more difficult in that we do not really know what organizations are, in the sense of having a single authoritative position from which they can be viewed. While many writers on organization attempt to offer such a position—for example, by defining organizations as groups of people who come together in pursuit of common goals— the reality is that to an extent we are *all* blind men and women groping to understand the nature of the beast. While we may be able to share our different experiences and even come to some consensus, we will never achieve that degree of certainty that is implicitly communicated in the Indian tale by the idea that it is they who are blind and we who have sight.

Stated in more conventional terms, there is a difference between the full and rich reality of an organization, and the knowledge that we are able to gain about that organization. We can know organizations only through our experience of them. We can use metaphors and theories to grasp and express this knowledge and experience, and to share our understandings, but we can never be sure that we are absolutely right. I believe we must always recognize this basic uncertainty.

A second important difference between the moral of the Indian tale and the problem of understanding organizations is that the very same aspect of organization can be many different things at the same time. Thus different ideas about organization do not stem just from the fact that like the blind men we are grasping different aspects of the beast, but because different dimensions are always intertwined. For example, a bureaucratic organization is simultaneously machinelike, a cultural and political phenomenon, an expression of unconscious preoccupations and concerns, an unfolded aspect of a deeper logic of social change, and so on. It *is* all these things at one and the same time. We can try to decompose organization into sets of related variables: structural, technical, political, cultural, human, and so forth; but we must remember that this does not really do justice to the nature of the phenomenon. For the structural and technical dimensions of an organization are simultaneously human, political, and cultural. The division between the different dimensions is in our minds rather than in the phenomenon.

To illustrate this point, I would like to take one of my favorite examples. The authoritarian owner of a small organization, concerned about his negative impact on employee morale and his general loss of control, has just returned from a course on human-resource management. He genuinely feels that he has had "a conversion experience" and wants to change his style of management to be more people-oriented. In an attempt to build closer and better relations with the workforce he decides to visit one of his factories. On the shop floor he makes a point of shaking hands with each employee. They are naturally surprised and don't quite know what to make of the situation, because "the boss" has always kept a clear distance and ruled with an iron hand.

Clearly, numerous different meanings are latent in the very same phenomenon—the handshake. The handshake is a symbolic gesture, an expression of a human-relations approach to management, possibly the beginning of a different and more democratic kind of political relationship within the firm, but also possibly the beginning of a new kind of employee control. The handshake embodies potentially contradictory meanings, e.g., of friendship, people-centeredness, manipulation, and control, just as the rationality of an organization can simultaneously have political and exploitative dimensions.

In trying to understand an organizational situation we have to be able to cope with these different and potentially paradoxical meanings, identifying them through some form of decomposition while retaining a sense of their interrelationship and essential integration.

This has obvious implications for the way we use the kind of analytical scheme developed in Chapter 10, and in making us aware of the dangers of theories that overcompartmentalize or decompose our understanding of organizations. I have emphasized that one of my main goals has been to develop *a way of thinking* that can cope with ambiguity and paradox. We must avoid the pitfalls of the blind-men syndrome. In using metaphors or other frames of reference to unravel the complexities of organizational life we can see certain metaphors fitting certain situations better than others (e.g., organization X is more machinelike than organization Y, department A is more holographic than department B, group C has a team-based culture while D is more adversarial), but we must always remember that aspects of every metaphor may be found in every situation.

The analytical scheme that I have developed is thus best understood as a sensitizing or interpretive process rather than as a model or static framework. Good analysis rests not just in spotting "what metaphor fits where" or "which metaphor fits best," but in using metaphor to unravel multiple patterns of significance and their interrelations. I believe that the best intuitive readings made by managers and other organizational members have the same quality. These individuals are open to the kind of nuance that stems from an appreciation that any given situation can be many different things at once.

Imaginization: organization as a way of thinking

Images and metaphors are not only interpretive constructs or ways of seeing; they also provide frameworks for action. Their use creates insights that often allow us to act in ways that we may not have thought possible before. I have tried to bring out this point in various ways, for example by demonstrating how the use of different metaphors can lead to different ways of organizing and managing, and in discussing the prescriptive functions of my approach to organizational analysis.

I now want to be more forthright in my position on the close links between thought and action and suggest that we could well begin to think about organization in a broader and more open way by using the word *imaginization* to provide us with a much more empowering view of the basic phenomenon.

As noted in Chapter 2, the word organization derives from the Greek *organon,* meaning tool or instrument. It is thus hardly surprising that the concept of organization is usually loaded with mechanical or instrumental significance. In coining the word *imaginization* my intention is to break free of this mechanical meaning by symbolizing the close link between images and actions. Organization is always shaped by underlying images and ideas; we organize as we imaginize; and it is always possible to imaginize in many different ways.

When we think about organization in this manner we are provided with a constant reminder that we are involved in a creative process where new images and ideas can create new actions. In the field of architecture new kinds of buildings have arisen from major revisions in the concepts underlying the building process. For example, the assumption that sturdy buildings depend on a satisfactory pattern of stress *compression* confines the architect to producing traditional structures. The idea that buildings can be held in place through appropriate patterns of *tension* gives rise to freer-flowing forms held in place by wires and buttresses. I believe that we can create similar revolutions in the way we organize by being aware that we are always engaged in *imaginization*.

Rather than just interpreting the way organizations are, this book also seeks to show how we can change the way they are. In recognizing the close links between thought and action in organizational life, we recognize that the way we "read" organizations influences how we produce them. Images and metaphors are not just interpretive constructs used in the task of analysis. They are central to the process of *imaginization* through which people enact or "write" the character of organizational life.

Bibliographic Notes

1: Introduction

This is a book about metaphor set within a metaphor: that of "reading organization." Intellectually, it develops the tradition pioneered by writers such as Pepper (1942) and Kuhn (1970) on the impact of root metaphors and cognitive paradigms on how we understand the world around us.

Specifically, the impetus for the book stemmed from my work on earlier projects, Burrell and Morgan (1979) and Morgan (1980, 1983a, 1983b, 1983c, 1984), each of which attempts to take a multisided view of organization. Whereas they were pitched at a theoretical level and directed at an academic audience, the present book attempts to develop the more practical implications of the basic ideas. My concern is to show how we can *use* the creative insights generated by metaphor to create new ways of understanding organization. In these notes, I sketch the foundations on which I build, elaborate points of special interest, and provide a trail of references for further reading.

On metaphor: There is a growing literature demonstrating the impact of metaphor on the way we think, on our language, and on systems of scientific and everyday knowledge. Aristotle was the first to identify the role of metaphor in the production of knowledge. In his *Rhetoric* he suggests that "midway between the unintelligible and the commonplace, it is metaphor which most produces knowledge," and in the *Poetics* he identifies the four tropes we now recognize as metaphor, metonymy, synecdoche, and irony. Each of these tropes can be understood as a variety of metaphor, but they play somewhat different roles (see, for example, White 1978; Morgan 1983b). In this work we will not worry about these distinctions, using the term metaphor to embrace the general process of image crossing whereby A is seen as B.

Vico (1968) in the early eighteenth century was the first to recognize the importance of metaphor and related tropes as modes of experience, and hence as having more than figurative significance. A number of philosophers in the nineteenth century, such as Nietzsche (1974), mention the importance of metaphor. But it is not until the work of twentieth-century philosophers like Cassirer (1946), Wittgenstein (1958), and others emphasizing language and other modes of symbolism in reality construction that these ideas acquire any prominence.

Over the last forty years, a number of important works have suggested that we must pay more attention to the role of metaphor and related tropes, including Black (1962), Boulding (1956a), Brown (1977), Burke (1962), Manning (1979), Pepper (1942), Schön (1963, 1979), and White (1978). Some of the most important contemporary debates are occurring in linguistics, hermeneutics, and psychoanalysis. Works such as Eco (1976), Jakobson and Halle (1956), Lacan (1966), and Lemaire (1977) are central to this debate. Collections of papers on metaphor, such as those by Ortony (1979) and Sacks (1979), present useful overviews of some of the issues.

The impact of metaphor on language and communication generally has been subjected to detailed analysis by Lakoff and Johnson (1980).

The role of metaphor in creative imagination and science has been treated in a number of popular and academic works. Koestler (1969) and Jonathan Miller (1978) are both outstanding in combining these dimensions.

Brown (1977) has shown the metaphorical basis of social theory. And my own work has explored the metaphorical basis of organization theory (Morgan, 1980, 1983b).

2: The machine metaphor

Mechanism in science: Many social theorists have noted that we live in a technological society dominated

by the needs of machines and mechanical modes of thought (e.g., Ellul, 1964; Giedeon, 1948; Mumford, 1934). The elements of mechanistic theory first appear in the ideas of the Greek "atomists" of the fifth
through third centuries B.C., such as Democritus and Leucippus.
They believed that the world was composed of indivisible particles in
motion in an infinite void, and that all form, movement, and change
could be explained in terms of the size, shape, form, and movement of
atoms. This mechanistic vision has influenced scientific thought right
into the twentieth century, and receives its fullest and most comprehensive expression in the contributions to physics of Sir Isaac Newton,
who developed a theory of the universe as a celestial machine. On the
way, numerous scientists invented and studied machines as a means of
understanding the laws of nature. Aristotle used mechanistic principles to understand the movement of animals, Archimedes (in Heath
1897), Galileo (1968), and others used machines to make important
contributions to mathematics and physics, and did much to advance
the idea that it is possible to build an objective science based on mechanistic principles. Galileo, for example, sought a science that could reduce all explanations of reality to a physical base, pursuing the
atomist's ideal of a universe that could be explained in terms of matter
in motion.

Mechanism in social theory: Within
the field of philosophy mechanistic ideas have exerted a powerful influence upon theories of the human mind and the nature of knowledge
and reality. The French philosopher Réne Descartes set important
foundations for these developments in his famous *Discourse on Method*
published in 1637, arguing for the separation of mind and body and
subject and object, in an attempt to place the process of human reasoning on as firm a basis as possible. Descartes, like Galileo and Newton,
built his views on the principles of atomism, believing that the material
world was to be understood in terms of the mechanical interaction and
movement of corpuscles originally created and set in motion by God.
He was fascinated with the study of automata and mechanical toys,
and contemplated the possibility of building mechanical men. Plants
and animals were viewed by Descartes as superior forms of machine.
Humans were viewed as being like machines, but distinguished by
their great capacity to use words and signs as a basis for discourse and
by their capacity to reason (Descartes 1968: 73-74).

The logic of Descartes's view of human nature was eventually developed to an extreme a century later by the French materialist Julien de
LaMettrie. In 1748, he published a book, *L'Homme Machine,* arguing
that man *is* a machine, that both body and soul are a product of mechanical processes, and that all human behavior is reducible to laws of
matter in motion. Instincts, actions, and the operation of the human

brain were thus seen as operating in accordance with completely deterministic laws, which allowed no room for voluntary behavior or subjective influence of any kind. His views were unpopular in many quarters, and he was forced at different times to leave his native Paris, and Holland, where *L'Homme Machine* was published. Interestingly, LaMettrie found a welcome in the court of Frederick the Great, where he was given a prominent position. There is thus an interesting and direct link between the mechanistic theories of the human being developed by Descartes and LaMettrie and the military practice of Frederick's Prussian army, which, as discussed in Chapter 2, actually attempted to reduce soldiers to automata who would obey instructions on command.

In social science the idea that man is a machine has exerted a powerful influence over behavioral psychology, especially through the idea that human beings are the product of environmental forces. These ideas were carried to modern psychology through the ideas of philosophers such as Hume, Locke, and Bentham, and receive their fullest expression in the stimulus-response psychology of B.F. Skinner (1953) and reinforcement theory. Arthur Koestler (1967) presents a comprehensive critique of this kind of approach to understanding human behavior. Schön (1963) presents an excellent analysis of how the principles of Newtonian physics have been used in psychological theories. The work of the influential social theorist Vilfredo Pareto (e.g., Pareto, 1935) provides a powerful illustration of how principles derived from mechanical sciences have been used to understand economics, politics, and society. And in the ideas of one of Frederick Taylor's followers, Henry Gantt (see Alford, 1934: 264-277), we find the mechanistic vision of social life carried to an extreme in his proposal for an organization called "The New Machine": "a conspiracy of men of science, engineers, chemists, land and sea-tamers and general masters of arts and materials" (p. 264). In this scheme all industry would be put under the control of engineers, who would design and run it with mechanical efficiency.

Mechanism in everyday life: With regard to the links between mechanism and everyday life, it is interesting to note how we have come to treat our bodies as machines. This is most evident in many approaches to physical fitness in which the primary aim is to "shape" the body, through jogging, calisthenics, body building, and gymnastics. Calisthenics were first developed by Swedish landowners wishing to make their peasants like soldiers, and gymnastics were developed in Germany in an attempt to prepare farmworkers for war. Modern sports are being increasingly "mechanized," the epitome being American football. This provides an almost perfect exposition of Taylor's principles of scientific management.

**Mechanism in organization theory—
Max Weber and bureaucratic organization:** Sociologist Max Weber (1946, 1947) discusses the parallels between mechanization and organization. In understanding his work it is important to realize that he was not interested in studying formal organizations as ends in themselves. Rather, he was concerned to understand the process of organization, which takes different forms in different contexts and in different epochs, as part of a wider social process. Thus, the bureaucratic form of organization was seen as but a manifestation of a more general process of rationalization within society as a whole, emphasizing the importance of means-ends relations.

There has been much misinterpretation of Weber's work in organization theory, especially with regard to his idea that the bureaucratic form of organization constitutes an ideal type. In Weber's work the concept of "ideal type" is used as a methodological tool for understanding many aspects of society. He believed that in order to understand the social world it was necessary to develop clear-cut concepts against which one could compare empirical reality. All of the ideal types that he developed were intended to serve this end. Thus he advocated using the concept of bureaucracy as an ideal type to capture a particular *form* of organization—that based on the *idea* of a machine—with a view to understanding the extent to which a society is bureaucratized. He recognized that the ideal type would not be found in practice in a pure form, since organizations would probably correspond with the ideal in varying degrees. Hence its purpose as a comparative tool. By using different ideal types to discern different forms of organization, he believed that one possessed a powerful methodology for understanding the social world.

Many of the misinterpretations relate to the fact that Weber's use of the concept "ideal" has been equated with the concept of best. Thus, Weber is often presented as endorsing bureaucracy as a best type of organization. This is completely inaccurate. Weber was skeptical about the merits of bureaucracy, and in no way intended the concept to be used in this way. One important reason why this misinterpretation has occurred is found in the fact that the publication of Weber's work in English followed the publication and popularization of the work of the classical management theorists, who had advocated that the bureaucratic approach to organization was the one best way of organizing. While Weber did not share this view, many organization theorists have interpreted him as belonging to the same school of classical management theory. They have understood his theory of bureaucracy and his use of the notion of ideal type through the lens provided by their understanding of the classical management theorists. As a result, the thrust and significance of his work has been placed in a completely inappropriate perspective. Most importantly, the fact that he understood organization as a process of domination has been completely overlooked (see Chapter 9). More often than not, he has been used as a "straw-man"—an advocate of the bureaucratic mode of organization—to be knocked down in the course of building theories that overcome the well-known limitations of bureaucracy. Unfortunately for Weberian sociology, even some of Weber's most constructive and accurate interpreters, such as Robert Merton (1968a), focus on the dysfunctions of the bureaucratic model in a way that has unintentionally fed the misinterpretations of Weber's stand on bureaucracy. This work and its implications for organization theory are discussed extensively by Burrell and Morgan (1979).

Stinchombe (1965) presents important insights on how the bureaucratic mode of organization emerges along with the mechanization of industry and the industrial revolution. George (1972) presents an extensive analysis of the history of management thought from prehistoric times, including good discussion of the writers who set the basis for classical management theory and scientific management. Adam Smith (1776) and Charles Babbage (1832) are worth reading as classic texts of the industrial revolution.

Classical management theory: Of the works of the classical management theorists, those of Fayol (1949), Mooney and Reiley (1931), and Gulick and Urwick (1937) have been among the most influential. Each illustrates how classical management theory is essentially a theory of machine design. More modern works such as Koontz and O'Donnell (1955) illustrate how these ideas have been carried forward to the present day and reinterpreted within the context of MBO, MIS, PPBS, and the like. Peter Drucker's (1954) work on MBO, which is much more participative than most treatments, is also worth consulting.

Scientific management: The principles of scientific management are set out by Taylor (1911). Important insights on the nature of the man and his ideas can be obtained by reading the biographies by Copley (1923) and Kakar (1970). Taylor emerges as a man with an obsessive vision backed by a determination to implement it at all costs. These aspects of his personality and background will be discussed in Chapter 9. A folklore has developed around Taylor and Taylorism that often confuses fact and fiction, a point that needs to be borne firmly in mind when reading Taylor's own writings. As Wrege and Perroni (1974) show, Taylor himself appears to have had what might be kindly described as a vivid imagination, creating elaborate tales that often bear little resemblance to other accounts of the same situations. Despite the fiction, the reality of the consequences of Taylor's ideas are beyond dispute. Braverman (1974) and

Worthy (1959) provide excellent critical accounts of the nature and significance of Taylorism in industrial management in both the United States and the USSR.

The Gilbreths' pioneering work on the study of human motion in the workplace is found in Frank Gilbreth's *Motion Study* (1911). The impact of scientific management on industrial engineering, industrial psychology, modern ergonomics, and work study can be seen in almost any modern text on industrial management. On a point of detail, it should be noted that while the work of all these theorists elaborates a mechanistic view of organization that is highly consistent in terms of detailed principles, minor disagreements did arise, such as between the principle of the unity of command and Taylor's principle of functional foremanship, which violated the principle that each subordinate should only have one boss.

Mechanistic organization in practice: The data relating to Henry Ford's introduction of assembly-line production are drawn from Sward (1948). He provides an excellent account of the background to assembly line production. The data on GM's Lordstown plant and Ford's at Wixom are drawn from Aronowitz (1973). Hailey (1971) and Frost, Mitchell, and Nord (1982) also present interesting ethnographic accounts of work experience in similar situations.

The problems encountered by mechanistic organizations in changing circumstances are explored in the classic study by Burns and Stalker (1961), and in Kanter's (1983) analysis of the problems of modern U.S. corporations.

March and Simon (1958) and Merton (1968a, 1968b) explore some of the dysfunctional aspects of bureaucracy.

The human problems resulting from mechanistic organization have been explored by Argyris (1957) and numerous other writers on the psychology of organization.

The distinction between functional (instrumental-bureaucratic) and substantial rationality has been developed by Karl Mannheim (1940).

The quotation from the Chinese sage Chuang-tzu is taken from Heisenberg (1958).

3: The organismic metaphor

Biology has developed as a systematic science concerned with the study and explanation of organic functioning. It studies the anatomy and physiology of living things and investigates the modes and conditions of their survival, reproduction, development, and decay. Biology classifies vital organisms into species, inquires into their geographic description, their lines of descent, and their evolutionary changes. What better description could there be of organization theory since the 1950s?

Biology and social theory: Biological thought has influenced social and organizational theory since at least the nineteenth century through the work of Spencer (1873, 1876, 1884), Durkheim, (1934, 1938, 1951), and Radcliffe-Brown (1952). These are the formative works that have influenced the powerful school of thought in sociology known as structural functionalism, brought into prominence in the 1950s and 1960s by Talcott Parsons (1951). A comprehensive discussion of this development and its relevance for the study of organization is presented by Burrell and Morgan (1979). Nisbet (1969) and Pepper (1942) discuss the impact of organic thought in more general terms.

Individual and organizational "needs": The influence of the organic metaphor on the analysis of individual and organizational "needs" can be seen in the classic accounts of the Hawthorne studies (Roethlisberger and Dickson, 1939; Mayo, 1933), and in the work of Maslow (1943), Argyris (1957, 1964), Alderfer (1969, 1972), McGregor (1960), and Herzberg et al. (1959). Good accounts discussing the work of the Tavistock Institute and the evolution of the sociotechnical systems movement can be found in Trist (1982), Trist and Bamforth (1951), Trist et al. (1963), and Rice (1958). Illustrations of how the sociotechnical perspective has been applied to theories of leadership and group behavior can be found in Blake and Mouton (1964) and Bales (1950).

Open systems theory: The concept of the "open system" has been elaborated through use of biological principles by von Bertalanffy (1950, 1968) and many others. J. C. Miller's (1978) mammoth work on "living systems" provides an excellent and thorough overview. Boulding (1956a) presents an excellent illustration of how systems theory can be applied to different levels of system that go beyond those of the biological organism. Virtually anything can be defined as a system by drawing a boundary. Hence the application of systems theory to psychology, social psychology, organization studies, and societal studies. The approach is a flexible one and open to a wide variety of interpretations. For an example of how basic systems theory can be applied to the study of organizations, see the works by Katz and Kahn (1978), Kast and Rosenzweig (1973), and Beer (1980). Emery (1969) provides an excellent overview of open-systems concepts.

The early development of systems theory was very much influenced by perspectives emphasizing equilibrium and homeostasis. In recent years, however, much more attention has been devoted to the analysis of instability. See, for example, Maruyama (1963) and Prigogine (1978, 1984) and the references on autopoiesis in my notes to Chapter 8. These new developments have carried systems thinking into a completely new realm, with very exciting new possibilities.

Contingency theory: The history of the contingency approach to organizational analysis is outlined in Burrell and Morgan (1979). The important works are by Burns and Stalker (1961), Woodward (1965), and Lawrence and Lorsch (1967a, 1967b). Miles (1980) presents an excellent overview of the implications of contingency theory for organizational choice. The important ideas on differentiation and integration are found in Lawrence and Lorsch (1967a, 1967b).

Good discussions on matrix organization are presented by Galbraith (1971), Kingdon (1973), Davis and Lawrence (1977), and Kolodny (1981).

The use of contingency theory for organizational development is very popular and takes various forms. Leavitt (1964), Kast and Rosenzweig (1973), and Nadler and Tushman (1977) provide illustrations. The approach offered in the present chapter elaborates the model developed by Burrell and Morgan (1979).

Bennis (1966) and Levinson (1972) present good illustrations of how the general concept of organizational health underlies the theory and practice of organizational development.

There is a growing literature identifying different species of organizations and distinguishing between different organizational characteristics. See, for example, Mintzberg (1979), McKelvey (1982a, 1982b), and Miller and Friesen (1984). The following provides an overview of the attempts to classify different organizational attributes:

Environment: A number of key characteristics have been identified, including the degree of stability or change, homogeneity-heterogeneity, interconnectedness between elements, abundance or scarcity of key resources, patterns of resource ownership, competition, symmetrical or assymetrical interdependence, political, legal, technological, economic, social, and market conditions. Turbulence, uncertainty, resource dependence, and specific contextual features have attracted much attention. See, for example, Dill (1958), Emery and Trist (1965), Hall (1982), Lawrence and Lorsch (1967a, 1967b), Pfeffer and Salancik (1978), Scott (1981), and Thompson (1967).

By Industry: Industrial classifications developed by governments (e.g., the U.S. Office of Management and Budget) provide detailed ways of distinguishing between public, private, and voluntary sector organizations, service, manufacturing, and retailing organizations, all

cross-tabulated according to industrial groups and industries producing specific products (see Office of Management and Budget
1972, Scott, 1981).

Strategy: Organizations may be classified according to the strategic
stance they adopt. Thus, Miles and Snow (1978) distinguish between reactor, defender, analyzer, and prospector organizations,
whereas Miller and Friesen (1984) and Emery and Trist (1965) identify other strategic patterns.

Structure: Organizations may be classified according to whether their
structures are bureaucratic-mechanistic, organic, matrix, function-
alized, divisionalized according to their authority base, size, and
their scores on various measuring scales (see Burns and Stalker,
1961; Chandler, 1962; Davis and Lawrence, 1977; Hall, 1982; Mintzberg, 1979; Pugh, Hickson, and Hinings, 1969; and Weber, 1947).

Technology: The core technology employed by an organization may be
used to explain many different organizational characteristics.
Among the classifications of technology are those which distinguish
between mass, process, and unit or small-batch production (Woodward 1965), the complexity and analyzability of work processes
(Perrow 1967), operations, knowledge, and materials technology
(Hickson, Pugh, and Pheysey, 1969), task interdependence
(Thompson, 1967), and stage of technological evolution (McKelvey
and Aldrich, 1983).

Employee Commitment: Organizations can be classified according to the
relationships developed between organization and employees. This
is crucially linked to the kind of motivation or use of power employed. For example, Etzioni (1961) distinguishes between coercive,
utilitarian, and normative organizations (e.g., prisons, business
firms, churches), based on alienative, calculative, and moral
involvement.

Key Beneficiary: "Cui bono?" Blau and Scott's (1962) typology of organizations focuses on the prime beneficiary, arguing that different
organizational characteristics are associated with the way organizations are controlled and rewards distributed. They distinguish between mutual benefit associations, business concerns, service
organizations, and commonwealth organizations in which the
prime beneficiaries are, respectively, rank and file members, owners
and managers, clients, and the public at large.

Empirical Configurations: Organizations may be classified according to
the way different variables cluster to form configurations, patterns,
or archetypes (Miller and Mintzberg, 1983). One way to identify
such configurations is to conduct case studies or empirical surveys
of as many organizations as possible, to see what patterns emerge.
McKelvey (1982a, 1982b), Mintzberg (1979), Miller and Friesen

(1984), Pinder and Moore (1978), and Pugh, Hickson,and Hinings (1969) provide illustrations of this approach.

Population ecology: The main works developing the population-ecology view of organizations are Aldrich (1979), McKelvey and Aldrich (1983), Hannan and Freeman (1977), and Freeman and Hannan (1983). They in turn draw upon the ideas of Hawley (1968) on human ecology, and Campbell (1969), who introduced the variety-selection-retention model to social science. Pfeffer and Salancik (1978) develop related ideas in terms of a resource dependence view of organization that has close links to the population ecology approach. Kimberley and Miles (1980) and Freeman (1982) have produced interesting ideas on organizational life cycles, tracing the birth, growth, development, and decline of organizations. Pennings (1982) has studied birth frequencies.

The debate between the population ecologists and the contingency theorists is very well represented by Astley and Van de Ven (1983) and by Lawrence and Dyer (1982).

Organizational ecology—the creation of shared futures: Eric Trist's work on organizational ecology can be found in Trist (1976, 1979, 1983), and Emery and Trist (1973). Epistemologically, there are strong links between his perspective and the theory of co-evolution developed by Bateson (1972, 1979). My notes to Chapter 8 on autopoiesis and "systemic wisdom" provide further references. Kenneth Boulding's view that evolution involves the "survival of the fitting" can be found in Boulding (1981). Kropotkin's (1903) early work on the relationship between evolution and mutual aid is also important, providing an impressive counterweight to the interpretations of Darwin that place emphasis on the role of competition in social evolution. The implications of the idea that organizations can evolve through collaboration as well as competition are developed by Astley (1984), Astley and Fombrun (1983), Fombrun and Astley (1983), and Van de Ven and Astley (1981). Also, see Vickers (1983).

4: The brain metaphor

Brains looking at brains! The study of the brain poses a unique problem in reflexivity and of knowledge construction, since we use brains to understand brains. Not surprisingly, the process has drawn on many different kinds of metaphor as scientists have searched for appropriate images to make sense of this complex part of anatomy. My analysis in this chapter draws on the work of Begley (1983), Burns (1968), Pribram (1971, 1976), and Taylor

(1979). Useful accounts of the holographic character of the brain are provided in Wilber (1982) and Ferguson (1980). Charles Hampden-Turner (1981) provides an outstanding account of the different metaphors that have shaped theories of the mind in science and social thought.

Under the influence of the findings of split brain research arising from the work of Roger Sperry (1968, 1969) and others, there has been much interest in understanding the implications of the functioning of the creative right and analytic left hemispheres (e.g., Mintzberg, 1976; and Taggert and Robey, 1981). The specialization of functions between these two hemispheres is important, but it is important not to underestimate the degree of interconnection as well. To reemphasize this here, it is worth noting that some scientists believe that there may be more interconnections in a single human brain than atoms in the universe. Despite all our theories, the simple fact is that the brain is as complicated as anything we know.

Brains and organizations as communication and decision-making systems: Compared with the complexity and mystery of modern brain research, use of the brain metaphor in organization theory is still in a humble stage of development. While managers have long recognized the importance of developing good systems of communication for transmitting relevant information to where it is needed, the idea of using the brain as a metaphor for organization creates exciting new possibilities. Whereas in traditional theories of organization, attention has been devoted to the way communication links are established between different elements of an organization, the brain metaphor helps us to appreciate that an organization can itself be regarded as a cognitive system, embodying a structure of thought as well as a pattern of action.

Reference has been made in Chapter 4 to the valuable work of Simon (1947) in initiating this line of investigation, and to the work of his early colleagues at Carnegie-Mellon University: March and Simon (1958), Cyert and March (1963), and those who have followed their lead: Thompson (1967) and Galbraith (1974, 1977). These works provide valuable insights on processes of organizational decision-making and organizational design.

A related approach to their "bounded rationality" view of organization is found in the work of a number of decision-making theorists and researchers who have focused on the process of "incrementalism" (e.g., Braybrooke and Lindblom, 1963; and Lindblom, 1959, 1968).

Over the last few years, James March, now at Stanford University, has launched a critique of the bounded rationality model for presenting an overly rational view of organization. He now argues that organizations may be more like "organized anarchies" and "garbage cans."

Discussions of these models of organization and decision-making are found in Cohen, March, and Olsen (1972), March (1981), and March and Olsen (1976).

Cybernetics: For an introduction to cybernetics it is best to start with Wiener (1967), McCorduck (1979), McCullouch (1974), and Warrick (1980) and then proceed to some of the classic works such as Wiener (1961), Ashby (1952, 1960), and Beer (1959, 1972). Useful overviews of concepts and ideas are provided by Buckley (1967, 1968), Steinbruner (1974), and Morgan (1982).

From a cybernetic perspective, everything can be understood in informational terms. It is no accident that the word "information" contains the word "form," for the cyberneticians believe that form rests in information, or difference. The mathematical basis of this proposition has been demonstrated by Spencer-Brown (1969) and its logic has been clearly described by Gregory Bateson (1972: 317-318) in the notion that a unit of information is a difference that makes a difference. Responsiveness to difference seems to be basic to all systems. We see this in the operation of a simple thermostat, and in the operation of more complex systems such as the human brain. Information systems map differences, exactly as a geographical map traces the difference between water and land, degrees of elevation, and other physical features of the terrain thus represented. Information rests in the communication of difference.

Developments in cybernetics and cybernetic technology have contributed greatly to our understanding of how systems learn. The work of Pask (1961) and Ashby (1952, 1960) on the nature of learning is important, and also the work of writers on the principles of self-organization and artificial intelligence (e.g., von Foerester and Zopf, 1962; McCorduck, 1979). Bateson (1972) has developed the concept of learning to learn.

Cybernetic epistemology: Although cybernetics is primarily seen as a technique for designing self-regulating systems, its basic insight that systems in the natural and social world can be understood as changing patterns of information has major epistemological implications. We have not had a chance to explore these in this chapter, but they lead to exciting new theories relating to the nature of control, causality, and the process of evolution. Bateson (1972, 1979), Gadalla and Cooper (1978), Maruyama (1963), Morgan (1982, 1983b), and Wilden (1979) discuss these, including the cybernetic theory of coevolution that critiques Darwin's rather one-sided and overmaterialistic interpretation of nature. Some of the implications of this cybernetic epistemology are discussed in Chapter 8.

Learning and learning to learn: Studies of organizational learning build around the work of Bateson (1972) and have been brought to prominence in the work of Argyris and Schön (1974, 1978), Argyris (1982), and Schön (1983). These works emphasize the importance of generating double-loop learning through the questioning of assumptions. Michael (1973) and Williams (1982) have presented comprehensive analyses of the need for learning in the planning process and indicated ways in which this might be achieved. The above works also give considerable attention to the barriers to learning created in many conventional approaches to organization. Vickers (1965, 1972) has also given considerable attention to the kind of inquiry that provides the basis for effective learning.

Cybernetic strategy: The argument in favor of developing a cybernetic strategy based on an avoidance of noxiants is developed in different ways by Michael (1973) and Morgan (1983c). The more we examine this principle, the more we come to see its key role in the evolution of form of all kinds. When we talk about adaptation or "good fit," we are referring to an absence of disjunction, i.e., any misfit between form and context has been removed. In any design process it is the misfit which draws attention and calls for correction. Design typically evolves through the elimination of noxiants, and, as architect Christopher Alexander (1964) has suggested, good design can be specified in terms of potential misfit variables. The process is guided by a vision of the end product, but the specific form emerges as a consequence of corrective actions that eliminate undesirable qualities.

Many human decisions evolve in a similar way as noxiants are eliminated. When we make decisions, we cut off undesirable courses of action (the word "decide" comes from the Latin *decidere* meaning "cut off"). The decision "yes" always implies a series of "nos." In these and other ways, the avoidance of noxiants underpins much of everyday life. We typically avoid what is unpleasant or threatening, carving a course to the future in the space that remains. Our most basic sensibility thus has a cybernetic quality of which we are often unaware. The logic of goal setting often tends to erode this quality, favoring a more linear process that tries to straighten the path between present and future.

Holographic organization: On holography it is worth consulting Bentov (1977), Bohm (1978, 1980a, 1980b), and Wilber (1982). As in the case of cybernetics the technical principles have all kinds of epistemological implications. For example, as Karl Pribram (in Wilber, 1982) has suggested, if we see holography as a basic organizing principle and recognize the holographic character of the brain, it takes but a small step to realize that perhaps the world *is* a hologram. This makes good sense, as if we accept that the brain is holographic, it is but a small extension of thought to suggest that it is a holographic element of a holographic whole. The work of Bohm and Pribram explores this possibility and promises to open the way to radically new modes of understanding. (See Chapter 8 for more discussion.)

As might be expected, the literature applying the holographic metaphor to organization is still in the process of development. Morgan and Ramirez (1984) show how the metaphor can be used to shape strategies of "action learning," and to create organizations with holographic characteristics. Morgan (forthcoming) explores the potential for holographic organization created by microprocessing technology. There is a growing literature on robotics and the effects of microprocessing on the workplace (see, for example, Birchall and Hammond, 1981; Pava, 1983).

The important distinction between organizational designs based on a redundancy of parts and a redundancy of functions was introduced by Emery (1967). The principle of requisite variety is developed in the work of Ashby (1952, 1960), and the principle of learning to learn derives from the work of Bateson (1972). The principle of minimum critical specification derives from Herbst (1974).

A comprehensive discussion of autonomous work groups can be found in Herbst (1962) and Susman (1976).

The parable of the watchmaker is based on Simon (1962). Ashby (1952: 192-204) develops a similar point on the relation between randomness and stability.

5: The culture metaphor

As far as the English language is concerned, culture is a modern concept, used in an anthropological and social sense to refer broadly to "civilization" and "social heritage" no earlier than 1871. This meaning of the word does not appear in an English dictionary until the 1920s. Its use within the German language is somewhat older, having made an appearance by 1800. Its increasing use within the social sciences has led to definitions of varying generality, which develop in a host of ways Tylor's (1871) view that "culture, or civilization . . . is that complex whole which includes knowledge, belief, art, law, morals, custom, and any other capabilities and habits acquired by man as a member of society." Kroeber and Kluckhohn (1952), in their classic work on the meaning and use of this concept within the social sciences, claim to have identified almost three-hundred definitions, and they provide a detailed analysis of one-hundred and sixty-four.

Culture and organization: There is a growing literature of relevance to understanding how organization can be understood as a cultural phenomenon. Durkheim (1934), Weber (1947), Parsons (1973), and Harris (1979) provide valuable sociological analyses. Durkheim (1934) is particularly valuable for understanding the relationship between culture and industrialization, while Kerr et al. (1964) explore the similarities in the structure of all kinds of industrial societies. Sahlins (1972) helps us to see the distinctive nature of modern society through comparisons with stone age society.

There is an enormous literature on the relationship between organization and culture from a cross-national perspective. See, for example, Child (1981), Cole (1979), Webber (1969), and Lammers and Hickson (1979). On the relation between culture and Japanese organization and management, see Abeglen (1974), Austin (1976), Dore (1973), McMillan (1984), Vogel (1979), and Yoshino (1968, 1976). The discussion presented in my chapter has drawn on Dore (1973), Ouchi (1981), Pascale and Athos (1981), Maruyama (1982), Sayle (1982), and Kamata (1982). The story of the Honda worker is taken from Peters and Waterman (1982).

The text discussion on American culture draws upon the analysis by Bateson (1972: 88-106). Numerous examples of his thesis regarding the prominence of exhibitionistic behavior in American culture are found in Peters and Waterman (1982).

Corporate culture and subculture: The possibility of studying organizations as cultures has been brought into prominence by a number of recent works, notably Deal and Kennedy (1982), Frost et al. (1985), Handy (1978), Jelinek et al. (1983), Kilmann et al. (1985), Marshall and McLean (1985), Pascale and Athos (1981), Peters and Waterman (1982), Pondy et al. (1983), Schein (1985), and Smircich (1983a, 1983b, 1983c). These works provide a comprehensive indication of some of the latest developments in this field.

The case study of the insurance company discussed here is based on Smircich (1983a, 1983b) and Smircich and Morgan (1982). The discussion of corporate culture at Hewlett-Packard draws on Ouchi (1981), Peters and Waterman (1982), and Wilkins (1983). The discussion of the corporate culture of ITT under Geneen draws on Sampson (1978) and Deal and Kennedy (1982). Michael Maccoby's characterization of the gamesman is found in Maccoby (1976).

On organizational countercultures or subcultures, see Turner (1971) and Martin and Siehl (1983). On occupational subcultures, see Van Mannen and Barley (1984). W. F. Whyte's study of status relations in the restaurant industry is found in Whyte (1948).

Creating organizational reality: Garfinkel (1967) discusses how we "accomplish" realities and Weick (1979) discusses the concept of enactment. These ideas draw on a long tradition of social thought, most often associated with the work of James (1950), Wittgenstein (1958), Schutz (1967), and Berger and Luckmann (1967). Useful discussions on the enactment of organizational culture can be found in Louis (1983) and Smircich (1983a). Huff (1982) and Smircich and Stubbart (1985) show how organizations enact their environments, a theme that will be explored again in Chapter 8. Sudnow's analysis of the enactment of realities in the judicial system is found in Sudnow (1965).

For a discussion of how language shapes organizational reality, see Bittner (1965), Evered (1983), Hummel (1977), and Silverman and Jones (1976). Hall (1959, 1960) has also drawn attention to the "silent language" of nonverbal forms and gestures.

The volumes by Frost et al. (1985), Kilmann et al. (1985), Pondy et al. (1983), and Schein (1985) contain many illustrations of the influence of stories, sagas, legends, rituals, ceremonies, and other attributes of culture in the enactment of reality.

The impact of leadership on corporate culture is discussed by Barnard (1938), Bennis and Nanus (1985), Peters (1978), Peters and Waterman (1982), Selznick (1957), Schein (1985), and Smircich and Morgan (1982). The notion of transformational leadership discussed by Burns (1978) is also important. The story about Picasso is drawn from Hampden-Turner (1981).

Discussions of the parallels between the use of managerial techniques and primitive magic draw on Devons (1961), Gluckman (1972), and an unpublished paper by Gimpl and Dakin (1983).

Meyer and Rowan (1977) provide an insightful analysis of the role of organizational structure as myth and ceremony.

The story about the Kwakiutl Indian's visit to New York is related by Levi-Strauss (1967) and Turner (1983).

The interpretation of the culture metaphor adopted in this chapter has been a broad one. Many of the ideas that we have discussed elaborate a cluster of insights that in principle could have been developed in their own right. For example, at various points in discussion we have referred to the idea that organizational activity can be understood as a language, the playing of a game, as drama, theater, or even as text. A preliminary indication of how these metaphors can be used to develop approaches to organizational analysis is provided by Morgan, Frost, and Pondy (1983). Goffman (1959), Mangham (1978), and Mangham and Overington (1983) illustrate the use of dramaturgical metaphor.

6: The political metaphor

Any discussion of politics and political systems must pay early reference to the work of Aristotle. His idea that politics is a way of creating order is central to political thought, showing how society can avoid degenerating into what Thomas Hobbes (1951) described as "a war of all against all." Most political philosophies, whether we are talking about the manipulative diplomacy of a Machiavelli, the anarchism of a Proudhon (1969), the elitism of a Mosca (1939), or the rationalism of a Popper (1945), are all centrally concerned with solutions to this problem of order. Almost any good text on political science can be consulted to obtain more background on the evolution of the Aristotelian view (e.g., Crick, 1964). Bottomore (1966) provides an excellent discussion of the relationship between elites, democracy, and society, and their general role in politics.

Organizations as systems of government: The idea of drawing the links between modes of organization and systems of political rule has been long appreciated by political scientists interested in understanding the political significance of organization and the relationship between organizations and the state. As a result, most of the systems of organizational rule explored in my chapter have been investigated in one way or another.

For example, on autocracy, see Michels (1949); on bureaucracy, see Weber (1947); on technocracy, see Galbraith (1967); and on approaches to industrial democracy and self-organization, see Vaneck (1975), Woodworth, Meek, and Whyte (1985). Discussions of the German approach to codetermination can be found in Agthe (1977), Bergmann (1975), Donahue (1976), Garson (1977), Mintzberg (1983), and Tivey (1978). On varieties of representative and direct democracy, see Emery and Thorsrud (1969), Coates and Topham (1970), and Coates (1976, 1981a, 1981b). Much of the literature in the field of industrial democracy is also vitally concerned with these issues, since many of the debates between labor and management hinge on issues relating to who has the right to rule and under what circumstances (see, for example, Fox, 1974). On the Lucas experiment see Wainwright and Elliott (1982).

The story on Henry Ford is taken from *Business Week*, April 1979. Lee Iacocca's (1984) autobiography confirms the details of this story and provides many interesting illustrations of how Henry Ford II has exercised a monarchial prerogative over company affairs.

Organizational politics: The idea of viewing organizations with a focus on the political actions of organizational members has become increasingly popular since the early 1960s. Important discussions can be found in Burns (1961), Burns and Stalker

(1961), Bower (1983), Crozier (1964), Jay (1967), March (1962), Murray and Gandz (1980), Pettigrew (1973), and Pfeffer (1978, 1981). The idea that organizational politics hinges on the relationship between interests, conflict, and power runs throughout this literature, at least in an implicit way. Useful discussions on how political action follows individual or group interests can be found in almost all these works.

Interests: Culbert and McDonough (1980) discuss how self-interest shapes organizational behavior. Downs (1967) provides a discussion of the types of political actors found in bureaucratic organizations: e.g., climbers, conservers, zealots, advocates, and statesmen. Useful discussions on the role of interest groups, cliques and coalitions in organizations can be found in Bacharach and Lawler (1980), Cyert and March (1963), Dalton (1959), Pfeffer (1981), Tichy (1973), and Wildavsky (1964).

Conflict: Useful discussions on organizational conflict can be found in Brown (1983), Filley (1975), Litterer (1966), and Pondy (1964, 1967). Much of the current literature on organizational conflict tends to draw upon the ideas first developed by Coser (1956) on the latent functions of social conflict. His work builds on important sociological insights developed by Simmel (1950) and Merton (1968a). A history of the background and evolution of sociological approaches to the analysis of conflict, and their impact on organization theory is provided by Burrell and Morgan (1979).

Discussions of the nature of interdepartmental and role conflict can be found in Dalton (1959), Morgan (1979), Crozier (1964), Pettigrew (1973), Lawrence and Lorsch (1967a, 1967b). Related discussions of role conflicts between bureaucrats and professionals can be found in Benson (1973), Corwin (1970), and Kornhauser (1963). On conflicts relating to the process of budgeting and resource allocation, see Hofstede (1967), Pondy (1964), and Wildavsky (1964). The case illustrations on conflicts relating to the setting of work standards are taken from Whyte (1955).

Power: The study of power has received long-standing treatment in the field of political science, and its nature has been the subject of great debate. The pluralist view of power draws on the work of Dahl (1957), Emerson (1962), and Lasswell (1936), and has been extended to the analysis of organizations in many different ways by Bacharach and Lawler (1980), Blau (1964), Crozier (1964), Cumming (1981), French and Raven (1968), Korda (1975), Kotter (1977), Mintzberg (1983), Pfeffer (1978), and in numerous collections of readings, such as Allen and Porter (1983). The adequacy of the pluralist view has been challenged through a number of radical critiques such as those of Bachrach and Baratz (1962, 1970), Burrell and Morgan (1979), Clegg (1975, 1979), Giddens (1979), and Lukes (1974).

The following references are useful in following up chapter discussion on specific sources of power. On formal authority, see Weber (1947) and Mouzelis (1975). On the control of scarce resources, see Emerson (1962), Pfeffer and Salancik (1978), and Pfeffer (1981). On the use of organization structure, rules, and regulations, see Crozier (1964), Hickson et al. (1971), Perrow (1979, 1984), Pettigrew (1973), and Pfeffer (1978, 1981). On the control of decision processes, see Bachrach and Baratz (1962, 1970), Lukes (1974), March and Simon (1958), Perrow (1979), and Pettigrew (1973). On the control of knowledge and information and the use of expert power and gatekeeping activities, see Crozier (1964), Easton (1965), Forester (1983), French and Raven (1968), Habermas (1970a, 1970b), Pettigrew (1973), and Wilensky (1967). On the control of boundaries, see Miller and Rice (1967), Thompson (1967), and Pfeffer (1981). Goffman (1967) contains a discussion of avoidance rituals. My discussion on the schismatic tendencies of organizations and how boundaries may be managed to protect the autonomy of individuals and departments draws on Morgan (1981), and the idea of loosely coupled systems draws on Weick (1976). On the ability to cope with uncertainty, see Hickson et al. (1971), Thompson (1967), and Pfeffer (1981). On the control of technology, see Crozier (1964) and Woodward (1965). On interpersonal alliances, networks, and coalitions see Pfeffer and Salancik (1978) and Pfeffer (1981). Kanter (1977) contains a useful discussion of the role of sponsors, mentors, and godfather figures. Literally hundreds of pieces of research since the Hawthorne studies (Roethlisberger and Dickson, 1939) have demonstrated the role and power of informal organization. On the control of "counterorganizations," see Galbraith (1962) on countervailing power, and Fox (1974) and Coates (1976, 1981a, 1981b) and Hyman (1975) on labor unionism. On symbolism and the management of meaning see Edelman (1971, 1977), Habermas (1970a, 1970b), Pondy et al. (1983), and Smircich and Morgan (1982). The discussion in the text on dramatism and impression management develops the work of Goffman (1959). Carr (1968) and Maccoby (1976) contain useful discussions of gamesmanship in organizations. On gender, see Millett (1969), Kanter (1977), and Sheppard (1984). On the structural factors that define the stage of action, see Bachrach and Baratz (1962, 1970), Clegg (1979), Giddens (1979), Gramsci (1971), and Lukes (1974). This topic is also explored in depth in Chapters 8 and 9 of the present work. On the empowering aspects of power see Freire (1970).

          Pluralism: On the origins of pluralism in political thought, see Bentley (1908), Figgis (1913), Follett (1918), Laski (1917, 1919), and Maitland (1911). The concept of pluralism has been brought to organization theory in many different ways and are discussed in detail by Burrell and Morgan (1979). The distinction between unitary and pluralist frames of reference has been developed by Ross (1958, 1969) and in the important works by Fox (1966, 1974). Fox (1974) and Burrell and Morgan (1979) develop the implications of the radical frame of reference.

The pluralist approach to conflict has its roots in Coser (1956) and has had an important impact on the history of both sociology and organization theory. Within organization theory, the focus has been on studying the functions of social conflict, and the skills of conflict management—see, for example, Brown (1983), Filley (1975), Robbins (1978), and Thomas (1976).

My analysis of rationality as a political concept benefited from the work of Lucas (1983), Perrow (1979), and the warnings issued by Silverman (1971) regarding the dangers of reifying the organization and its goals. My critique of organizations as functionally integrated systems, also explored in the conclusions to Chapter 3, builds on the work of Gouldner (1973) and Morgan (1981), and general sociological analyses of the dysfunctions of bureaucracy. Burrell and Morgan (1979: 184-189) provide a review of this work. Discussion of the relationship between power, personality, and human motivation is developed by Nietzsche (1976), Adler (1927), Horney (1942), Lips (1981), Nord (1978), and McClelland (1975). The manipulative and gamelike aspects of power are explored in books such as Korda (1975) and Kennedy (1980). Literature relating to the radical critique of pluralism is further explored in Chapter 9 of the present work.

7: The psychic prison metaphor

The idea that people create worlds which then imprison them has proved a popular theme in social thought and literature. It is explored in Shakespeare's *Othello,* in Herman Melville's *Moby Dick,* and in the cries of alienation that pervade the novels of Beckett (1958, 1965), Camus (1946), Kafka (1953, 1973), and Sartre (1938, 1966). The ideas expressed in these and other works draw upon a long history of social thought stretching back to Plato. This now receives its most forceful treatment in the intellectual schemes developed by Freud, Marx, and other contributors to what Burrell and Morgan (1979) have described as the radical humanist paradigm.

Plato was among the first to intellectualize the predicament of human beings as prisoners of their thoughts and actions. His allegory of the cave, found in Book VII of the *Republic,* has provided an evocative image that has inspired many to explore the relationship between illusion and reality. The works of Freud, Jung, and various "critical theorists" have developed new attacks on the basic problem, linking the idea that humans become trapped by their preoccupations, images, and ideas with the need for radical critique of this situation. This is the essential foundation of the radical humanist tradition, which builds from the idea that while individuals create their reality, they often do so in confining and perhaps alienating ways. In this sense, the image of the psychic prison radicalizes many of the ideas discussed in Chapter 5 on the notion of culture, suggesting that the enactments, accomplishments, and language games that shape everyday life often serve hidden purposes, and can be much more confining and oppressive than typically presumed.

On ideology: My original aim in writing this chapter was to explore two aspects of the psychic prison: one associated with the unconscious, and the other with the role of ideology. However, the problem of making the chapter a manageable one has led me to focus on the former. The issue of ideology is thus not given the attention it truly deserves. Indeed, a strong case can be made for the idea that the metaphor of "organization as ideology" should be developed in its own right. This would require that we attempt to understand how organizational life reflects a process of *power-based reality construction*, and to trace how people become trapped by ideas that serve specific sets of interests. In addition, it would be necessary to understand the ideological links between organizational life and social life more generally, and to focus on the general problem of human alienation. Much of the work of Karl Marx on the theory of alienation and the work of the Frankfurt school on "critical theory" would be relevant to this endeavor.

Those who wish to explore this area should consult Marx (1975), Marx and Engels (1846, 1848), Fromm (1961), McLellan (1973), Meszaros (1970), and Ollman (1976). Baxter (1982) presents an excellent theoretical discussion of modern theories of alienation and also an excellent bibliography. Burrell and Morgan (1979), Jay (1973), and Held (1980) present a discussion of the work of the Frankfurt school of critical theory. Members of this school (e.g., Horkheimer, 1972; Horkheimer and Adorno, 1973) have launched a wide-ranging critique of the ideological processes that imprison humans in alienating modes of existence. Building on the idea that manmade society is dominating its members, they have sought to reveal the political significance of culture as a socially constructed reality that is seen and experienced as concrete and "real" in its nature and effects.

Cognitive traps: In organization theory the idea of challenging taken-for-granted ways of thinking is becoming well-established, especially in the work of theorists recognizing the role of paradigms and metaphors in shaping how we think (e.g., Burrell and Morgan, 1979; Morgan, 1980; Schon, 1963, 1979). At a practical level this has developed into the ideas that problem solutions depend on the way problems are framed, and that we can develop methodologies to escape cognitive traps by engaging in dialectical and other modes of critical thinking (e.g., Mason and Mitroff, 1981). The process of framing and reframing involved here underpins the processes of learning to learn discussed in Chapter 4, and can help avoid the problem of "groupthink" identified by Janis (1972).

Freud and the unconscious: The literature on the Freudian approach to the unconscious is enormous. In order to understand Freud's view on the theory of repression, it is important to consult his essays (in *The Complete Works of Sigmund Freud*) on "The Unconscious" (Vol. 14), on "Repression" (Vol. 14), and the "Introductory Lectures on Psychoanalysis" (Vols. 15 and 16). On the links between the unconscious and culture see "Totem and Taboo" (Vol. 13), "Civilization and Its Discontents" (Vol. 21), and "The Future of an Illusion" (Vol. 21). Fromm (1971), Brown (1959), Hampden-Turner (1981), Frey-Rohn (1974), and Mitchell (1974) provide excellent overviews of Freud's work.

In interpreting Freudian work it is important to note the division in Freudian circles between conservative and radical wings. The former tend to be preoccupied with the role of psychoanalysis as an instrument of control, whereas the latter see psychoanalysis as a potentially liberating force. The difference is splendidly discussed in Fromm (1971). Among the more important radical Freudians one should note the work of Eric Fromm (1942, 1961, 1962, 1971), Karen Horney (1967), Melanie Klein (1965, 1980, 1981), R.D. Laing (1965), and Wilhelm Reich (1933, 1961, 1972a, 1972b). Numerous social theorists have built on and developed these insights, particularly Norman O. Brown (1959) and members of the so-called Frankfurt School of social thought, notably Horkheimer (1972), Horkheimer and Adorno (1973), Habermas (1972), and Marcuse (1955, 1964, 1970).

Organization and repressed sexuality: Freud's ideas on the development of sexuality are presented in *Three Essays on the Theory of Sexuality* (Vol. 7) and in *Character and Anal Eroticism* (Vol. 9). The latter article presents initial ideas leading to the theory of characterology, as developed by Abraham (1927), Reich (1972), and Fromm (1971). In understanding the role of sexuality in Freudian theory it is important to recognize that sexuality was linked to the concept of primitive and aggressive forces of life and death, as well as with forms of eroticism. It is also important to remember that in many discussions Freud's interpretation of anal eroticism is much oversimplified, being reduced to a concern for the relationship between anal desires and toilet training. In point of fact, Freud believed that anal sexuality was the focus of many aspects of bodily eroticism, displaced into the anal region. Norman O. Brown (1959) presents an excellent discussion of this, together with a detailed exposition of the Freudian theory on the relations between wealth, money, and faeces, and the links that Freud drew between anal sexuality and the death instinct.

My analysis of the anal-compulsive character of Frederick Taylor draws on information in the biographies by Copley (1923) and Kakar (1970). In case we think Taylor an exception, it is important to note that other key figures in developing the work ethic on which industrial society has been built share many of Taylor's personality characteristics. For example, the biographies of Henry Ford, Benjamin Franklin, Martin Luther, and many of the Quakers in England and North America reveal excellent examples of people dominated by concerns that have roots in unconscious anal preoccupations. See, for example, Zaleznik and de Vries (1975) and Jardim (1970). In their different ways, they contributed to the development of social relations that inhibited the expression of gential sexuality in favor of the expression of sublimated anal sexuality.

Brown's *Life Against Death* (1959) provides an intriguing analysis of how the rise of capitalism seems linked with characteristics of the anal personality. In particular, his essay on the role of anality in the life and ideas of Martin Luther and the rise of Protestantism deserves special attention. As is well known, Max Weber (1958) has linked Protestantism and the rise of capitalism. Brown's contribution is to show how Luther's support for capitalism through the Protestant movement is quite unintended. In a remarkable analysis, Brown reveals that Luther received the great illumination that led him to the doctrine of justification by faith while on the privy. He shows that Luther perceived a link between money, faeces, and the devil, and saw the devil as being the lord of capitalism. Luther was thus critical of capitalism, viewing usury as the devil and usurers as serving the devil's cause. He also saw a certain inevitability in the ways of the world, believing that the world was in bondage to the devil. Hence the principle of being true in one's calling and of receiving salvation through faith, rather than by attempting to find salvation in the present world. Brown's psychoanalytic interpretation of Luther's underlying motives thus provides an interesting twist to Weber's thesis, suggesting that Protestantism sanctioned capitalism by default, in a way that was probably opposite to Luther's intentions.

On the role of sexual repression and the rise of formal organization, see Burrell (1984), Cleugh (1963), Taylor (1954), and Foucault (1979a, 1979b). See Chatov (1981) on the links between repressed sexuality and governmental and other forms of regulation, and Schwartz (1982) on the links between anal eroticism and compulsive job involvement.

Good discussions on the relationship between narcissism and contemporary society can be found in Lasch (1979) and Walter (1983). For an analysis of the relationship between personality types and power, see McClelland (1975). For an analysis of the relation between character types and managerial styles, see Maccoby (1976).

One of the interesting questions embedded in discussions about organization and sexuality is whether it is possible to achieve a repression-free mode of organization. Such an ideal has been advocated by Marcuse (1955), and also underlies the vision of certain anarchistic theories, such as those of Stirner (1963). In Fromm's (1971) view, such theorists are searching for an infantilistic utopia where there are no limits on gratification. For example, he suggests that Marcuse ignores conflict and tragedy as human realities, and that his dream of a nonrepressive society confuses the Freudian notion of repression with the idea of political suppression or oppression. In the Freudian view, there seems an inherent conflict between the satisfaction of libidinal drives and the requirements of civilized organization. As Fromm notes, humans seem to face a choice between instinctual satisfaction and barbarism. Sometimes the balance achieved between these competing principles leads to neurosis, and at other times to modes of happy adjustment.

The patriarchal family: For discussion of the significance of patriarchy and the patriarchal family, see Bachofen (1968), Engels (1972), Coward (1983), Fromm (1971), and Reich (1968). Mitchell (1974) provides an excellent discussion of the Oedipus complex from a woman's point of view, and Dodson-Gray (1982) has presented an analysis of the links between patriarchy and modern society.

Death and immortality: On the links between death and immortality, see Becker (1973), Freud's *Beyond the Pleasure Principle* (C.W. Vol. 18), Lifton and Olson (1975), and Rank (1950). Denhardt (1981) and Schwartz (1985) begin to develop the organizational implications of these views.

Defenses against anxiety: For Melanie Klein's approach to psychoanalysis and object relations, see Klein (1965, 1980, 1981). Her essays "Notes on Some Schizoid Mechanisms" (1980: 1-24) and "Our Adult World and Its Roots in Infancy" (1980: 247-263) are particularly important for the discussion presented in my chapter. Guntrip (1961) presents an excellent introduction to her work. Discussions of Bion's theory of leadership and group behavior can be found in Bion (1959) and Pines (1985).

Jaques (1955) discusses how social systems act as defenses against anxiety, and Menzies (1960) applies this idea in the analysis of nursing. Chatov (1981) discusses the idea of regulatory sadism.

Zaleznik's work on power relations, leadership, and the unconscious can be found in Zaleznik (1970) and Zaleznik and Kets deVries (1975). Other research studies on how fear, envy, anger, and other impulses are often projected elsewhere can be found in Lowenberg (1972) and Eagle and Newton (1981). Kets deVries and Miller (1984) investigate these issues in detail. The book contains excellent case material and goes a long way toward showing how the influence of the unconscious gives rise to different varieties of organization, lending great support to the idea that it may be possible to develop a "new contingency theory of organization" based on an understanding of unconscious processes.

The theory of transitional objects: The work of Winnicott on transitional objects can be found in Winnicott (1958, 1964, 1971). Harold Bridger of the Tavistock Institute has developed the implications of this for organizational analysis and organizational change, though as yet there is no published work in this area.

Jung, shadow, and archetypes: The work of Jung on psychoanalysis and the unconscious is, like Freud's, voluminous and wide ranging. Among the numerous volumes of his *Collected Works* those on *Psychological Types, Analytical Psychology,* and the *Structure and Dynamics of the Psyche* are most relevent for the ideas discussed in my chapter. Extracts from these works are presented in Jung (1971), which also contains a useful editorial by Joseph Campbell. Good overviews of Jung's most important ideas can be found in Jung (1964, 1967), Whitmont (1969), and Frey-Rohn (1974). These are especially useful for understanding the Jungian position on archetypes. In particular, Frey-Rohn discusses many definitions of Jung's use of the notion of archetype in a clear way. Neumann (1954), Maccoby (1976), Frye (1957), and Thompson (1971) illustrate the role of archetypes in social life. Bettleheim (1977) analyzes fairy tales. Mitroff and Kilmann use Jung's psychological types to analyze patterns of reasoning and thought. And the relevance of Jung's work for organizational analysis has been explored by Denhardt (1981), Ingalls (1979), Mitroff (1984), and McSwain and White (1982). Hirsch and Andrews (1983) have illustrated how the language of corporate takeovers is often dominated by archetypal visions of rape, conquest, pillage, and romantic union. Smith and Simmons (1983) have shown how the dynamics of a case of organizational change followed the pattern of a fairy tale about Rumplestiltskin.

The idea of viewing the unconscious as a black hole is explored by Delahanty and Gemill (1982).

Eric Trist's discussion of how workers may leave "badness" in the systems in which they work can be found in Trist (in press).

8: The flux metaphor

This chapter develops a view that has received little attention in organization theory. It takes its point of departure from the ideas of Heraclitus, which have much in common with the ancient Chinese philosophy of Taoism. Despite Heraclitus's important influence on the evolution of Western science and social thought, his ideas can only be understood and read through secondary sources. Wheelwright (1959) provides an excellent overview.

Implicate and explicate orders and modern realist philosophy: Bohm's analysis of the relations between the implicate and explicate order is presented in Bohm (1980a) and in a number of important articles, especially Bohm (1978, 1980b). His idea that the implicate order is an enfolded domain of potentiality has close links with the holographic metaphor discussed in Chapter 4. Bohm uses holonomic and other metaphors to express his point of view. For example, he invites us to envisage the universe as an unfolding set of relations such as those found in a piece of symphony music, in which different notes and instruments evolve in relation to create a sound encoded in the implicate order of the musical score.

In appreciating Bohm's theory it is important to realize that he places considerable emphasis on the creativity inherent in the implicate order. Indeed, he has suggested that this realm may be sheer creativity, a set of potentialities that become explicate in a probabilistic way. He stresses that the implicate and explicate orders are in interaction, and may produce and reproduce form through a cycle of projection, injection, and reprojection. The forms realized in the explicate order are thus permitted a degree of autonomy and self-rule, but are always regarded as dependent on deeper forces within the implicate order for their existence. Under appropriate conditions, certain explicate orders become likely or possible, realizing the logic of the system. This aspect of the theory has much in common with the work of Prigogine (1978, 1984) and Sheldrake (1981).

Bohm's analysis of relations between implicate and explicate orders parallels the distinction drawn in modern realist philosophy by Bhaskar (1978) and Outhwaite (1983) between three domains of reality: the empirical, the actual, and the real. The thrust of their "realist" analysis is to suggest that our reality is shaped by generative mechanisms in the domain of the real, and that the domains of the actual and the empirical are in effect realized tendencies that lend specific form to processes in this other domain. This kind of analysis searches for an explanation of the deep structure of social life, and provides a means of reinterpreting the role and significance of the unconscious, culture, and other generative social forces. It has a great deal in common with more materialistic theories that stress how society "unfolds" in accordance with some kind of structural logic.

Autopoiesis: The theory of autopoiesis was first developed in Chile in the 1960s and early 1970s by Maturana and Varela. The core works are Maturana and Varela (1980), which provides an excellent though very difficult and technical overview of concepts, and Varela (1979), which applies the theory to biology. Other useful expositions can be found in Varela (1975, 1976, 1984), Varela and Johnson (1976), Harries-Jones (1983, 1984), and Ulrich and Probst (1984).

The theory of autopoiesis has many implications for the analysis of living systems of all kinds, whether biological, cognitive, or social. In the manner of general systems theory, it seeks to unite and transcend discipline boundaries using the simple but remarkably powerful notion that all systems look at themselves and regulate their functioning through a process analogous to thought. It is in this sense that Maturana and Varela can describe living as a process of cognition and view cognition as a biological process. They view the basic cognitive operation as that of making distinctions, as does Spencer-Brown (1969). Maturana and Varela argue that by specifying distinctions we make entities distinct from their background. Since this process can proceed in many possible directions, the notion of a complete system is thus rather arbitrary. Any unity, such as a biological system, can be differentiated into cells, organs, etc., by drawing further distinctions. And moving in the opposite direction, we can draw distinctions between an individual organism and its background, and create differentiations within its background. The whole process of specifying differences (i.e., the process of differentiation) is based upon this simple cognitive process, which is the basis of all form and specifies the organization of a system.

The ideas developed by Maturana and Varela have much in common with Bateson's (1972, 1979) views on coevolution and the idea that nature thinks and mind evolves, and with Touraine's (1977) work on the self-production of society. Similar ideas on the nature of self-referential systems have also been offered in very different contexts by Godel (1962) and Hofstadter (1979, 1983). My own work on the nature of epistemology (Morgan, 1983) also explores a similar theme. The point in my chapter about confusing and mixing the domain of organization with that of explanation is made by Harries-Jones (1984).

As yet there is little organizational literature developing the autopoietic perspective, though Ulrich and Probst (1984) have made a useful start. Touraine's analysis of the self-production of society has obvious relevance, though his work is not specifically based on the theory of autopoiesis. Bateson's (1972) analysis of the pathology of conscious purpose points to the lack of recursive awareness in much decision making, and has much in common with the pathologies of egocentric self-imagery discussed in my chapter. My own work on corporate strategy (Morgan, 1982) presents an approach that has much in common with the autopoietic viewpoint. Rapoport's (1960) work on fights, games and debates is important in developing collaborative strategies (also, see Hafstadter, 1983).

Prigogine's worked on self organizing systems can be found in Prigogine (1978, 1984) and in Jantsch (1980) and Jantsch and Waddington (1976).

It should be noted that in much of my discussion about organizations as autopoietic systems I have talked about *organizations* maintaining their identity. This is an oversimplification, since, strictly speaking, organizations do not think and act: organizational members do this, and what we recognize as the organization is a product of their thoughts and actions. When we talk about an organization acting, or sustaining its identity, it would thus be more correct to do so in terms of the key people involved.

Mutual causality: the second cybernetics: A discussion of the theory of mutual causality is presented by Maruyama (1963) and Buckley (1967). Maruyama's discussion of "the second cybernetics" is of crucial importance in allowing cybernetic theory to break free of the steady state models that dominated early development of the discipline. Useful applications of his theory are found in Maruyama (1982). Also see Forester's (1961) work on the dynamics of global systems. The Club of Rome report *Limits to Growth* is authored by Meadows et al. (1972) and contains the tale of the Persian courtier. Maruyama's analysis of runaway systems in nature, such as the crack collecting water and the development of a homogeneous plain, are taken from Maruyama (1963).

An analysis of the schismatic properties of social systems in which positive feedback relations transform and often destroy existing relations can be found in Bateson (1936, 1972) and in Morgan (1981).

Systemic wisdom: Bateson's discussion of the epistemology of systemic wisdom can be found in Bateson (1972). Vickers (1965, 1972) develops a related notion through his concept of "appreciation." Gadalla and Cooper (1978) and Morgan (1982, 1983c) apply these notions in developing new epistemologies for management and corporate strategy. Wilden (1972) presents a difficult theoretical discussion of issues related to the epistemology of systemic wisdom. His view that causes cause causes to cause causes is taken from this source. Weick (1979) provides good illustrations of how social systems can be managed through the modification of feedback loops.

Dialectics and Marxian analysis: Most books on Eastern philosophy provide good discussions of Taoism. The *I Ching* and the *Chuang-Tzu* make interesting reading. Capra (1975) also provides an excellent discussion of Eastern philosophy and its links with modern science.

The concept of dialectics has made a contribution to a wide variety of social thought. Recall, for example, Jung's use of the "unity of opposites" discussed in Chapter 7. Extensive discussions of the Hegelian approach to dialectics can be found in Hegel (1892, 1929), Findlay (1958), Kaufman (1965), McLellan (1973), and Wetter (1958).

Marx's description of his own use of the dialectic can be found in the *Postface* to the second edition of *Capital*, though he does not devote any extensive description to the nature of the method, preferring to illustrate its use in practice. Ernest Mandel's introduction to Volume I of Marx's *Capital* (Marx, 1976) also provides an informative discussion. As noted in Chapter 8 of Marx's dialectical method, this has been subjected to a wide range of interpretation (see, for example, Althusser, 1969; Colletti, 1975a, 1975b; Engels, 1873, 1876, 1886; Godelier, 1972; Lefebvre, 1968a, 1968b; Lenin, 1936; Plekhanov, 1961; Markovic, 1974; Meszaros, 1972; Novack, 1966; and Wetter, 1958). Marx's friend, Frederick Engels, for a long time stood as the authoritative source of interpretation of the Marxist dialectic. Apart from rival interpretations provided early by Lenin (1936) and Lukacs (1971), which sought to recognize and revive the importance of the Hegelian influence on Marx, it is only recently that the overly deterministic trend set in motion by Engels has begun to be reversed. With Engels, Marx's dialectical method was characterized as dialectical materialism and eventually presented as being equivalent to a historical materialism in which the laws of society are equivalent to the laws of nature. In the view of many, Engels's work has done a disservice to the development of Marxist theory, lending it a much more deterministic flavor than Marx probably intended.

An interesting perspective can be gained on the varieties of Marxism and other radical social theories by focusing on the various elements of the dialectic presented in Exhibit 8.6. Very often, these different aspects of the dialectic are developed in a somewhat isolated and extreme form. As discussed in my chapter, Marx's own work emphasizes their interconnection, explaining how the struggle of opposites (principle one) sets the basis for change, which, through the negation of the negation (principle two), becomes evolutionary, until the intensity or quantity of change precipitates a qualitative change in the system as a whole (principle three). Developed separately, these three dialectical principles give rise to (a) theories focusing on change through contradiction (principle one; e.g., Allen, 1975); (b) anarchistic theories that *celebrate* the act of negation (principle two) and its creative potential (e.g., Bakunin 1950, 1964; Stirner, 1963); and (c) revolutionary or catastrophic theories that focus on the inevitability of revolutionary change (principle three), often to understand how revolution can best be brought about, as in varieties of vulgar or revolutionary Marxism (Bukharin, 1962, 1972). Yet another branch of radical thought focuses on documenting the opposition inherent in the dialectic, building on a theme of domination to be examined in Chapter 9.

In addition to consulting *Capital* itself, especially Volume I, the reader interested in obtaining a grip of Marxian economics should consult Mandel (1962), and analyses of the contradictions of capitalism offered by Godelier (1972), Baran and Sweezy (1966), Benson and Jenkins (1978), Glyn and Sutcliffe (1972), Habermas (1973), Holloway and Picciotto (1978), O'Connor (1973), and Offe (1972, 1974, 1975, 1976). Mandel (1962) provides an excellent analysis of the concept of surplus value and of the contradictions that arise from the quest for surplus value.

Mandel's discussion of the links between wealth and theft can be found in Mandel (1962: 83-88). Marx's explanation of how capitalism helps to create its demise by organizing the working class as a byproduct of its organization of production can be found in *Capital* Vol. 1, Ch. 32).

An appreciation of the dialectical nature of Marx's work shows that many interpretations of Marx are far too deterministic. The idea that economics is a *determining* force in social life, or that technology *determines* social structure does not do justice to the dialectical point of view. Dialectics shows us that in discussing such relations we are always talking about two sides of the same phenomenon; the one side depends on the other. They thus tend to be coproduced, rather than existing in a linear causal relation in which one leads to the other.

Good illustrations of the dialectical mode of organizational analysis can be found in the work of Allen (1975), Benson (1983), Braverman (1974), and Heydebrand (1977, 1983). Such works show how we can begin to understand how dialectical contradictions lie at the source of recurrent crises in the modern world, and how we can begin to deal with them.

My analysis of how contradictions between professional, administrative, and economic logics of change are shaping the U.S. judicial system draws on Heydebrand and Seron (1981) and Heydebrand (1983).

Adam Smith's view of the "invisible hand" is found in Smith (1776).

Reframing the study of change: Few organization theorists have devoted attention to understanding the *nature* of change. Analyses tend to be descriptive (e.g., Burns and Stalker, 1961) or analytical (e.g., Lawrence and Lorsch, 1967a; Thompson, 1967; Aldrich, 1979), but do not show how and why change occurs. Emery and Trist's (1965) analysis of the causal texture of environments begins to address this task, as does Maruyama's (1963) analysis of positive and negative feedback systems and the forms of dialectical analysis offered in my chapter. In attempting to study the nature of change, it is necessary to move to an analysis of change at the level of what Russell and Whitehead (1913) describe as a higher "logical type." This switch in frame of reference promises to make a major contribution to organization theory in the future. An understanding of the deep structure of organization and an ability to reframe problems in ways that overcome existing contradictions also depend on creating a similar switch in perspective.

9: The domination metaphor

Reports on domination in the corporate world, especially with regard to how organizations often have a negative impact on human beings and the environment, appear regularly in most newspapers and current affairs magazines. The evocative illustrations presented at the beginning of this chapter are drawn from the following sources: Zwerdling (1971) discusses the topic of food pollution; the data on pollution in the Great Lakes Basin is drawn from local data sources and figures presented at professional conferences; the data on health hazards at work is drawn from annual reports of the International Labor Organization; data on the relationship between multinationals and the Third World is provided by Hayter (1981). Numerous other references on these issues will be presented in later sections of this chapter.

The domination metaphor brings the seamy side of organizational life to the center of our attention and invites us to examine the extent to which it must be regarded as an intrinsic aspect of the way we organize. Insofar as these topics are treated in organization theory, they are often viewed as unfortunate and for the most part unintentional side effects or as issues that have a bearing on the ethics of organization and the relationship between business and society. In viewing the domination metaphor as a primary framework for organizational analysis, the discussion in this chapter attempts to make these issues mainstream in the sense that they should be dominant in our consideration of the nature and success of organization in modern society. For example, many otherwise excellent companies often have very questionable records with regard to their effect on the environment, on the workforce in their factories, and in their effect on the Third World. While having developed a distinguished status in terms of certain aspects of internal management practice, there is also often a seamy side to this excellence that is completely ignored.

Domination in history: It is instructive to analyze the origins of organization in ancient society and, in particular, to understand how the rise of organization is associated with the generation of economic surplus and accompanied by a more general process of social stratification. From the earliest times there seems to be a relationship between organization and domination in the form of class rule. See, for example, the analyses of ancient and prehistoric societies offered by Childe (1946), Kautzky (1982), Wittfogel (1957) and Sahlins (1972). My data on the building of the Great Pyramid at Giza is taken from the *Encyclopaedia Britannica*. George (1972) also offers useful discussions of the forms of organization used in ancient society, and an overview of the evolution of management practice to the present day.

It is fascinating to observe how the development of organization occurs alongside the development of slavery or the control of one group or class by another and with the development of military power. And it is interesting to note how the mode of organization employed often varied from one situation to another. For example, slaves were not extensively used in purely agricultural societies in ancient days because of the communal nature of agriculture and the difficulty of enforcing people to take the great care required in the cultivation process. Their main use was in the context of domestic work, workshops, mines, and building, where effective systems of supervision could be most easily developed. From the earliest of times, therefore, the contingency idea that different types of organization and management are required in different circumstances has been well understood. As is argued in my chapter, the evolution of modern society has been accompanied by changes in the mode of domination employed, there being a shift away from the use of raw exploitation to what Max Weber would describe as more subtle forms of domination. An appreciation of the historical process through which this has occurred is thus very instructive for understanding organizations in the present day.

Weber, Michels, and Marx—founders of radical organization theory: Max Weber's analysis of the links between organization and social domination are found throughout his extensive writings, notably in Weber (1946, 1947, 1949, 1961, 1968). McNeil (1978), Mouzelis (1975), and Salaman (1978) present excellent discussions of this aspect of his work with a focus on the problem of understanding modern organizations. Weber was very much aware of the intimate connection between the development of bureaucratization and the role of the state in society, and has provided an excellent basis for understanding the growth of "corporatism" in capitalist and noncapitalist societies. Important discussions of these ideas and other post-Weberian developments can be found in Miliband (1973) and Benson (1975). In viewing the role of the state as an aspect of a wider process of domination in society, the work of Weber has much affinity with that of Marx, and many organization theorists have contributed useful insights by exploring this interface. Burrell and Morgan (1979) provide an extensive discussion of this in their analysis of their "radical structuralist paradigm."

Weber's views on bureaucracy as an iron cage can be found in Weber (1946: 228). Robert Michels's views on the iron law of oligarchy can be found in Michels (1949). Perrow (1979) provides an excellent discussion of the way organizations engage in strategies of domination, both internally and in relation to their environment.

For a discussion of Marx's analysis on how domination is embedded in the quest for surplus value, see my discussion in Chapter 8 and the references provided in the bibliographical notes to that chapter. On the links between the work of Marx and Weber, see Burrell and Morgan (1979) and Salaman (1978).

Organization, class, and control: Most modern discussions of the relationship between organization, class, and control draw on Weberian or Marxist theories in one way or another (see, for example, Clegg and Dunkerley, 1980; Clegg, 1981; Salaman, 1979, 1981). My discussion of the evolution of the working class in Britain draws on Thompson (1968), and of the evolution of wage labor in the United States on Gordon, Edwards, and Reich (1982). For a discussion of the process of deskilling and the degradation of work, see Braverman (1974) and Wood (1982). Gordon, Edwards, and Reich (1982) present an excellent discussion of the proletarianization of the workforce in the United States, and Blackburn and Mann (1979) provide an excellent analysis of the role of the working class in the labor market in Britain. The figures quoted in my chapter on the number of manual workers that exercise less skill in their jobs than in driving to work and the extent to which there is an interchangeability of skills in the workplace are derived from this source.

For a discussion of ideas on the dual nature of primary and secondary labor markets, see Berger and Piore (1980), Piore (1979), and Gordon, Edwards, and Reich (1982). For a discussion of the segmentation of labor markets, see Gordon et al. (1982), Edwards et al. (1975), Edwards (1979), Williamson (1981), and Friedman (1977). Friedman (1977) and Edwards (1979) are particularly useful in illustrating the different strategies of managerial control relating to different labor markets.

For a discussion of the role of migrant workers in the modern economy, see Castles and Kosack (1973), Piore (1979), Power and Hardman (1978), and Berger and Mohr (1975). Gordon et al. (1982) contains a useful discussion of the role of blacks in the U.S. workforce.

Other discussions of the links between capitalism and domination in the labor process can be found in Goldman and VanHouten (1977), Gorz (1985), Marglin (1976), and Buroway (1979). The analyses of Marglin (1976) and O'Connor (1973) also provide useful political-economic explanations of contemporary organizational structure and the division of labor. Salaman (1979) provides a useful analysis of how the labor process can be seen as a process of domination and focuses on the resistance presented by the workforce. Foucault (1979a, 1979b) presents a useful analysis of the history of control, tracing links between the school, the army, the prison, and the factory. Perrow (1979) provides a discussion of the role of unobtrusive controls in organization, and Friedman (1977) provides a good discussion of how organizations often attempt to control their employees in the primary labor market through systems of "responsible autonomy."

Hazardous work: Marx's vivid account of the horrors of early capitalism is found in *Capital*, (chap. 10). All my quotes are taken from this source. There is a growing literature on the hazards of modern work situations. See, for example, Ashford (1976), Berman (1978), Epstein (1978), Follman (1978), Frost et al. (1982), Navarro and Berman (1983), Nelkin and Brown (1984), Reasons et al. (1981), Sayles and Strauss (1981), Scott (1974), Tataryn (1979), Viscusi (1983), and Wright (1973). My data are drawn from these sources and the original reports cited therein. Details on the asbestos "cover up" can be found in Reasons et al. (1981), the problems of asbestos production in Ontario in the Royal Commission Report on Health and Safety (1984) and those in the Third World in Navarro and Berman (1983). The *Washington Post* article on brown lung disease is by Baker (1980).

My data on occupational accidents and diseases are confined to the United States and Canada, since international comparisons become extremely misleading. The scope and coverage of these kinds of statistics vary considerably from one country to another and between industries within any given country. Even the basic concept of the recordable occupational injury varies. Comparisons with Third World countries are particularly difficult because the available statistics are unreliable. They are generally produced as a byproduct of administrative work processes and regulations, and are often uncoordinated with regard to the requirements of occupational health and safety. Anyone wishing to examine these statistics further is referred to the *International Labour Organization Statistical Year Book*. This produces the best statistics that are available and also gives a good guide to some of the qualifications that need to be made in interpretation.

For an overview of the literature relating to occupational sources of stress and related illness, see Burke and Weir (1980), Cooper and Marshall (1976), and Cooper and Payne (1980). For a discussion of the problems relating to workaholism, see Oates (1971), Machlowitz (1978), and Feinberg and Dempewolf (1980). Frost et al. (1982) present a useful collection of readings relating to this area of work.

The radical frame of reference: As discussed in Chapter 6, the concept of the radical frame of reference as a description of organizational reality and as an ideology for guiding organizational practice derives from the work of Fox (1974). Over the last ten years or so, a great deal of literature has been produced that is firmly consistent with this point of view, and does much to help us understand how organizations become radicalized and the strategies that are adopted to advance antagonistic ends. Much of the best literature is British, since it is here that the battle lines between management and workers have often been most clearly drawn. For example, for an illustration of workers' perspectives on the logic of the profit motive and alternatives and its relevance for understanding the loss of jobs, industrial decline, and the need for industrial revitalization, see Bryer, Brignall, and Maunders (1982), Levie et al. (1984), Massey and Mergaw (1982), and the results of the workers' inquiry conducted by the Trades Councils for Coventry, Liverpool, and Newcastle (1980). As part of the radical response to managerial control, many unions have attempted to develop alternative plans and alternative work systems. See, for example, Coates (1978, 1981a, 1981b) and Wainwright and Elliott (1982). For a discussion of related economic strategies, see Holland (1975) and Hughes (1981). Many radical interpretations of the nature of the labor process are available on both sides of the Atlantic. For example, see Braverman (1974), Gorz (1985), Hyman (1975), and Levidon and Young (1981).

Multinationals: The literature on the activities of multinational corporations is now voluminous. The United Nations and Stopford et al. (1980) publish many valuable statistics on a regular basis. My data relating to the current size of multinational corporations are drawn from the United Nations' 1983 report on transnational corporations in world development.

As will be evident from the debate presented in my chapter, different writers on the multinationals tend to present different perspectives on their operation, according to whether they are advocates or critics. A good all-round view can be achieved by consulting some of the following works: Brandt (1980), Brooke and Remmers (1970), Casson (1983), Goldberg and Negandhi (1983), Grunberg (1981), Gunnermann (1975), Kujawa (1975), Lall (1983), Medwar and Freese (1982), Mirow and Maurer (1982), Tavis (1982), Thomas (1979), Servan-Schreiber (1968), and Wilczynski (1976). Sampson (1978) provides an excellent analysis of the international operations of ITT and has interesting information on other organizations as well. My data on industrial concentration are taken from the U.S. Conglomerate Hearings and from the 1985 Statistical Abstract of the U.S. Department of Commerce (also, see Mizruchi, 1982).

Goldberg and Negandhi (1983), Grunberg (1981), and Gunnermann (1975) present interesting statistics and case studies on the role of multinationals as world powers. Mirow and Maurer (1982) present excellent case studies of the role of cartels in the world economy. Brooke and Remmers (1970) provide a useful discussion of the strategies adopted by multinationals in dealing with their environment.

Good critical accounts of how the multinationals have exploited the world economy can be found in Hayter (1981), George (1976), and Bello et al. (1982). Hayter is particularly useful in presenting numerous pieces of data and case studies, and is the source of many of the statistics that I have presented on the international operations of multinational corporations. The influential Brandt report (1980) has also provided a valuable source of data.

For an excellent critical discussion of how decision making in large corporations can have major negative impacts on whole communities, see the analysis of the cutbacks in the British steel industry presented by Bryers et al. (1982), and the case studies on profit-oriented divestment decisions presented by Grunberg (1981).

Alfred Chandler's discussion of how the visible hand of management has replaced the invisible hand that Adam Smith saw guiding competitive market economies is found in Chandler (1977).

The case study on Dow Chemical in Chile is drawn from Gunnerman (1975).

10: The art of organizational analysis

Intellectually, this chapter owes much to the work of social scientists such as Gregory Bateson (1972, 1979),

Thomas Kuhn (1970), Donald Schon (1963, 1979), and Geoffrey Vickers (1965, 1972), and to the general principles of dialectical thinking. I have used a related approach for dealing with the problems of the paradoxical properties of social research (Morgan, 1983).

11: Imaginization

The overall approach I have developed in this book builds on a host of assumptions about the nature of reality and knowledge. The concept of *imaginization* symbolizes my position: I believe that we are active in constructing our worlds; that we can benefit from greater awareness of the processes through which this occurs; and that we can become simultaneously more reflective and more proactive in shaping the way social reality unfolds. At the same time, I recognize that the theory of enactment can be taken too far in the sense that it can lead to an extreme subjectivism. I believe in a position that attempts to recognize the paradox that reality is simultaneously subjective and objective. We *engage* objective realities subjectively: by putting ourselves into what we "see," in a way that actually influences what we see. The process can be understood as one of "engagement" and "co-production," involving both subjective constructions and concrete interactions between real "others." I have explored aspects of this position in greater depth elsewhere (Morgan, 1983a).

My concept of *imaginization* seeks to develop a proactive attitude in relation to the way organizations are and how they could be. I believe that people can change organizations and society, even though the perception and actuality or power relations passed down through history may at times make change difficult. Prescriptively, I would thus like us all to recognize that reality is made, not given; to recognize that our seeing and understanding of the world is always *seeing as*, rather than a *seeing as is*; and to take an ethical and moral responsibility for the personal and collective consequences of the way we see and act in everyday life, difficult though this may be.

Consistent with this view of the world, I have an inclination to favor certain metaphors over others (though in writing this book I have tried to be conscious of and minimize this inclination). I favor general use of the psychic-prison metaphor (broadened in interpretation to take account of the role of ideology) to free people from the traps of favored ways of thinking and to unleash their power and creativity. I favor the culture metaphor as a means of emphasizing the importance of enactment processes, and the political metaphor for decoding webs of interest and power relations. I favor the brain metaphor because of the fundamental challenge it presents to the bureaucratic mode of organization, and the flux and transformation metaphor for highlighting the tendencies and contradictions built into our general way of life. I believe that the domination metaphor helps us to confront the gross exploitation and inequality on which so many of our organizations build. I value aspects of the mechanistic and organismic metaphors for some of the practical insights they offer when used in a contingency mode, and am favorably disposed to the possibility of developing an ecologically based framework for interorganizational development.

Consistent with my overall orientation, I firmly believe that we need to break the hold of bureaucratic thinking and to move toward newer, less exploitative, more equal modes of interaction in organizations.

My selection of metaphors considered in this book is inevitably partial. While I have tried to discuss some of the most important metaphors shaping how we organize at present, others deserve attention, and others may claim more prominence than they have been given. For example, some may argue that I should have given more explicit attention to the military metaphor or to ideas of organizations as teams, anarchies, ideologies, prisons, theaters, and so on. However, these and other metaphors can easily be incorporated in any actual analysis within the general style of metaphorical thinking that I have tried to develop.

My analysis and discussion have raised many questions that constraints of space and time have obliged me to ignore. For example, there is a need to explain the power and attractiveness of different metaphors beyond what I have been able to achieve in my general discussions of strengths and limitations—to explain why certain metaphors have exerted such great influence and to understand their role as ideological constructs. There is a need to address the question of whether some metaphors give too much prominence to a managerial view of organization that eliminates more democratic possibilities. And there is a need to give serious attention to whether the kind of managerial thinking that I've tried to develop will serve actually to change organizations, or will entrench existing patterns of control. Further critical study of these and other questions will place in broader perspective the issues that I have raised and the merits of the approach to analysis that I have advocated.

Bibliography

Abeglen, J. G. *The Japanese Factory*. Glencoe, IL: Free Press, 1974.

Abraham, K. *Selected Papers*. London: Hogarth Press, 1927.

Ackoff, R. L. and F. E. Emery. *On Purposeful Systems*. Chicago: Aldine, 1972.

Adler, A. *Understanding Human Nature*. New York: Greenburg, 1927.

Agthe, K. E. "Mitbestimmung: Report on a Social Experiment." *Business Horizons*, 5-14, 1977.

Ahituv, N. and S. Neumann. *Principles of Information Systems for Management*. Dubuque, IA: W.C. Brown, 1982.

Alderfer, C. P. "A New Theory of Human Needs." *Organizational Behavior and Human Performance*, 4: 142-175, 1969.

Alderfer, C. P. *Existence, Relatedness and Growth*. New York: Free Press, 1972.

Aldrich, H. *Organizations and Environments*. Englewood Cliffs, NJ: Prentice-Hall, 1979.

Alexander, C. *Notes on the Synthesis of Form*. Cambridge: Harvard University Press, 1964.

Alford, L. P. *Henry Lawrence Gantt, Leader in Industry*. New York: Harper & Row, 1934.

Allen, R. W. and L. W. Porter (eds.) *Organizational Influence Processes*. Glenview, IL: Scott Foresman, 1983.

Allen, V. L. *Social Analysis: A Marxist Critique and Alternative*. London: Longman, 1975.

Althusser, L. *For Marx*. London: New Left Books, 1969.

Althusser, L. and E. Balibar. *Reading Capital*. London: New Left Books, 1970.

Argyris, C. *Personality and Organization*. New York: Harper & Row, 1957.

Argyris, C. *Integrating the Individual and the Organization*. New York: John Wiley, 1964.

Argyris, C. *Reasoning, Learning and Action*. San Francisco: Jossey-Bass, 1982.

Argyris, C. and D. A. Schon. *Theory in Practice*. San Francisco: Jossey-Bass, 1974.

Argyris, C. and D. A. Schon. *Organizational Learning: A Theory of Action Perspective*. Reading, MA: Addison-Wesley, 1978.

Aristotle. *On the Movement of Animals*. Cambridge, MA: Harvard University Press, 1937.

Aristotle. *The Politics*. Oxford: Clarendon, 1946.

Aristotle. *Rhetoric*. Oxford: Oxford University Press, 1946a.

Aristotle. *The Poetics*. Cambridge: Cambridge University Press, 1968.

Aronowitz, S. *False Promises*. New York: McGraw-Hill, 1973.

Ashby, W. R. *Design for a Brain*. New York: John Wiley, 1952.

Ashby, W. R. *An Introduction to Cybernetics*. London: Chapman & Hall, 1960.

Ashford, N. *Crisis in the Workplace: Occupational Disease and Injury*. Cambridge, MA: MIT Press, 1976.

Ashton, D. S. "U.S. Investments in Canada." *Worldwide P&I Planning*, September, 1968.

Astley, W. G. "Toward an Appreciation of Collective Strategy." *Academy of Management Review*, 9: 526-535, 1984.

Astley, W. G. and C. J. Fombrun. "Technological Innovation and Industrial Structure: The Case of Telecommunications," pp. 205-229 in *Advances in Strategic Management*. Greenwich, CT: JAI Press, 1983.

Astley, W. G. and A. H. Van de Ven. "Central Perspectives and Debates in Organization Theory." *Administrative Science Quarterly*, 28: 245-273, 1983.

Atkinson, A. B. *The Economics of Inequality*. New York: Oxford University Press, 1983.

Austin, L. (ed.) *Japan: The Paradox of Progress*. New Haven, CT: Yale University Press, 1976.

Babbage, C. *On the Economy of Machinery and Manufactures*. London: Charles Knight, 1832.

Bachofen, J. J. *Myth, Religion, and Mother-Right*. London: Routledge & Kegan Paul, 1968.

Bacharach, S. B. and E. J. Lawler. *Power and Politics in Organizations*. San Francisco, Jossey-Bass, 1980.

Bachrach, P. and M. S. Baratz. "Two Faces of Power." *American Political Science Review*, 56: 947-952, 1962.

Bachrach, P. and M. S. Baratz (eds.) *Power and Poverty*. New York: Oxford University Press, 1970.

Bailey, A. "Coronary Disease: The Management Killer." *Journal of General Management*, 3: 72-80, 1973.

Baker, K. "Textile Industry vs. Brown Lung." *The Washington Post*, November 28: 19, 1980.

Bakunin, M. *Marxism, Freedom and the State*. London: Freedom Press, 1950.

Bakunin, M. *The Political Philosophy of Bakunin*. New York: Free Press, 1964.

Bales, R. F. *Interaction Process Analysis*. Cambridge, MA: Addison-Wesley, 1950.

Baran, P. and P. M. Sweezy. *Monopoly Capital*. New York, Monthly Review Press, 1966.

Barnard, C. *The Functions of the Executive*. Cambridge, MA: Harvard University Press, 1938.

Baron, H. "The Demand for Black Labor," pp. 368-381 in R.C. Edwards, M. Reich, and D. Gordon (eds.) *Labor Market Segmentation*. Lexington, MA: D. C. Heath, 1975.

Bateson, G. *Naven*. Cambridge: Cambridge University Press, 1936.

Bateson, G. *Steps to an Ecology of Mind*. New York: Ballantine Books, 1972.

Bateson, G. *Mind and Nature*. New York: Bantam Books, 1979.

Baxter, B. *Alienation and Authenticity*. London: Tavistock, 1982.

Becker, E. *The Denial of Death*. New York: Free Press, 1973.

Beckett, S. *Endgame*. New York: Faber, 1958.

Beckett, S. *Waiting for Godot*. New York: Faber, 1965.

Beer, M. *Organization Change and Development*. Santa Monica, CA: Goodyear, 1980.

Beer, S. *Cybernetics and Management*. New York: John Wiley, 1959.

Beer, S. *Brain of the Firm*. New York: Herder & Herder, 1972.

Begley, S. J. and R. Sawhill. "How the Brain Works." *Newsweek*, February 7: 40-47, 1983.

Bello, W., D. Kinley, and E. Elinson. *Development Debacle: The World Bank in the Philippines*. San Francisco: Institute for Food and Development Policy, 1982.

Bendix, R. *Work and Authority in Industry*. New York: John Wiley, 1956.

Bennis, W. G. *Changing Organizations*. New York: McGraw-Hill, 1966.

Bennis, W. G. and B. Nanus. *Leaders: The Strategies for Taking Charge*. New York: Harper & Row, 1985.

Benson, J. K. "The Analysis of Bureaucratic-Professional Conflict." *Sociological Quarterly*, 14: 376-394, 1973.

Benson, J. K. "The Interorganizational Network as a Political Economy." *Administrative Science Quarterly*, 20: 229-249, 1975.

Benson, J. K. "A Dialectical Method for the Study of Organizations," pp. 331-346 in Gareth Morgan (ed.) *Beyond Method*. Beverly Hills, CA: Sage, 1983.

Benson, J. K. and C. J. Jenkins. "Interorganizational Networks and the Theory of the State." Presented at the American Sociological Association Meetings, San Francisco, 1978.

Bentley, A. F. *The Process of Government*. Cambridge, MA: Harvard University Press, 1980.

Bentov I. *Stalking the Wild Pendulum*. New York: Dutton, 1977.

Berger, J. and J. Mohr. *A Seventh Man*. Harmondsworth: Penguin, 1975.

Berger, P. and T. Luckmann. *The Social Construction of Reality*. Garden City, NY: Anchor, 1967.

Berger, S. and M. Piore. *Dualism and Discontinuity in Industrial Societies*. New York: Cambridge University Press, 1980.

Bergmann, A. E. "Industrial Democracy in Germany—The Battle for Power." *Journal of General Management*, 20-29, 1975.

Berman, D. M. *Death on the Job*. New York: Monthly Review Press, 1978.

Bettleheim, B. *The Uses of Enchantment: The Meaning and Importance of Fairy Tales*. New York: Vintage, 1977.

Beynon, H. *Working for Ford*. London: Allen Lane, 1973.

Bhaskar, R. *A Realist Theory of Science*. Hassocks, Sussex: Harvester Press, 1978.

Bion, W. R. *Experiences in Groups*. New York: Basic Books, 1959.

Birchall, D. W. and V. J. Hammond. *Tomorrow's Office Today*. New York: John Wiley, 1981.

Bittner, E. "On the Concept of Organization." *Social Research*, 32: 239-255, 1965.

Black, M. *Models and Metaphors*. Ithaca, NY: Cornell University Press, 1962.

Blackburn, R. M. and M. Mann. *The Working Class in the Labor Market*. London: Macmillan, 1979.

Blake, R. and J. S. Mouton. *The Managerial Grid*. Houston: Gulf Publishing, 1964.

Blau, P. M. and W. R. Scott. *Formal Organizations*. San Francisco: Chandler, 1962.

Blau, P. M. *Exchange and Power in Social Life*. New York: John Wiley, 1964.

Blauner, R. *Alienation and Freedom*. Chicago: University of Chicago Press, 1964.

Bohm, D. "The Implicate Order: A New Order for Physics." *Process Studies*, 8: 73-102, 1978.

Bohm, D. *Wholeness and the Implicate Order*. London: Routledge & Kegan Paul, 1980a.

Bohm, D. "The Enfolded Order and Consciousness," in G. Epstein (ed.) *Studies in Non-Deterministic Psychology*. New York: Human Sciences Press, 1980b.

Boland, R. J. and R. Hoffman. "Humor in a Machine Shop," pp. 187-198 in L. Pondy, P. Frost, G. Morgan, and T. Dandridge (eds.) *Organizational Symbolism*. Greenwich, CT: JAI Press, 1983.

Bottmore, T. B. *Elites and Society*. Harmondsworth: Penguin, 1966.

Boulding, K. E. *The Image*. Ann Arbor: University of Michigan Press, 1956a.

Boulding, K. E. "General Systems Theory—The Skeleton of Science." *Management Science*, 2: 197-208, 1956b.

Boulding, K. E. *Evolutionary Economics*. Beverly Hills, CA: Sage, 1981.

Bower, J. "Managing for Efficiency, Managing for Equity." *Harvard Business Review*, 83-90, August 1983.

Brandt, W. *North-South: A Program for Survival*. Cambridge, MA: MIT Press, 1980.

Braverman, H. *Labor and Monopoly Capital*. New York: Monthly Review Press, 1974.

Braybrooke, D. and C. E. Lindblom. *A Strategy of Decision*. New York: Free Press, 1963.

Brooke, M. Z. and H. L. Remmers. *The Strategy of Multi-National Enterprise*. New York: American Elsevier, 1970.

Brown, B. *Marx, Freud, and the Critique of Everyday Life*. New York: Monthly Review Press, 1973.

Brown, L. D. "Managing Conflict Among Groups," pp. 225-237 in D. A. Kolb, I. M. Rubin, and J. McIntyre (eds.) *Organizational Psychology*. Englewood Cliffs, NJ: Prentice-Hall, 1983.

Brown, N. O. *Life Against Death*. Middletown, CT: Wesleyan University Press, 1959.

Brown, R. H. *A Poetic for Sociology*. New York: Cambridge University Press, 1977.

Bryer, R., T. J. Brignall, and A. R. Maunders. *Accounting for British Steel*. London: Gower Press, 1982.

Buckley, W. *Sociology and Modern Systems Theory*. Englewood Cliffs, NJ: Prentice-Hall, 1967.

Buckley, W. (ed.) *Modern Systems Research for the Behavioral Scientist*. Chicago: Aldine, 1968.

Bukharin, N. *Imperialism and World Economy*. London: Merlin, 1972.

Bukharin, N. *Historical Materialism: A System of Sociology.* New York: Russell & Russell, 1962.

Burke, K. *A Grammar of Motives and a Rhetoric of Motives.* Cleveland, OH: Meridian, 1962.

Burke, K. "Dramatism," in D. Sills (ed.) *International Encyclopaedia of the Social Sciences.* New York: Macmillan, 1968.

Burke, R. J. and T. Weir. "Coping with the Stress of Managerial Occupations," pp. 299-335 in C. L. Cooper and R. Payne (eds.) *Current Concerns in Occupational Stress.* London: Wiley, 1980.

Burns, J. M. *Leadership.* New York: Harper & Row, 1978.

Burns, R. D. *The Uncertain Nervous System.* London: Arnold, 1968.

Burns, T. and G. M. Stalker. *The Management of Innovation.* London: Tavistock, 1961.

Burns, T. "Micropolitics: Mechanisms of Organizational Change." *Administrative Science Quarterly,* 6: 257-281, 1961.

Buroway, M. *Manufacturing Consent.* Chicago: University of Chicago Press, 1979.

Burrell, G. "Sex and Organizational Analysis." *Organization Studies,* 5: 97-118, 1984.

Burrell, G. and G. Morgan. *Sociological Paradigms and Organizational Analysis.* London: Heinemann Educational Books, 1979.

Business Week Reporters. "Ford After Henry II: Will He Really Leave?" *Business Week,* April 30: 62-72, 1979.

Campbell, D. T. "Variation and Selective Retention in Socio-Cultural Evolution." *General Systems,* 16: 69-85, 1969.

Camus, A. *The Outsider.* London: Hamilton, 1946.

Capra, F. *The Tao of Physics.* New York: Wildwood House, 1975.

Carr, A. Z. *Business as a Game.* New York: Mentor, 1968.

Cassirer, E. *Language and Myth.* New York: Dover Publications, 1946.

Casson, M. *The Growth of International Business.* London: Allen & Unwin, 1983.

Castles, S. and G. Kosack. *Immigrant Workers and Class Structures in Western Europe.* New York: Oxford University Press, 1973.

Chandler, A. *Strategy and Structure.* Cambridge, MA: MIT Press, 1962.

Chandler, A. *The Visible Hand.* Cambridge, MA: Harvard University Press, 1977.

Chatov, R. "Cooperation Between Government and Business," pp. 487-502 in P. C. Nystrom and W. H. Starbuck (eds.) *Handbook of Organizational Design.* New York: Oxford University Press, 1981.

Child, J. "Culture, Contingency and Capitalism in the Cross-National Study of Organizations," pp. 303-356 in B. Staw and L. L. Cummings (eds.) *Research in Organizational Behavior.* 1981.

Childe, V. G. *Man Makes Himself.* London: Fontana, 1946.

Clegg, S. *Power, Rule and Domination.* London: Routledge & Kegan Paul, 1975.

Clegg, S. *The Theory of Power and Organization.* London: Routledge & Kegan Paul, 1979.

Clegg, S. "Organization and Control." *Administrative Science Quarterly,* 26: 545-562, 1981.

Clegg, S. and D. Dunkerley. *Organization, Class and Control.* London: Routledge & Kegan Paul, 1980.

Cleugh, J. *Love Locked Out: An Examination of the Irrepressible Sexuality of the Middle Ages.* New York: Crown, 1963.

Coates, K. *The New Worker Cooperatives*. Nottingham: Spokesman Books, 1976.
Coates, K. (ed.) *The Right to Useful Work*. Nottingham: Spokesman Books, 1978.
Coates, K. *Work-Ins, Sit-Ins and Industrial Democracy*. Nottingham: Spokesman Books, 1981a.
Coates, K. *How to Win*. Nottingham: Spokesman Books, 1981b.
Coates, K. and T. Topham. *Worker Control*. London: Panther, 1970.
Cohen, M. D., J. G. March, and J. P. Olsen. "A Garbage Can Model of Organizational Choice." *Administrative Science Quarterly*, 17: 1-25, 1972.
Cole, R. E. *Work, Mobility and Participation: A Comparative Study of American and Japanese Industry*. Berkeley: University of California Press, 1979.
Colletti, L. *From Rousseau to Lenin*. London: New Left Books, 1972.
Colletti, L. "A Political and Philosophical Interview." *New Left Review*, 86: 3-28, 1974.
Colletti, L. "Introduction," pp. 7-56 in K. Marx, *Early Writings*. London: Allen Lane, 1975a.
Colletti, L. "Marxism and the Dialectic." *New Left Review*, 93: 3-29, 1975b.
Cooper, C. L. and J. Marshall. "Occupational Sources of Stress: A Review of the Literature Relating to Coronary Heart Disease and Mental Ill-health." *Journal of Occupational Psychology*, 49: 11-28, 1976.
Cooper, C. L. and R. Payne (eds.) *Current Concerns in Occupational Stress*. New York: John Wiley, 1980.
Copley, F. B. *Frederick Taylor: Father of Scientific Management*, 2 vols. New York: Harper & Row, 1923.
Corwin, R. G. *Militant Professionalism*. New York: Appleton-Century-Crofts, 1970.
Coser, L. A. *The Functions of Social Conflict*. New York: Routledge & Kegan Paul, 1956.
Coward, R. *Patriarchal Precedents: Sexuality and Social Relations*. London: Routledge & Kegan Paul, 1983.
Crick, B. *In Defense of Politics*. Harmondsworth: Penguin, 1964.
Crozier, M. *The Bureaucratic Phenomenon*. London: Tavistock, 1964.
Culbert, S. and J. McDonough. *The Invisible War: Pursuing Self-Interest at Work*. Toronto: John Wiley, 1980.
Cumming, P. *The Power Handbook*. Boston: CBI Publishing, 1981.
Cyert, R. M and J. G. March. *A Behavioral Theory of the Firm*. Englewood Cliffs, NJ: Prentice-Hall, 1963.
Dahl, R. A. "The Concept of Power." *Behavioral Science*, 2: 201-215, 1957.
Dalton, M. *Men Who Manage*. New York: John Wiley, 1959.
Davis, S. M. and P. R. Lawrence. *Matrix*. Reading, MA: Addison-Wesley, 1977.
Deal, T. E. and A. A. Kennedy. *Corporate Cultures*. Reading, MA: Addison-Wesley, 1982.
Delahanty, F. and G. Gemill. "The Black Hole in Group Development." Presented at the Academy of Management Meetings, New York, 1982.
Denhardt, R. B. *In the Shadow of Organization*. Lawrence, KA: Regents Press, 1981.
Descartes, R. *Discourse on Method*. London: Penguin, 1968.
Devons, E. "Statistics as a Basis for Policy," pp. 122-137 in *Essays in Economics*. London: Allen & Unwin, 1961.
Dill, W. R. "Environment as an Influence on Managerial Autonomy." *Administrative Science Quarterly*, 2: 409-443, 1958.

Dodson-Gray, E. *Patriarchy as a Conceptual Trap*. Wellesley, MA: Roundtable Press, 1982.

Donahue, T. R. "Collective Bargaining, Codetermination, and the Quality of Work." *World of Work Report*, 1, 1976.

Dore, R. *British Factory, Japanese Factory*. London: Allen & Unwin, 1973.

Dore, R. "Introduction," pp ix-xi in S. Kamata (ed.) *Japan in the Passing Lane*. New York: Pantheon, 1982.

Downs, A. *Inside Bureaucracy*. Boston: Little, Brown, 1967.

Drucker, P. F. *The Practice of Management*. New York: Harper & Row, 1954.

Dunnette, M. D. (ed.) *Handbook of Industrial and Organizational Psychology*. Chicago: Rand McNally, 1976.

Durkheim, E. *The Division of Labour in Society*. London: Macmillan, 1934.

Durkheim, E. *The Rules of Sociological Method*. New York: Free Press, 1938.

Durkheim, E. *Suicide*. New York: Free Press, 1951.

Eagle, J. and P. M. Newton. "Scapegoating in Small Groups." *Human Relations*, 34: 283-301, 1981.

Easton, D. A. *A Systems Analysis of Political Life*. New York: John Wiley, 1965.

Eccles, T. *Under New Management*. London: Pan Books, 1981.

Eco, U. *A Theory of Semiotics*. Bloomington: Indiana University Press, 1976.

Edelman, M. *Politics as Symbolic Action*. Chicago: Markham, 1971.

Edelman, M. *Political Language: Words That Succeed and Policies That Fail*. New York: Academic Press, 1977.

Edwards, R. C. *Contested Terrain*. New York: Basic Books, 1979.

Edwards, R. C., M. Reich, and D. Gordon (eds.) *Labor Market Segmentation*. Lexington, MA: D.C. Heath, 1975.

Ellul, J. *The Technological Society*. New York: Alfred A. Knopf, 1964.

Emerson, R. M. "Power-Dependence Relations." *American Sociological Review*, 27: 31-40, 1962.

Emery, F. E. (ed.) *Systems Thinking*. Harmondsworth: Penguin, 1969.

Emery, F. E. and E. Thorsrud. *Form and Content in Industrial Democracy*. London: Tavistock, 1969.

Emery, F. E. and E. L. Trist. "The Causal Texture of Organizational Environments." *Human Relations*, 18: 21-32, 1965.

Emery, F. E. and E. L. Trist. *Toward a Social Ecology*. London: Tavistock, 1973.

Engels, F. *The Origins of the Family, Private Property and the State*. London: Lawrence & Wishart, 1972.

Engels, F. *Dialectics of Nature*. London: Lawrence & Wishart, 1873.

Engels, F. *Anti-Duhring*. London: Martin Lawrence, 1876.

Engels, F. *Ludwig Feuerbach and the Outcome of Classical German Philosophy*. London: Martin Lawrence, 1886.

Epstein, S. S. *The Politics of Cancer*. San Francisco: Sierra Club Books, 1978.

Epstein, S. "The Unconscious, the Preconscious, and the Self-Concept," in J. Suls and A. Greenwald (eds.) *Psychological Perspectives on the Self*. Hillsdale, NJ: Erlbaum, 1983.

Etzioni, A. *A Comparative Analysis of Complex Organizations*. New York: Free Press, 1961.

Evered, R. "The Language of Organization: The Case of the Navy," pp. 125-143 in L. Pondy et al. (eds.) *Organizational Symbolism*. Greenwich, CT: JAI Press, 1983.

Fayol, H. *General and Industrial Management*. London: Pitman, 1949.

Feinberg, M. R. and R. F. Dempewolf. *Corporate Bigamy*. New York: William Morrow, 1980.

Ferguson, M. *The Aquarian Conspiracy*. New York: J.P. Tarcher, 1980.

Figgis, J. N. *Churches in the Modern State*. London: Longmans, 1913.

Findlay, J. N. *Hegel: A Re-Examination*. London: Allen & Unwin, 1958.

Filley, A. C. *Interpersonal Conflict Resolution*. Glenview, IL: Scott Foresman, 1975.

Follett, M. P. *The New State*. London: Longmans, 1918.

Follman, J. F. *The Economics of Industrial Health: History, Theory, Practice*. New York: Amacom, 1978.

Fombrun, C. J. and W. G. Astley. "Strategies of Collective Action: The Case of the Financial Services Industry," pp. 125-129 in *Advances in Strategic Management*. Greenwich, CT: JAI Press, 1983.

Forester, J. W. *Industrial Dynamics*. Cambridge, MA: MIT Press, 1961.

Forester, J. "Critical Theory and Organizational Analysis," pp. 234-246 in G. Morgan (ed.) *Beyond Method: Strategies for Social Research*. Beverly Hills, CA: Sage, 1983.

Foucault, M. *Discipline and Punish*. New York: Vintage, 1979a.

Foucault, M. *The History of Sexuality*. London: Allen Lane, 1979b.

Fox, A. "Industrial Sociology and Industrial Relations." *Royal Commission on Trade Unions and Employers' Associations*. London: HMSO, 1966.

Fox, A. *Beyond Contract: Work, Power and Trust Relations*. London: Faber & Faber, 1974.

Freeman, J. and M. T. Hannan. "Niche Width and the Dynamics of Organizational Populations." *American Journal of Sociology*, 6: 1116-1145, 1983.

Freeman, J. "Organizational Life Cycles and Natural Selection Processes," in B. M. Staw and L. L. Cummings (eds.) *Research in Organizational Behavior*. Greenwich, CT: JAI Press, 1982.

Freire, P. *The Pedgogy of the Oppressed*. New York: Herder and Herder, 1970.

French, J.R.P. and B. Raven. "The Bases of Social Power," in D. Cartwright and A. Zander (eds.) *Group Dynamics*. New York: Harper & Row, 1968.

Freud, S. *The Complete Psychological Works of Sigmund Freud*. London: Hogarth Press, 1953.

Frey-Rohn, L. *From Freud to Jung*. New York: Putnam, 1974.

Friedman, A. L. *Industry and Labour: Class Struggle at Work and Monopoly Capitalism*. London: Macmillan, 1977.

Fromm, E. *Marx's Concept of Man*. New York: Ungar, 1961.

Fromm, E. *Beyond the Chains of Illusion: My Encounter with Marx and Freud*. New York: Trident Press, 1962.

Fromm, E. *The Crisis of Psychoanalysis*. New York: Cape, 1971.

Frost, P. J., V. F. Mitchell, and W. R. Nord (eds.) *Organizational Reality*. Santa Monica, CA: Goodyear, 1982.

Frost, P. J., L. F. Moore, M. R. Louis, C. C. Lundberg, and J. Martin. *Organizational Culture*. Beverly Hills, CA: Sage, 1985.

Fry, E. H. *The Politics of International Investment*. New York: McGraw-Hill, 1983.

Frye, N. *Anatomy of Criticism*. Princeton, NJ: Princeton University Press, 1957.

Frye, N. *The Great Code: The Bible and Literature*. Toronto: Academic Press, 1982.

Gadalla, I. E. and R. C. Cooper. "Toward an Epistemology of Management." *Social Science Information*, 17: 349-383, 1978.

Galbraith, J. K. *American Capitalism*. Boston: Houghton Mifflin, 1962.

Galbraith, J. K. *The New Industrial State*. London: Hamish Hamilton, 1967.

Galbraith, J. R. "Matrix Organization Designs: How to Combine Functional and Project Forms." *Business Horizons*, 14: 29-40, 1971.

Galbraith, J. R. "Organization Design: An Information Processing View." *Interfaces*, 4: 28-36, 1974.

Galbraith, J. R. *Organization Design*. Reading, MA: Addison-Wesley, 1977.

Galileo, *Discourses on Two New Science*. Evanston, IL: Northwestern University Press, 1968.

Garfinkel, H. *Studies in Ethnomethodology*. Englewood Cliffs, NJ: Prentice-Hall, 1967.

Garson, G.D. "The Codetermination Model of Worker's Participation: Where Is It Leading?" *Sloan Management Review*, 63-78, 1977.

Geertz, C. *The Interpretation of Cultures*. New York: Basic Books, 1973.

George, C. S. *The History of Management Thought*. Englewood Cliffs, NJ: Prentice-Hall, 1972.

George, S. *How the Other Half Dies: The Real Reasons for World Hunger*. Harmondsworth: Penguin, 1976.

Giddens, A. *Central Problems in Social Theory*. London: Macmillan, 1979.

Giedeon, S. *Mechanization Takes Command*. New York: Oxford University Press, 1948.

Gilbreth, F. B. *Motion Study*. New York: Van Nostrand, 1911.

Gimpl, M. L. and S. Dakin. "Management and Magic." New Zealand: University of Canterbury, 1983. (unpublished)

Gladwin, T. N. and I. Walter. *Multinationals Under Fire*. New York: John Wiley, 1980.

Gluckman, M. (ed.) *The Allocation of Responsibility*. Manchester: Manchester University Press, 1972.

Glyn, A. and B. Sutcliffe. *British Capitalism, Workers and the Profits Squeeze*. Harmondsworth: Penguin, 1972.

Godel, K. *On Formally Undecidable Propositions*. New York: Basic Books, 1962.

Godelier, M. "Structure and Contradiction in Capital," pp. 334-368 in R. Blackburn (ed.) *Ideology in Social Science*. London: Fontana/Collins, 1972.

Goffman, E. *The Presentation of Self in Everyday Life*. Garden City, NY: Doubleday, 1959.

Goffman, E. *Interaction Ritual*. Garden City, NY: Doubleday, 1967.

Goldberg, W. H. and A. R. Negandhi (eds.) *Governments and Multinationals: The Policy of Control Versus Autonomy*. Cambridge, MA: Oelgeschlager, Gunn, & Hain, 1983.

Goldman, P. and D. Van Houten. "Managerial Strategies and the Worker." *The Sociological Quarterly*, 18: 108-125, 1977.

Gomez, P. and G. Probst. "Organizational Closure in Management: A Complementary View to Contingency Approaches." Presented to the American Society for Cybernetics, Philadelphia, 1984.

Gordon, D. M., R. C. Edwards, and M. Reich. *Segmented Work, Divided Workers*. New York: Cambridge University Press, 1982.

Gorz, A. *Paths to Paradise*. London: Pluto Press, 1985.

Gouldner, A. "Reciprocity and Autonomy in Functional Theory," pp. 190-225 in A. W. Gouldner (ed.) *For Sociology*. Harmondsworth: Penguin, 1973.

Gramsci, A. *Selections from the Prison Notebooks*. London: Lawrence & Wishart, 1971.

Grunberg, L. *Failed Multinational Ventures: The Political Economy of International Divestments*. Lexington, MA: D.C. Heath, 1981.

Guillet de Monthoux, P. *Action and Existence: Anarchism for Business Administration*. New York: John Wiley, 1983.

Gulick, L. and L. Urwick (eds.) *Papers in the Science of Administration*. New York: Institute of Public Administration, Columbia University, 1937.

Guntrip, H. *Personality Structure and Human Interaction*. New York: International University Press, 1961.

Gunnermann, J. P. (ed.) *The Nation-State and Transnational Corporations in Conflict*. New York: Praeger, 1975.

Habermas, J. "On Systematically Distorted Communications." *Inquiry*, 13: 205-218, 1970a.

Habermas, J. "Towards a Theory of Communicative Competence." *Inquiry*, 13: 360-375, 1970b.

Habermas, J. *Knowledge and Human Interests*. London: Heinemann Educational Books, 1972.

Habermas, J. *Legitimation Crisis*. London: Heinemann Educational Books, 1973.

Hackman, J. R. and J. L. Suttle. *Improving Life at Work*. Santa Monica, CA: Goodyear, 1976.

Hailey, A. *Wheels*. Garden City, NY: Doubleday, 1971.

Hall, E. T. *The Silent Language*. Garden City, NY: Doubleday, 1959.

Hall, E. T. "The Silent Language in Overseas Business." *Harvard Business Review*, 38: 87-96, 1960.

Hall, R. H. *Organizations: Structure and Process*. Englewood Cliffs, NJ: Prentice-Hall, 1982.

Hampden-Turner, C. *Maps of the Mind*. New York: Macmillan, 1981.

Handy, C. *Gods of Management*. London: Pan Books, 1978.

Hannan, M. T. and J. H. Freeman. "The Population Ecology of Organizations." *American Journal of Sociology*, 82: 929-964, 1977.

Harding, M. E. *The I and the Not I: A Study in the Development of Consciousness*. Princeton, NJ: Princeton University Press, 1965.

Harris, M. L. *Cultural Materialism*. New York: Random House, 1979.

Harries-Jones, P. "Human Judgement and Conversation Theory: The Significance of Gregory Bateson's Concept of Co-Evolution." Toronto: York University, 1983. (unpublished)

Harries-Jones, P. "The Other Side of the Mirror: Communication as Presentation." Toronto: York University, 1984. (unpublished)

Hawley, A. H. "Human Ecology," pp. 328-337 in D. Sills (ed.) *International Encyclopedia of the Social Sciences*. New York: Macmillan, 1968.

Hayter, T. *The Creation of World Poverty: An Alternative View to the Brandt Report*. London: Pluto Press, 1981.

Heath, T. L. *The Works of Archimedes*. Cambridge: Cambridge University Press, 1897.

Hegel, G.W.F. *The Logic of Hegel*. Oxford: Clarendon, 1892.

Hegel, G.W.F. *Science of Logic*. London, 1929.

Heisenberg, W. *A Physicist's Conception of Nature*. London: Hutchinson, 1958.

Held, D. *Introduction to Critical Theory*. Berkeley: University of California Press, 1980.

Herbst, P. G. *Autonomous Group Functioning*. London: Tavistock, 1962.

Herbst, P. G. *Socio-Technical Design*. London: Tavistock, 1974.

Herzberg, F., B. Mausner, and B. Snyderman. *The Motivation to Work*. New York: John Wiley, 1959.

Heydebrand, W. V. "Organizational Contradictions in Public Bureaucracies: Toward a Marxian Theory of Organizations." *Sociological Quarterly*, 18: 83-107, 1977.

Heydebrand, W. V. "Organization and Praxis," pp. 306-320 in G. Morgan (ed.) *Beyond Method*. Beverly Hills, CA: Sage, 1983.

Heydebrand, W. V. and C. Seron. "The Double-Bind of the Capitalist Judicial System." *International Journal of the Sociology of Law*, 9: 407-436, 1981.

Hickson, D. J., D. S. Pugh, and D. C. Pheysey. "Operations Technology and Organization Structure: An Empirical Reappraisal." *Administrative Science Quarterly*, 14: 378-397, 1969.

Hickson, D. J., C. R. Hinings, C. A. Lee, R. E. Schneck, and J. M. Pennings. "A Strategic Contingencies Theory of Intra-Organizational Power." *Administrative Science Quarterly*, 16: 216-229, 1971.

Hirsch, P. M. and J. Andrews. "Ambushes, Shootouts, and Knights of the Roundtable: The Language of Corporate Takeovers," pp. 145-155 in L. Pondy et al. (eds.) *Organizational Symbolism*. Greenwich, CT: JAI Press, 1983.

Hobbes, T. *Leviathan*. London: Basil Blackwell, 1951.

Hodge, B., R. Fleck, and C. B. Honess. *Management Information Systems*. Reston, VA: Reston Publishing, 1984.

Hofstadter, D. R. *Gödel, Escher, Bach*. New York: Basic Books, 1979.

Hofstadter, D. R. "Metamagical Themas." *Scientific American*, 248: 16-26, 1983.

Hofstede, G. H. *The Game of Budget Control*. Assen, Netherlands: Van Gorcum, 1967.

Holland, S. *The Socialist Challenge*. London: Quartet, 1975.

Holloway, J. and S. Picciotto (eds.) *State and Capital: A Marxist Debate*. London: Arnold, 1978.

Hopkins, T. K. and I. Wallerstein. *World-System Analysis*. Beverly Hills, CA: Sage, 1982.

Horkheimer, M. *Critical Theory: Selected Essays*. New York: Herder, 1972.

Horkheimer, M. and T. Adorno. *Dialectic of Enlightenment*. London: Allen Lane, 1973.

Horney, K. *Self-Analysis*. New York: Norton, 1942.

Horney, K. *Feminine Psychology*. New York: Norton, 1967.

Huff, A. S. "Industry Influences on Strategy Reformulation." *Strategic Management Journal*, 3: 119-131, 1982.

Hughes, J. *Britain in Crisis*. Nottingham: Spokesman Books, 1981.

Hummel, R. *The Bureaucratic Experience*. New York: St. Martin's, 1977.

Hyman, R. *Industrial Relations: A Marxist Introduction*. London: Macmillan, 1975.

Iacocca, L. *An Autobiography*. New York: Bantam, 1984.

Ingalls, J. D. *Human Energy*. Austin, TX: Learning Concepts, 1979.

Jakobson, R. *Selected Writings*. The Hague: Mouton, 1956.

Jakobson, R. and M. Halle. *Fundamentals of Language*. The Hague: Mouton, 1962.

James, W. *The Principles of Psychology*. New York: Dover, 1950.

Janis, I. L. *Victims of Groupthink*. Boston: Houghton Mifflin, 1972.

Jantsch, E. *Design for Evolution*. New York: Braziller, 1975.

Jantsch, E. *The Self-Organizing Universe*. Oxford: Pergamon, 1980.

Jantsch, E. and C. Waddington. *Evolution and Consciousness*. Reading, MA: Addison-Wesley, 1976.

Jaques, E. "Social Systems as a Defence Against Persecutory and Depressive Anxiety," pp. 478-498 in M. Klein (ed.) *New Directions in Psycho-Analysis*. London: Tavistock, 1955.

Jardin, A. *The First Henry Ford: A Study in Personality and Business Leadership*. Cambridge, MA: MIT Press, 1970.

Jay, M. *The Dialectical Imagination*. London: Heinemann, 1973.

Jay, P. *Management and Machiavelli*. London: Hodder & Stoughton, 1967.

Jelinek, M., L. Smircich, and P. Hirsch (eds.) "Organizational Culture." *Administrative Science Quarterly*, 28, 1983.

Jung, C. G. *Collected Works*. London: Routledge & Kegan Paul, 1953.

Jung, C. G. *Man and His Symbols*. London: Aldus Books, 1964.

Jung, C. G. *Memories, Dreams, Reflections*. London: Routledge & Kegan Paul, 1967.

Jung, C. G. *The Portable Jung*. New York: Viking Press, 1971.

Kafka, F. *The Trial*. Harmondsworth: Penguin, 1953.

Kafka, F. *The Castle*. New York: Secker, 1973.

Kakar, S. *Frederick Taylor: A Study in Personality and Innovation*. Cambridge, MA: MIT Press, 1970.

Kamata, S. *Japan In The Passing Lane*. New York: Pantheon, 1982.

Kanter, R. M. *Men and Women of the Corporation*. New York: Basic Books, 1977.

Kanter, R. M. *The Change Masters*. New York: Simon & Schuster, 1983.

Kast, E. and J. E. Rosenzweig. *Contingency Views of Organization and Management*. Chicago: Science Research Associates, 1973.

Katz, D. and R. L. Kahn. *The Social Psychology of Organizations*. New York: John Wiley, 1978.

Kaufman, W. *Hegel*. London: Weidenfeld & Nicholson, 1965.

Kautsky, J. H. *The Politics of Aristocratic Empires*. Chapel Hill: University of North Carolina Press, 1982.

Kennedy, M. M. *Office Politics: Seizing Power and Wielding Clout*. New York: Warner Books, 1980.

Kerr, C., J. T. Dunlop, F. H. Harbison, and C. A. Myers. Industrialism and Industrial Man. London: Oxford University Press, 1964.

Kets de Vries, M. and D. Miller. *The Neurotic Organization*. San Francisco: Jossey-Bass, 1984.

Kiernans, E. *Globalism and the Nation State*. Toronto: CBC Enterprises, 1984.

Kilmann, R. H., M. J. Saxton, and R. Serpa (eds.) *Gaining Control of the Corporate Culture*. San Francisco: Jossey-Bass, 1985.

Kimberley, J. R. and R. H. Miles. *The Organizational Life Cycle*. San Francisco: Jossey-Bass, 1980.

Kingdon, D. R. *Matrix Organization*. London: Tavistock, 1973.

Klein, M. *Contributions to Psycho-Analysis: 1921-1945*. London: Hogarth Press, 1965.

Klein, M. *Envy, Gratitude and Other Works*. London: Hogarth Press, 1980.

Klein, M. *Love, Guilt and Reparation and Other Works*. London: Hogarth Press, 1981.

Koestler, A. *The Ghost in the Machine*. London: Hutchinson, 1967.

Koestler, A. *The Act of Creation*. London: Hutchinson, 1969.

Kolodny, H. "Managing in a Matrix." *Business Horizons*, 17-24, March 1981.

Koontz, H. and C. O'Donnell. *Principles of Management*. New York: McGraw-Hill, 1955.

Korda, M. *Power: How to Get It, How to Use It*. New York: Random House, 1975.

Kornhauser, W. *Scientists in Industry*. Berkeley: University of California Press, 1963.

Kotter, J. P. "Power, Dependence and Effective Management." *Harvard Business Review*, July-August 1977.

Kreckel, R. "Unequal Opportunity Structure and Labor Market Segmentation." *Sociology*, 14: 525-550, 1980.

Kroeber, A. L. and C. Kluckhohn. *Culture: A Critical Review of Concepts and Definitions*. New York: Vintage, 1952.

Kropotkin, P. A. *Mutual Aid*. New York: McLure, Phillips, 1903.

Kuhn, T. S. *The Structure of Scientific Revolutions*. Chicago: University of Chicago Press, 1970.

Kujawa, D. (ed.) *International Labor and the Multinational Enterprise*. New York: Praeger, 1975.

Lacan, J. *Ecrits*. Paris: Seuil, 1966.

Laing, R. D. *The Divided Self*. Harmondsworth: Penguin, 1965.

Lakoff, G. and M. Johnson. *Metaphors We Live By*. Chicago: University of Chicago Press, 1980.

Lall, S. (ed.) *The New Multinationals: The Spread of Third World Enterprises*. New York: John Wiley, 1983.

LaMettrie, J. *L'Homme Machine*. London: Owen, 1748.

Lammers, C. J. and D. Hickson (eds.) *Organizations Alike and Unalike*. London: Routledge & Kegan Paul, 1979.

Lasch, C. *The Culture of Narcissism*. New York: Warner Books, 1979.

Laski, H. J. *Studies in the Problem of Sovereignty*. New Haven, CT: Yale University Press, 1917.

Laski, H. J. *Authority in the Modern State*. New Haven, CT: Yale University Press, 1919.

Lasswell, H. D. *Politics: Who Gets What, When, How*. New York: McGraw-Hill, 1936.

Lawler, E. E. *Motivation in Work Organizations*. Monterey, CA: Brooks/Cole, 1973.

Lawrence, P. R. and D. Dyer. *Renewing American Industry*. New York: Free Press, 1982.

Lawrence, P. R. and J. W. Lorsch. *Organization and Environment*. Cambridge, MA: Harvard Graduate School of Business Administration, 1967a.

Lawrence, P. R. and J. W. Lorsch. "Differentiation and Integration in Complex Organizations." *Administrative Science Quarterly*, 12: 1-47, 1967b.

Leavitt, H. J. "Applied Organizational Change in Industry: Structural, Technical and Human Approaches," in W.W. Cooper, H.J. Leavitt and M. W. Shelly (eds.) *New Perspectives in Organization Research*. New York: John Wiley, 1964.

Lefebvre, H. *Dialectical Materialism*. London: Jonathan Cape, 1968a.

Lefebvre, H. *The Sociology of Karl Marx*. London: Allen Lane, 1968b.

Lemaire, A. *Jacques Lacan*. London: Routledge & Kegan Paul, 1977.

Lenin, V. I. "On Dialectics," in *Selected Works*. London, 1936.

Levidon, L. and B. Young (eds.) *Science, Technology and the Labour Process*. London: Blackrose Press, 1981.

Levie, H. D., and N. Lorentzen (eds.) *Fighting Closures*. Nottingham: Spokesman Books, 1984.

Levinson, H. *Organizational Diagnosis*. Cambridge, MA: Harvard University Press, 1972.

Levi-Strauss, C. *The Scope of Anthropology*. New York: Johnathan Cape, 1967.
Lifton, J. and E. Olson. *Living and Dying*. New York: Bantam, 1975.
Lindblom, C. E. "The Science of 'Muddling Through.'" *Public Administration Review*, 19: 78-88, 1959.
Lindblom, C. E. *The Policy-Making Process*. Englewood Cliffs, NJ: Prentice-Hall, 1968.
Lips, H. M. *Women, Men, and the Psychology of Power*. Englewood Cliffs, NJ: Prentice-Hall, 1981.
Litterer, J. A. "Conflict in Organization: A Re-Examination." *Academy of Management*, 9: 178-186, 1966.
Louis, M. R. "Organizations as Culture-Bearing Milieux," pp. 39-54 in L. Pondy et al. (eds.) *Organizational Symbolism*. Greenwich, CT: JAI Press, 1983.
Lowenberg, P. "Love and Hate in the Academy." *Centre Magazine*, 4-11, September 1972.
Lucas, R. "Combining Political and Cultural Analyses of Organizations." Toronto: York University, 1983. (unpublished)
Lukacs, G. *History and Class Consciousness*. London: Merlin, 1971.
Lukes, S. *Power: A Radical View*. London: Macmillan, 1974.
Maccoby, M. *The Gamesman*. New York: Simon & Schuster, 1976.
Machiavelli, N. *The Prince*.
Machlowitz, M. *Workaholics*. Reading, MA: Addison-Wesley, 1978.
Maitland, F. W. *Collected Papers*. Cambridge: Cambridge University Press, 1911.
Mandel, E. *Marxist Economic Theory*. London: Merlin, 1962.
Mangham, I. *Interactions and Interventions in Organizations*. New York: John Wiley, 1978.
Mangham, I. and M. Overington. "Dramatism and the Theatrical Metaphor," pp. 219-233 in G. Morgan (ed.) *Beyond Method*. Beverly Hills, CA: Sage, 1983.
Mannheim, K. *Man and Society in an Age of Reconstruction*. London: Routledge & Kegan Paul, 1940.
Manning, P. K. "Talking and Becoming: A View of Organizational Socialization," pp. 239-256 in J. Douglas (ed.) *Understanding Everyday Life*. Chicago: Aldine, 1970.
Manning, P. K. "Metaphors of the Field: Varieties of Organizational Discourse." *Administrative Science Quarterly*, 24: 660-671, 1979.
Mao Tse Tung. *On Contradiction*. Peking: Foreign Language Press, 1937.
March, J. G. "The Business Firm as a Political Coalition." *Journal of Politics*, 24: 662-678, 1962.
March, J. G. "Decision Making Perspective: Decisions in Organizations and Theories of Choice," pp. 205-244 in A. Van de Ven and W. Joyce (eds.) *Perspectives on Organization Design and Behavior*. New York: John Wiley, 1981.
March, J. G. and H. A. Simon. *Organizations*. New York: John Wiley, 1958.
March, J. G. and J. P. Oslen. *Ambiguity and Choice in Organizations*. Bergen: Universitetsforlaget, 1976.
Marcuse, H. *Eros and Civilization*. Boston: Beacon Press, 1955.
Marcuse, H. *One-Dimensional Man*. Boston: Beacon Press, 1964.
Marcuse, H. "Freedom and Freud's Theory of Instincts," in *Five Lectures: Psychoanalysis, Politics and Utopia*. Boston: Beacon Press, 1970.
Marglin, S. A. "What Do Bosses Do?" pp. 13-54 in A. Gorz (ed.) *The Division of Labor*. Hassocks: Harvester Press, 1976.

Markovic, M. *From Affluence to Praxis*. Ann Arbor: University of Michigan Press, 1974.

Marshall, J. and A. McLean. "Exploring Organization Culture as a Route to Organizational Change," pp. 2-20 in V. Hammond (ed.) *Current Research in Management*. London: Francis Pinter, 1985.

Martin, J. and C. Siehl. "Organizational Culture and Sub-Culture: An Uneasy Symbiosis." *Organizational Dynamics*, 12: 52-64, 1983.

Marx, K. *Early Writings*. Harmondsworth: Penguin, 1975.

Marx, K. *Capital*. Harmondsworth: Penguin, 1976.

Marx, K. and R. Engels. *The German Ideology*. London: Lawrence & Wishart, 1846.

Marx, K. and R. Engels. "The Manifesto of the Communist Party," pp. 35-63 in K. Marx and R. Engels, *Selected Works*. London: Lawrence & Wishart, 1848.

Maruyama, M. "The Second Cybernetics: Deviation Amplifying Mutual Causal Processes." *American Scientist*, 51: 164-179, 1963.

Maruyama, M. "Mindscapes, Management, Business Policy, and Public Policy." *Academy of Management Review*, 7: 612-619, 1982.

Maslow, A. H. "A Theory of Human Motivation." *Psychological Review*, 50: 370-396, 1943.

Maslow, A. H. *Toward a Psychology of Being*. New York: Van Nostrand, 1968.

Mason, R. O. and I. Mitroff. *Challenging Strategic Planning Assumptions*. New York: John Wiley, 1981.

Massey, D. and R. Meegan. *The Anatomy of Job Loss*. London: Methuen, 1982.

Maturana, H. and F. Varela. *Autopoiesis and Cognition: The Realization of the Living*. London: Reidl, 1980.

Mayo, E. *The Human Problems of an Industrial Civilization*. New York: Macmillan, 1933.

McClelland, D. *Power: The Inner-Experience*. New York: John Wiley, 1975.

McCorduck, P. *Machines Who Think*. San Francisco: Freeman, 1979.

McCulloch, W. S. "Recollections of the Many Sources of Cybernetics." *Forum*, 6, 1974.

McGregor, D. *The Human Side of Enterprise*. New York: McGraw-Hill, 1960.

McKelvey, B. "Guidelines for the Empirical Classification of Organizations." *Administrative Science Quarterly*, 20: 509-525, 1982a.

McKelvey, B. *Organizational Systematics: Taxonomy, Evolution, Classification*. Berkeley: University of California Press, 1982b.

McKelvey, B. and H. Aldrich. "Populations, Natural Selection and Applied Organizational Science." *Administrative Science Quarterly*, 28: 101-128, 1983.

McLellan, D. *Karl Marx: His Life and Thought*. London: Macmillan, 1973.

McMillan, C. J. *The Japanese Industrial System*. Berlin: Walter de Gruyter, 1984.

McNeil, K. "Understanding Organizational Power: Building on the Weberian Legacy." *Administrative Science Quarterly*, 23: 65-90, 1978.

McSwain, C. J. and O. F. White, Jr. "The Case for Lying, Cheating, and Stealing: Organization Development as an Ethos Model for Management Practice." Presented at the Academy of Management meetings, New York City, 1982.

McWhinney, W. "Resolving Complex Issues." Los Angeles: Fielding Institute, 1982. (unpublished)

Meadows, D. H., D. L. Meadows, R. Randers, and W. Behrens. *The Limits to Growth*. New York: Universe Books, 1972.

Medawar, C. and B. Freese. *Drug Diplomacy*. London: Social Audit, 1982.

Menzies, I. "A Case Study in the Functioning of Social Systems as a Defence Against Anxiety." *Human Relations*, 13: 95-121, 1960.

Merton, R. K. *Social Theory and Social Structure*. New York: Free Press, 1968a.

Merton, R. K. "Manifest and Latent Functions," pp. 73-138 in *Social Theory and Social Structure*. New York: Free Press, 1968b.

Meszaros, I. *Marx's Theory of Alienation*. London: Merlin, 1970.

Meszaros, I. *Lukacs' Concept of Dialectic*. London: Merlin, 1972.

Meyer, J. W. and B. Rowan. "Institutionalized Organizations: Formal Structure as Myth and Ceremony." *American Journal of Sociology*, 83: 340-363, 1977.

Michael, D. N. *On Learning to Plan-and Planning to Learn*. San Francisco: Jossey-Bass, 1973.

Michels, R. *Political Parties*. New York: Free Press, 1949.

Miles, R. H. *Macro Organizational Behavior*. Santa Monica, CA: Goodyear, 1980.

Miles, R. E. and C. C. Snow. *Organizational Strategy, Structure and Process*. New York: McGraw-Hill, 1978.

Miliband, R. *The State in Capitalist Society*. London: Quartet, 1973.

Miller, A. *Death of a Salesman*. New York: Viking, 1949.

Miller, D. and P.H. Friesen. *Organizations: A Quantum View*. Englewood Cliffs, NJ: Prentice-Hall, 1984.

Miller, D. and P. H. Friesen. "Archetypes of Strategy Formulation." *Management Science*, 24: 921-933, 1978.

Miller, D. and H. Mintzberg. "The Case for Configuration," pp. 57-73 in G. Morgan (ed.) *Beyond Method: Strategies for Social Research*. Beverly Hills, CA: Sage, 1983.

Miller, E. J. and A. K. Rice. *Systems of Organization*. London: Tavistock, 1967.

Miller, J. *The Body in Question*. New York: Jonathan Cape, 1978.

Miller, J. G. *Living Systems*. New York: McGraw-Hill, 1978.

Millett, K. *Sexual Politics*. New York: Avon, 1969.

Mills, T. "Europe's Industrial Democracy: An American Response." *Harvard Business Review*, 56, 1978.

Mintzberg, H. *The Nature of Managerial Work*. New York: Harper & Row, 1973.

Mintzberg, H. "Planning on the Left Side and Managing on the Right." *Harvard Business Review*, 54: 49-58, 1976.

Mintzberg, H. *The Structuring of Organizations*. Englewood Cliffs, NJ: Prentice-Hall, 1979.

Mintzberg, H. *Power In and Around Organizations*. Englewood Cliffs, NJ: Prentice-Hall, 1983.

Mirow, K. R. and H. Maurer. *Webs of Power: International Cartels and the World Economy*. Boston: Houghton Mifflin, 1982.

Mitchell, J. *Psychoanalysis and Feminism*. New York; Pantheon, 1974.

Mitroff, I. I. *Stakeholders of the Mind*. San Francisco: Jossey-Bass, 1984.

Mitroff, I. I. and R. H. Kilmann. "On Organizational Stories," in R. H. Kilmann,, L. R. Pondy, and D. P. Slevin (eds.) *The Management of Organization Design*. New York: American Elsevier, 1976.

Mitroff, I. I. and R. H. Kilmann. *Methodological Approaches to Social Science*. San Francisco: Jossey-Bass, 1978.

Mizruchi, M. *The American Corporate Network, 1904-1974*. Beverly Hills, CA: Sage, 1982.

Mooney, J. C. and A. P. Reiley. *Onward Industry*. New York: Harper & Row, 1931.

Morgan, G. "Internal Audit Role Conflict: A Pluralist View." *Managerial Finance*, 5: 160-170, 1979.

Morgan, G. "Paradigms, Metaphors and Puzzle Solving in Organization Theory." *Administrative Science Quarterly*, 25: 605-622, 1980.

Morgan, G. "The Schismatic Metaphor and Its Implications for Organizational Analysis." *Organization Studies*, 2: 23-44, 1981.

Morgan, G. "Cybernetics and Organization Theory: Epistemology or Technique?" *Human Relations*, 35: 521-538, 1982.

Morgan, G. (ed.) *Beyond Method: Strategies for Social Research*. Beverly Hills, CA: Sage, 1983a.

Morgan, G. "More on Metaphor: Why We Cannot Control Tropes in Administrative Science." *Administrative Science Quarterly*, 28: 601-607, 1983b.

Morgan, G. "Rethinking Corporate Strategy: A Cybernetic Perspective." *Human Relations*, 36: 345-360, 1983c.

Morgan, G. "Opportunities Arising from Paradigm Diversity." *Administration and Society*, 16: 306-327, 1984.

Morgan, G. "Organizational Choice and the New Technology," in D. Morley and S. Wright (eds.) *Eric Trist in Canada*. Forthcoming.

Morgan, G. and R. Ramirez. "Action Learning: A Holographic Metaphor for Guiding Social Change." *Human Relations*, 37: 1-28, 1984.

Morgan, G., P. Frost, and L. Pondy. "Organizational Symbolism," pp. 3-35 in L. Pondy et al. (eds.) *Organizational Symbolism*. Greenwich, CT: JAI Press, 1983.

Mouzelis, N. *Organization and Bureaucracy* (2nd ed.). London: Routledge & Kegan Paul, 1979.

Mumford, L. *Technics and Civilization*. New York: Harcourt Brace Jovanovich, 1934.

Murray, V. and J. Gandz. "Games Executives Play: Politics at Work." *Business Horizons*, 1980, 11-23.

Myers-Briggs, I. *Manual for the Myers-Briggs Type Indicator*. Princeton, NJ: Educational Testing Service, 1962.

Nadler, D. A. and M. L. Tushman. "A General Diagnostic Model for Organizational Behavior: Applying a Congruence Perspective," in J. R. Hackman, E. E. Lawler, and L. W. Porter (eds.) *Perspectives on Behavior in Organizations*. New York: McGraw-Hill, 1977.

Navarro, V. and D. M. Berman (eds.) *Health and Work Under Capitalism*. New York: Baywood Publishing, 1983.

Negandhi, A. R. "External and Internal Functioning of American, German, and Japanese Multinational Corporations: Decision-Making and Policy Issues," in W. H. Goldberg and A. R. Negandhi (eds.) *Governments and Multinationals*. Cambridge, MA: Oelgeschlager, Gunn, & Hain, 1983.

Nelkin, D. and M. S. Brown. *Workers at Risk*. Chicago: University of Chicago Press, 1984.

Neumann, E. *The Origins and History of Consciousness*. Princeton, NJ: Princeton University Press, 1954.

Nichols, T. *Ownership, Control and Ideology*. London: Unwin, 1980.

Nietzsche, F. *The Gay Science*. New York: Vintage, 1974.

Nietzsche, F. *The Will to Power*. New York: Vintage, 1976.

Nisbet, R. A. *Social Change and History*. London: Oxford University Press, 1969.

Nord, W. "Dreams of Humanization and the Realities of Power." *Academy of Management Review*, 3: 674-679, 1978.

Northrup, H. R. and R. L. Rowan. *Multinational Collective Bargaining Attempts*. Philadelphia: University of Pennsylvania Press, 1979.

Novack, G. *An Introduction to the Logic of Marxism*. New York: Merit, 1966.

Oates, W. *Confessions of a Workaholic*. New York: Harper & Row, 1971.

O'Connor, J. *The Fiscal Crisis of the State*. New York: St. Martin's, 1973.

Offe, C. "Advanced Capitalism and the Welfare State." *Politics and Society*, 2: 479-488, 1974.

Offe, C. "Class Rule and the Political System." *German Political Studies*, 1: 31-57, 1974.

Offe, C. "The Theory of the Capitalist State and the Problem of Policy Formation," in L. N. Lindberg et al. (eds.) *Stress and Contradiction in Modern Capitalism*. Lexington, MA: D.C. Heath, 1975.

Offe, C. *Industry and Inequality*. London: Arnold, 1976.

Office of Management and Budget. *Standard Industrial Classification Manual*. Washington, DC: Government Printing Office, 1972.

Ollman, B. *Alienation: Marx's Conception of Man in Capitalist Society*. Cambridge: Cambridge University Press, 1976.

Ortony, A. "Why Metaphors Are Necessary and Not Just Nice." *Educational Theory*, 25: 45-53, 1975.

Ortony, A. (ed.) *Metaphor and Thought*. Cambridge: Cambridge University Press, 1979.

Ouchi, W. A. *Theory Z: How American Business Can Meet the Japanese Challenge*. Reading, MA: Addison-Wesley, 1981.

Outhwaite, W. "Toward a Realist Perspective," pp. 321-330 in G. Morgan (ed.) *Beyond Method*. Beverly Hills, CA: Sage, 1983.

Pareto, V. *The Mind and Society*. New York: Harcourt Brace Jovanovich, 1935.

Parsons, T. *The Social System*. New York: Free Press, 1951.

Parsons, T. "Culture and Social System Revisited," in L. Schneider and C. M. Bonjean (eds.) *The Idea of Culture in the Social Sciences*. Cambridge: Cambridge University Press, 1973.

Pascale, R. and A. Athos. *The Art of Japanese Management*. New York: Warner Books, 1981.

Pask, G. *An Approach to Cybernetics*. New York: Harper & Row, 1961.

Pava, C. *Managing New Office Technology*. New York: Free Press, 1983.

Pennings, J. M. "Organizational Birth Frequencies: An Empirical Investigation." *Administrative Science Quarterly*, 27: 120-144, 1982.

Pepper, S. C. *World Hypotheses*. Berkeley: University of California Press, 1942.

Perrow, C. "A Framework for the Comparative Analysis of Organizations." *American Sociological Review*, 32: 194-208, 1967.

Perrow, C. *Complex Organizations: A Critical Essay*. New York: Random House, 1979.

Perrow, C. *Normal Accidents*. New York: Basic Books, 1984.

Peters, T. J. "Symbols, Patterns and Settings." *Organizational Dynamics*, 7: 3-22, 1978.

Peters, T. J. and R. H. Waterman. *In Search of Excellence*. New York: Harper & Row, 1982.

Pettigrew, A. M. *The Politics of Organizational Decision-Making*. London: Tavistock, 1973.

Pfeffer, J. *Organization Design*. Arlington Heights, IL: AHM, 1978.

Pfeffer, J. *Power in Organizations*. Marshfield, MA: Pitman, 1981.
Pfeffer, J. *Organizations and Organization Theory*. Marshfield, MA: Pitman, 1982.
Pfeffer, J. and G. R. Salancik. *The External Control of Organizations: A Resource Dependence Perspective*. New York: Harper & Row, 1978.
Pinder, C. and L. Moore. "The Resurrection of Taxonomy to Aid the Development of Middle-Range Theories of Organizational Behavior." *Administrative Science Quarterly*, 24: 99-118, 1978.
Pines, M. *Bion and Group Psychotherapy*. London: Routledge & Kegan Paul, 1985.
Piore, M. *Birds of Passage: Migrant Labor in Industrial Society*. London: Cambridge University Press, 1979.
Plato, *The Republic*. Oxford: Clarendon, 1941.
Plato, *The Laws*. London: Heinemann, 1926.
Plekhanov, G. V. *Selected Philosophical Works*. London: Lawrence & Wishart, 1961.
Pondy, L. R. "Budgeting and Intergroup Conflict in Organizations." *Pittsburgh Business Review*, 1964.
Pondy, L. R. "Organizational Conflict: Concepts and Models." *Administrative Science Quarterly*, 12: 296-320, 1967.
Pondy, L. R., P. Frost, G. Morgan, and T. Dandridge (eds.) *Organizational Symbolism*. Greenwich, CT: JAI Press, 1983.
Popper, K. R. *The Open Society and Its Enemies*. London: Routledge & Kegan Paul, 1945.
Power, J. and A. Hardman. *Western Europe's Migrant Workers*. London: Minority Rights Group, 1978.
Presthus, R. *The Organizational Society*. New York: St. Martin's, 1978.
Pribram, K. *Languages of the Brain*. Englewood Cliffs, NJ: Prentice-Hall, 1971.
Pribram, K. "Problems Concerning the Structure of Consciousness," in G. Globus et al. (eds.) *Consciousness and the Brain*. New York: Plenum, 1976.
Prigogine, I. "Time, Structure and Fluctuations." *Science*, 201: 777-795, 1978.
Prigogine, I. *Order Out of Chaos*. New York: Random House, 1984.
Proudhon, P. J. *Selected Writings*. London: Macmillan, 1969.
Pugh, D. S., D. J. Hickson, and C. R. Hinings. "An Empirical Taxonomy of Work Organizations." *Administrative Science Quarterly*, 14: 115-126, 1969.
Radcliffe-Brown, A. R. *Structure and Function in Primitive Society*. London: Cohen & West, 1952.
Rank, O. *Psychology and the Soul*. Philadelphia: University of Pennsylvania Press, 1950.
Rapoport, A. *Fights, Games and Debates*. Ann Arbor: University of Michigan Press, 1960.
Ravn, I. "Notes on the Emergence of Order." Philadelphia: Wharton School, University of Pennsylvania, 1983. (unpublished)
Reasons, C. E., L. L. Ross, and C. Paterson. *Assault on the Worker*. Toronto: Butterworth, 1981.
Reich, M. "The Development of the Wage Labor Force," pp. 179-185 in R. C. Edwards, M. Reich, and T. Weisskopf (eds.) *The Capitalist System*. Englewood Cliffs, NJ: Prentice-Hall, 1978.
Reich, W. *The Mass Psychology of Fascism*. New York: Farrar, Straus, Giroux, 1933.
Reich, W. *The Function of the Orgasm*. New York: Panther, 1961.

Reich, W. *The Sexual Revolution*. New York: Farrar, Straus, Giroux, 1968.
Reich, W. *Character Analysis*. New York: Farrar, Straus, Giroux, 1972a.
Reich, W. *Dialectical Materialism and Psychoanalysis*. London: Socialist Reproduction, 1972b.
Rice, A. K. *Productivity and Social Organization*. London: Tavistock, 1958.
Robbins, S. P. "Conflict Management, and Conflict Resolution Are Not Synonymous Terms." *California Management Review*, 21: 67-75, 1978.
Roethlisberger, F. J. and W. J. Dickson. *Management and the Worker*. Cambridge, MA: Harvard University Press, 1939.
Ross, N. S. "Organized Labour and Management: The U. K.," in E. M. Hugh-Jones (ed.) *Human Relations and Modern Management*. North Holland: Elsevier, 1958.
Ross, N. S. *Constructive Conflict*. Edinburgh: Oliver & Boyd, 1969.
Royal Commission on Matters of Health and Safety Arising from the Use of Asbestos in Ontario. *Report*. Toronto: Ontario Government Bookstore, 1984.
Russell, B. and A. N. Whitehead. *Principia Mathematica*. Cambridge: Cambridge University Press, 1913.
Sacks, S. (ed.) *On Metaphor*. Chicago: University of Chicago Press, 1979.
Sahlins, M. *Stone Age Economics*. London: Tavistock, 1972.
Salaman, G. "Towards a Sociology of Organizational Structure." *Sociological Quarterly*, 26: 519-554, 1978.
Salaman, G. *Work Organizations: Resistance and Control*. New York: Longman, 1979.
Salaman, G. *Class and the Corporation*. London: Fontana, 1981.
Sampson, A. *The Sovereign State of ITT*. New York: Stein & Day, 1978.
Sapir, E. *Culture, Language and Personality*. Berkeley: University of California Press, 1949.
Sartre, J. *Nausea*. Harmondsworth: Penguin, 1938.
Sartre, J. P. *Being and Nothingness*. New York: Washington Square Press, 1966.
Sayle, M. "The Yellow Peril and the Red Haired Devils." *Harper's*, November: 23-35, 1982.
Sayles, L. R. and G. Strauss. *Managing Human Resources*. Englewood Cliffs, NJ: Prentice-Hall, 1981.
Schattschneider, E. E. *The Semi-Sovereign People*. New York: Holt, Rinehart & Winston, 1960.
Schein, E. *Oganizational Culture and Leadership*. San Francisco: Jossey-Bass, 1985.
Schön, D. A. *Invention and the Evolution of Ideas*. London: Tavistock, 1963.
Schön, D. A. *Beyond the Stable State*. New York: Random House, 1971.
Schön, D. A. "Generative Metaphor: A Perspective on Problem Setting in Social Policy," pp. 254-283 in A. Ortony (ed.) *Metaphor and Thought*. Cambridge: Cambridge University Press, 1979.
Schön, D. A. *The Reflective Practitioner*. New York: Basic Books, 1983.
Scott, R. *Muscle and Blood*. New York: Dutton, 1974.
Schutz, A. *Collected Papers I: The Problem of Social Reality*. The Hague: Martinus Nijhoff, 1967.
Schwartz, H. S. "Job Involvement as Obsession-Compulsion." *Academy of Management Review*, 7: 429-432, 1982.
Schwartz, H. S. "The Usefulness of Myth and the Myth of Usefulness." *Journal of Management*, 11: 31-42, 1985.

Scientific American. *The Brain: A Scientific American Book.* San Francisco: Freeman, 1979.

Scott, W. R. *Organizations: Rational, Natural and Open Systems.* Englewood Cliffs, NJ: Prentice-Hall, 1981.

Selznick, P. *Leadership in Administration.* New York: Harper & Row, 1957.

Servan-Schreiber, J-J. *The American Challenge.* New York: Atheneum, 1968.

Sheldrake, R. *A New Science of Life.* London: Bland & Briggs, 1981.

Sheldrake, R., R. Weber, and D. Bohm. "Conversations." *Re-Vision,* 5: 23-48, 1982.

Sheppard, D. "Image and Self-Image of Women in Organizations." Presented to the Annual Conference of the Canadian Research Institute for the Advancement of Women, Montreal, 1984.

Silverman, D. *The Theory of Organizations.* London: Heinemann Educational Books, 1971.

Silverman, D. and J. Jones. *Organizational Work.* London: Macmillan, 1976.

Simmel, G. *The Sociology of Georg Simmel.* New York: Free Press, 1950.

Simon, H. A. *Administrative Behavior.* New York: Macmillan, 1947.

Simon, H. A. "The architecture of complexity." *Proceedings of the American Philosophical Society,* 106: 467-482, 1962.

Sinclair, U. *The Jungle.* New York: Grosset & Dunlap, 1906.

Skinner, B. F. *Science and Human Behavior.* New York: Macmillan, 1953.

Smircich, L. "Organizations as Shared Meanings," pp. 55-65 in L. Pondy et al. (eds.) *Organizational Symbolism.* Greenwich, CT: JAI Press, 1983a.

Smircich, L. "Studying Organizations as Cultures," pp. 160-172 in G. Morgan (ed.) *Beyond Method: Strategies for Social Research.* Beverly Hills, CA: Sage, 1983b.

Smircich, L. "Concepts of Culture and Organizational Analysis." *Administrative Science Quarterly,* 28: 339-358, 1983c.

Smircich, L. and G. Morgan. "Leadership: The Management of Meaning." *Journal of Applied Behavioral Studies,* 18: 257-273, 1982.

Smircich, L. and C. Stubbart. "Strategic Management in an Enacted World." *Academy of Management Review,* 10: 724-736, 1985.

Smith, Adam. *The Wealth of Nations.* London: Stratton and Cadell, 1776.

Smith, K. K. and V. M. Simmons. "A Rumplestiltskin Organization: Metaphors on Metaphors in Field Research." *Administrative Science Quarterly,* 28: 377-392, 1983.

Spencer, H. *The Study of Sociology.* London: Kegan Paul & Tench, 1873.

Spencer, H. *Principles of Sociology.* London: Williams & Norgate, 1876.

Spencer, H. *The Principles of Biology.* London: Williams & Norgate, 1884.

Spencer-Brown, G. *Laws of Form.* New York: Dutton, 1969.

Sperry, R. W. "Hemisphere Deconnection and Unity in Conscious Awareness." *American Psychologist,* 23: 723-733, 1968.

Sperry, R. W. "A Modified Concept of Consciousness." *Psychological Review,* 76: 532-536, 1969.

Steinbrunner, J. *The Cybernetic Theory of Decision.* Princeton, NJ: Princeton University Press, 1974.

Stinchcombe, A. L. "Social Structure and Organizations," pp. 142-193 in J. G. March (ed.) *Handbook of Organizations.* Chicago: Rand McNally, 1965.

Stirner, M. *The Ego and His Own.* New York: Libertarian Book Club, 1963.

Stopford, J. M., J. H. Dunning, and K. O. Itaberich. *The World Directory of Multinational Enterprizes.* New York: Facts on File, 1980.

Sudnow, D. "Normal Crimes: Sociological Features of the Penal Code in a Public Defender Office." *Social Problems*, 12: 255-276, 1965.

Susman, G. *Autonomy at Work*. New York: Praeger, 1976.

Sward, K. *The Legend of Henry Ford*. New York: Rinehart, 1948.

Taggart, W. and D. Robey. "Minds and Managers: On the Dual Nature of Human Information Processing and Management." *Academy of Management Review*, 6: 187-196, 1981.

Tataryn, L. *Dying for a Living: The Politics of Industrial Death*. Ottawa: Deneau & Breenberg, 1979.

Tavis, L. A. *Multinational Managers and Poverty in the Third World*. Notre Dame, IN: University of Notre Dame Press, 1982.

Taylor, F. W. *Principles of Scientific Management*. New York: Harper & Row, 1911.

Taylor, G. R. *Sex in History*. New York: Vanguard, 1954.

Taylor, G. R. *The Natural History of the Mind*. New York: Dutton, 1979.

Thomas, K. W. "Conflict and Conflict Management," pp. 889-935 in M. D. Dunnette (ed.) *Handbook of Industrial and Organizational Psychology*. Chicago: Rand McNally, 1976.

Thomas, K. W. "Toward Multi-dimensional Values in Teaching: The Example of Conflict Behaviors." *Academy of Management Review*, 12: 484-490, 1977.

Thomas, S. *The Multi-National Companies*. Hove: Wayland Publishers, 1979.

Thomas, W. I. *Social Behavior and Personality*. New York: Social Science Research Council, 1951.

Thompson, E. P. *The Making of the English Working Class*. London: Pelican, 1968.

Thompson, J. D. *Organizations in Action*. New York: McGraw-Hill, 1967.

Thompson, W. I. *At the Edge of History*. New York: Harper & Row, 1971.

Thorsrud, E. "Policy-Making as a Learning Process," in A. B. Cherns et. al. (eds.) *Social Science and Government Policies and Problems*. London: Tavistock, 1972a.

Thorsrud, E. *Workers' Participation in Management in Norway*. Geneva: Institute for Labour Studies, 1972b.

Tichy, N. M. "An Analysis of Clique Formation and Structure in Organizations." *Administrative Science Quarterly*, 18: 194-208, 1973.

Tivey, L. *The Politics of the Firm*. New York: St. Martin's, 1978.

Touraine, A. *The Self-Production of Society*. Chicago: University of Chicago Press, 1977.

Trades Councils of Coventry, Liverpool, Newcastle, and North Tyneside. *State Intervention in Industry: A Workers' Inquiry*. Coventry: Trades Council, 1980.

Trist, E. L. and K. W. Bamforth. "Some Social and Psychological Consequences of the Longwall Method of Coal Getting." *Human Relations*, 4: 3-38, 1951.

Trist, E. L. "A Concept of Organizational Ecology." *Australian Journal of Management*, 2, 1976.

Trist, E. L. "New Directions of Hope: Recent Innovations Interconnecting Organizational, Industrial, Community and Personal Development." *Regional Studies*, 13: 439-451, 1979.

Trist, E. L. "The Evolution of Sociotechnical Systems as a Conceptual Framework and as an Action Research Program," pp. 19-75 in A. H. Van de Ven and W. F. Joyce (eds.) *Perspectives on Organization Design and Behavior*. New York: John Wiley, 1982.

Trist, E. L. "Referent Organizations and the Development of Inter-Organizational Domains." *Human Relations*, 36: 269-284, 1983.

Trist, E. L. "Culture as a Psycho-Social Process." *Human Relations*, in press.

Trist, E. L., G. W. Higgin, H. Murray, and A. B. Pollock. *Organizational Choice*. London: Tavistock, 1963.

Turner, B. A. *Exploring the Industrial Sub-Culture*. London: Macmillan, 1971.

Turner, S. "Studying Organization Through Levi Strauss's Structuralism," pp. 189-201 in G. Morgan (ed.) *Beyond Method*. Beverly Hills, CA: Sage, 1983.

Tushman, M. L. and D. A. Nadler. "Implications of Political Models of Organization," pp. 177-190 in R. Miles (ed.) *Resource Book in Macro Organizational Behavior*. Glenview, IL: Scott Foresman, 1980.

Tylor, E. B. *Primitive Culture*. London: John Murray, 1871.

Ulrich, H. and G.J.B. Probst (eds.) *Self-Organization and Management of Social Systems*. New York: Springer-Verlag, 1984.

United Nations. *Transnational Corporations in World Development: Third Survey*. New York: United Nations, Center on Transnational Corporations, 1983.

Vaill, P. B. "Process Wisdom for a New Age." *ReVision*, 7: 39-49, 1984.

Van de Ven, A. H. and W. G. Astley. "Mapping the Field to Create a Dynamic Perspective on Organization Design and Behavior," pp. 427-468 in A. H. Van De Ven and W. F. Joyce (eds.) *Perspectives on Organization Design and Behavior*. New York: John Wiley, 1981.

Vanek, J. *Self Management*. Harmondsworth: Penguin, 1975.

Van Maanen, J. and S. R. Barley. "Occupational Communities: Culture and Control in Organizations," in B. Staw and L. L. Cummings (eds.) *Research in Organizational Behavior*. Greenwich, CT: JAI Press, 1984.

Varela, F. "Not One, Not Two." *Co-Evolution Quarterly*, 1976.

Varela, F. *Principles of Biological Autonomy*. Amsterdam: Elsevier, 1979.

Varela, F. "Two Principles of Self-Organization," in H. Ulrich and G. Probst (eds.) *Self-Organization and Management of Social Systems*. New York: Springer-Verlag, 1984.

Varela, F. and D. Johnson. "On Observing Natural Systems." *Co-Evolution Quarterly*, Summer: 26-31, 1976.

Vickers, G. *The Art of Judgement*. London: Chapman & Hall, 1965.

Vickers, G. *Value Systems and Social Process*. London: Tavistock, 1972.

Vickers, G. *Human Systems Are Different*. New York: Harper & Row, 1983.

Vico, G. *The New Science*. Ithaca, NY: Cornell University Press, 1968.

Viscusi, W. K. *Risk by Choice: Regulating Health and Safety in the Workplace*. Cambridge, MA: Harvard University Press, 1983.

Vogel, Ezra. *Japan as Number One*. Cambridge, MA: Harvard University Press, 1979.

von Bertalanffy, L. "The Theory of Open Systems in Physics and Biology," *Science*, 3: 23-29, 1950.

von Bertalanffy, L. *General Systems Theory: Foundations, Development, Applications*. New York: Braziller, 1968.

von Foerester, H. and G. W. Zopf (eds.) *Principles of Self-Organization*. New York: Pergamon, 1962.

Wainwright, H. and D. Elliott. *The Lucas Plan: A New Trade-Unionism in the Making?* London: Allison & Busby, 1982.

Wall Street Journal. "Palace Revolt Forced Henry Ford to Remove Knudsen as President." *Wall Street Journal*, September 17, 1969.

Wallerstein, I. *The Modern World-System*. New York: Academic Press, 1974.

Wallerstein, I. *The Capitalist World Economy*. London: Cambridge University Press, 1979.

Walter, G. A. "Psyche and Symbol," pp. 257-271 in L. Pondy et al. (eds.) *Organizational Symbolism*. Greenwich, CT: JAI Press, 1983.

Walton, R. E. and J. M. Dutton. "Managing Inter-Departmental Conflict: A Model and Review." *Administrative Science Quarterly*, 14: 73-82, 1969.

Wamsley, G. L. and M. N. Zald. *The Political Economy of Public Organizations*. Lexington, MA: D.C. Heath, 1973.

Ward, C. *Anarchy in Action*. London: Allen & Unwin, 1973.

Warrick, P. S. *The Cybernetic Imagination in Science Fiction*. Cambridge, MA: MIT Press, 1980.

Watson, L. *Lifetide*. New York: Simon & Schuster, 1979.

Webber, R. A. (ed.) *Culture and Management*. Homewood, IL: Irwin, 1969.

Weber, M. *From Max Weber* (eds., H. Gerth and C. W. Mills). New York: Oxford University Press, 1946.

Weber, M. *The Theory of Social and Economic Organization*. London: Oxford University Press, 1947.

Weber, M. *The Methodology of the Social Sciences*. New York: Free Press, 1949.

Weber, M. *The Protestant Ethic and the Spirit of Capitalism*. New York: Scribners, 1958.

Weber, M. *General Economic History*. New York: Collier, 1961.

Weber, M. *Economy and Society: An Outline of Interpretive Sociology*. New York: Bedminster, 1968.

Weick, K. E. "Educational Organizations as Loosely Coupled Systems." *Administrative Science Quarterly*, 21: 1-19, 1976.

Weick, K. E. *The Social Psychology of Organizing*. Reading, MA: Addison-Wesley, 1979.

Wetter, G. E. *Dialectical Materialism*. London: Routledge & Kegan Paul, 1958.

Wheelwright, P. *Heraclitus*. Princeton, NJ: Princeton University Press, 1959.

White, H. *The Tropics of Dicourse*. Baltimore: Johns Hopkins University Press, 1978.

White, L. *Human Debris: The Injured Worker in America*. New York: Seaview/Putnam, 1983.

White, O. F. and C. J. McSwain. "Transformational Theory and Organizational Analysis," pp. 292-305 in G. Morgan (ed.) *Beyond Method*. Beverly Hills, CA: Sage, 1983.

Whitmont, E. C. *The Symbolic Quest*. New York: Putnam, 1969.

Whyte, W. F. *Human Relations in the Restaurant Industry*. New York: McGraw-Hill, 1948.

Whyte, W. F. *Money and Motivation*. New York: Harper & Row, 1955.

Wiener, N. *Cybernetics*. Cambridge, MA: MIT Press, 1961.

Wiener, N. *The Human Use of Human Beings*. Boston, MA: Houghton Mifflin, 1967.

Wilber, K. (ed.) *The Holographic Paradigm and Other Paradoxes*. Boulder, CO: Shambhala, 1982.

Wilczynski. *The Multinationals and East-West Relations*. London: Macmillan, 1976.

Wildavsky, A. *The Politics of the Budgetary Process*. Boston: Little, Brown, 1964.

Wilden, A. *System and Structure*. London: Tavistock, 1972.

Wilensky, H. L. *Organizational Intelligence*. New York: Basic Books, 1967.

Wilkins, A. L. "Organizational Stories as Symbols Which Control the Organization," pp. 81-92 in L. Pondy et al. (eds.) *Organizational Symbolism*. Greenwich, CT: JAI Press, 1983.

Williams, T. A. *Learning to Manage Our Futures*. New York: John Wiley, 1982.

Williamson, I. (ed.) *The Dynamics of Labor Market Segmentation*. New York: Academic Press, 1981.

Winnicott, D. W. "Transitional Objects and Transitional Phenomena," in *Collected Papers*. London: Tavistock, 1958.

Winnicott, D. W. *Playing and Reality*. London: Tavistock, 1971.

Winnicott, D. W. *The Child, the Family and the Outside World*. Harmondsworth: Penguin, 1964.

Wittfogel, K. A. *Oriental Despotism*. New Haven, CT: Yale University Press, 1957.

Wittgenstein, L. *Philosophical Investigations*. Oxford: Basil Blackwell, 1958.

Wittgenstein, L. *Tractatus Logico-Philosophicus*. London: Routledge & Kegan Paul, 1961.

Wood, S. (ed.) *The Degradation of Work?* London: Hutchinson, 1982.

Woodward, J. *Industrial Organization: Theory and Practice*. London: Oxford University Press, 1965.

Woodworth, W., C. Meek, and W. F. Whyte. *Industrial Democracy*. Beverly Hills, CA: Sage, 1985.

Worthy, J. C. *Big Business and Free Men*. New York: Harper & Row, 1959.

Wrege, C. D. and A. G. Perroni. "Taylor's Pig-Tale." *Academy of Management Journal*, 17: 6-27, 1974.

Wright, H. B. "Health Hazards of Managers." *Journal of General Management*, 2: 9-13, 1973.

Wright, J. P. *On a Clear Day You Can See General Motors*. New York: Avon, 1979.

Yoshino, M. Y. *Japan's Managerial System: Tradition and Innovation*. Cambridge, MA: MIT Press, 1968.

Yoshino, M. Y. *Japan's Multinational Enterprises*. Cambridge, MA: Harvard University Press, 1976.

Zaleznik, A. "Power and Politics in Organizational Life." *Harvard Business Review*, 48: 47-60, 1970.

Zaleznik, A. and M. Kets de Vries. *Power and the Corporate Mind*. Boston: Houghton Mifflin, 1975.

Zeleny, M. *Autopoiesis, Dissipative Structures and Spontaneous Social Order*. Boulder, CO: Westview, 1980.

Zmud, R. W. *Information Systems in Organizations*. Glenview, IL: Scott Foresman, 1983.

Zwerdling, D. "Food Pollution." *Ramparts*, June: 35-37, 1971.

Index

About the Author

Gareth Morgan is well known for his contributions to social research. A pioneer in developing creative approaches to organization theory, he has authored and edited a wide range of books and articles, including *Beyond Method, Sociological Paradigms and Organizational Analysis,* and *Organizational Symbolism.* He holds degrees from the London School of Economics and Political Science, the University of Texas at Austin, and the University of Lancaster. He sits on the editorial boards of the *Academy of Management Review, Administration and Society,* the *Journal of Management,* and *Organization Studies.* He has lectured at over forty universities in Europe and North America and has held a number of visiting appointments. He is now Professor of Administrative Studies at York University, Toronto.